MORAL ENGINES

Exploring the Ethical Drives in Human Life

Edited by

Cheryl Mattingly

Rasmus Dyring

Maria Louw

Thomas Schwarz Wentzer

berghahn
NEW YORK · OXFORD
www.berghahnbooks.com

Published in 2018 by
Berghahn Books
www.berghahnbooks.com

© 2018 Cheryl Mattingly

Library of Congress Cataloging-in-Publication Data

A C.I.P. cataloging record is available from the Library of Congress

British Library Cataloguing in Publication Data

A catalogue record for this book is available from the British Library

ISBN 978-1-78533-693-5 hardback
ISBN 978-1-78533-694-2 ebook

Contents

Contents

MORAL ENGINES

Wyse Series in Social Anthropology

Editors:
James Laidlaw, William Wyse Professor of Social Anthropology, University of Cambridge, and Fellow of King's College, Cambridge
Maryon McDonald, Fellow in Social Anthropology, Robinson College, University of Cambridge
Joel Robbins, Sigrid Rausing Professor of Social Anthropology, University of Cambridge, and Fellow of Trinity College, Cambridge

Social Anthropology is a vibrant discipline of relevance to many areas – economics, politics, business, humanities, health and public policy. This series, published in association with the Cambridge William Wyse Chair in Social Anthropology, focuses on key interventions in Social Anthropology, based on innovative theory and research of relevance to contemporary social issues and debates. Former holders of the William Wyse Chair have included Meyer Fortes, Jack Goody, Ernest Gellner and Marilyn Strathern, all of whom have advanced the frontiers of the discipline. This series intends to develop and foster that tradition.

MORAL ENGINES

Exploring the Ethical Drives in Human Life

Edited by

Cheryl Mattingly

Rasmus Dyring

Maria Louw

Thomas Schwarz Wentzer

berghahn
NEW YORK · OXFORD
www.berghahnbooks.com

Published in 2018 by
Berghahn Books
www.berghahnbooks.com

Library of Congress Cataloging-in-Publication Data

A C.I.P. cataloging record is available from the Library of Congress

British Library Cataloguing in Publication Data

A catalogue record for this book is available from the British Library

ISBN 978-1-78533-693-5 hardback
ISBN 978-1-78533-694-2 ebook

Prologue

Cheryl Mattingly

It is no accident that the editors of this volume are comprised of two anthropologists and two philosophers. This book is the result of a history of conversation between the two disciplines that is, on the one hand, quite local, an Aarhus centred dialogue that has developed over the last quarter-century. Even at its most local, it has never been a solely Danish conversation however. Rather, Aarhus has provided a nurturing space for a gradually developing international conversation. I'm sure there are many stories to tell about how and why this has happened or continues to build with increased momentum. The ones I will tell are, quite frankly, shaped by my own particular experience of what has been an extraordinarily rich personal history with Aarhus philosophers and anthropologists.

I'm indulging in a markedly autobiographical foreword for two reasons. Some readers might find it interesting to catch a behind the scenes glimpse – from one participant's perspective – of how this conversation has grown, where interdisciplinarity became challenging, how it provoked. It also allows me, as an American who has been invited repeatedly to think with Aarhus scholars, to acknowledge some of those who are not represented in this volume but who have been crucial in cultivating an interdisciplinary exchange between philosophy and anthropology that, I think, is truly groundbreaking. The provocations we anthropologists and philosophers have confronted in various Aarhus forums are surely not unique. I suspect that my stories will resonate with scholars in either discipline who have also embarked on collaborative ventures. Unquestionably, there has been a recent *rapprochement* between the two fields, at least in some quarters. In anthropology, and in some corners of philosophy, there has been a reach across the aisle to see what kind of new thinking about things like morality, experience, and even philosophical anthropology a collaborative effort might yield. Our introductory chapter recounts some of this interdisciplinary work.

As an anthropologist, I can speak best to the anthropology side where this wider conversation is particularly evident – and pertinent – because of anthropology's ethical turn. One of the interesting features of this current anthropological moment is that in giving such explicit attention to ethics, and debating what might properly constitute it, many anthropologists have turned to philosophy (especially moral philosophy and phenomenology) for inspiration. Every anthropological piece in this collection reflects this philosophical engagement. While there have always been some anthropologists who have taken philosophy very seriously in their work, a new collective enthusiasm reflects another kind of turn in the discipline as a whole. It marks a contrast from earlier decades, which have often been characterized by suspicion of philosophy's universalisms, abstractions and western egocentrism. As is well known, philosophy has served as a useful intellectual adversary against which one could pitch challenging claims about the moral (or social) diversity of human life, based most often upon close investigation of non-western communities. For some of us, the contemporary *rapprochement* is evident not only in an ever more serious use of philosophical texts but also a far more ambitious attempt to develop a new kind of anthropology, a 'philosophical anthropology'.

On the philosophy side there are also some movements toward anthropology where an 'ethnographic turn' has been developing. As Wentzer documents in his chapter in this volume, this philosophical reach outside the discipline is not altogether new. Wentzer retraces a specific history of German thought in the first half of the twentieth century which saw itself as offering a revived philosophical anthropology. The twentieth-century German tradition 'attempted to deal with the human in a way that avoids both naturalistic reductionisms and idealist shortcomings' but defends a 'philosophical take on the human' (p. 211). It drew widely from a broad range of disciplines, including biology and anthropology, in order to develop a more adequate account of the human, recognizing that philosophy was not equipped to address this question by itself. In this sense it was, Wentzer notes, a movement akin to Wittgenstein's call to get 'back to the rough ground'.

The Story of an Introduction: A Destabilizing Border Event

The introductory chapter of this volume involved a cooperative writing venture that, rather to our surprise, demanded an enormous amount of discussion, writing and rewriting of key sections. Our joint task has sometimes felt like navigating a minefield of potential misunderstandings. And it has been an ambitious project. Although the topic of this volume is ethics, and more specifically the question of 'ethical drives', it is also an entry into the still nascent creation of a reinvented philosophical anthropology. (Several of the chapters in this volume make explicit what is entailed in speaking of our collaborative work as a form of philosophical anthropology. Wentzer's chapter is particularly helpful in this regard.) It took us a full year to complete our introduction, and not only for the usual reason that collaborations among busy people tend to create delays. It pushed me, and I think it pushed us all, to think beyond our familiar vocabularies and comfort zone of ideas.

This propulsion into the unfamiliar was generally precipitated by small hermeneutic difficulties that looked, initially, as though they should be easy to resolve. An example: how to translate terms like 'fundamental' or 'essential' from a phenomenological philosophical framework into a sociocultural anthropological one? Rasmus Dyring had used both these terms freely in one section of our draft. I objected. After some to-ing and fro-ing, we ultimately dropped the term 'essential' and used 'fundamental' sparingly so that we would not be read as embracing philosophy's penchant for metaphysical essentialisms that anthropology has so vociferously critiqued. But our discussions and confusions over word choice did not merely reflect the politics of addressing multiple disciplinary audiences. Something more was at stake, reminding me that there is a reason philosophers like Dilthey and especially Gadamer have viewed 'understanding' and its necessary corollary 'misunderstanding' as a basic mode of human experience.

I will try to convey a sense of this 'at stakeness' through one of Thomas Wentzer's responses.[1] In an email to the rest of us, he notes that we editors, in our oral discussions and in our communications with contributing authors, had sometimes used the term 'fundamental' to indicate the level of reflection we wanted them to engage in when writing their chapters: 'to indicate that our take [in this book] urges all contributors to address explicitly what they otherwise silently might presuppose'. But the tricky part, Thomas noted, was that because a word like 'fundamental' belongs to the conceptual family 'fundament', readers (especially anthropologists) might mistake us for advancing something 'foundationalist' when reading so much about 'fundamentals'. Thomas reflected upon how differently this vocabulary plays in Heideggerian phenomenology. 'Being a Heideggerian, to me this word (fundamental) actually does not indicate metaphysical foundationalism ('old fashioned conceptual armchair philosophy'), but a hermeneutical enterprise to settle some horizon of understanding of what we are talking about. In this sense, the word indicates the horizon within which the domain of the ethical can be located, the guiding thread that leads our understanding to begin with. Asking thusly means to pose "fundamental questions"'. However, Thomas doubted that 'non-Heideggerians (i.e., normal people) would join [his] connotations', hence the danger of the term.

For me, one of Thomas' 'normal people' whose grip on Heidegger is by no means assured, this minor dilemma over word phrasing began to seem like a gift. Could my engagement with Rasmus and Thomas help me to address a concern that has haunted me since I began to do anthropology? Namely, how could I be wedded to particulars, including intimate relationships and biographical selves (which my kind of ethnography insists upon), and at the same time lay claim to something like universals concerning 'the human condition'?

How could a deep engagement with singularities, including the humble events of everyday family life that have often been the focus of my attention, provide a privileged avenue to life's big questions? How could I justify an intuition that the kind of human condition universals – or 'fundamentals' – I was after could be disclosed through textually representing irreducible particularities? Especially because my particulars so often concerned small matters and little histories invisible from the stage of world history? If, within phenomenology, a term like 'fundamental' could indicate something that was not substantive and fixed but operated as an 'indicator' of a 'horizon of understanding' within which a conversation might take place, could a concrete particular (for example, a description of a mother dropping her child off for a first day of school in a wheelchair) function in the same way? That is, could Thomas' description of 'fundamentals' as 'horizons of understanding' speak to problems that are not necessarily his (or Heidegger's) concern? Could they help me to articulate what ethnographic particulars might offer? If so, this could not be because I simply 'applied' a Heideggerian understanding of everydayness to my ethnographic depictions of some community's small practices. (In fact, my fieldwork often seemed to challenge Heidegger's ontological depiction of the everyday.)

What Thomas' note suggested to me was a way to consider a more radical possibility that I have been entertaining for a long time without feeling equipped to justify or even articulate – that I was not merely *using* philosophy but *doing* philosophy. A Heideggerian understanding of fundamentals might provide a lens through which to consider how and why ethnographic particulars could be transformed from mere 'facts' of the substantive kind into windows that open onto 'horizons of understanding', that is, vistas in which conversations might be had. Of course, my dogged concern with the philosophical import of the ethnographic particular is not a new problem for philosophically engaged anthropologists. (Geertz's work quickly comes to mind, as does Michael Jackson's for a more recent example.) But my little story of how I glimpsed an idea (or a potential idea)[2] about how to address this via a small struggle over word choice illustrates how quickly we co-writers found ourselves grappling with very big issues.

Undertaking this book has forced all of us, as editors, to consider what claims we could make about anthropology as a (kind of) philosophical enterprise and about philosophy – at least of a certain sort – as a (kind of) anthropological enterprise. What has haunted me also pervaded our discussions in writing this introduction as we sought to outline and justify our claims. Annoyingly (for the anthropologists) it seemed much easier to justify what philosophy had to offer anthropology than the reverse. But all of us were quite clear that we were rejecting some familiar roles the two disciplines are often assigned. We were certainly repudiating the view that anthropology is, at best, some kind of applied philosophy that imports philosophical abstractions and cavalierly air drops them onto ethnographic scenes. Nor were we happy with the idea that anthropology plays a merely negative role of critique, providing 'exotic' counter-examples to refute philosophical universals (however useful that may sometimes be). We also dismissed the more benign idea that anthropology is good for fleshing out armchair philosophical examples. Nor, it should be said, did we want to confine philosophers to armchairs.

By contrast to all these recognizable roles, we have grandly claimed to be doing something more radical in our collaboration, using our dialogue between the two disciplines to sketch and defend a border inquiry that, we argue, is necessary for an adequate exploration of ethical drives. We try to articulate some features of this borderland inquiry between anthropology and philosophy. Our sketch is sometimes descriptive, elucidating in a thematic way the shape of the current dialogue (especially among anthropologists where it has developed in a far more pronounced way). But sometimes we take a bolder stand that has the ring of a kind of manifesto, a prescriptive challenge. Border inquiry should not merely enrich, we contend, but destabilize and call into question each discipline's familiar ways of thinking about what propels us into ethical life in the first place. (Since we make this case extensively in the introduction, I won't rehearse it further here.)

There was one heady moment in our writing process when we offered one of our more far-reaching claims. We stated that we were promoting a kind of disciplinary role reversal: anthropologists would ask questions and create concepts of the philosophical sort (or were already doing so) and philosophers would create (or were already creating) anthropological style thick descriptions in posing their questions. As I reviewed our exalted prose, I had a sobering moment. Were we leading readers to anticipate chapters the likes of which they had never seen before? Were we promising some whole new type of prose and style of argument? Or, at the least, would they be unable to tell the philosophers and the anthropologists apart, so role-reversing were we? Well, no. The anthropological contributors pretty much articulated their arguments through analyses of detailed ethnographic examples and the philosophers pretty much made their cases through discussions within the philosophical tradition. Despite this difficulty, none of us wanted to drop our most ambitious assertions. Instead, we added a necessary caveat. We amended our prose to emphasize that we are indicating where we think this border inquiry might, even should, go. You could say we are gesturing toward a horizon of thought.

Quite appropriately, to my mind, we have placed this whole gesturing enterprise under the umbrella of a sheltering metaphor, the 'moral engine'. Maria Louw must be credited with the book's guiding image. She suggested it to me several years ago as a comment to a talk I had given and the trope struck a chord with us all. As we have struggled to see what claims we could make, and become inspired with the vistas this project has opened, it has made particular sense to call upon a metaphor to connote the hazy terrain in which we have ventured.

Local History: The Aarhus Story

The 'engine' that has propelled this particular volume can be traced not only to disciplinary wide shifts (especially in anthropology) but also to a more local history, quite specific to Aarhus. One beginning is the establishment, in 1990, of a unique interdisciplinary network at Aarhus University: Health, Humanity and Culture. This network, which continues to thrive, has involved philosophers, ethnologists and psychologists. It was founded by an Aarhus philosopher, Uffe Juul Jensen, and continues to have its home in philosophy, though involving a wide range of disciplines. The impetus behind this network was the very strong belief that philosophy could not, by itself, think through crucial issues like health (or suffering) without reaching out to create a cross-disciplinary conversation that not only spanned different disciplines but also involved health practitioners. This might sound familiar – just applied philosophy. But this was not how this network was conceived. Rather, the idea was that even to do philosophy well, it was necessary not only to know the history of key concepts and thinkers (its scholastic feature), but also to know how these concepts intersected with the 'rough ground' of everyday practices. Scholars working across a broad range of disciplines were often invited to participate in network seminars and workshops.

The existence of this volume can be partly traced back to one such invitation, given to me back in 1991. This initial invitation led to a partnership with Uffe Jensen and the network that has been involved in co-organizing international seminars of anthropologists and philosophers (and many other disciplines, especially psychology) to collectively think through topics related to health and ethics. While *Moral Engines* is not about health per se, it is not surprising that the connection of bodily suffering to ethics is foregrounded in several chapters. (Four of the eight contributors work in medical anthropology, broadly conceived: Throop, Zigon, Meinert and Mattingly.) Ethics has become increasingly central to anthropology in part because so many anthropologists have explored the ethical precarities engendered by health problems ranging from diagnosable conditions to the suffering that results from structural or societal level violence.

The Aarhus history of conversation can be traced to some other developments. In 2009, the anthropology and philosophy faculty at Aarhus organized a conference on *Trust and Hope* that attracted a large international as well as local audience. One result of that conference was an innovative set of dialogues between anthropology and philosophy (which included two editors of this volume, Wentzer and Mattingly), published as *Anthropology and Philosophy: Dialogues on Trust and Hope* (Berghahn Books 2015, Liisberg, Pedersen and Dalsgaard, editors). This 2009 conference also precipitated the inauguration of a discussion group of the anthropology and philosophy faculty, who met at irregular intervals and jokily referred to themselves as the 'Philanthropes'. All four editors of this volume have been core members of this group.

More proximally, this volume has been inspired by a series of conferences that were organized under the auspices of Aarhus University's Institute of Advanced Studies (AIAS) during the years that I had a senior fellowship there. AIAS, under the leadership of Morten Kyndrup, provided not only funding but also crucial organizational support for three conferences to which prominent anthropologists and philosophers in ethics and phenomenology were invited. We four editors were co-organizers of all the conferences. The first conference, on moral experience, was held in the autumn of 2013. The second, much larger 'Moral Engines' conference took place in June 2014. A third conference, on Philosophical Anthropology, held June 2015, involved a number of the same scholars invited to the 'Moral Engines' conference. The chapters gathered in this book are not, in any sense, conference papers. Every one has been extensively developed and revised; in fact, several bear little or no connection to the paper originally delivered. However, it is worth mentioning these events because they have helped to generate a community of dialogue that is by no means finished. Already during the 2014 symposium, there was a sense among participating speakers that we were onto something, that we could find ways to talk across our disciplines in order to think better together. The interdisciplinarity so frequently touted by universities, and so frequently a disappointing and empty slogan, seemed to be actually possible. Out of this sense of possibility, and the commitment among us to continue our thinking together, this volume was born.

Cheryl Mattingly
May 2017
Los Angeles

Notes

1. Although Thomas is not listed as an author of the introduction, he read and commented on several iterations of it.
2. I try to articulate this insight in a manuscript, currently under review, entitled 'Ordinary Possibility, Transcendent Immanence and Responsive Ethics: A Philosophical Anthropology of the Small Event'. It is being reviewed as part of a special issue of HAU entitled 'Reinventing Philosophical Anthropology.' Thomas Wentzer and I are co-editing. The special issue as a whole is also currently under review.

1

The Question of 'Moral Engines'
Introducing a Philosophical Anthropological Dialogue

Rasmus Dyring, Cheryl Mattingly and Maria Louw

In the last two decades there has been a virtual explosion of anthropological literature arguing that ethics or morality (we use the terms interchangeably)[1] should be considered a central dimension of human practice. Much important and genre-defining work has already been done on the topic of ethics, including a number of original and complex analyses of ethical life and its predicaments. However, one question that has not always been made explicit is this: what actually commits and drives us to understand our lives in ethical terms? This question is both ethnographically underexplored and theoretically underdeveloped. In other words, what remains to be adequately thematized is why, and on what grounds, human beings qualify certain experiences and registers of life as ethically important ones. With the trope of 'moral engines' as an analytical lodestar, this volume sets out to pose the fundamental question of the ethical drives in human life.

The attraction of approaching this question via a metaphor is that it highlights its mysterious character – an ethical drive may move us but where it comes from or why it carries such potency and force often eludes neat definition. Throughout this volume, this riddle is explored from various points of departure steeped in different vocabularies, including philosophical phenomenology and vocabularies rooted in the experiences of anthropologists' diverse interlocutors. As anthropologists have frequently contended, attending to a range of voices, practices and experiences across a wide spectrum of societies may teach us something as fundamental about the human condition as the western philosophical tradition offers.

This introduction is devoted to the task of qualifying what is entailed in the proposed exploration of 'moral engines'. This task will be approached as follows. Section One makes the case for why a consideration of ethical drives seems to demand a borderland inquiry that crosses anthropology and philosophy. Section Two situates the question of ethical drives within a brief overview of how ethics and morality have been explored in anthropology and makes the case for why, despite a wealth of current scholarship, this question still needs to be asked. It also identifies certain organizing themes that have emerged in the current theoretical debates in anthropology that are especially pertinent to addressing it.

Section Three broadly outlines a framework consisting of three quite different approaches that can be taken in considering what might constitute moral engines. We return to these approaches later in the chapter but briefly introduce them here. One approach, to put it a bit crudely, stresses 'moral facts'. While opposing reductionist and social deterministic understandings of 'moral facts' in order to clear a space for undetermined ethical action, this approach foregrounds some notion of sociocultural dynamics and structures as important catalysts of the ethical drive. A second approach emphasizes 'moral experience' and finds in the first-person perspective certain irreducible ethical dynamics. This approach tends to stress the excessiveness of experience, the way that ethical experience can elude attempts to capture it through a society's normative structures, dynamics or concepts. A third approach argues that an inquiry into the drives or impulses that prompt ethical life needs to be connected to an ontological inquiry into the existential roots of the ethical and into the human condition as such. Relying widely on existential phenomenology and the German tradition of philosophical anthropology, this latter approach insists that the question of moral engines must be posed as a radical anthropological question. The chapters in this volume variously elaborate each of these approaches, sometimes combining more than one. Like any schematic, our tripartite division is necessarily simplified and intended for heuristic purposes. Notably, these approaches are not mutually exclusive. In fact, we will argue that there is an essential complementarity among the three foci and that this complementarity offers a powerful analytic lens through which to explore ethical drives.

Section One: Moral Engines as a Borderland Inquiry

This volume is the result of the editors' insistence on the need for a close interdisciplinary collaboration between anthropology and philosophy when exploring the domain of ethics. This is not a new position, especially on the part of anthropologists. However strained this disciplinary relationship might at times be, many of the protagonists in the bourgeoning anthropology of ethics have pointed out that the anthropological investigation of the ethical requires a special dialogue with the philosophical tradition, if not a heightened philosophical sensitivity (notably Laidlaw 2014, Lambek 2010a, Mattingly 2014,

Zigon 2009). Some of the authors contributing to this volume even stress this interdisciplinary affinity to the extent that the anthropology of ethics and morality is only truly possible as a new kind of philosophical anthropology.[2]

The philosophical incitement at the heart of the anthropological turn to ethics shows itself most obviously when core terms like 'ethics' or 'morality' are put into play because these invariably invoke a plethora of related concepts. That is, core concepts not only serve central as analytical 'tools' for the anthropologist but, put in the terminology of hermeneutics, they establish conceptual horizons that include other central concepts and analytical frameworks. These conceptual horizons point toward an ontological level of inquiry, though this is not always made explicit. To briefly illustrate, we call on four of these 'grounding' conceptual connections to suggest the ontological profundity of the problematics inherent in the question of moral engines: virtue, possibility, the ordinary (or immanence) and freedom. All of these are frequently invoked in the current anthropological literature or have been forcefully put forward as central to anthropology's investigations of ethical life.

The notion of virtue, which plays a central role in the anthropologies of morality taking their cues from virtue ethics (be they Aristotelian or Foucauldian in orientation), implies, on the one hand, some notion of selfhood (a *psychē* or subjectivity) as the seat of ethical character and the agentive locus of ethical orientation, and, on the other hand, some understanding of the place and status of the human self in relation to the (sociocultural) world. What is important in the present context is to acknowledge that once the question of 'moral engines' is thematized, this basic relationship between selfhood and world quickly shows itself to be highly charged theoretically. In other words, the understanding, and the allocation, of ethical drive, of ethical teleology if you will, is brought to bear on how the ontological relationship between self and world is construed.

From an ancient Aristotelian perspective, ethical teleology is part and parcel of a cosmological teleology, which means that the individual human being, as a *zoon logon echon* that has its place within a 'logically' ordered cosmos, is naturally endowed with a drive toward a higher degree of completion and in this sense a natural drive toward the good and a catalogue of virtues in and through which human excellence is actualized.[3] Beyond the ancient world such a 'metaphysical biology', as MacIntyre argues in *After Virtue*, becomes untenable[4] (MacIntyre 1985: 162). Both in MacIntyre's neo-Aristotelian account of virtue ethics and in Foucault's account of ethics, which is not exactly a moral philosophical doctrine, but conceived rather in terms of a history of ethical thought, the self is expressly cleared of an innate teleology. For the former, ethical selfhood is narratively constructed and infused with ethical orientation by the reigning historical traditions. For the latter, the ethical subject 'is not a substance. It is a form...' (1997: 290), which means that the concrete ethical subject emerges from a generative relationship with the ethical norms and rules that are imposed on the subject 'by his culture, his society, and his social group' (Foucault 1997: 290–91, cf. 1992: 26–27).

Emptying the individual human self of a naturally constituted ethical drive thus entails that the original impetus of the ethical, the 'moral engine', must now be located elsewhere; in the world, in social dynamics or structures, in a tradition or in a culture that impress on the individual self a certain type of ethical teleology. But where the impetus of the ethical is located immediately has profound consequences for the understanding of the range and limits of ethical possibility and for the understanding of the relationship of such modal categories as possibility, reality and necessity. If it is indeed tradition, as MacIntyre holds (in *After Virtue*), or culture, as Foucault holds, that harbors ethical teleology, will ethical possibility be fundamentally constrained by a given moral reality? Or is ethical striving, despite its origin within a given historical context, nonetheless capable of striving beyond, i.e. transcending, a given moral reality?

Such questions have prompted contemporary anthropologists writing about ethics to explore possibility at individual, interpersonal and societal levels. These questions also immediately bear upon the question of the immanence of ethics to human agency – on ordinary ethics. This has proved a lively topic in continuing anthropological discussions as anthropologists have wrestled with questions like: is there something transcendent about ethics or is it fully embedded in the everyday? If it is fully embedded, does this doom it to being reducible to a particular society's normative structures and practices? (Because this issue has been so crucial in anthropological debates, we return to it in more detail in Section Two.)

This line of thinking leads to another vexed concept and domain of inquiry: freedom. Although many anthropologists have eschewed this term in their formulations (with notable exceptions), most do insist that there is an indeterminacy to ethical life and that the ethical cannot be subsumed unproblematically within an already demarcated social structure in the manner of a straightforward socialization process. But this advocacy of indeterminacy does raise the question of ethical freedom. Put most strongly, the very notion of ethics itself, some would argue, presupposes freedom, or at least a kindred notion of non-determined potentiality, not merely as impetus but as its condition of possibility. As James Faubion writes – without, however, pursuing this lead – there seems to be a mutual implication between ethics and freedom from which he sees 'no escape' (2011: 37–38; for an extensive exploration of this mutual implication, see Dyring, chapter 6 in this volume and Dyring, under review). This implication is perhaps most pointedly stressed by James Laidlaw, when he famously proclaimed that 'an anthropology of ethics will only be possible – will only be prevented from constantly collapsing into general questions of social regularity and social control – if we take seriously, as something requiring ethnographic description, the possibilities of human freedom' (Laidlaw 2002: 315). This raises the methodological and epistemological question: how is ethnographic description of 'the possibilities of human freedom' possible? But given the contested ontological status and the highly elusive – perhaps even illusive – character of 'human freedom', this question is impossible to separate from the equally fundamental question: what is human freedom? In other words, the methodological and epistemological question seems to be inseparably tied in with an ontological question. Hence, taking seriously 'the possibilities of human freedom' would seem to require also taking seriously the implicated philosophical problematics.

This exceedingly brief discussion of four recurring concepts in the anthropology of ethics is intended to illustrate that once the question of moral engines is thematized, it registers an accompanying conceptual horizon that, as it unfurls, goes beyond what can be addressed epistemologically or methodologically. It presses inquiry into very basic ontological considerations about the human condition as such. This might seem merely to suggest that anthropologists need to rely upon philosophers (as professional experts in ontology) to guide them in their inquiry into the ethical. But this is not our point. Rather, we are suggesting the necessity of a more mutually interdependent sphere of inquiry at the level of ontology – a borderland inquiry.

Destabilizing the Terrain

But what do we mean by a borderland inquiry? And what don't we mean? Certainly, we are resisting a disciplinary role delineation in which the anthropologists' task in the conversation is to provide thick descriptions and/or strange 'facts' to philosophy. Historically, this role division has marked one predominant way in which the dialogue between the two disciplines has unfolded. Each discipline uses the other, in rather eclectic fashion, to establish more authority (Clifford 1988). Anthropology has turned to philosophy in order to be able to say something more authoritatively about the human condition, and philosophy has turned to anthropology in the search of empirical authority. This mutual borrowing and authority building (however useful at times) falls short of a proper dialogue that destabilizes knowledge.

It is certainly true that few contemporary philosophers engage seriously with the wealth of ethnographic descriptions and theoretical explications to discover the potential they harbour for a more complex, but also more subversive and critical conceptual development. Despite this philosophical reluctance, there are some notable instances in the history of western philosophy, where it is exactly the insistence on taking seriously alterity and cultural diversity that brings about new philosophical orientations. In some respects this was already the impetus of Herder's objection to the philosophical obsession with reason as a universal, transcendental faculty and his turn toward the historical, cultural, linguistic development of the human being (Herder 2004). In early twentieth-century philosophy, Wittgenstein's preoccupation with Frazer's Golden Bough is worth mentioning and along the same lines also Winch and MacIntyre's debates on the status of rationality vis-à-vis, for instance, magical practices (Winch 1964; Wittgenstein 1993). Bernard Williams has written of the 'ethnographic stance' and the possibilities of inter-cultural understanding (1986: 203) and most recently Jonathan Lear (2006) has founded an exploration of possibilities of ethics in times of cultural devastation on anthropological accounts of the traditional Crow way of life.

By calling on these examples, we might seem to suggest something more modest than we intend. These cases most clearly illustrate how a borderland conversation may occur when philosophers take up anthropological depictions of exotic alterities, including alternative forms of epistemology or ontology, not simply to bolster empirical authority but to challenge or expand philosophical positions. Without discounting the value of this, we are suggesting something even more radical: a combined effort to bring our disciplinary resources to bear so that we can pursue, empirically as well as theoretically, a decentring kind of dialogue.

We aim to contribute to a more genuine dialogue that promotes this creative, destabilizing potential. This borderland inquiry urges us, in varying degrees, to take up 'roles' generally associated with the other discipline, challenging the usual idea that there are some people who are anthropologists and can provide the ethnography and other people who are philosophers and can do the ontological analysis. Our excursion into 'moral engines' propels us into a position in which not only human indeterminacy but also non-essentialism in general is recognized. We, each in our own discipline, are pushed to break with the disciplinary essentialisms that all too often become an obstacle in our interdisciplinary discussions; the disciplinary essentialisms that urge us to assume the roles of gatekeepers whenever someone from another discipline dares step onto our turf.

This role reversing, or role expanding, border inquiry is very much a work in progress and may not always be apparent in the chapters that follow. Readers will find that the anthropological chapters contained here are, by and large, steeped in culturally specific particulars and anthropology's trademark thick description. The philosophical contributions, by and large, are not. Because anthropological contributors draw so heavily upon the vocabularies and traditions of philosophy in doing so, the interdisciplinary nature of thought may be more apparent in their chapters than in the philosophical ones. These philosophically infused contributions reflect a precedent in the discipline, especially as anthropologists try to explore cultural and personal possibility as ontological matters.

Several authors in anthropology have already noted the necessity of venturing into this borderland with philosophy in questions pertaining to possibility and the practical transcendence of prevailing social structures. Michael Jackson, for example, describes his project of existential anthropology as an endeavour toward an ethnographically grounded philosophical anthropology, that 'abandon[s] the substantive idea of the universal' (*in casu* a human substance with a fixed essence) and 'focus[es] on the universalizing impulse that inspires us to transgress parochial boundaries, push ourselves to the limit, and open ourselves up to new horizons through strategies that take us beyond ourselves' (2013: 20, see also Jackson and Piette 2015). Vincent Crapanzano, to offer another example, sees an impetus for his project of a literary-philosophical anthropology in the 'problem of cultural creativity' and the fact that sociocultural anthropological research has tended to ignore individual 'imaginative processes' – in fact, '[t]he individual has always been something of an embarrassment in anthropology' (2004: 1). Criticizing the social sciences for sacrificing the singular to the general and for an 'implicit if not explicit emphasis on determinism', Crapanzano's philosophical anthropology is intended instead to address 'human creativity, transgressive possibility, and imaginative play', and ultimately 'to address the question of human freedom, however delusional that freedom may be' (2004: 6; for another important, literarily and philosophically inspired defence of singularity and anti-determinism from an anthropological perspective, see also Rapport 1997).

The edited book *Anthropology and Philosophy: Dialogues on Trust and Hope* (Liisberg et al. 2015) offers a recent example of creative acts of dialogue and even co-writing between philosophers and anthropologists.[5] And there are also a few earlier examples of this kind of collaborative effort. Despite these creative forays, what anthropology might offer philosophy in a destabilizing kind of way is far less well articulated. In the context of this volume, one kind of answer arises: because we emphasize what might be called the sources or conditions for morality (rather than simply morality's cultural content or practice), anthropological contributions reveal how concrete instantiations of ethical life speak to ontological matters. Generally speaking, from an anthropological perspective, ontology and ethics are not to be addressed merely abstractly or only via consultation with the western philosophical canon. Approaching ethical drives empirically opens up the whole conceptual horizon of inquiry because it illuminates the diversity of human responses that can serve as answers or responses to the call of the ethical. As Karen Sykes put it, cultural phenomena can be understood as answers to questions we might think of as philosophical – for her, the 'big questions' are ontological, that is, 'What is life?' questions. She argues that anthropologists ought to see their studies of culture as 'answers' or 'responses' to such ontological questions (2010: 169, see also Leistle 2016 for further elaboration of this line of thinking). Mattingly (under review) argues that in an analogous way the anthropological contribution to ethical matters, when put in conversation with phenomenological philosophy, reveals how culturally shaped 'moral facts' and 'moral experiences' are socially situated responses to existential or ontological ethical questions.

Anthropological approaches that highlight the 'experiential excesses' of ethical life are especially suitable for exposing the ontological indeterminacy of the ethical domain. Many anthropologists would claim that investigations into the 'actual' or empirical are also investigations into the possible. This claim can be contrasted with the distinction between anthropology and philosophy that, for example, Lear makes in his beautiful book, *Radical Hope* (2006; see also Dyring in this volume). In this well-known work, Lear distinguishes his inquiry into possibility from anthropological considerations of what actually happened – in his case to the Crow peoples when the buffalo (and their traditional way of life) disappeared. However, for anthropologists, at least after the hermeneutical turn, there has been a profound doubt about our ability to get at 'what really happened' which stems exactly from the experiential excesses of the anthropological encounter: the direct and disturbing experience of the limits of our familiar concepts.

These excesses arise not only in the confrontation with radically different worlds and ontologies, but also, and more importantly, in the confrontation with situations in which interlocutors themselves find that their own words and familiar concepts fail to adequately capture their experiences. Or, put more positively, there is a richness of ethical experience that seems to speak to what cannot be said, what might or might not have happened, what might or might not happen, in ways that simply exceed and elude structures of meaning. While we claim that this excessiveness at the empirical level is a gift for philosophy, it must be acknowledged that it has rarely been received as such. It is perhaps just these elusive disturbances, these 'alien moons of reason' (cf. Därmann 2005) that ethnography introduces that have so often sidelined it from philosophy. How is all this alterity and excess to be accounted for conceptually, even formally?

But the challenge of conceptual disturbance afflicts anthropology as well. Anthropology, as already noted, continues to lean heavily upon western scholarly traditions, including philosophy.[6] Anthropologists cannot be congratulated for being, somehow, more conceptually imaginative than philosophers. Both disciplines suffer from difficulty in getting past received assumptions. Despite the discipline's longstanding insistence on contesting western styles of thought, anthropologists still find themselves confronted with the problem of how to listen. How can one attend to the voices and world views of interlocutors so that these voices press insistently enough to disrupt one's own received ways of thinking? How can one's field experiences, styles of representation and theory building prompt a reconsideration of 'our' (philosophy's or anthropology's) most basic assumptions and starting points? Certainly, these are not new questions or troubles for anthropology.

Our ambition here, which can by no means be fully realized, is to use this borderland inquiry to aid in creative destabilization. A conversation between the two is mutually beneficial when it can address this inevitable limitation. A useful recent example is anthropologist Veena Das' discussion of Wittgenstein's interpretation of Frazer's The Golden Bough:

> Wittgenstein's great insight into Frazer's The Golden Bough was that Frazer is unable to see that the feeling of dread that he attributes to the past dark crimes committed by savages is related to his own constricted imagination of the life of the other ... Wittgenstein's remarks of Frazer ... are oriented to make us consider

existence as always being capable of being more, or other, than its present realizations. (2015: 79–80)

Here we have an anthropologist (Das) drawing upon a philosopher (Wittgenstein) to contest the imaginative failure of an earlier anthropologist (Frazer). Das finds that it is the philosopher who is able to see potentiality in the lives of Frazer's 'savages' in ways that Frazer, himself, is apparently blind to.

One example from the philosophy side, especially pertinent for this volume, is the way that Heidegger's phenomenological terminology might be reconsidered in light of ethnographic accounts of the everyday across a wide diversity of cultural contexts. Ethnography has the potential to provide thick descriptions (interpretations of other people's interpretations, as Geertz [1973] formulated it)[7] that render the concrete, ontic scene of the phenomenological, ontological investigation infinitely more profound than the conflated, average everydayness described in *Being and Time*. For phenomenology, an ethnographic vantage point that emphasizes the excessiveness of ordinary lived life entails an originary decentring of philosophical analysis. Ethnographic analysis may further disturb long-standing distinctions between reflection and everyday practical immersion or the 'natural attitude' by exploring how reflection can occur precisely through immersion in practical life (Mattingly [under review]; Mattingly and Jensen 2015; Mattingly 2014). Broadly speaking, ethnographic analysis reveals the inability of philosophical analysis to grasp everything in clear and distinct concepts and thus dethrones logical analysis as a 'first science'.

While Heidegger's critique of the western metaphysical tradition to a large extent remains a movement internal to this tradition, notably as an exploration of its origins and the estranged resources of these origins, later continental philosophers – such as Levinas, Foucault, Derrida, Nancy – while not exactly drawing on ethnography, would be more open to the importance of instances of radical alterity that are irreducible to any intellectual tradition, yet constitutively at work at the core of human life (see Raffoul in this volume). In contemporary phenomenology, however, Bernhard Waldenfels seems to be the most open to the importance of engaging directly with the anthropological tradition in order to get a deeper understanding of the role of unassumable alterity or alienness in the very constitution of homely and familiar orders and in the very constitution of the ethical subject (Waldenfels 1999). We will return to Waldenfels's responsive phenomenology of the alien later in this introduction.

Section Two: Moral Engines and Anthropology's Ethical Turn – A Brief History of Core Themes and Debates

Around the turn of the millennium, several prominent anthropologists, quite independently of each other, started criticizing the discipline for having been reluctant to deal with morality and ethics other than as epiphenomena which should be explained by reference to something else and presumably something more profound (e.g. social structure or economic and political interests) or, alternatively, as norms and values which dictate peoples' behaviour, and called for situating moral experience, practice, reasoning and judgment at the centre of what anthropology should be concerned with and for refining our theoretical tools for doing so (Faubion 2001; Heintz 2009; Howell 1997; Kleinman 1999; Lambek 2008, 2010a; Sykes 2009; Zigon 2007, 2008). Furthermore, a number of anthropological monographs were published which had morality and ethics as their central theme (see for example Basso 1996; Hirschkind 2006; Mahmood 2005; Rasanayagam 2011; Robbins 2007; Rogers 2009).

An early landmark was James Laidlaw's Malinowski Memorial Lecture in 2001 (Laidlaw 2002), which programmatically called for an anthropology of ethics and freedom. As touched upon above, Laidlaw argued that in order for anthropology to develop a more informed theoretical reflection on the nature of ethics, it would be necessary to break with the Durkheimian understanding of morality which had so thoroughly permeated anthropological thought on the issue, leading anthropologists to equate the moral and the social, and find a way to describe the possibilities of human freedom. Most anthropologists who have since contributed to the anthropology of ethics and morality have agreed to some extent with this idea that we need to move beyond the Durkheimian legacy and similar theories of morality with strongly collectivist underpinnings (Lambek 2010a, 2010b, this volume; Zigon 2007, 2008; Mattingly 2012, 2014; for a notable exception, see Yan 2011). However, there has been less agreement about what this movement beyond the Durkheimian 'moral facts' would imply and which alternative concepts of ethics and morality should inform it.

While the body of literature is growing rapidly, which makes it a somewhat difficult task to give a clear outline of the field and distinguish unequivocally the various trends within it, there are certain themes and positions that have played central and structuring roles since the beginning of the ethical turn. One central theoretical influence is Foucault, whose thinking has been enormously influential on anthropology's ethical turn. Foucauldian inspired approaches have been at the forefront of its theoretical development from the very beginning (notably Faubion 2001, 2011; Laidlaw 2002, 2014, this volume; Mahmood 2005).

At the same time, a second inspiration has been an orientation toward Aristotelian ethical thought, both in dialogue with and, sometimes, in clear opposition to the aforementioned Foucauldian take on ethics (for an influential example of the latter, see Mattingly 2012). Philosophy of language has provided a third major theoretical source of inspiration, especially among the proponents of the influential 'ordinary ethics' approach. Here Wittgenstein's and Austin's thoughts on the self-structuring capacity of language have played an important role, not least in dialogue with Cavell's interpretations and further developments of these ideas (notably Das 2007, 2012; Lambek 2010a,

2010b, this volume). A fourth recurring source of inspiration has been phenomenological and hermeneutic philosophy (Mattingly 2010, this volume; Throop 2010, 2012, 2014, this volume; Zigon 2007, this volume).

In addition to this plethora of sources of inspiration, some key debates have begun to crystallize. Laidlaw (this volume: 175) suggests that the current debate in the anthropology of ethics should be seen as organized along the 'fault lines' emerging around a number of questions frequently recurring in the literature: who (or what) acts as an ethical subject? Is ethics immanent or not? Is freedom a necessary component of ethical life, and if so, what kind of freedom? The question of immanence that Laidlaw points to has been an especially contentious one, and Laidlaw's aforementioned chapter usefully reviews some of the crucial claims that have been made on various sides of this. On the ordinary side are those who argue for the pervasiveness of ethical life because 'human action is always subject to criteria of evaluation', and is part of practical reasoning, as Lambek contends (Laidlaw this volume: 182) or because it runs through the 'un-dramatic actions' of 'apparently unremarkable people in modest circumstances' and is largely tacit, as Das argues (ibid.). For others, ethics proper cannot be linked to the habitual or everyday but should be reserved for moments of disturbance, or even societal level break-down, when norms can no longer be unproblematically followed, provoking conscious, and reflective consideration of those norms. Zigon's (2007) early work is a notable example of this position. A third position, in which Laidlaw places his own work, sees the ethical as a kind of range, a gradation that moves between the tacitness of in-the-midst action and relatively more explicit moments, often characterized by a 'standing back' from action posture. According to Laidlaw, this variation can also be extended to collective entities, including an entire society's ethical life. He argues that 'ethical reflection is more concerted in some settings and institutions ... and is subject at times to intensification' (ibid: 184).

A related point of contention concerns whether or not ethics needs to be distinguished from morality. For example, in their highly influential work, Keane (2016) and Laidlaw (2014, this volume) both invoke Bernard Williams' distinction between the ethical (involving the question 'how should one live') and morality, which refers 'to a subset of answers to that general ethical question' that have been developed in particular historical times and places. These scholars find this distinction extremely useful in supporting a comparative analysis of different historically produced moral systems. Ethics may be an existential matter but how it is shaped – through morality systems – is a historical and even classically anthropology matter. For other reasons, a number of scholars have resisted this division. Lambek, for instance, finds this vocabulary problematic because those advocating it tend to remove ethics from everyday life. He calls upon Aristotle's claim that 'wise judgment entails reflection and feeling', 'can occur before, during, and after the act' (this volume: 141) and is thoroughly ordinary. It does not make sense, from Lambek's perspective, to make a strong demarcation between habitual convention (glossed as 'morality') and a stepping out of action kind of evaluation (glossed as 'ethics'). Along different lines, Mattingly has identified the most notable division in the difference between authors who proceed from a poststructuralist or Foucauldian analytical framework, focusing on how moral selves are shaped within particular discursive regimes, and authors who, like herself, proceed from a first-person perspective, emphasizing moral life in more experiential and interpersonal terms as a struggle often characterized by doubt and ambiguity (Mattingly 2012 and 2014).

Section Three: The Question of 'Moral Engines' as a Radical Anthropological Project – Three Approaches to 'Moral Engines'

Although the sources of inspiration and thematic debates within anthropology are readily visible in the anthropological contributions to the book, our particular point of departure, and the borderland nature of our inquiry, leads us to identify some rather different 'fault lines' than those Laidlaw (this volume) considers. By asking the authors to engage the question of what the moral drives in human life are, where they are located and how they present themselves to us, we have asked them to make explicit the most basic dimensions of their respective approaches to the ethical.

As noted earlier, we have identified three categories or kinds of answers to the question of what constitutes an ethical drive: 1) some authors focus primarily on the concrete instantiation and social shape of the moral in such phenomena as values, criteria and standards; 2) some authors stress the features of moral experience and the experiential dimensions of being ethically committed or confronted by an ethical demand; and 3) finally, some authors explore the existential roots of morality as a way to investigate what it is to be human. In distinguishing these three analytic strategies, one of our objectives is to help to clarify certain theoretical and ontological assumptions about the ethical that often remain unthematized in current anthropological debates. A related aim is to examine how apparently diverging approaches to the most foundational registers of ethical life may reveal complementary, and thus ontologically enmeshed, aspects of the same phenomena.

As can easily be recognized, each of these strategies addresses the question of ethical drives from a somewhat different angle. Naturally, this entails a prioritization of the aspects of the phenomenon under consideration, and perhaps even certain analytical blind spots. Hence, a cautionary point to stress is that none of the approaches can stand alone in providing an exhaustive account of the 'moral engines' in practical life. Rather, a sufficiently rich exploration of something as complex and multifarious as moral life, and the impulses and drives that charge it, demands multiple viewpoints, however uneasily they may sometimes sit with one another. Bringing multiple frameworks to bear, as we do here, is intended to allow those aspects of ethical life naturally foregrounded within one given framework to complement and even cross-pollinate with the others. Indeed, such complementarity and cross-pollination can be seen in several of the individual chapters. Each of them, even when largely showcasing one approach, is intent on rendering the moral scene in complex ways and thus none of them fall exclusively and without residue within one of the three categories. Despite this overlap, we have, for reasons of theoretical clarity, chosen to group the chapters under the heading of that general approach which an individual chapter most illuminates.

We describe them below in an order that begins with the most well-known anthropological approach (emphasizing what we have called 'moral fact') because this is the one most obviously situated in the discipline's long history of concern with the structures of social communities. However, we should note that this is not the order of the chapters in the volume itself. Here, we open with the chapters that contribute most directly to a 'moral experience' approach. These speak most obviously to the kind of borderland inquiry that this book, as a whole, takes up, which is situated between phenomenological philosophy and anthropology.

First Approach: Moral Engines and 'Moral Facts'

One way of approaching the question of moral engines, very familiar to anthropologists, considers the concrete instantiations of the moral or ethical in such phenomena as values, criteria and ethical standards. Despite the aforementioned break with the Durkheimian understanding of morality that in many respects inaugurated the anthropology of ethics and morality, this first approach retains some degree of affinity with the Durkheimian focus inasmuch as it seeks to preserve some version of the category of 'moral facts', of cultural, historical, discursive schematics that grant certain practical possibilities. At the same time, it infuses this focus with a sensitivity to the ethical and practical dynamics that participate in establishing obligations and commitments, establishing certain forms of subjectivity and in preventing or furthering cultural change. Hence, we should not, as Joel Robbins warns us, 'throw out the Durkheimian baby with the bathwater of too rigid models of cultural reproduction' (Robbins 2007: 295). Rather, as Michael Lambek points out in one of the already 'canonical' texts in the anthropology of ethics, once the emphasis in the investigation of social phenomena is shifted from a focus on rules and regulations in the classical, positivist Durkheimian sense to an Aristotelian focus on action and practical judgment, there is 'no great methodological danger in dissolving the ethical into the social...' (Lambek 2010a: 28).

Three chapters foreground such overall approaches to the question of moral engines. Lambek's chapter focuses on the performative constitution of ethical criteria as that which sets up the standards whence practical, moral obligation arises and according to which concrete acts and, moreover, practical life on the whole can be judged. In arguing for ethics as immanent, he recognizes an affinity with Durkheim, but with important differences. 'Where Durkheim saw morality as a function of rules or structure', Lambek proposes seeing it as a matter of 'action and criteria', believing that this offers a 'less static, less determined, and less mechanical' picture than the one so often associated with Durkheim (this volume: 139). Lambek calls upon Aristotle to propose what he calls a 'middle path' between a view of ethics that treats it as correct rule following and another view that treats is a courageous willingness to 'ignore, subvert, or transcend rules' (ibid.). He finds in Aristotle's theory of practice judgment a 'middle path' that recognizes that circumstances demand judgments about what actions to take where the correctness of judgments cannot be ascertained in any straightforward sense but are open to debate and challenge. As Aristotle points out, 'the good or right thing to do in a given set of circumstances, or how to do it, is not always obvious' (ibid.: 140). He finds Aristotle's notion of 'balance' useful in considering what is demanded by good judgment; one must find the right balance (among various claims to our attention, desire, interests, etc.) to fit the circumstances.

Robbins undertakes an exploration of cultural values and, more specifically, of where in our practical everyday worlds they can be said to reside. Robbins finds Durkheim a useful thinker for exploring the role of values, recalling Durkheim's suggestion that moral facts are 'ones that awaken in people a combined sense of both duty and desire' (Robbins this volume: 155). He notes that anthropologists have often relied on Durkheim's emphasis on the moral as a generator of duty and obligation but he suggests that we might take up a less explored Durkheimian-inspired path by investigating the connection of the moral to desire – 'the desire we have to do what is good' (ibid.). Thus Robbins aims to offer us a rough sketch of moral social psychology.

Both Lambek and Robbins address the question of 'moral engines' by focusing on how the concrete instantiations of the moral or the ethical can be said to harbour some kind of binding and hence obligatory force; i.e. how criteria come to commit, how values make their claim. Laidlaw's work can also be seen as retaining some of the concerns addressed by Durkheim, although strongly disputing the sociologist's neglect of the role of freedom in morality. Laidlaw wants to be able to continue to carry out some version of the comparative ethnographic project that was inspired by Durkheim's social vision while avoiding social determinism. Laidlaw's invocation of Williams' distinction between ethics and morality allows him to preserve a place for continued and deepened comparative exploration of the social contours of moral life. Laidlaw also calls upon recent work by Jonathan Lear to shore up this comparative ambition in a way that moves beyond the traditional Durkheimian project, proposing a research programme in comparative analysis that foregrounds not merely morality systems but ethical capacities (treated as conscious evaluative reflection). Laidlaw poses the following question: 'When – under what social and political conditions – might people's capacity for reflection be encouraged and when might it be discouraged?' He suggests an ethnographic inquiry that would consider 'the forms, constraints, and possibilities of ethical life under diverse political regimes and circumstances ... the possibilities of ethical life they respectively promote and inhibit' (Laidlaw this volume: 190).

Webb Keane's recent and already influential work, *Ethical Life* (2016), addresses at least part of Laidlaw's proposed agenda for comparative inquiry into the constraints and possibilities of ethical reflection under various social and political conditions. Although Keane is not a contributor to this collection, he is worth some discussion because he offers a significant articulation of how such a comparative project might be carried out. His ethical framework bears some important resemblances to Laidlaw's; it also highlights the capacity for ethical evaluation, or as he puts it 'accountability'. He argues that ethical reflexivity, in the form of evaluation and accountability, is pervasive. He focuses on the minute social exchanges that comprise everyday life to reveal this. The central reflexive property of social interaction he examines is the ability to take an outsider (or third-person) perspective on oneself. Such perspective taking, he contends, is ubiquitous in ordinary social interaction and it is essential to ethics, it is part of the very ordinary call to be accountable for ourselves and our actions. He explores the kinds of social conditions that 'induce reflexivity' (2016: 25) by introducing the felicitous concept of ethical affordance.

The very term 'affordance' draws attention to the way that social situations and cultural semiotics need not be thought of as deterministic but rather as offering a set of potentialities embedded in everyday action ('A chair may invite you to sit but it does not determine that you will sit' [2016: 28]). Ethical affordances, according to Keane, are 'the opportunities that any experiences might offer as people evaluate themselves, other persons, and their circumstances' (2016: 31). For example, he notes the presence of multiple ethical worlds that characterize many (if not all) people's lives, whatever the community. He argues that the co-existence and clashes of 'historically constituted ethical worlds' provide 'crucial stimuli to moral reflection' (2016: 124). In proposing his notion of ethical affordances, Keane takes up the 'Durkheim problem' by treating 'moral facts' not as straightforward causes of ethical behaviour but rather as resources that are, in different times and places, socially available.

Second Approach: Moral Engines and Human Experience

A second way to approach the question of 'moral engines' is to focus on the very experience of being the sort of creatures for whom not only biological and economic necessity, but also the practical necessity of ethical demands, make claims. The main analytical unit of this kind of approach is thus what is often called moral experience (see Kleinman 1999, 2006; Zigon and Throop

2014). In this approach the ethical is investigated by examining closely the experiential and often affective registers of ethical praxis. As Zigon and Throop have recently put it,

> [a] focus on experience foregrounds the fact that our existence as humans is framed by our particular perspectives, vantage points, and embodied emplacements within a given social world. The aspectual, partial, perspectival, situated, horizon-defined, and horizon-defining modes of being that characterize our existence as humans, as well as the particular forms of revealing and concealing associated with them, is thus necessarily implicated in a turn to examine the experience of morality. (Zigon and Throop 2014: 6)

Whereas the first approach to the question of moral engines sketched above engages critically with the 'moral facts' of ethical standards, criteria and values and the dynamics in which they are established, this second, experiential approach to the ethical is to a greater extent directed towards what in phenomenology has been termed the facticity of human existence; that is, towards the very 'fact' that we are always already, as Zigon and Throop describe it above, thrown into a world, and towards the ethical ramifications of the burdensome or boring, anxious or joyous, or regrettable, despairing or perhaps disappointed experience of this, the 'thrownness' of our being.

One important characteristic of the ethicality of human life foregrounded in this perspective is a poignant sense of being committed ethically; a sense of commitment that oftentimes is neither easily accounted for nor necessarily transparent and meaningful to those undergoing it, nor easily answered, let alone, satisfied, however viscerally one feels one ought to adhere to it. In all such cases it becomes manifest that it is experience itself, as Kleinman puts it, that is moral because experience here 'is the medium of engagement in everyday life in which things are at stake and in which ordinary people are deeply engaged stake-holders who have important things to lose, to gain, and to preserve' (Kleinman 1999: 8).

This experiential approach provides another register for exploring how the ethical infiltrates everyday life, one that also takes us some distance from unconscious rule-following. Throop's chapter, for example, concerns regret as a 'mooded' response to our life situations and to our past. Like many other contributors, he depicts the ethical in relation to some kind of striving toward the 'best possible' life, in other words, some orientation to the good. This is a matter of 'thinking well of oneself' (or striving to) but it should not be treated as a kind of thinking so much as a form of affectivity. He introduces 'regret' as a way to consider this. In offering regret as a mood that is also a form of attunement to the worlds we inhabit, he suggests that the ethical is a pervasive aspect of everyday life. However, in drawing upon Husserl and Heidegger's phenomenology, Throop introduces a quite different vocabulary and perspective for thinking about the ordinariness of ethical life than we find among some of the other anthropological contributors in this volume. (See Lambek, in this volume, for an illuminating contrast.) If moods like regret represent something dispositional, even immanent, the immanence they reveal has a highly subjunctive quality. Regret, Throop argues, is linked to a desire for a different world (Troop this volume: 68). If a mood tells us about dominant, socially shared, modes of practical life, it does so through an indirect path because it foregrounds how people situate themselves in relation to possible lives – ones that they did not live and perhaps even ones that are no longer culturally available. In the vocabulary of Wentzer (in this volume), it speaks of an 'immanent transcendence'.

Louw's chapter also suggests this quality of 'immanent transcendence' that belongs to everyday life, offering an extended meditation on the complexity of moral emotions among Uzbek Sufis. She paints a deeply, even tragically, paradoxical ethical scene in which the Uzbeks have come to try to re-embrace their Muslim religious heritage after seventy years of Soviet rule and its suppression. For them, the embracing also reveals the depth of loss in which they no longer know how to be 'real Sufis'. Louw insists from the beginning that in speaking about their religious experience, she is not locating it in some transcendent realm beyond ordinary life but in terms of a this worldly virtue ethics. She asks such questions as: how is religion lived in ordinary life? How is it interlaced with other ethical concerns and commitments? How does it help to shape moral emotions? For the Uzbeks she has come to know, the ethical shows up in everyday life through paradoxes.

Remorse, as the visceral emotional presence of paths not taken and lives not lived, is the central theme of Louw's chapter. She takes up Derrida's concept of the ghostly presence of something that has disappeared and yet still haunts the present: 'Haunting describes the seething presence of what appears not to be there, the ghost or apparition being a form through which something barely visible or lost makes itself known' (Louw this volume: 90). Louw draws from this to develop the notion of a haunted ethics: 'the moral choices one did not make, but could have made; the moral acts one did not engage in, but could have engaged in; and the moral person one did not become but could have become – in short, by the moral potential in all that which is discarded in the search for moral perfection' (ibid.). Her investigation into ethical remorse underscores that the status of everyday ethics is precarious because the moral foundations are shaky (ibid.: 84).

Meinert offers yet another portrait of an everyday ethics that is neither mundane nor unconsciously habitual. Rather, in her ethnographic case, ordinary activities become the vehicle for extraordinary moral acts. Meinert takes us to postwar Northern Uganda, where the everyday serves as a moral and cultural resource for this task of creating a space for living; crucially, in her account, this demands acts of forgiveness. She argues that forgiveness has become an essential task for Northern Ugandans as they try to resettle into their old social communities. The everydayness of these actions, and the mundane cultural resources that they rely upon, reveal the everyday as a precarious venture and as posing a certain relentless ethical demand: it is an Every

Day (Meinert this volume: 100). While in this postwar period there have been highly public and extraordinary measures aimed at forgiveness, most notably extensive rituals and criminal trials which have been highly publicized by the media, these are not practices that people seem to trust very much to achieve anything. Rather, it is through more humble, less visible acts that the rebuilding of community relies. Meinert insists that in this ethnographic situation, morality is not a taken for granted matter, some kind of 'unconscious cultural compulsion' (ibid.: 101). She finds it more useful to adopt Robbins' discussion of the ethical as a field of values which may attract but certainly do not compel people to act in light of them. She also argues that in this situation, these Ugandans have a heightened awareness of the morality of every single action that is taken. This situation of heightened attention also creates potentiality; new possibilities for community making arise.

Some proponents of neo-Aristotian ethical approaches who foreground moral experience bring in narratological theory to examine the emplotment of moral experience and the particular temporal organization that ethical teleology grants human experience. This has been much more common in philosophy than anthropology. In her chapter, Mattingly argues that in promoting a narrative version of the self, virtue ethics philosophers have tended to offer an overly coherent picture of self-becoming. In taking up this narrative self, Mattingly sets out to confront the limitations of its usual formulation. Drawing upon an ethnographic of one mother facing the death of her young child, she argues that if we are to attend to the excessiveness of the ethical demand, as phenomenologists insist, and if we call upon narrative to consider this, then narrative must be able to offer something more complex and more ambiguous than self as sameness over time or as mere linear progression (in a novice to expert fashion). The narrative self that Mattingly proposes is more like an experimental self, someone who, in response to ethical demands, engages in narrative experiments, actively living out 'imaginative variations that destabilize narrative identity' (Ricoeur 1988: 249).

Because the chapters in this section give prominence to an experiential approach to the question of moral engines, they also emphasize (ethnographically and philosophically) a first-person perspective. A conceptual figure that recurs in several of them, where the authors attempt to capture the practical experience of being drawn into moral matters or ethical quandaries, is the figure of responsiveness. Accordingly, ethical phenomena might be described in terms of acts and stories or moods, even dreams and hauntings, that are performed, told or that arise in response to some ethical demand that encroaches in all registers of existence to make its claim. Bernhard Waldenfels, the German phenomenologist who more than any other philosopher has pursued the dynamics of human responsiveness, writes of the logic of such responsive phenomena, that when struck by an ethical or existential demand, 'I cannot not respond … even so, it is still I who engage with or evade it' (Waldenfels 2006: 109, our translation).

This responsive logic entails several important aspects. First, such demands in a sense single out their addressees, strike them in their singularity; the ethical situation arises here and now and demands of exactly me or us that we engage with or evade it. Secondly, they institute a sphere of practical necessity; whether I attempt to meet the demand or evade it, I still respond to it. Thirdly, such demands can never be mastered and assimilated to one's own being or practical agenda, and hence they can never be adequately satisfied and ultimately quenched. Any response can at best be an approximating attempt to meet the demand. Several chapters in this volume point to instances of moral experience in which ethical demands faced by informants exceed the latter's capacities or the practical acts that may be taken to respond to them. Not surprisingly, such moral experiences are often heavily laden with pathos and manifest in affects like nostalgia and regret, as examined by Jason Throop (2014 and this volume), in the disappointment with or despair in the face of improbable or failed moral experiments, as found in Cheryl Mattingly's work (2014, this volume), in the precarious experience of a call for forgiveness that makes a relentless demand but never really fulfils its promise of restoring trust, as explored in Lotte Meinert's chapter (this volume), or in the spectral experience of ethical inadequacy which Maria Louw explores in her chapter on the hauntology of discarded ethical possibilities (this volume).

Finally, as a fourth aspect of the responsive logic we find responsive freedom, which is explicitly addressed in Rasmus Dyring's chapter (this volume). The idea here is that although I cannot 'not' respond when struck by ethical or existential demands, it is nonetheless 'I' who have to respond in my own name. As Waldenfels points out, this procedure of finding a proper answer is always, potentially at least, *erfinderisch*; that is to say, a creative, experimental, inventive process that supersedes the limits of the given order of things and opens new horizons (Waldenfels 2006: 118). With originary creativity lodged in the responsive dynamic, a notion of freedom enters into the exploration of moral experience, which, contrary to highly contested Enlightenment notions of freedom as pure, unaffected, willing, of independent, autonomous individuality, is a kind of freedom that is found to begin elsewhere than in the individual, a freedom that inheres in the very process of responding to something beyond one's command and power.

Dyring addresses responsive freedom by calling attention to the role of possibility and its relation to the ethical in both philosophy and anthropology. He sees some convergences but also some differences. He identifies four ways in which freedom and underdetermined possibility, whether explicitly invoked or implicitly presumed, play a role in the anthropology of ethics: (1) as an exercise or practice rather than an a priori fact of nature or transcendental reason; (2) as an activity that 'takes place within a range of culturally granted possibilities'; (3) as an aspect of character formation; and (4) as something that entails a degree of reflectivity and consciousness (Dyring this volume: 120). While agreeing with the anthropology of ethics in this emphasis on possibility, Dyring argues that it should be supplemented with more radical considerations of the ontological relationship between such modal categories as the real and the possible and the existential conditions of possibility of the concrete ethical possibilities that afford themselves in a given situation. Dyring has to proceed carefully here. He does not want to appear to align with a notion of conditions of possibility in the Kantian sense – that is, the 'a priori conditions that make possible empirical experience' – conditions unavailable to experience. Rather, as a phenomenologist, Dyring argues that the conditions of possibility are experientially available.

He calls upon both Jonathan Lear and Kierkegaard to make his case. He notes that possibility in Lear's well-known case of the Crows is not directed to 'intentional, deliberative action' but to another register characterized by a 'pathos of anxiety' and a 'posture of hope' (ibid.: 122). This register is better explored in a Kierkegaardian sense in which freedom becomes actual in anxiety. Anxiety is a special term here that does important analytic work. Unlike fear, which is about something, freedom – made actual in anxiety – 'has no object, it is an experience that experiences no definite thing … and as such it harbours an experiential disclosure of possibility as such' (ibid.: 123). Focusing on an unsettling experience prompted by a peculiar artwork, Dyring explores this anxiety and its relation to the dynamics of responsive freedom. (For further discussion of the notion of responsive freedom, but as related to the ethical concept of responsibility, see Raffoul in this volume.)

The notion of ethical responsiveness that comes to the fore between the various authors who, with more or less theoretical explication, describe the ethical as procedures of responding has a wider span than is captured by an ethics that focuses only on reflective and intentional responses. Ethical responsiveness in this experiential sense resonates immediately with all registers of human existence. This is why pathos, sentiments, moods also play such prominent roles in this perspective. The frequent use of the idiom of responsiveness, hence, explicitly or implicitly, holds a potential for the development of notions of freedom that emphasize other experiential dimensions than the more intellectualist dimensions of reflectivity.

Third Approach: Moral Engines and the Human Condition

A third approach to the question of moral engines emerges when exploring the relationship between ethics – and the ethical broadly speaking – and what is held to be the specifically human. The strategy here is to explore whether, and if so, how, ethical drive and the urgency of ethical demands can be traced to the very conditions of human existence as such. This third path has a strong affinity with the second in the sense that it builds upon the exploration of ethical phenomena through experience-near ethnographic and phenomenological means, but posing it as a distinctive third strategy suggests another way that anthropology and philosophy can be in fruitful conversation. It is not surprising that the ethical turn in anthropology has also been a turn (and sometimes a return) to philosophy. This volume highlights anthropological engagements with ordinary language philosophy, philosophy of action, virtue ethics, political philosophy, and existential and phenomenological traditions. But what becomes clear in putting anthropological considerations of the ethical alongside philosophical ones is how much this recent anthropological work has the potential to reinvigorate the radical philosophical anthropological questions: what is the human being? What characterizes human existence as such?

Not surprisingly, the three contributing phenomenological philosophers (Wentzer, Raffoul and Dyring) are most concerned to articulate what is at stake in this ambition to address the question of the human from the perspective of responsive phenomenology. However, the anthropological contributors to this volume who highlight the importance of experience for ethical life also draw inspiration from the existential phenomenological tradition. They illustrate the phenomenological point that the being-committed that arises with the factical experience of the lived human life is established neither on the collective level as a collection of facts, rules and regulations, nor in a causal sequence as the necessary consequence of a given cause. Rather, this being-committed channels, at its core, an irreducible demand that emanates from finite, singular human existence as such. This radical existential dimension that resides just below the surface of the experiential focus indicates strongly what these anthropological investigations might fruitfully contribute to a philosophical anthropology of the human condition.

Zigon's chapter is an anthropological contribution that explicitly connects this experiential focus to claims about the human condition, and as such raises questions addressed most thoroughly by the two philosophical chapters in Section Three. Though grounded within his ethnographic material, Zigon directly argues the importance of considering the question of 'the human' in relation to any project to articulate ethics. However, he expresses this ambition in a particularly cautionary way and as a challenge to any version of metaphysical humanism that might creep into a consideration of ethical life. He contrasts 'an ethical imperative for human existence' with the 'metaphysical humanism' that he believes characterizes not only much of moral philosophy but also, increasingly, anthropology's studies of ethics. He recognizes that both the notion of dwelling and the vocabulary of dignity 'make claims about the essential "nature" of being human' (Zigon this volume: 203) but the status of these claims is very different, he argues. Metaphysical humanists assert the notion of a 'predefined human with very specific characteristics and capacities' while the sort of ethical imperative he proposes does not do so. He proposes 'dwelling' as a useful way to understand human life because it involves a simpler and less normatively freighted 'claim that to be human is to be intimately intertwined with a world for which one is concerned and which is concerned, in turn, for it' (ibid.: 204). Zigon's concern is to create or borrow from vocabularies that help us to see human existence as a space of possibility, including in ways that do not tie us to moral vocabularies that seem to presuppose too much about what it means to be human or to be an ethical being.

Wentzer's chapter is particularly useful as an entry into a philosophical discussion of a responsive ethics that directly addresses the question of what it means to be human. He takes on the task of noting points of convergence but also some crucial differences between his responsive approach and some dominant positions within anthropology. He outlines three primary claims that characterize a responsive approach: 1) that life is characterized by an essential human indeterminacy; 2) that the ethical claims we face exceed our ability to respond or even to account for them through our normative categories; and 3) most centrally that exploring the ethical demands a first-person phenomenology in order to illuminate these first two conditions, namely 'being in a state of ontological indeterminacy and ethical overload' (Wentzer this volume: 215).

As he explores these three claims, Wentzer comes to some important conclusions that distinguish his phenomenological approach from some of the frameworks taken up within the anthropology of ethics, and can be seen in some of the other chapters in this volume. While he recognizes that the notion of the human as undetermined developed in German philosophical anthropology does entail some 'elements about human agency and freedom' (ibid.: 218), the issue of freedom as connected to 'reason, consciousness or language' are not presupposed in it. Rather, human freedom is linked to this existential condition of indeterminacy as an ontological condition coupled with the burden of action – 'we have to lead a life instead of just living it' (ibid.: 219). Humans are 'world-open creatures that are not bound to an environment but released to the world' (ibid.: 218). This release carries with it the burden that responsivity entails. 'Responsiveness is the name for a way to cope with one's fragile and finite existence that captures our being called upon to act anyway' (ibid.: 222).

There are certainly some key differences between the way that many anthropologists have been considering matters like the role of freedom and normativity in ethical life and what Wentzer proposes here. However, as he develops his thesis, Wentzer does not emphasize difference so much as points of convergence or resonance. He finds the ethnographic insistence of anthropology, especially when it is taken up as a kind of 'existential anthropology', particularly important. As he puts it: 'Maybe one may say that existential anthropology actually indicates the intersection between philosophical anthropology and ethnography, approachable from both ends, with the first-person-perspective and a sensitivity for the universal relevance of lived experience with its ethical quandaries as its vantage point' (ibid.: 219).

Francois Raffoul's chapter sharpens our understanding of what a phenomenological portrait of ethics can contribute to an investigation of what it means to be human as a responsive being. Among all the chapters, his is most explicit in setting up a contrast between the kind of philosophical anthropology that builds upon an existential picture of human life and one that draws upon Kant's seminal formulations. Raffoul contrasts two notions of responsibility (as a foundational ethical concept) and the distinct ethical scenes that surround them. Both treat responsibility as the heart of ethics but in very different, perhaps even irreconcilable, ways. The traditional version links responsibility to accountability. It is credited primarily to Kant, though with a reach that goes back to Aristotle and Plato. The other, which Raffoul favours, arises from post-Nietzschean phenomenological philosophy. Here, responsibility is linked to responsiveness: the 'motif of the call'.

Several motifs characterize the phenomenological picture of responsibility that Raffoul draws. Notably, all of these portray responsibility in terms of the experience of responding, as befits a phenomenological approach. First, it is, in the first instance, passive. We are responsible not because we are able to begin something but because of a prior something that initiates – we are exposed 'to an event that does not come from us and yet calls us' (Raffoul this volume: 236). Second, responsibility is not, primarily (or at all), directed to the self. It certainly cannot be characterized by an effort of self-mastery of some sovereign subject. Rather, it involves a response to an other, an alterity that makes its demands. Third, the demands made upon us exceed our capacity. Responding – or responding adequately – is, in an important sense, impossible. Thus the call for care is also a burden that exposes our own finitude (ibid.: 236). If we are free, Sartre tells us, we are 'condemned to be free' (ibid.: 238). Our vulnerability to our own finitude, in the face of impossible or excessive demands, reveals why the whole notion of responsibility as accountability is utterly flawed. It does not make sense to presume that we can use our reason to respond adequately in ways that could be justified after the fact. This picture simply fails to understand the deeper, ontological nature of how responsibility engages us. Finally, we are responsible for a future – for what is to come – but this future has an openness we can never fully envision or control. Rather, it is characterized by an unforeseeability; it is unapproachable even as we approach it (ibid.: 240). We can think about the future in an immediate eventful sense, the way we are 'respondents, not absolute beginners' in any situation, or we can consider this in a more long-term sense as when we consider the future of our children and the next generations, or the fate of the planet. Whatever the horizon, our vulnerability and finitude is exposed.

Conclusion

To sum up and state things in their boldest terms, the trope of moral engines suggests that inquiry into the ethical has its natural home neither in anthropology nor philosophy alone but in a borderland between them. The point of entering this borderland is not to provide a general overview of philosophical and anthropological theories of morality and ethics. Rather, by exploring the question of what drives or propels ethical life, this volume aims to generate scholarly, interdisciplinary debate on a topic that has not yet been given the theoretical attention that its importance warrants.

Our suggestion has been that a preliminary way of addressing the question of moral engines opens if we follow the intuition that this inquiry into the 'engine' in ethical and moral matters is an inquiry into their drives or impulses, including the ontological or existential roots of the ethical as such. Hence, this kind of inquiry entails an effort to shed light on the urgency, the imperative quality or the practical necessity with which such matters present themselves to us, and to place analytical emphasis on the questions of the constitution of this urgency, of the status of such imperative qualities, of whence comes this practical necessity or commitment so poignantly felt in ethical dilemmas.

This kind of inquiry provides a vantage point for critically questioning the most commonly deployed ethical concepts. In fact, there is a thread of critique about received ethical concepts running through many of the contributing chapters. For anthropologists, this is often spurred on by the experiential excesses of the ethnographic encounter itself. Implicitly or explicitly, authors ask: do dominant vocabularies of morality do justice to the particular ethical demands people face? Are these vocabularies capable of grasping the properly ethical drive unfolding in human practice? The commitment to experience-nearness, so central to anthropological research, is thus not abandoned with the turn toward the fundamental question of moral engines and the venture into the borderlands between anthropology and philosophy. Even the more philosophical contributions in this volume remain true to this commitment by stressing phenomenological analysis as opposed to logical deductions and simplistic thought experiments. Hence, contributors – both anthropologists and philosophers – draw upon complicating ethnographic or aesthetic cases, suggesting potential paths for a conceptual development that might be better equipped to address the ethical dimensions and moral engines of human life.

Cheryl Mattingly, Ph.D. is Professor of Anthropology in the Department of Anthropology at the University of Southern California. She was a Dale T. Mortensen Fellow at Aarhus University's Institute of Advanced Studies (2013– 2015) and is a 2017 recipient of a John Simon Guggenheim fellowship. She has been the PI and Co-PI on federally funded grants from National Institutes of Health, Maternal and Child Health and the Department of Education. She has received numerous awards from the American Anthropological Association, including the Victor Turner Book Prize for *Healing Dramas and Clinical Plots* (Cambridge 1998), the Stirling Book Prize for *The Paradox of Hope: Journeys Through a Clinical Borderland* (2010, University of California Press), the New Millennium Book Prize for *Moral Laboratories: Family Peril and the Struggle for a Good Life* (2014, University of California Press), and the Polgar Essay Prize for 'In Search of the Good: Narrative Reasoning in Clinical Practice' (1998).

Rasmus Dyring is Assistant Professor at the Department of Philosophy and History of Ideas, Aarhus University. In dialogue with the anthropology of ethics, Dyring's research aims at foregrounding the existential dimensions of ethical life. He has published several articles on this subject, for instance, 'A Spectacle of Disappearance' (*Tropos*, 2015).

Maria Louw is Associate Professor at the Department of Anthropology, Aarhus University. She is the author of 'Everyday Islam in Post-Soviet Central Asia' (Routledge, 2007) and a number of other publications focusing on religion, secularism, atheism and morality in Central Asia.

Notes

1. In this introductory chapter, while we do not distinguish 'morality' from 'ethics' as concepts, we recognize that several of the contributing authors, for various theoretical reasons, do make such a distinction. We briefly discuss some of these reasons in a later section of the introduction.
2. Several of the authors contributing to this volume will feature in the special issue 'The Human Condition: Reinventing Philosophical Anthropology' (edited by Cheryl Mattingly and Thomas S. Wentzer), forthcoming in *HAU: Journal of Ethnographic Theory*.
3. Aristotle's doctrine of ethical teleology is not mechanistic. Ethical striving is natural, but excellence does not happen merely by nature (*physei*) or by chance for that matter. Ethical virtue requires continuous habituation and cultivation of a disposition of the soul (*hexis proairetikē*) that enables the virtuous person to conceive rightly a given moment of action and choose the act appropriate to it.
4. Notably, in his later work *Dependent Rational Animals* (1999), MacIntyre revises his position, reverting to one closer to Aristotle's original thinking, by founding his ethics in the animal condition of the human being. It is worth pointing this out because it shows how MacIntyre's reconsideration speaks to the whole question of what constitutes an ethical drive. Acknowledging that tradition and social roles can only provide ethical orientation, but not an ethical drive as such, MacIntyre now looks to nature and natural vulnerability for an account of what we are here calling a moral engine of ethical cultivation and comportment. He admits that 'no account of the goods, rules and virtues that are definitive of our moral life can be adequate that does not explain ... how that form of life is possible for beings who are biologically constituted as we are' (1999: x).
5. It is notable that two of the editors of *Moral Engines*, Mattingly and Wentzer, have chapters in the *Anthropology and Philosophy* collection. In one sense, it provided inspiration for this edited collection despite the difference in topic and tone. (See the prologue for further discussion of this.)
6. Here we leave aside the longer history of the philosophical roots of the discipline of anthropology, cf. Adams 1998.
7. Of course, it should not be forgotten that Geertz' articulation of ethnography as thick description is deeply indebted to philosopher Gilbert Ryle, exemplifying yet again the dizzying interpenetration of philosophy and anthropology.

References

Adams, William Y. 1998. *The Philosophical Roots of Anthropology*. Stanford: CSLI Publications.

Basso, Keith. 1996. *Wisdom Sits in Places: Landscape and Language among the Western Apache*. Albuquerque: University of Mexico Press.

Clifford, James. 1988. 'On Ethnographic Authority', in *The Predicament of Culture: Twentieth-Century Ethnography, Literature and Art*. London: Harvard University Press, pp. 21–55.

Crapanzano, Vincent. 2004. *Imaginative Horizons: An Essay in Literary-Philosophical Anthropology*. Chicago: The University of Chicago Press.

Das, Veena. 2007. *Life and Words: Violence and the Descent into the Ordinary*. Berkeley: University of California Press.

———. 2012. 'Ordinary Ethics', in Didier Fassin (ed.), *A Companion to Moral Anthropology*. Oxford: Wiley-Blackwell, pp. 133–49.

———. 2015. 'What does Ordinary Ethics Look Like?', in M. Lambek, V. Das, D. Fassin and W. Keane (eds), *Four Lectures on Ethics*. Chicago: Hau Press.

Därmann, Iris. 2005. *Fremde Monde der Vernunft: Die ethnologische Provokation der Philosophie*. Munich: Wilhelm Fink Verlag.

Dyring, Rasmus. (under review). 'From Moral Facts to Ethical Facticity: On the Problem of Freedom in the Anthropology of Ethics', *HAU: Journal of Ethnographic Theory*. Special Issue: 'The Human Condition: Reinventing Philosophical Anthropology', ed. Cheryl Mattingly and Thomas Schwarz Wentzer.

Faubion, James. 2001. 'Toward an Anthropology of Ethics: Foucault and the Pedagogies of Autopoiesis', *Representations* 74: 83–104.

———. 2011. *An Anthropology of Ethics*. Cambridge: Cambridge University Press.

Foucault, Michel. 1992. *The Use of Pleasure: The History of Sexuality II*, transl. Robert Hurley. London: Penguin Books.

———. 1997. 'The Ethics of the Concern for Self as a Practice of Freedom', in Paul Rabinow (ed.), *Ethics, Subjectivity, and Truth: Essential Works of Foucault 1954–1984. Volume 1*. New York: New Press, pp. 281–301.

Geertz, Clifford. 1973. *The Interpretation of Cultures*. New York: Basic Books.

Heintz, Monica. 2009. *The Anthropology of Moralities*. New York: Berghahn Books.

Herder, Johann G. 2004. 'Treatise on the Origin of Language', in *Philosophical Writings*. Cambridge: Cambridge University Press.

Hirschkind, Charles. 2006. *The Ethical Soundscape: Casette Sermons and Islamic Counter-Publics*. New York: Columbia University Press.

Howell, Signe. 1997. *The Ethnography of Moralities*. London: Routledge.

Jackson, Michael D. 2013. *Lifeworlds: Essays in Existential Anthropology*. Chicago: The University of Chicago Press.

Jackson, Michael D. and Albert Piette. 2015. *What is Existential Anthropology?* New York: Berghahn Books.

Keane, Webb. 2016. *Ethical Life: Its Natural and Social Histories*. Princeton, NJ: Princeton University Press.

Kleinman, Arthur. 1999. *The Tanner Lectures on Human Values*, Vol. 20, ed. G.B. Peterson. Salt Lake City: University of Utah Press.

———. 2006, *What Really Matters: Living a Moral Life amidst Uncertainty and Danger*. Oxford: Oxford University Press.

Laidlaw, James. 2002. 'For an Anthropology of Ethics and Freedom', *Journal of the Royal Anthropological Institute* 8: 311–32.

_____. 2014. *The Subject of Virtue. An Anthropology of Ethics and Freedom.* Cambridge: Cambridge University Press.

Lambek, Michael. 2008. 'Value and Virtue', *Anthropological Theory* 8: 133–57.

_____. 2010a. 'Introduction', in Michael Lambek (ed.), *Ordinary Ethics: Anthropology, Language and Action.* New York: Fordham University Press, pp. 1–38.

_____. 2010b. 'Toward an Ethics of the Act', in Michael Lambek, *Ordinary Ethics: Anthropology, Language and Action.* New York: Fordham University Press, pp. 39–63.

Lear, Jonathan. 2006. *Radical Hope: Ethics in the Face of Cultural Devastation.* Cambridge, MA: Harvard University Press.

Leistle, Bernhard. 2016. 'Responsivity and (some) other Approaches to Alterity', *Anthropological Theory* 16(1): 48–74.

Liisberg, Sune, E. Pedersen and A.L. Dalsgaard. 2015. *Anthropology and Philosophy: Dialogues on Trust and Hope.* New York: Berghahn Books.

MacIntyre, Alasdair. 1985. *After Virtue*, 2nd corrected edition with postscript. London: Duckworth.

_____. 1999. *Dependent Rational Animals.* Chicago: Open Court.

Mahmood, Saba. 2005. *Politics of Piety: The Islamic Revival and the Feminist Subject.* Princeton: Princeton University Press.

Mattingly, Cheryl. 2010. *The Paradox of Hope: Journeys through a Clinical Borderland.* Berkeley: University of California Press

_____. 2012. 'Two Virtue Ethics and the Anthropology of Morality', *Anthropological Theory* 12(2): 161–84.

_____. 2014. *Moral Laboratories: Family Peril and the Struggle for a Good Life.* Oakland, CA: University of California Press.

_____. (under review). 'Ordinary Possibility and Responsive Ethics: A Philosophical Anthropology of the Small Event', in *The Human Condition: Reinventing Philosophical Anthropology.* Guest co-editors, Cheryl Mattingly and Thomas Wentzer. *HAU: Journal of Ethnographic Theory.*

Mattingly, Cheryl and Uffe Juul Jensen. 2015. 'What Can We Hope For? An Exploration in Cosmopolitan Philosophical Anthropology', in S. Liisberg, E. Pedersen and A. Dalsgaard (eds), *Anthropology and Philosophy: Dialogues on Trust and Hope.* New York: Berghahn Books, pp. 21–56.

Nussbaum, Martha. 1986. *The Fragility of Goodness: Luck and Ethics in Greek Tragedy and Philosophy.* Cambridge: Cambridge University Press.

Rapport, Nigel. 1997. *Transcendent Individual: Towards a Literary and Liberal Anthropology.* New York and London: Routledge.

Rasanayagam, Johan. 2011. *Islam in Post-Soviet Uzbekistan: The Morality of Experience.* Cambridge: Cambridge University Press.

Ricoeur, Paul. 1988. *Time and Narrative*, vol. 3, trans. Kathleen Blamey and David Pellauer. Chicago: Chicago University Press.

Robbins, Joel. 2004. *Becoming Sinners: Christianity and Moral Torment in a Papua New Guinea Society.* Berkeley: University of California Press.

_____. 2007. 'Between Reproduction and Freedom: Morality, Value, and Radical Cultural Change', *Ethnos* 72: 293–314.

Rogers, Douglas. 2009. *The Old Faith and the Russian Land: A Historical Ethnography of Ethics in the Urals.* Ithaca: Cornell University Press.

Sykes, Karen. 2009. *Ethnographies of Moral Reasoning: Living Paradoxes of a Global Age.* New York: Palgrave Macmillan.

Skykes, Karen 2010. '"Ontology Is Just Another Word for Culture": Motion Tabled at the 2008 Meeting of the Group for Debates in Anthropological Theory, University of Manchester.' S. Venkatesan (ed). *Critique of Anthropology* 30: 152–200.

Throop, C. Jason. 2010. *Suffering and Sentiment: Exploring the Vicissitudes of Experience and Pain in Yap.* Berkeley: University of California Press.

_____. 2012. 'Moral Sentiments', in Didier Fassin (ed.), *A Companion to Moral Anthropology.* Oxford: Wiley-Blackwell, pp. 150–68.

_____. 2014. 'Moral Moods', *Ethos* 42(1): 65–83.

Waldenfels, Bernhard. 1999. *Vielstimmigkeit der Rede.* Frankfurt a. M.: Suhrkamp Verlag.

_____. 2006. *Schattenrisse der Moral.* Frankfurt a. M.: Suhrkamp Verlag.

Williams, Bernard. 1986. 'Reply to Simon Blackburn', *Philosophical Books* 27(4): 203–208.

Winch, Peter. 1964. 'Understanding a Primitive Society', *American Philosophical Quarterly* 1(4): 307–324.

Wittgenstein, Ludvig. 1993. 'Remarks on Frazer's Golder Bough', in *Philosophical Occasions: 1912–1951.* Indianapolis: Hackett Publishing Company.

Yan, Yunxiang. 2011. 'How Far Away can we Move from Durkheim? – Reflections on the New Anthropology of Morality', *Anthropology of this Century* 2. Available online at http://aotcpress.com/articles/move-durkheim-reflections-anthropology-morality/.

Zigon, Jarrett. 2007. 'Moral Breakdown and Ethical Demand: A Theoretical Framework for an Anthropology of Moralities', *Anthropological Theory* 7: 131–50.

_____. 2008. *Morality: An Anthropological Perspective.* Oxford: Berg.

_____. 2009. 'Within a Range of Possibilities: Morality and Ethics in Social Life', *Ethnos: Journal of Anthropology* 74(2): 251–76.

Zigon, Jarrett and Jason Throop. 2014. 'Moral Experience: Introduction', *Ethos* 42(1): 1–15.

PART I

Moral Engines and Human Experience

2

Ethics, Immanent Transcendence and the Experimental Narrative Self

Cheryl Mattingly

Introduction

The framing question of this volume is: how should we think about the moral engines of ethical life? It might be argued that an engine is a highly problematic metaphor to capture moral life and its exigencies. An engine suggests something powerful, Lambek (this volume) protests, and it seems to privilege one version of ethics, a driving, striving sort of effort. Admittedly, its kinship with all things mechanical resonates uncomfortably with the host of industrial tropes that have infiltrated western modernity's considerations of just about everything. Yet I find this ungainly figure alluring precisely because it conjures something that pushes, propels with a force that is easy to lose control of, a force with its own mysterious energy. I too think of an engine as something powerful, even dangerous, excessive. Placed in the right kind of machine, it can run you over. While other contributors to this volume sometimes prefer other figures, 'tracks' for Michael Lambek, 'roots' for Thomas Wentzer, I will see what I can say about what it means when your most deeply cherished commitments propel you, as if from the outside, toward destinations you may not have imagined or ever wanted to go.

   In taking up this question, I will bring three intellectual traditions into conversation. Two of them are central to the chapters in this volume.[1] One tradition has roots in anthropology's longstanding concern with the sociocultural features of ethical life and their more recent problematization in anthropology's 'ethical turn'. (For many anthropologists, this problematization has also involved a serious engagement with moral philosophy.) The other is rooted in phenomenological philosophy, in particular the tradition that foregrounds human responsiveness to what is often called the 'ethical demand'. My chapter considers what a responsive phenomenology can offer to an ethical framework that takes the social 'facticity' of ethical life seriously, including the norms and values it so deeply shapes, while at the same time registering the existential excess of an ethical demand that cannot be adequately captured by reference to pre-existing social norms. The third tradition I consider is philosophy's virtue ethics, with its focus on the singularity, individuality and the socially embedded qualities of moral experience. More specifically, this chapter considers how we might rethink the 'narrative self', including ethical self-formation as a narrative activity, by bringing insights from all three of these traditions to bear.

But first, some difficulties. Both sociocultural anthropology and phenomenology raise challenges for a notion of a 'narrative self' along the lines that virtue ethics philosophers have frequently proposed. Anthropologists and phenomenologists typically insist that any individual human is, in an important sense, 'derivative', as Raffoul (this volume) puts it, an 'I' who 'always comes after' (Raffoul, p. 246). Anthropology takes this derivative feature from the primacy of a sociocultural world that precedes any individual, a world into which she is born. Phenomenological philosophers propose their derivative 'I' against a Kantian 'I' – the autonomous and responsible subject 'who is the cause of his or her actions through the freedom of the will' (Raffoul, p. 233). Rather than an agent being a 'cause', in the sense that Kant presumes, the phenomenological self is 'in the first instance, passive' (Raffoul, p. 237) because it is always a response to a prior something that initiates. We are exposed 'to an event that does not come from us and yet calls us' (Raffoul, p. 236).

Both anthropological and phenomenological traditions have tended to downplay not just the Kantian autonomous individual but the individual altogether. There is an obvious logic to this. If the individual self is derivative, it makes sense to give analytic primacy to the sociocultural conditions that precede and shape an individual's ethical life (in the anthropological picture) or the experiential features of this 'call to respond' (in the phenomenological one). Despite this persuasive logic, I have found it worrisome. In my own previous work, I have argued that even if it is correct to treat the individual as analytically secondary, there is a cost to diminishing the individual self as a site of ethical experience and a causal agent. Isn't it possible to reject an autonomous, self-mastering, freely choosing 'I', while still preserving a self who acts and bears a historical singularity?

I have found moral philosophy's virtue ethics a more hospitable home for developing insights about ethical self-formation characterized by the singularity of selves and circumstances. Narrative has played an important role in depicting this. Virtue ethics also challenges this Kantian self but continues to follow Aristotle in foregrounding an 'I' – even a narrative self – as a central site of ethical work. Narrative singularity represents what I believe to be crucial both for an existential picture of ethical responsiveness and a sociocultural picture that resists reduction to mere socialization. Attending to the narrative singularities of self and circumstance can help to challenge the hegemony of social norms as well as deepen the phenomenological insistence on the fragile, precarious and finite character of ethical responsiveness.

My primary concern in this chapter is to rethink the kind of narrative self so often presumed by virtue ethics philosophers, one that – to my mind – lays too much stress on coherence. Any coherence portrait of the self is too simplistic. If we are to attend to the excessiveness of the ethical demand and if we call upon narrative to do so, then a narrative self must be conceived as something more complex and ambiguous than self as sameness over time or as mere linear development suggests.[2] The narrative self I will propose is more like an experimental self, one who, in response to ethical demands, engages in narrative experiments with her own becoming. She actively lives out 'imaginative variations that destablize narrative identity' (Ricoeur 1988: 249).

This chapter is divided into several parts. The first section situates my own claims within recent anthropological discussions of ethics. I am particularly interested in the way that ethical intentionality has been conceived, how anthropologists have attempted to put forward some version of intentional and reflective agents while trying to avoid committing themselves (in any strong sense) to the idea of the individual ethical actor. I propose a robust personal and narrative self as a contrast figure, foregrounding 'longer term intentions' and the small histories (personal and interpersonal) that are its temporal home. The second section locates this narrative self in philosophy's virtue ethics, where it has been espoused most explicitly. The third section addresses the difficulties with a narrative self that is tied too closely to self-coherence. I offer, instead, an experimental and responsive self – a self characterized by immanent transcendence. Here, I bring together both phenomenology and Ricoeur's discussion of literary narratives as laboratories for ethical experiment in ways of living. The fourth section turns, more specifically, to the question of moral engine(s). My proposal for one such moral engine is 'care of the intimate other', a project that is self-defining, that calls for intentional commitments that last over time, and that is frequently ethically fraught. I draw upon one case example where I take up my claims about the experimental narrative self in ethnographic context. I consider the way in which one mother, faced with the death of her young daughter, experiments with how to respond to the existential – and excessive – demands this poses to her and the kind of self this situation seems to call for.[3]

The Problem of Ethical Intentions:
An Anthropological Conversation

The question of what prompts ethical life or ethical intentionality would likely have been far easier for anthropologists to answer just a few decades ago. For most anthropologists, the overall answer could be stated with relative ease:

society and its normative demands. Of course, ascertaining the ethnographic specifics of what those demands were and how they exerted their moral force was not at all a straightforward matter in light of the sheer diversity of human communities. In recent decades, reference to widely shared and communally distinct normative moral orders has been problematized by the demise of holistic notions of culture, rising attention to globalization, and the incorporation of analyses of political and economic factors as key shapers of societal norms. But still, the role of social convention (however it came to exist and be shored up), or what some anthropologists sometimes call the morality system (Fassin 2015; Laidlaw 2002), tended to be held responsible for the ethical life of its community.

Perhaps the first thing to notice about recent anthropological discussions of ethics is how much this has changed. Morality systems still play a crucial role but these are no longer considered sufficient to explain things. Many anthropologists working within the ethical turn are attempting to put two pictures of ethical life together: the version that focuses on the 'social constraints of morality, the norms imposed by society', and 'the individual dimensions of ethics, the freedom each person has to deliberate and to decide, and the inner experience through which ethical subjects are formed' (Fassin 2015: 176). Rather than treating them as antithetical, the ambition is to see how these two understandings of ethical life can help to inform one another. For many scholars, this has meant an increased emphasis not only on the classic (Durkheimian) problem of how humans, through society's primary influence, acquire a kind of 'second nature' that 'can even overcome "first nature"' but also (unlike Durkheim) on the human 'capacity to reflect on and evaluate one's actions as part of this second nature' (Das et al. 2014: 16, also citing McDowell 1994).

However, once one tries to incorporate Fassin's 'individual dimensions' (which include notions of freedom and inner experience), a whole new set of problems arises. A key concern has to do with intentionality and how it figures into ethics. For most anthropologists, it is a simple fact that much of our life, including our moral life, depends upon ordinary, tacit actions that do not require any conscious deliberation. And yet, within recent writings on ethics, even those anthropologists most enthusiastic about acknowledging this unconscious feature of ordinary morality resist placing the ethical fully within the tacit. To do so risks returning to dominant anthropological views of ethical life, again reducing ethics to mere social conformity.

Laidlaw (2014), whose earlier writings (especially 2002) have helped to foster such widespread interest in ethics, has insisted that if we accept that the ethical is tied to the capacity to reflectively evaluate our circumstances in a conscious way, this demands that we have some account of human freedom. For Laidlaw (2014, this volume), the ethical sphere includes the capacity to engage in some sort of second order reflection on the norms themselves, a reflective act that requires one be able step out of the scene of action. While many anthropologists have expressed uneasiness with his adoption of freedom as a key term because of its particularly western (and Kantian) associations (Lambek 2015; Das et al. 2014; Keane 2014, 2016), or think the dichotomy between freedom and convention is too overdrawn, most would acknowledge that there needs to be some room for conscious reflection in any ethical framework.

This line of thinking raises an immediate question: how is it possible to defend an account of ethics that is both broadly shared in a relatively untroubled way and yet calls upon some notion of reflexivity? Many anthropologists have claimed to be investigating 'ordinary ethics', to borrow Lambek's (2010, 2015) vocabulary. For those who contend that ethical life is pervasive and ordinary, it has been especially important to address the puzzle of how ethics can be reflective (or at least have an unremarkable potentiality for reflexivity), and yet not typically be in conscious awareness. A corollary problem is how to address the obvious fact that people may be self-deceiving. Keane puts the challenge as follows: 'If people do not have the consistency of character they think they have, and if their acts are not due to the reasons they give for them, but character and action are shaped by processes that lie beyond their awareness, then what role does awareness play in ethical life?' (2016: 244).

Anthropologists have tackled this difficult question in several distinct, though not always mutually exclusive, ways. One approach stresses the important notion that ethics are, in some sense, public (Lambek 2015, this volume). Thus, even if ethical stances are out of the conscious awareness of a particular person at the individual level, they are nevertheless available because they are shared and known within a community. They show up in the form of 'judgments that circulate across a community, or act descriptions that endure from one generation to the next' (Keane 2016: 244). As Keane puts it, even if people are not necessarily consciously acting, they could, if necessary, back up their 'ethical intuitions' with ethical descriptions that others within their community will be expected to also condone, understand, agree with, or at least recognize as ethical positions.

A second approach demarcates a sphere of ethics proper that emerges only in rare circumstances. Anthropologists adopting this line of thinking are especially keen to differentiate morality (as a societal structure of norms that operates more or less unconsciously) from a conscious domain of ethics. Zigon's (2008, 2011) influential notion of the 'moral breakdown' is a very good example of this. Life moves along more or less unproblematically, Zigon argues, except under very special conditions in which there is such an impasse in how to go on, how to act. Under such conditions what is ordinarily merely habitual and out of view suddenly comes into conscious awareness. Taken for granted norms suddenly become problematized, demanding explicit attention and review. A third (and often related) strategy has allowed anthropologists to make a significant place for conscious reflection by shifting attention from everyday routine activity to a much grander temporal arc, to social history, in which visible and consequential ethical instabilities or even transformations occur at a societal level (Zigon 2011; Keane 2016).

Longer-Term Intentions and Virtue Ethics: History with a small 'h'

My own strategy has been to consider the reflective properties of ethical life not as tied to immediate decisions or even crisis points (though these may arise), but to another pervasive feature of ordinary life – the fact that people make long-term, even life-long commitments to projects and significant others and these bring with them ethical entailments that carry a great deal of force (Mattingly 2014a, b, c). A focus on longer-term intentions in ethical life is congruent with philosophy's virtue ethics.

Although this tradition of moral philosophy is increasingly familiar for an anthropological audience, I will briefly sketch a few points which are particularly salient for my argument. Virtue ethics, the moral philosophy most associated with Greek and Roman antiquity (especially Aristotle), has enjoyed a revival in philosophy since the mid-twentieth century. Much of the impetus behind this revival can be credited to Anglo-American moral philosophers who wanted to challenge the psychologically 'thin' moral selves presupposed in utilitarian and deontological schemes. Its focus on the good, or the good life, concerns more than mere human survival and certainly more than hedonistic pleasure. Rather, it speaks to what we could call human flourishing. Happiness or flourishing cannot be equated with a mere subjective feeling of pleasure or contentment but is better understood as a 'life worth living', a life that is practiced within a social community. Lear's discussion of 'thoughtful desire' illuminates the motivational complexity of this ethical scheme. Lear shows us how, for Aristotle, desire – unlike mere 'appetites' – is part and parcel of deliberative decision-making (1988: 165). One attraction of virtue ethics for anthropologists is that it emphasizes the role of social practices in cultivating the moral self. This is appealing for a discipline that takes the cultural to be more fundamental and primary than the individual.[4]

Despite this rootedness in social practice, philosophical virtue ethics (of various stripes) has placed a certain analytic premium on the individual self. I find this an indispensable addition even for an anthropological ethics rooted primarily in the social. From my perspective, it is also one which is seriously undertheorized,[5] even among anthropologists drawing from virtue ethics philosophers. To bring the individual into the picture in a more adequate way, we need to attend not only to large-scale histories or to micro-level interactions (though these are certainly important) but also to another unit of analysis. This is history on a smaller scale, the history of intentionality that comprises a personal life or a small unit (like a household) who share life over time. From this vantage point it is possible to explore the more conscious side of ethical intentionality as well as attempts at ethical innovation.

Stating this in even stronger terms, and as I have argued elsewhere (Mattingly 2012, 2014a), I do not see how to adopt a virtue ethics approach without some robust portrait of a personal self who is entwined in intimate, personal, self-defining relationships. Several moral philosophers who currently play an important role in informing anthropologists (e.g. Bernard Williams, Charles Taylor, Hannah Arendt, Aristotle) have been particularly eloquent in stressing the personal as a crucial site of ethics, not as an optional addition, but as fundamental to ethical life (Williams 1981; Taylor 1989). For a number of contemporary moral philosophers, Aristotle inspires a more useful portrait of ethics than its primary alternatives – utilitarianism and Kantianism – because Aristotle's ethics are grounded both in the particularities of self and the particularities of situation. Cavell puts it this way: as compared to utilitarianism 'Aristotle emphasizes *myself*, this individual, this development of my character, as the touchstone of goodness and rightness – so forcefully and continuously that some have found his theory to be an ethics of selfishness, not a morality at all' (Cavell 2004: 357). In contrast to Kant's *a priori*, universal principle, Aristotle focuses on 'individual circumstances ... here it is the exercise of my perception of a situation – not an intellectual grasp of necessity, but an empirical judgment ... of practical intelligence ... that determines the course I shall take' (Cavell 2004: 357).

This attention to the individual can also be felt in the influential work of Bernard Williams who argues that the self is ethically constituted by commitments that are not just personal but irreducibly individual. He uses friendship as an example. Our friends are not merely interchangeable with one another, Williams points out, but are quite specific individuals with whom we share histories. This is a significant point since friendship has been taken in some moral philosophies (e.g. Aristotle's) as essential for an ethically flourishing life.

Obviously, I am not the first anthropologist to notice this attention to individuals. So, why have anthropologists skirted (theoretically if not ethnographically) the individual and the small histories of personal lives? This is evidence of a kind of internal conflict about whether it is really analytically necessary for an anthropological virtue ethics to posit a singular individual in any strong or 'thick' sense. On the one hand, this promotes a focus on ethical experience, reflection and responsibility, presumably a good thing. But it also raises the spectre of an individualist humanism that many anthropologists have been keen to distance themselves from (Mahmood 2005; Faubion 2001). And some fear such a focus will weaken the kind of moral investigation that has been a traditional anthropological strength, indeed a contribution, to moral philosophy, namely the comparative investigation of cultural norms, morality systems and prescribed subject positions across a widely diverse range of societies.

It is quite usual even for anthropologists proposing some version of virtue ethics (that is an ethics that places a premium on the self-cultivation of virtues over time) to distance themselves from the individual as a key site of ethical projects (Keane 2016; Mahmood 2005; Faubion 2001). It is certainly important to rid ourselves of the highly problematic and improbable autonomous 'I', but there is a real cost in removing individuals altogether as sites of ethical action and experience. The straw man of the 'autonomous I' has made it difficult to explore the first-person 'I' as a relational being or to attend to the small histories that, in my own ethnographic work at any rate, are of crucial analytic importance for ethics.

Making conceptual room for individuals who are not coterminous with the social roles they inhabit or the mere product of normative ethical practices offers an important dividend in our exploration of ethical life cross-culturally. Introducing morally complex and nuanced agents into our schemes can also illuminate situations of ethical awareness and reflection that show up in intimate spaces even when they are not visible on a world stage. Equally important, following lives through their particular histories and shadowy ambiguities can reveal sources of ethical vulnerability that accompany fragile projects of becoming.

The Enduring Narrative Self

Many virtue ethics philosophers have advocated a narrative version of the self, one who endures over time. In philosophy, proposals for a coherent or enduring self, as well as a narrative self, were the subject of much debate a few decades ago (especially between the mid-1980s and mid-1990s) which continue to this day. It seems to me that some notion of a narrative self – who has a historical singularity – is also analytically indispensable for any virtue ethics. That is, a strong or 'thick' version of a narrative self is indispensable for an ethics that can do justice to the complexity of the ethics of practical action as well as the cultivation of character.

Indeed, moral philosophers advocating a 'thick moral self', whether directly inspired by Aristotle or not, portray that self as a biographical and diachronic moral agent. So, for Williams, 'ground projects' are self-constituting because who we are as particular persons is formed by an at-stakeness in the world that lasts over time and serves as a morally self-defining compass. Along analogous lines, Charles Taylor declares that our self-interpretations are bound up with 'what is of significance' to us (1989: 34). For Taylor, as for Williams, 'significance' assumes a moral cast because it depends upon what Taylor calls an 'orientation to the good' (1989: 34). Thus, the good life, the committed life, and a person's self-understanding of who he or she is, are all bound up together.

One might ask why the individual, treated as a narrative self, shows up so prominently in philosophy's virtue ethics. The simplest answer is that it is an analytical necessity. Virtue ethics cannot do without the notion of the arc of a life and some kind of biographical integrity. The whole notion of cultivating one's character depends upon it. An individual agent is a historical being, one who persists over time and is imbued with a complex internal life. This is what philosophers have called a 'thick' (that is, socially embedded, historically singular, enduring and emotionally complex) self rather than a 'thin' or 'fractured' one. Such a self is analytically demanded if ethics is concerned with 'the cultivation of character, the training of moral emotions, the centrality of intention, motive and the inner life,' and a focus 'not only on isolated acts of choice, but also, and more importantly, on the whole course of an agent's moral life, its patterns of commitment, conduct, and also passion' (Hursthouse 1999: 170).

There is a temporality to our ethical projects, in other words, that leads many scholars to insist that there is an inherent narrativity to ethical practice and its self-constituting nature. A narrative sense of self is not an 'optional extra,' Taylor contends. Drawing on Heidegger's construal of the temporal structure of being, he states: 'In order to have a sense of who we are, we have to have a notion of how we have become, and of where we are going' (Taylor 1989: 47). We cannot operate without this minimal narrative understanding of our lives. Iris Murdoch calls us 'moral pilgrims,' a conceit that speaks to the quest-like narrative structure of this moral self that is always in the process of becoming. Commitments and projects have a history and, in taking them up or responding to them, we become part of a history. Cultivating virtues as part of these commitments and projects belongs to a task of moral becoming and this, too, implies the narrativity of moral life. MacIntyre, especially in *After Virtue*, offers perhaps the most well-known version of the narrative, historically embedded self (1981).[6]

However, one cannot speak unproblematically about something like a narrative self. Anthropologists have often, and for good reason, been wary of it. One primary objection is that a narrative portrait of the self implies too much coherence, as though life unfolded in the orderly manner of a temporally unified whole, complete with beginning, middle and end. Even as anthropologists turn to this revived virtue ethics within moral philosophy, they often tend to distance themselves from this coherence portrait and offer a more pluralistic or fractured conception. They have also distanced themselves from an individualist self that the notion of the biographical life story may seem to imply. I propose a version of a narrative self that I believe addresses at least some of the critiques directed against it, while strengthening what is truly important and valuable about it.

The Responsive and Experimental Narrative Self

I emphasize narrative not in order to espouse a coherent life but to expose a responsive one, a life where one is sometimes compelled to confront the excessiveness of the ethical demand. What I want to suggest is that such a demand seems to call for self-making as a kind of moral experiment in perceiving and attempting to realize any 'best good.' Responsive phenomenology highlights an imperative to act in an asymmetrical relationship between the ethical demands that face us (paradigmatically stated as 'how should one live?') and our ability to answer them, as Wentzer (this volume) explains. The ethical demand is in this way excessive; it 'exceeds the limits of norms and values' (Wentzer, p. 213). We may try our best, but this best is not the same thing as doing what is good, even by our own lights. Thus, the presence of the ethical demand can be felt as an 'immanent urge to transcend any given option towards its presumably better state or alternative'; it can be characterized by an immanent transcendence (Wentzer, p. 213). The ethical demand is also inescapable, it 'is not a perspective that an agent is free to choose or to dismiss' (Wentzer, p. 215).

What is it about narrative that makes it so useful in capturing a self who confronts the excessiveness of the ethical demand? Stories have the power to foreground this very asymmetry. Narratives, in the form of literary works and everyday speech acts, teach us about the suspenseful and the subjunctive. Ricoeur's extended consideration of the literary narrative and its relation to lived experience highlights this capability. Narrative identity, as lived experience, is neither stable nor seamless: 'it is always possible to weave different, even opposed, plots of our lives' (1988: 248). This instability is exposed in narrative texts which can render life unfamiliar: 'the practice of narrative lies in a thought experiment by means of which we try to inhabit worlds foreign to us' (1988: 249). Paradoxically, as I will try to illustrate ethnographically, this foreignness may include aspects or versions of ourselves that we would, in more direct or explicit espousals, reject as moral possibilities. Such narrative thought experiments may be engendered through stories we read or hear, which is Ricoeur's point, or by dramatic events we experience and even help to create, which is my point.

The kinds of narrative that Ricoeur has in mind are artistic or historical achievements to be found especially in works of art rather than in life as lived. However, we should not consider narrative texts and the narratives qualities of self experience to be antithetical. Rather, I would say (although putting it in different, or at least stronger, terms than Ricoeur might agree with) that narrative is needed to consider the temporality of the self because our lived experience is already narratively prefigured in ways that narrative discourse can distil. Literature can bring into stark relief the radical contingency that is already present in lived experience.[7] The realization of our fragile and finite place in the world, and of our paradoxical character as a being who changes and yet remains, in some ways, the same, is precisely what I think a narrative understanding of the self emphasizes.

Narratives offer a picture of identity that is a 'discordant concordance'. From a narrative perspective, as developed by Ricoeur, rather than depicting a self whose coherence is the result of sameness over time (what Ricoeur calls 'concordance'), coherence speaks to a complex synthesis, even a tension, between the concordant elements of life and its discordant ones (paradigmatically 'reversals of fortune'). A narrative identity is characterized by this discordant concordance. Narrative reveals this aspect of identity because a story offers, at once, a 'manifold of events', which can be discordant, but also 'the temporal unity of the plot'. The plot is, in fact, a configuring feature which includes both this episodic dispersion and also a unification over time – of time. As Ricoeur puts it: 'configuration' to this art of composition which mediates between concordance and discordance' (1992: 141).

Ricoeur argues persuasively for the advantage of thinking about the unity of a life not in terms of commitments to 'life-plans', as MacIntyre does, but through narrative. As Ricoeur points out: 'Life plan emphasizes the agentive, even the voluntary and willful aspect of action' (1992: 178). But narrative 'places its accent on the organization of intention, causes and chance that we find in all stories'. By bringing 'chance' and reversals of fortune into the picture, it allows us to recognize suffering as well as action. Ethically, it calls attention to what Nussbaum has described as the 'fragility of the goodness of human action' (cited in Ricoeur 1992: 178).

Narrative Selves and Moral Engines: Care of the Intimate Other

How might this narrative self, characterized as a discordant and fluid concordance, formed by chance as well as by intentional acts, be helpful in framing the question of moral engines? How might this portrait also reveal the asymmetry of the ethical demand? To answer these questions, I offer one particular 'moral engine': care of intimate others. What kind of forward movement does this moral engine engender? Family love can be a highly troubled moral practice that makes strenuous demands upon the self and requires the cultivation of virtues that can seem (or actually be) unattainable. While I can't take up the prolific literature around family love and care that has recently emerged in feminist studies and the rethinking of classic anthropological work on kinship, it is worth noting that this literature emphasizes the ethical complexity surrounding practices of relatedness (Borneman 2001; Rapp and Ginsburg 2001, 2011; Horton 2009; Edwards in Venkatesan et al. 2011; Zigon 2013; Mattingly 2014b.[8] In feminist literature, 'care ethics' stresses responsibilities, relationships, intersubjectivity, the circumstantiality of ethics and activity rather than rights, rules and abstract reasoning (Tronto 1993). It also ethically privileges a 'connected self' rather than an 'autonomous self'.

Projects of intimate care are certainly only one kind moral engine that may exert force upon us. And such projects obviously do not hold universally with equal strength. But it is difficult to imagine any human society (and perhaps even some non-human ones) where this task of care of significant others is not central and does not raise deeply felt ethical concerns, demands to respond, to be responsible. Such care also foregrounds the kind of ethical work that lasts over time, enduring for years at a stretch, if not a whole lifetime. Thus, it speaks especially well to intentions that cannot be reduced to momentary choice but rather to longer term and even lifelong projects.

In my own work following African American families raising children with significant disabilities and chronic illnesses, family care is revealed through a multitude of small 'moral experiments' in everyday life which are only recognizable as part of larger ethical projects (Mattingly 2014a). The parents (or grandparents) in these families often find themselves propelled to imagine and try to transform their lives because of these projects of care. In exploring the moral complexity of projects of care that parents undertake in circumstances that are fraught and uncertain, what becomes apparent is that it often seems impossible to find any 'best good' that is worth acting upon, but where, nonetheless, people continue to care about and struggle to obtain some version of a good life. The work of care can engender moral demands to cultivate virtues to be, for example, a 'good enough' parent, provoking critical self-examination and attempts to transform the practical engagements and commitments of oneself, one's family, even one's community. When placed within small histories (the lives of individuals and families, for example), the experimental qualities of these projects of care, and of self-making in light of them, can be brought to light. I do not mean for this talk of experiments to imply an overly goal directed, agentive self. Rather, my point will be to stress self-experience as both indeterminate and excessive.

Cultivating an Experimental Narrative Self: Andrena Faces Death

To illustrate some of these points ethnographically, I turn to Andrena. Her actions and experiences do not reveal a narratively coherent self so much as a narratively paradoxical and even experimental one. When I first met Andrena, it was in the hospital room of a large Los Angeles hospital in the spring of 1997.[9] She was seated next to her four-year old daughter, Belinda, who was recovering from surgery, a still small form in the hospital bed. It was just one month after Andrena had heard the news that Belinda not only had cancer, but cancer of the 'worst kind'. Upon finding that her daughter has this 'worst kind' of brain cancer, Andrena cried out in disbelief, 'I'm dreaming, I'm dreaming, I'm dreaming!' Life reversed itself in an instant. What should be a nightmare is what is real. Her nightmare set the stage for an earlier book (Mattingly 2010b).

With Belinda's illness, Andrena faced not only her own fears, but also a sense of her family's betrayal. Life had changed dramatically for everyone. As a result of the surgery, Belinda was suddenly altered. She had to wear a large helmet to protect her head. She was confined to a wheelchair. She lost a substantial amount of her hearing. When she spoke at all, it was in short, halting sentences, or in the sharply tempered commands of a two-year-old. Often she seemed lost in a world all of her own. Suddenly, the family was faced with a severely disabled little girl. Even in the best scenarios, it was not clear how severe or long-lasting these impairments would be. The dramatic alteration of a bright and talkative child caused unbearable pain for the family. And, as families sometimes do under the press of misery, they fell apart.

Before Belinda's illness, she had lived in a home of six. There were her parents, her adult older sister and her husband, and her nephew – who was a year older than her and as close as any brother. Within months after the diagnosis, their home dissolved. In Andrena's mind, the rest of the family had all 'run away', and she found herself in a small apartment with just Belinda.

In an early interview she put it this way:

> We were just kinda like sad about my little girl and it seemed like I was the only one willing to accept it. Because now it's only the two of us, my little girl and myself. The other ones, they kind of moved out on me ... It just seemed like they couldn't take it. Which I couldn't take it either. But, you know, she's my daughter and I thought I was responsible for her. And there was times when I wanted to go in different directions too, but I couldn't. Because I said, 'I want to see this thing through with her'.

Andrena cannot 'go in different directions' but commits to 'see[ing] this thing through'. And yet, what will she do if her daughter dies? How will she be able to bear it? 'When I first found out about my daughter I wanted to kill myself. I didn't want to be here if my daughter, if she wasn't going to make it, you know? And I just – and I just kept saying "I don't want to be here"'.

From her moral perspective, which is deeply informed by her evangelical Christian background, suicide is not an option for an ethical life. Thus, she is confronted by the ethical imperative to become a different sort of person, not only because suicide is morally repugnant for her but because she feels impelled to re-envision her own life so that she can see her daughter differently. She was horrified that she was not seeing her daughter in the right way. 'I was looking at her, I was already making her gone, you know? Talking like that, I was, just already making her gone'.

When Andrena faces the situation with her daughter, it is in this sense that she is thrown headlong into a moral struggle to cultivate a new kind of good life, a life worth living even under these most blighted of circumstances. As James Laidlaw, Joel Robbins and others have recently pointed out, a focus on the good does not presume that people are necessarily motivated to be good (rather than, say malicious or cruel) or that they are never misled by violent or callous ideologies. Rather, the cultural point is that moral striving seems to matter to people in all sorts of societies and making evaluative interpretations about what is good is a pervasive feature of social life. What constitutes the good life may vary widely from society to society, but it is difficult to imagine any community where this does not matter or where, if it has ceased to be important, this does not seem problematic for its members (Mattingly 2014a). But the notion of evaluation does not fully encompass the Aristotelian inspired version of one's ethical situation that I call upon here.

In response to the despair Andrena faces upon hearing her daughter's diagnosis, she tries to create a good life for them and avert the threat of moral tragedy which is posed to her by her own desire to commit suicide. Through a series of experiments, Andrena simultaneously nurtures multiple and mutually exclusive life plots. She actively cultivates uncertainty. She acts in such a way that several plotlines are promoted which are, in fact, contradictory. She shapes moments with Belinda that further the most hopeful story, the one in which the chemotherapy and radiation and surgery work, the tumour does not grow back, and Belinda gets a chance to grow up. But Andrena and Belinda also participate in other activities that force them to experience the dreaded story, one where Belinda will not live to see another birthday.

Emplotting A Hopeful Narrative

Andrena cultivates many moments that figure as episodes in an arduous yet promising healing journey. There is the terrifying diagnosis, Andrena's shock and depression and the disintegration of the family. But then there is an answer from Andrena: her determination to re-envision her life and her future in a narrative of hope, of possibility. Whatever else, she declares, her daughter was not 'already gone', and she seems to have refused to allow herself that future story. She prays for strength to reimagine her future in this more hopeful way, to be with her child on this journey, wherever it may take them.

And she takes practical steps. She rids her small living and dining room space of furniture, except a couch she pushes to one side in order to create (with Kmart purchases) a kind of combination rehabilitation room/indoor play area in order to carry out the home therapy programmes as directed by her daughter's occupational and physical therapists. Her daughter gets stronger, even relearning how to walk again several months after the surgery that saved her life but confined her to a wheelchair.

Andrena's determination to live out a narrative of hope becomes a central mission of her life. One Halloween illustrates Andrena's efforts to cultivate a rich life with Belinda wherever she can. On this Halloween I had promised to come for a visit. She had dressed Belinda in a favourite bunny costume and I brought a plastic pumpkin filled with candy so we could have an indoor celebration since Belinda was too sick to trick or treat with other children. I made a videotape of that Halloween and gave a copy to Andrena that she and her daughter watched and rewatched. The part they both liked best was my recording of Belinda's grumpiness at being urged by her mother to climb the stairs to her slide set and show me how she can slide. This was a hard task for her since she had lost much of her balance and strength. She didn't want to do it and sat forlornly picking through her candy. But when her mother provoked her repeatedly, 'You can't get up all those stairs Belinda, I know you can't!' Belinda finally rejoined with frustration: 'Yes, I can. I *can* do it'. And she did, wobbling but determined. Her annoyance turned to glee when she made it to the top and sailed down the slide, grinning madly in her bunny costume. Every time they watched this part of the video, Andrena laughed and laughed. This was a moment both ordinary (a usual child's activity) and extraordinary because it was increasingly rare.

Embracing Despair: Befriending Drea

In the midst of the cultivation of these little experiments in normalcy, Andrena does something I found very puzzling. She befriends Drea, another mother in the study. The surprise is that Drea's child is near death. The even greater surprise is that this child's diagnosis and even her oncologist are the same as Belinda's. But most puzzling for someone like Andrena is that Drea is vocal about giving up on herself as well as on her child's recovery. Drea is drowning in her own sorrow and despair. Andrena repeatedly told me she had refused to see some of her friends who thought she should 'just let Belinda go'. Though it might seem that Andrena insists upon a simple optimism, this is belied by her simultaneous efforts to face an opposing future story, creating experiences and taking actions that compel her to recognize a much darker possibility.

When Sashi, Drea's daughter, fell into a coma at home, Andrena not only visited her, but took Belinda on one of her visits. Andrena recounted how Belinda had climbed into the bed with Sashi, put her arms around her, and just lay down beside her. Together, Andrena and Belinda pre-experience Belinda's probable death. Less than a year later, Belinda will be the little girl lying at home on a bed in a coma. One way of seeing this relationship is that Drea confronts Andrena, not so much through what she says, but through her own stance of unrelenting rage. Andrena actively rejects the company of close family and friends who urge her to begin 'letting go' of her daughter but she actively pursues a friendship with a mother who has begun to let go of her dying daughter, not gracefully, under God's guidance, but in fury.

Experimenting with Life and Death

Though Andrena hoped for a cure, ultimately healing came to mean something very different. It marked, instead, another episode in a narrative where she herself was transformed from a distraught, even suicidal mother to someone who came to volunteer at the hospital where her daughter was treated, helping other parents whose children were critically ill. She became a guide through an unbearable journey.

Andrena did a number of things while Belinda was alive that helped her to construct 'hope in the crossroads', so to speak. This crossroads marked three paths with their accompanying hopes: hope her child would live; hope she could find a reason to live even if her child died; and hope that if her child died this could be a 'good death' after a 'good life', however brief. These paths are not only divergent but, in the case of the first two, are mutually contradictory. Furthermore, the cultivation of each of these paths feeds the task of narrative re-envisioning that Andrena set for herself soon after she confronted Belinda's diagnosis. There are two paths that Andrena feels morally impelled to avoid, and both of these 'tempt' her when she begins the journey through suffering engendered by Belinda's illness. One is to 'run away' rather than stay by Belinda's side through the illness. This is the unthinkable abandonment, behaviour she laments in other family members – most notably her husband. She would never physically leave her daughter. But for Andrena, abandonment is also seeing her daughter through despairing eyes, as though she were 'already gone'. The other path, she fears, will tempt her too much, that she will kill herself if her daughter does not live. Her determination to find some way to hope reveals her belief that hope is the only path that might lead her away from what she finds ethically untenable, her own self-destruction. However, hope that rests on the happy ending of cure is too flimsy. This will not do.

The task of narrative re-envisioning she undertakes propelled her to move towards death in order to embrace life. She 'practiced' becoming intimate with death when she befriended Sashi and Drea. And she brought Belinda into this practice as well. In a telling exchange that painfully highlights this movement, Drea and Andrena once joked about how much of Drea's chicken Belinda ate on one of their visits. Andrena rejoiced at this rare moment when Belinda took pleasure in food, a greedy childish moment in the kitchen while another child lay in a coma in the next room. If this is to be a narrative of hope, hope itself must come to mean something different.

Four Years Later

In the months and years after Belinda's death Andrena struggled to make a new life for herself. She vowed never to return to her old job as a receptionist in a car dealership. That life was over. She did part-time work caring for the children of two well to-do families, chauffeuring them to various after-school events and, in general, mothering them in the absence of their very busy professional parents. She had to move from the apartment where she had lived since Belinda's sickness, because once her daughter died, she no longer received benefits that allowed her to pay the rent. Because Section 8 housing (housing for the poor) has become increasingly defunded in Los Angeles during recent years, she decided to move to a town about an hour's drive from central LA where she was born and raised, and where her older daughter and other members of her family still lived. There she managed to find a decent apartment that she could afford.

What she defined as her main job didn't pay her anything at all. She was a relentless volunteer for the hospital where her child was treated, working with a family cancer group which raised money for the hospital and to support cancer treatment. She became a central figure in this advocacy group, and she hoped that they would consider bringing her on as a paid liaison to work with other families. They had one funded position, but instead the family advocacy group hired another mother, a wealthy white woman whose child had also recently died. Andrena spoke to me several times about her disappointment. She felt there was something unfair about this decision; she put in more hours than anyone and worked with more families (crossing race and ethnic lines) providing support and advice. Indeed, whenever I visited her, there were always families whose children were in the hospital on the phone with her. Although she was careful not to couch her disappointment in openly racial terms, she clearly wondered whether this was in part a racial decision. 'You know there aren't so many blacks who go to this hospital anymore', she told me. 'The area's changed too. Now it's much more Hispanic'. She left unspoken, though hinted at, the growing tension that has arisen between Latinos and blacks in South Central Los Angeles in the past decade as Latinos have gradually moved into neighbourhoods that were once African American strongholds.

Andrena's economic situation grew much worse when the primary family who had been paying her to care for their children suddenly moved to Hawaii. She was searching for other families who might hire her, but the bills were piling up. Early one morning in November 2003, three weeks after I had been to her fiftieth birthday party, I got a call from her twenty-eight-year-old daughter. 'My mom's died', her daughter told me. 'We just found her last night. The funeral will be this Friday'. I simply couldn't believe it. 'What?', I asked. 'How can this be? How can she be dead? I just saw her'. 'I know', her daughter replied. But she said it quietly, I realized after I hung up. She didn't even sound very surprised. Andrena's blood pressure had been very high, dangerously high, since Belinda's illness. She kept joking to me that she really needed to start dieting, but she couldn't seem to find the energy. Could she have had a sudden stroke? A heart attack? Or had she done something more deliberate?

Andrena's funeral was packed. Every seat was taken, and people stood in the back and around the seats of the church located in the heart of the South Central neighbourhood where Andrena had grown up. There were Latino families, black families, and even a few whites as well. The speeches were charged not only with sadness and fondness but also with anger. There were funny and touching stories from childhood friends, family members, some of the parents Andrena had befriended at the hospital. There were a few frustrated and even bitter stories as well. A niece asked with angry tears: 'Why did she just have to help everyone else and not ask for help herself? Why didn't she lean on us? Why didn't she take better care of herself?' Several people nodded as she spoke.

Conclusion: The Excessive Ethical Demand and the Discordant Narrative Self

If we speak of the evaluation of moral goods or deliberation in regard to what Andrena does, this may suggest that her own reasoning and deliberated actions are adequate to meet the moral challenges her child's illness presents. But this language has too much in it of a rational agent and the sufficiency of guiding norms. Instead, there is every evidence of an existential situation of ethical excess. If we speak in the normative vocabulary that governs notions of the good life in Andrena's moral communities, language of the good mother, or the good Christian, this doesn't catch the radical way in which her situation puts her out of bounds. It is, as she sometimes said to me, 'too much'. 'Too much' must be responded to anyway, and so she does, resourcefully, persistently, in the face of 'reversals of fortune' that are even more relentless. To speak in the vocabulary of the ancients, she is plagued by bad luck. And still, as the phenomenologists say, she must not only live her life but lead it. She is responsible to respond.

In Andrena's case, responsiveness does not merely include single acts in the face of particular situations but, in an even more fundamental way, her attempt to reshape her very character, to refashion her longer term intentions, so that 'too much' can not only be bearable, but the source of a new ethical possibility, an immanent transcendence that signals not merely a promise or potentiality but also a demand. A narrative portrait of the self that conceives of self-coherence or unity as a 'discordant concordance' privileges the temporal complexity of this responsive project. She does not merely live out one life story; she finds herself in the unsure position of being situated among several possible plots and all at once. Her unfolding life does not merely embody discordance – things do keep falling apart – but she actively cultivates it through destabilizing actions that intensify the uncertainty she faces. That is, strikingly, she creates uncertainty, seeking out experiences and events that speak to multiple futures and multiple possible selves. As her life shows us, lived time has its lines and measures, it marches forward, but these lines are often hazy, roads marked by signposts seen through a fog. Haziness may even be cultivated, as Andrena seems to do, not in order to avoid seeing what is ahead, but in order to face it.

Even her death is marked by a haziness, a striking inconclusiveness. The bare facts, as I came to know them, strongly suggest suicide. But what kind of narrative ending does this turn out to be? Is it a moral failure, as she initially saw it and as most of her community regarded it? Or did her project of moral becoming include the cultivation of a new potentiality, a God whose mercy might include forgiveness for taking her own life after her long years of struggle, who might allow her to reunite with her beloved lost daughter? Did facing her daughter's death come to include this as a possible ethical response? I have puzzled over my last encounters with her, especially those just weeks before her death and I continue to wonder about this. My final speculations here are obviously inconclusive, even suspiciously 'redemptive' in tone. I introduce them not to save Andrena from a verdict of moral failure and self-condemnation but to underscore how a life may be haunted by a discordance that defies any attempt to resolve it into a simple meaningful unity. Illuminating a suspenseful self, rather than a consistent one, is perhaps the primary configuring gift a narrative portrait can offer.

Acknowledgments

I would like to thank the Aarhus Institute of Advanced Studies, at Aarhus University, for its generous support during my period as a Dale T. Mortensen fellow. I also want to thank my long-term research collaborator, Mary Lawlor, who knew Andrena well. Finally, I gratefully acknowledge extensive funding from the National Institutes of Health (HD38878) that allowed my collaborators and I to carry out the ethnographic research that informs the empirical material for this chapter.

Cheryl Mattingly, Ph.D. is Professor of Anthropology at the University of Southern California. She was a Dale T. Mortensen Fellow at Aarhus University's Institute of Advanced Studies (2013–2015) and is a 2017 recipient of a John Simon Guggenheim fellowship. She has been the PI and Co-PI on federally funded grants from National Institutes of Health, Maternal and Child Health and the Department of Education. She has received numerous awards from the American Anthropological Association, including the Victor Turner Book Prize for *Healing Dramas and Clinical Plots* (Cambridge 1998), the Stirling Book Prize for *The Paradox of Hope: Journeys Through a Clinical Borderland* (University of California 2010), the New Millennium Book Prize for *Moral Laboratories: Family Peril and the Struggle for a Good Life* (University of California 2014), and the Polgar Essay Prize for 'In Search of the Good: Narrative Reasoning in Clinical Practice' (1998). Her other books include: *Clinical Reasoning in a Therapeutic Practice* (1994); *Narrative and the Cultural Construction of Illness and Healing* (2000), co-edited with Linda Garro, and *Narrative, Self and Social Practice* (2009), co-edited with Uffe Juul Jensen.

Notes

1. In the introduction and prologue to this volume, we describe some of the historical antecedents of this conversation between these two traditions, including the way in which it has been taken up in Aarhus.
2. While I can't take it up in this chapter, elsewhere (2012, 2014) I have argued that the 'pedagogical self 'proposed by anthropologists, especially those following Foucault's virtue ethics of 'care of the self', also faces this coherence problem.
3. A more extended version of this case is published elsewhere (Mattingly 2014a), although in this chapter I subject the same ethnographic material to a rather different analysis, drawing upon the phenomenology of responsivity.
4. For Aristotle, a flourishing ethical life was only possible for people who had some freedom over their choices and their actions, were capable of acting on their assessments of the good, and had sufficient economic security so that life's necessities were secure.
5. An important exception is Nigel Rapport's extended and original considerations of the individual (cf. Rapport 1997, 2003).
6. While MacIntyre makes a persuasive case for a narrative self, his stress on traditions and the various histories to which an individual belong make it possible to read his individual as someone completely pre-formed by these traditions. Although this is not my

interpretation of MacIntyre's claims, Laidlaw (2014) may be correct in complaining that MacIntyre's influence in anthropology has prompted a version of the moral self that is thoroughly acculturated. See also the introductory chapter, this volume, for a discussion of this problem in relation to both MacIntyre and Foucault.

7. Ricoeur would probably find that I have put things too strongly, drawing too close a parallel between lived experience and narrated experience. His magisterial meditation on time (the three-volume *Time and Narrative* series) can be understood as an attempt to respond to what he considers the inadequacy of phenomenology in its conceptualization of human temporality. He argues both that it is impossible to consider human time without narrative – 'there can be no thought about time without narrated time' – and that thinking requires the mediated discourse of narrative: 'temporality cannot be spoken in the direct discourse of phenomenology, but rather requires the mediation of the indirect discourse of narration' (1988: 241). A considerable amount of his analysis critiques what he sees as the best phenomenological attempts to describe temporal lived experience in all its immediacy. The semantic innovation that especially literary narratives afford is important to his argument.

8. Feminists scholars across a broad range of disciplines have added impetus to the development of an ethics of intimate care through their long-standing contention that care has been neglected within Western moral theory. They have argued for an ethics of care distinct from dominant moral theory's ethics of impartial justice (Gilligan 1982; Tronto 1993). But notice that this does not presume an autonomous self – in fact, such a ground project highlights a self that is deeply relational.

9. The case story I tell here is an amended version, truncated in some places and elaborated in others, of writing about Andrena that has been published elsewhere (2010, 2014a). Extensive passages of this case are quoted verbatim from this earlier published material.

References

Arendt, H. 1958. *The Human Condition*. Chicago: University of Chicago Press.

Borneman, J. 2001. 'Caring and to Be Cared For: Displacing Marriage, Kinship, Gender, and Sexuality', in James Faubion (ed.), *The Ethics of Kinship*. New Jersey: Rowland and Littlefield, pp. 29–46.

Butler, J.P. 2005. *Giving an Account of Oneself*. New York: Fordham University Press.

Carr, D. 1991. *Time, Narrative, and History*. Bloomington: Indiana University Press.

Cavell, S. 2004. *Cities of Words: Pedagogical Letters on a Register of the Moral Life*. Cambridge: Harvard University Press.

Das, V., M. Jackson, A. Kleinman and B. Singh. 2014. 'Experiments Between Anthropology and Philosophy: Affinities and Antagonisms', in V. Das, M. Jackson, A. Kleinman and B. Singh (eds), *The Ground Between*. Durham, NC: Duke University Press, pp.1–26.

Edwards, Jeanette. 2009. In Venkatesan, Soumhya, Jeanette Edwards, Rane Willerslev, Elizabeth Povinelli and Perveez Mody 2011. 'The Anthropological Fixation with Reciprocity Leaves No Room for Love: 2009 Meeting of the Group for Debates in Anthropological Theory'. *Critique of Anthropology* 31 (3): 210–250.

Fassin, D. 2014. 'True Life, Real Lives: Revisiting the Boundaries Between Ethnography and Fiction', *American Ethnologist* 41(1): 40–45.

———. 2015. 'Troubled Waters: At the Confluence of Ethics and Politics.' in M. Lambek, V. Das, D. Fassin and W. Keane. *Four Lectures on Ethics: Anthropological Perspectives*. Chicago: Hau Books, pp 175–210.

Faubion, J. 2001. *The Ethics of Kinship: Ethnographic Inquiries*. Lanham: Rowman and Littlefield.

Forster, E.M. 1927. *Aspects of the Novel*. New York: Mariner Books.

Foucault, Michel. 1997. *Ethics: Subjectivity, and Truth: Essential Works of Foucault 1954–1984*, Vol. 1, ed. Paul Rabinow, trans. Robert J. Hurley. New York: New Press.

Gilligan, Carol. 1982. *In a Different Voice*. Cambridge: Harvard University Press.

Heidegger, M. 1977. 'Letter on Humanism', *Basic Writings* 204: 39.

Horton, Sarah 2009. 'A Mother's Heart is Weighed Down with Stones: A Phenomenological Approach to the Experience of Transnational Motherhood'. *Culture Medical Psychiatry* 33: 21–40.

Hursthouse, Rosalind. 1999. *On Virtue Ethics*. New York: Oxford University Press.

Keane, W. 2014. 'Freedom, Reflexivity, and the Sheer Everydayness of Ethics'. Comment on: 'Laidlaw, James. 2014. *The Subject of Virtue: An Anthropology of Ethics and Freedom*. Cambridge: Cambridge University Press'. HAU: *Journal of Ethnographic Theory* 4(1): 443–57.

_____. 2016. *Ethical Life: Its Natural and Social Histories*. Princeton, NJ: Princeton University Press.

Laidlaw, James. 2002. 'For an Anthropology of Ethics and Freedom', *Journal of the Royal Anthropological Institute* 8(2): 311–32.

_____. 2014. *The Subject of Virtue: An Anthropology of Ethics and Freedom*. Cambridge: Cambridge University Press.

Lambek, M. 2010. 'Toward an Ethics of the Act', in Michael Lambek (ed.), *Ordinary Ethics: Anthropology, Language, and Action*. New York: Fordham University Press, pp. 39–63.

_____. 2015. *The Ethical Condition: Essays on Action, Person, and Value*. Chicago: University of Chicago Press.

Lambek, M., V. Das, D. Fassin and W. Keane. 2015. *Four Lectures on Ethics: Anthropological Perspectives*. Chicago: Hau Books.

Lear, Jonathan. 1988. *Aristotle: The Desire to Understand*. Cambridge: Cambridge University Press.

MacIntyre, A. 1981. *After Virtue*. Notre Dame: University of Notre Dame Press.

Mahmood, Saba. 2005. *Politics of Piety: The Islamic Revival and the Feminist Subject*. Princeton: Princeton University Press.

Mattingly, C.F. 2010. *The Paradox of Hope: Journeys Through a Clinical Borderland*. Berkley: University of California Press.

_____. 2014a. *Moral Laboratories: Family Peril and the Struggle for a Good Life*. Berkeley: University of California Press.

_____. 2014b. 'Love's Imperfection: Moral Becoming, Friendship and Family Life', ed. Jason Throop and Valerio Simoni, S*pecial Issue: Friendship, Morality and Experience*: *Suomen Antropologi: Journal of the Finnish Anthropology Society* 39(1): 53–67.

_____. 2014c. 'The Moral Perils of a Superstrong Black Mother', *Ethos: Journal of the Society of Psychological Anthropology* 42(1): 119–38.

_____. 2017. 'Autism and the Ethics of Care: A Phenomenological Investigation into the Contagion of Nothing' *Ethos*.

McDowell, John 1994. *Mind and World*. Cambridge, MA: Harvard University Press.

Nussbaum, M. and Amartya Sen (eds). 1993. *The Quality of Life*. New York: Oxford University Press.

Rapp, R. and F. Ginsburg. 2001. 'Enabling Disability: Rewriting Kinship, Reimagining Citizenship', *Public Culture* 13(3): 533–56.

_____. 2011. 'Reverberations: Disability and the New Kinship Imaginary', *Anthropological Quarterly* 84(2): 379–410.

Rapport, Nigel 1997. *Transcendent Individual: Towards a Literary and Liberal Anthropology.* London and New York: Routledge.

_____. 2003. *I am Dynamite: An Alternative Anthropology of Power.* London and New York: Routledge Ricoeur, Paul. 1988. *Time and Narrative*, vol. 3, trans. Kathleen Blamey and David Pellauer. Chicago: Chicago University Press.

Ricoeur, Paul. 1992. *Oneself as Another.* Chicago: University of Chicago Press.

Taylor, Charles. 1989. *Sources of the Self: The Making of the Modern Identity.* Cambridge: Harvard University Press.

Tronto, J.C. 1993. *Moral Boundaries: A Political Argument for an Ethic of Care.* London: Routledge.

Williams, B. 1981. *Moral Luck: Philosophical Papers.* Cambridge: Cambridge University Press.

Zigon, J. 2008. *Morality: An Anthropological Perspective.* New York: Berg.

_____. 2011. *HIV is God's Blessing: Rehabilitating Morality in Neoliteral Russia.* Berkeley: University of California Press.

_____. 2013. 'Human Rights as Moral Progress? A Critique', *Cultural Anthropology* 28(4): 716–36.

3

Being Otherwise
On Regret, Morality and Mood

C. Jason Throop

An Endless Struggle to Think well of Oneself

In her recent book *Resonance* (2013), Unni Wikan argues, paraphrasing T.S. Elliot, that moral experience is existentially defined by an 'endless struggle to think well of oneself'. Arising from an interplay between compelling concerns and concrete social conditions, such struggles give shape, Wikan maintains, to the shifting trajectories of our lives as lived. A 'struggle to think well of oneself' is thus, she argues, a significant aspect of what moral experience is and entails. And yet, Wikan critically asks, is it ever truly accurate to say that moral experience is simply a struggle to 'think'? Is moral life not also characterized by an affective struggle as well? When, in other words, is a struggle to think also a struggle to feel? How do emotions give rise to, or shape, the sense of struggle itself? In short, how is such a sense of struggle affected by those various feelings, sentiments, and moods that are intimately tied up with our efforts to morally inhabit the existential conditions into which we find ourselves thrown?

Building upon my recent theorizing of mood and morality, this chapter will focus upon the moral and mooded dimensions of experiences of regret. While regret is a complex phenomenon that is certainly not limited to a manifestation in mood, mooded aspects of regret illuminate an expanse of moral concern that significantly texture our struggles to 'think well of ourselves' in a modality of being otherwise. In this regard, I will engage the question of how the mooded dimensions of regret are implicated in shaping our orientation to, what Edmund Husserl termed in the context of his phenomenological ethics, a striving toward 'the best possible' (*das Bestmögliche*) (Husserl 1989:33; see also Steinbock 1995: 202–203). That such possibilities for being are not only oriented to the future in the context of an anticipation of becoming otherwise[1] but may also arise in an opening up and re-inhabiting of the past to engage with possibilities that might have been, is a particular aspect of the ethics of the 'best possible' that I will foreground in my discussion of regretful moods below. Like other moods of possibility (e.g. despair, anxiety, boredom, hope, etc.), such regretful moods are, I argue, particular forms of attunement to the specific worlds we inhabit and the shifting moral currents that are always palpably coursing through them (see Throop 2012, 2014, 2015a). A central claim of this chapter is thus that morally inflected moods of possibility like regret should be understood as core moral engines driving the variegated texture of ethical life.

'A Horrible Disease'

> I think that diabetes is a horrible disease. I think it is the *worst* kind. I don't know maybe there are worse, maybe the ones who have cancer will say that cancer is the worst, but diabetes, it controls you. Everything you do, everything you eat, all of it, everything. If my sugar is high then I tend to be very forgetful, I can't think well at all. I don't like that. And for a while … I felt really horrible. I used to think that I had a really sharp mind, but now when my sugar goes high I become forgetful. I say to myself 'I think I might be going crazy'. Maybe I'm slowly … ah, what … slowly becoming mentally ill or cr…crazy? I don't know.

These words were uttered to me by a forty-eight year-old Yapese woman named Thiil in the context of an interview I conducted with her in the summer of 2009, focusing on her ongoing struggles to manage the degenerative physical and psychological effects of Type 2 diabetes. An extremely smart, witty and confident woman who had at one time worked for the Yap State Department of Public Health, Thiil first found out that she was afflicted with the disease in her late thirties, although she believes now in retrospect that she had been suffering with the illness for quite some time before that.

When she first received her diagnosis, Thiil was shocked. As she put it, 'I was in denial'.

> When I went to see the doctor and he confirmed that I was diabetic I didn't take medicine. I didn't *take* medicine. I guess I could not believe that I was diabetic. I keep thinking that something is wrong. It can't be true. I have never been fat in anytime of my life. I'm not the kind of person who drinks [alcohol] or who smokes. I thought I was healthy and that I had taken care of my life and my health. I thought, it can't be true because I don't drink, … and I take care of my health, so something is wrong somewhere. It can't be true that I am diabetic.

Refusing to take her medication, her physical condition gradually worsened. As she continued to deteriorate, feeling increasingly weak, dizzy, and tired, she began to acknowledge that the doctor might be right after all. Her first response to accepting her diagnosis was not compliance, however; she still refused to take the medication that had been prescribed for her. Instead she shifted from denial to anger as she began blaming her family for her suffering. As she explained, 'On my mother's side there are a lot of my uncles who are diabetic.' In fact, three of her four maternal uncles were afflicted with the disease. Audibly and visibly embodying her anger as she spoke, voiced raised and face flushed, Thiil recalled, 'I would go home, at that time I was staying with my mother and helping her, and I was mad, mad. "I'm sick and it's all your fault, you and your brothers, and your family, there is diabetes on that side!"' Thiil was not alone in her suffering, however. Six of her nine siblings were also diabetic.

A Dire Situation

The fact that Thiil's family had been so deeply affected by Type 2 diabetes, with so many of its members living with the diminished possibilities for flourishing brought on by the disease, reflects a worldly condition that resonates with the experience of many other families living in Yap. A small volcanic island located in the Western Caroline Islands with a population of 7,391 inhabitants (Yap Branch Statistics Office 2002), Yap is currently the site of the administrative capital of Yap State, one of four States that comprise the Federated States of Micronesia. According to records of hospital admission reporting for 2003, endocrine, metabolic and nutritional diseases (of which Type 2 diabetes comprised the overwhelming majority of cases) were deemed responsible for 1208 hospital admissions in all of the Federated States of Micronesia (FSM). This number had almost doubled in only three years after the first time that figures were collected in 2000.[2] In a more recent study examining available aggregate data on 'non-communicable disease' in Yap State between 2000 and 2010, Type 2 diabetes was found to be the third leading cause of death on the island (Ichiho et al. 2013). Unfortunately, it may not be long before such mortality rates increase still higher, given that prevalence rates are still on the rise. According to the *IDF Atlas of Diabetes* (6th edition), the Federated States of Micronesia currently ranks second out of 219 countries for the highest diabetes prevalence rates in the world.[3] Clearly, Type 2 diabetes in particular, and endocrine, metabolic and nutritional diseases broadly configured, are a very serious problem in the FSM, as they have been recognized to be throughout the Pacific region (McLennan and Ulijaszek 2015).

The increasingly dire situation in the FSM is by all accounts also evident in other communities in the so-called 'developing world', as well as in economically marginalized communities in so-called 'first-world nations', where epidemiological rates of diabetes and metabolic disorders have grown exponentially (Popkin 2015). Currently morbidity and mortality rates associated with diabetes (both Type 1 and Type 2), as well as various other metabolic diseases, are viewed by numerous medical specialists to be of epidemic global proportions (ibid; see also Garro 1995, 1996; Joe and Young 1993). For many Pacific Island communities, however, the epidemic of metabolic disorders like diabetes has been made all the worse by limited access to adequate health care facilities, an increased reliance upon foreign foodstuffs (often in the form of canned goods, rice, Ramen noodles, and high-fat content and low-quality meats such as turkey tail), and limited information about available nutritional and medical treatment options (see Gewertz and Errington 2010). Notably, within Yapese communities themselves, individuals explicitly recognize that a shift from local to non-local foods is one of the key causes underlying the rising rates of *mar nib beech* ('new illnesses') on the island, of which diabetes and cancer are deemed to be the most prevalent and most harmful (cf. Garro 1995, 1996). Such a shift is also considered by many to be a deeply troubling ethical issue given the extent to which these transformations have unsettled longstanding traditional moral concerns associated with the cultivation, harvesting, preparation and ingestion of local foods (see also Throop 2010).

Traditionally, fundamental moral dimensions of personhood were intimately linked with a complicated set of ritualized productive, consumptive and ascetic practices. In this context, food was understood as a tangible manifestation of intergenerational histories of effortful work upon the land (see Egan 1998; Labby 1976; Throop 2010). Embodied efforts to cultivate the land permeated the status and relative 'purity' of both the land and the food that it produced. Conversely, persons who worked upon the land and ingested the foods grown upon it were imbued with the political and moral qualities of previous generations, which significantly included the spirits of ancestors who needed to be continually consulted, propitiated and appeased. The ebb and flow of everyday life, one's personal status and identity, as well as one's moral standing within the community, were thus mediated through attempts at controlling, through ritual and other means, the necessary and inevitable interactions between spirits, people, food and lands that were differentially distributed along a continuum of 'purity' (Lingenfelter 1979). In this capacity, food was a vital vehicle for expressing and defining relationships according to a dynamic continuum of forces that range between 'pure' (*tabugul*) and 'impure' (*taqay*) poles. Whether understood in terms of power differentials between chiefs and their servants, status-based distinctions between age-grades and genders, the various life historical and developmental stages marking the temporal expanse extending between birth and death, or the intergenerational circulation of personal names which give individuals rights to speak for and use particular parcels of land, Yapese social life was understood as a reflection of attempts at carefully controlling the politically and ethically consequential interplay of these oppositional forces.

Today, for many in the community, the rise of 'new illnesses' like diabetes is viewed as a salient indication of the extent to which access to foreign foods has disrupted histories of possibility for moral flourishing as sedimented in the land and the food grown upon it. Historical transformations, as much as personal inclinations, have thus often been explicitly deemed responsible for bringing about conditions in which possibilities for health, viability, and flourishing have been significantly diminished in contemporary Yap.

'I keep thinking, 'I had no chance!'

As the months wore on and the intensity of Thiil's anger eventually subsided, she found herself subjected to a hard to described feeling. She did not feel well physically, it was true. However, she was also feeling affectively unsettled and uncertain. 'What did I do to deserve this?' was a constant refrain running through her mind. The more she reflected upon her past and the more she learned about the disease, the more it gradually dawned on Thiil that her mother and her family were not solely to blame for the onset of her illness. As she explained,

> it is not her fault. Its ... I was predisposed to becoming a diabetic, but I chose an unhealthy lifestyle, junk food, food from the store that I ate that's why it came quick. But my brothers and sisters who are older they ate local food more than processed food. Even my two alcoholic brothers they like taro and if you give them rice they don't really like it. Even though they drink almost every day, they probably have a bad liver, but they don't have diabetes. And today there are nine of us, six of us are diabetic, my sister who lives off island and my two alcoholic brothers are not diabetic ... I think that being raised, being the youngest, I [always] got what I wanted. 'You eat some taro'. 'I don't want taro'. 'Then what are you going to eat?' So up until now that is why, I had my way [I was stubborn] and it is [why it was] easy [for me] to become diabetic.

Acknowledging that her desire for soda, ramen noodles, rice, spam and canned meat was a significant trigger for the onset of the disease, Thiil often found herself regretfully dwelling on thoughts about how things might have turned out differently if she had not been so willful and had instead listened to her caregivers and eaten more local food as a child. She was also very upset with herself for not initially accepting her diagnosis, for refusing to take her medicine for so long, and overall for not taking better care of herself when she was younger. She was especially troubled by the fact that even during the time she worked at the Department of Public Health, where she had actually helped to run some informational programmes on diabetes, she did not pay closer attention to the way she was living her own life.

> I keep thinking, 'I had no chance!' I ate a lot of rice and drank cola every day. I should have, at the time when I was working at Public Health, taken time to learn about the different diseases instead of just, ah ... just making sure that they were administering the program and making sure that services we were providing were good ... but I didn't take time for that. So, what would have happened at that time [if I would have done that]? It might have helped me, but maybe not...

Even though she believed that she had no chance, Thiil was still haunted by the possibility that things could have gone differently for her if she had only paid better attention at work and been able to better manage her cravings for store bought foods. And indeed, Thiil often referred to her illness as a 'lifestyle disease', a biomedically-based framing that stems directly from those same local public health efforts to raise awareness about the disease that she initially ignored. Such a framing of her illness, at least at first glance, foregrounds what Linda Garro has characterized to be a biomedically configured choice-based account of 'individual responsibility for health' (1995: 38) that is often inherent in medicalized responses to so-called 'lifestyle diseases' like Type 2 diabetes. To the extent that these framings highlighted the optative dimensions of her affliction and its treatment, and hence also her own self-responsibility for those putative 'choices', Thiil's regret was arguably at least partially configured and/or amplified by such biomedical framings of her illness. Regardless of what or who is to blame for the onset and trajectory of her illness, however, Thiil found herself recurrently facing on a daily basis the existential fact that her struggle (*cham ko laem*) with diabetes continues. As a result, she recurrently finds herself in a battle against her own desires and yearnings and she expends great effort to be 'disciplined' enough to eat better, exercise, and take care of her body. As she lamented to me,

> Right now my diet is not very good ... With this illness you have to be very disciplined ... [4 sec] ... to ah ... [5 sec] ... to be on top of it and manage it really well and control it. Sometimes I feel like I'm fighting with my sickness to see who will control who. Will I control diabetes or will diabetes control me? It's always a struggle, every day. Sometimes, if I win and I feel good and I feel ... but other days like when someone brings ice cream into the house, if there is ice cream, I love chocolate, if vanilla ice cream, sometimes I can resist it, [but] if it is chocolate, I cannot. Sometime I can do it, but sometimes I think I will just have a little, I have been good all this time, maybe ... I deserve to have a little bit of chocolate ice cream. But sometimes it's not just a little bit. I eat it and I really like the taste and it has been a long time since I've had any [laughs] ... maybe later ... maybe later I'll have a little bit ... but then I will feel lethargic and my head feels heavy. But then I think I will just have a little bit and after I'll grab a machete and go out and clean around the path so I will burn it off. But it doesn't happen that way.

Intertwined with her anticipated, ongoing and recollected struggles to 'control' her desires, 'manage' her illness, and lead a 'healthy life' – each of which are orientations to self-responsibility for illness that have a clearly recognizable biomedical signature and provenience – was a discernable affective stance that took the form of an indistinct and yet at times still quite palpable mood that recurrently oriented her to what could have been, and might yet still be, possibilities for her being and becoming otherwise. Far from a simple reproduction of a biomedical choice-based account of 'individual responsibility for illness' (Garro 1995), however, her mood disclosed an attunement to broader social, historical and interpersonal conditions shaping the overall course of her life and the trajectory of her illness. While never using the Yapese term that comes closest to the English 'regret' – *kal'ngaen*, literally a 'misfortunate happening in the mind' – Thiil's mooded attunement to the trajectory and conditions of her life as lived evoked strong resonances with what I will argue today are the mooded and moral dimensions of experiences of regret.

The Persistence of the Possible

Given the extensive anthropological work devoted to exploring such moral sentiments as guilt, shame, anger, resentment, care, compassion, sympathy and pity, it is surprising that very little attention has been paid to the topic of regret in the discipline (see Fassin 2013; Humphrey and Hürelbaatar 2005; Scheper-Hughes 2005; Wilce 2005; Wool under review).[4] This omission is especially striking in light of the recent ethical turn in anthropology, which has sought to critically rethink ethical and moral dimensions of human existence (see Fassin 2012; Faubian 2011; Laidlaw 2013; Lambek 2010; Mattingly 2014; Robbins 2004; Zigon 2007, 2011; Zigon and Throop 2014). And yet, as the psychologist Janet Landerman notes in her now landmark study, *Regret: The Persistence of the Possible* (1993), anthropologists are not alone in failing to explicitly and systematically examine the experience of regret. As she put in 1993, 'Unlike related matters, such as depression, guilt, and shame, regret has only recently received scholarly attention.'

In an article published almost fifteen years after Landerman's book, the philosopher Jeanne Peijnenburg (2007) argues that while there have been an increasing number of philosophical and psychological studies of regret since the mid- to late 1980s, the majority of these have been 'decision-theoretic' in nature. Such studies take regret to be a form of counter-factual thinking, often focusing in particular on so-called 'regret aversion', which refers to ways that 'people try to avoid future regrets by anticipating their possible occurrence' (2007: 296). In comparison to the growing number of such decision-theoretic accounts, there are very few analyses of the experience of regret in either discipline, Peijnenburg argues. And yet, in her estimation, the existing

> meager phenomenological analyses of regret have a predominantly ethical flavor; and, in the wake of Bernard Williams (1976), many philosophers see regret as a 'moral remainder,' an unfortunate but unavoidable byproduct of moral dilemmas or other situations in which we are forced to choose between displeasing alternatives. (Peijnenburg 2007: 296)

Of the spattering of work on regret in anthropology, two notable contributions include Nancy Scheper-Hughes' reflections on racialized articulations of regret and 'political remorse' amongst perpetrators and victims of violence in post-Apartheid South Africa (2005) and Zoe Wool's (under review) yet to be published research on ambivalent orientations toward the 'unthinkability' of regret as perceptibly present at the 'edges' of narratives voiced by American veterans undergoing rehabilitation after traumatic injury in the Iraq war. Perhaps the most extensive anthropological account of regret, however, is advanced in Caroline Humphrey and Ujeed Hürelbaatar's work on so-called 'agent regret' as evidenced in thirteenth-century historical documents discussing the rise of the Mongolian empire at the time of Chinggis Khan.

Building upon the philosophical insights of Bernard Williams, Amelie Oksenberg Rorty, and Martha Nussbaum, Humphrey and Hürelbaatar focus on detailing the contours of so-called 'agent regret', that is the 'declarations of regret by a particular subject about action he or she has taken' (2005: 3). Agent regret as a form of 'painful reflection on action' is for these authors an inherently moral and ethical phenomenon, for it concerns the 'interpenetration of singular reflection on "what is done" with moral judgments prevailing in historically and culturally specific contexts' (2005: 4). To put it succinctly, 'agent regret' is thus taken to be a painfully reflexive moral emotion focused on the actions of a subject who reflects on 'how much better if it would have been otherwise'. Remaining agnostic to the types, qualities or character of acts that may be deemed regrettable, as well as the situations and contexts within which such acts arise, Humphrey and Hürelbaatar suggest that regret is more than simply a 'moral remainder'. In contrast, it is an 'anterior capacity' that potentiates 'ethical reflection on one's actions' (2005: 18).[5]

As an 'anterior capacity for ethical reflection' that articulates with various acts, events, conditions and experiences, regret is therefore taken by these, and other scholars, to be a moral engine that is inherently multiplex in nature. As Landerman phrases it, 'regret is a many-faceted thing. Bridging past and present, interior and exterior, actual and possible, the cognitive and the emotional, the individual and the collective' (1993: xviii). Often understood as related to a range of moral sentiments that span from guilt to remorse to repentance, regret may often also intertwine with, and take on the tonalities of other affects, emotions and moods, such as anger, bitterness, anxiety, depression or despair. Moreover, regret not only arises in the wake of orientations to acts taken or not taken, decisions made or not made, and opportunities pursued, passed over or missed, but is also, as Peijnenburg argues, accompanied by a particular underlying desire, namely the desire 'for a world different from the actual one' we are currently inhabiting (2007: 296). To this extent, at least, regret may at times extend anticipatory tendrils to experiences of nostalgia, fantasy, hope and utopian reverie.

The multifaceted nature of regret is further illuminated by its etymology. The English 'regret' stems from the Middle English *regretten*, from Old French *regreter*, 'to lament'. Both are perhaps derived from combining the intensifier *re-*, 'again', with either the Old Norse (*grata*), Old English (*graetan*), or Proto-Germanic (**gretan*) stems, which each signified 'to moan, weep, groan, sob' (American Heritage Dictionary, Online Etymology Dictionary). According to the American Heritage Dictionary, regret can thus be variously defined as:

tr.v. 1. To feel sorry, disappointed or distressed about. 2. To feel sorrow or grief over; mourn. – n. 1. A sense of loss and longing for someone gone. 2. Distress over a desire unfulfilled or an action performed or not performed. 3. An expression of grief or disappointment. 4. *Plural.* A courteous declining to accept an invitation.

When compared to other nouns of so-called 'mental distress' that are taken to be its synonyms, such as 'sorrow, grief, anguish, woe, heartache', the American Heritage Dictionary suggests that 'regret has the broader range of meanings, from mere disappointment in not being able to do something to painful sense of loss, bitterness, or longing for something lost or done or left undone' (ibid.).

The broad range of meanings and intensities of feeling associated with the concept, alongside its etymological ties to loss, mourning and lament, suggests that regret, while a many-faceted, ethically salient, and at times highly reflexive phenomenon, still bears within its range of experiential potentialities significant qualities of affect, sentiment and mood. And yet, it seems when looking at recent work on regret in philosophy and psychology, as well as the notably sparse reflections on regret in anthropology, that there has been a covering over of regret's mooded dimensions. In my estimation, this covering over has in part followed in the wake of regret being taken up most focally by scholars working to advance normative, communicative and/or decision theoretic ethical accounts. In the context of a phenomenological anthropological analysis of morality, however, it is imperative that the affective and mooded dimensions of regret be rendered more clearly visible.

Mood, Attunement, Morality

In an article recently published in a special issue of the journal *Ethos* focused on the topic of 'moral experience' that Jarrett Zigon and I co-edited, I set out to highlight what I take to be the unique moral space claimed by moods such as regret (Throop 2014; see also Throop 2017). As Martin Heidegger observed, 'a mood assails us. It comes neither from the "outside" nor the "inside", but arises out of being-in-the-world, as a way of such being' (Heidegger 1927/1962: 176). Neither precisely of the self nor of the world, as a form of intermediary experience (Throop 2009a), moods are seldom the end point of our reflection. They are instead, more often, the existential medium through which our reflections take shape. As the anthropologist Valentine Daniel suggests, moods connote 'a state of feeling – usually vague, diffuse, and enduring, a disposition toward the world at any particular time yet with a timeless quality to it' (2000: 333). As a vague, yet enduring 'disposition toward the world', a mood provides the existential expanse within which reflection is deployed (Throop 2014; see also Ram 2015). Reflection is inflected in moods. And moods, I argue, are often (though not always) implicated in our moral concerns.

Inhabiting a dispersed temporal and conscious expanse that lies somewhere between unrecognized sedimented habits and more ephemeral and accessible thoughts and feelings, moods traffic in zones of indeterminacy that may, given the right context, still yet coalesce into more or less marked objects of our attention (cf. Geertz 1973; Throop 2009b). The persisting and yet unsettled quality of moods is morally significant. Resisting easy articulation, moods may allow us to hold ambivalent, unresolved or contradictory assessments of our moral life in a semi-reflective expanse that may or may not result in permanent transformations of our being. As such, moods implicate moral concerns that are linked to residues of past experience and yet are still open to subjunctive possibilities for future transformation.[6] A mood is not moral transformation achieved, however. Nor is it the past as *fait accompli*. In a mood, past moral concerns are in the process of being worked through and are still potentially open to change. And yet, a mood persists. Importantly, moods are existential modes of engaging with moral problems in such a way that they remain viscerally bound to our being. In short, mood is our being, being affected and attuned.

As Sara Ahmed argues, 'if we are always in some way or another moody, then what we will receive as an impression will depend on our affective situation' (2010: 40; see also Ahmed 2014). That is, what we attend to, and how we attend it, will be organized, at least in part, by our moods. Moreover, as Zigon suggests in his own contribution to our recent *Ethos* volume, the forms of attunement giving rise to such 'affective situations' are in fact fundamental aspects of the 'ontological conditions' that make moral life itself possible. Drawing from Heidegger, Zigon explains,

> attunement manifests itself as the potentiality to become engaged with and become entangled in diverse and particular relationships that makes possible the vast diversity of ways of living we find in the social world. This engagement and entanglement is best conceived as having-fallen-upon Da-sein as a nexus rather than actively sought. Attunement, in this sense, is not done by an individual who psychologically adjusts; rather, attunement in the ontological sense is that foundational capacity that allows relationships to assemble … attunement is what allows Da-sein to be a being that is initially and always a being-in-relationships. (2014: 22)

As Heidegger himself argues, one of the foundational ways that attunement manifests itself experientially is in the context of moods. In disclosing our attunement to the world, moods thus reveal the various and shifting ways that we register our conditioned existence. Significantly, such a mooded form of attunement is one that Edmund Husserl characterized as an 'unclear intentionality' (Lee 1998): unclear, because moods are not tethered to specific things or circumstances that are evident in the immediate situations or contexts we find ourselves in. They articulate instead with more encompassing and indistinct conditions of reality that exceed whatever particular aspect of the world a given subject may be focused upon in a given moment. According to Husserl, moods, therefore, have 'the function of illuminating the world and, for this reason, he compares mood to light' (Lee 1998: 115). The horizon that is disclosed in a mood is the horizon within which any given object, act, event, subject or situation arises – this mood-illuminated horizon is what Husserl termed the 'world-horizon' (Lee 1998: 115). Indeed, as the phenomenologist Matthew Ratcliffe explains, we 'can only have objects of experience insofar as we already find ourselves in a world, and we would not find ourselves in a world at all without mood' (2013: 159; see also Ratcliffe 2015). Moods thus reveal the ongoing, more and less conscious, ways in which we are always already responsive to the worldly situations within which we find ourselves thrown. And crucially for the argument that I am advancing in the context of this chapter, moods may also, as Ratcliffe observes, 'determine the kinds of possibility we are open to' (2015: 57).

The various moods that may arise from our ongoing attunement to the ways we find ourselves-in-the-world are forms of affection that transect, organize and potentiate our more reflexive forms of engagement. According to the existential psychoanalyst Medard Boss, the forms of attunement disclosed in the context of a particular mood are thus 'at any given time the condition of our openness for perceiving and dealing with what we encounter; the pitch at which our existence, as a set of relationships to objects, ourselves, and other people, is vibrating' (Boss 1979; cited in Ahmed 2014). In Husserl's terms, such forms of vibrational affection arise from those constitutive processes of passive synthesis that he characterizes as a pre-predicative form of 'becoming that makes being [itself] possible' (Steinbock 1995: 34; Husserl 2001).

For instance, regretful moods arising from an attunement to the painful potentialities of being that are taken up in a modality of orienting to what could have been otherwise, diffusely permeate and potentiate more reflexive orientations to specific regrets. In finding ourselves attuned to a mooded orientation to the painful possibility that things could have been different, we may thus thematically foreground particular situations, historical conditions and life events as regrettable. Such regretful moods then play important roles in organizing our attention as it variously shifts to focus upon differing aspects of the situations, events, happenings, actions and relationships we find ourselves always already inhabiting (see Throop 2003, 2009a, 2010, 2015b; Throop and Duranti 2015).

As a mood, therefore, regret flows through situations, becoming variously prominent in one's experience by recurrently orienting in more and less conscious ways our attention to a painful assessment of events, actions and situations that could have gone differently and could been otherwise. This is not, as the philosopher Anthony Steinbock points out, a remorseful holding on to the past (2014: 143). Instead, regret entails an opening up again of possibilities that were once in the world – in this case a world already lived but revisited and lived again, now through a rather different vantage point and affective tonality.[7] Significantly, such mooded dimensions of regret are intimately tied, I argue, to what Husserl termed in the context of his phenomenological ethics an orientation to the optimality of 'the best possible' (*das Bestmögliche*).

The Best Possible

Husserl's phenomenological analysis of an ethics of the 'best possible' was first articulated in his early writings on ethical transformation and renewal, which were written at the invitation of the Japanese periodical *The Kaizo* between the years of 1922 and 1924 (see Husserl 1989; Steinbock 1995: 200). Particularly significant for the connection I wish to make here between mooded dimensions of regret and our moral lives as lived, are traces in these manuscripts of what Anthony Steinbock has characterized to be Husserl's initial efforts to outline a so-called 'generative' ethics.

Arising in the life worlds of beings who are embedded in an ongoing flow of overlapping and shifting generations of predecessors, contemporaries and successors, ethical generativity is founded upon the dynamic intertwining of habituality, historicity, normativity and optimality that together may potentiate an orientation to the 'best possible' in any given situation. It is, Husserl suggests, such an ongoing optimal orientation to the 'best possible' that founds the potentiality of continually 'renewing our life' (Steinbock 1995: 203).

For Husserl, the 'best possible' is not to be mistaken for an orientation to a singular outcome to be realized, a fixed goal to be achieved, or a concrete end to be pursued. Its optimality is always oriented instead to an openness to possibility for renewing one's life. Such possibilities for renewal are not solely of relevance for the individuals living through them, however. As Steinbock explains, 'Ethically, I am responsible not only for my own becoming but for the generation of an ethical context that I take up and in which I am inextricably involved' (1995: 204).

In engaging in possibilities of renewing my life, I am thus also opening up possibilities to re-enliven, to re-inhabit, and perhaps in so doing to transform, even if only slightly, the inherited standards, norms and values that in part shape the lived dimensions of what Husserl termed a given community's 'homeworld'. What is thus considered to be optimal here for Husserl is an ongoing process of opening the most 'richness and diversity' possible in the context of those traditions, situations and contexts that we find ourselves immersed in, living through, and that we inherit as historical beings. '[R]ealizing the optimal in the ethical life' for Husserl, as Steinbock explains, therefore 'means renewing the cultural community in its *historical* self-transformation, its institutions, organizations, and cultural goods of every kind: In short, the best possible of the homeworld is the *renewal of its generative force*' (1995: 204–205, emphasis in original).

Taking up, living through, renewing, making our own, and thus necessarily in part transfiguring systems of values, norms and goals is not, in Husserl's analysis, only evident in explicitly marked moments in which our taken for granted orientation to the world is somehow unsettled by a problem, ethical or otherwise. Renewal also arises, he observes, precisely in our efforts to carry on 'the sedimented system of values and goals *as* taken for granted ... [in the process] reawakening a generative community' (Steinbock 1995: 205). This is thus not only, in Zigon's terms, a reclaiming of a 'comfortable' orientation to the world that follows in the wake of a moment of moral breakdown and ensuing ethical reflection. It is also very much an ongoing transformational potentiality of ethical generativity that takes shape by means of our unthematized attunements to the familiar 'styles of life' embedded in our homeworld.

It is quite significant to note here then, that such a generative take on ethics is situated at the nexus of a dynamic tension between the dead weight of repetition, the ongoing flow of recurrent everyday practices, and the opening up of existential possibilities and new horizons of being. That possibilities for being are not only oriented to ongoing present concerns, or the future in anticipation of becoming otherwise, but also arise in an opening up and re-inhabiting of the past, even if painfully so, to engage with the possibilities that might have been, is a particular aspect of the ethics of the 'best possible' that mooded dimensions of regret disclose.

'Going Into a Darkness'

I … never thought to make it a big deal that I have this disease and [that] I have to take care of myself [as a result], because I don't know much about it. Just, just that it was something that I thought would come and go. So after a while I lost weight and I developed some … sometimes I get so lazy, I want to sleep, and I don't feel like … ahh … doing this and this you know. Sometimes I'm so weak and I, I, sometimes I … shake and stuff like that. So I kept on doing what I've been doing, what I'm usually doing, I used to drink a lot of alcohol, and eat whatever I want to eat without really being careful about what is good for me or what is not. I just [kept doing what I always did], and, and, the disease keep on, it's getting, getting worse, and after a while my early, my early, around 30 or 32 or 30 I began to feel that I, that the … that my eyes are getting so blurred you know, when I look at things, I think that there is something wrong with my vision the way I look at things, and ah, and ah I'm getting so skinny. And something I also noticed that I, that when there is a blister or when there is a small cut it takes a while to get healed so, so, so I keep on asking people … what is really going on with me? That is when I learned that, learned a little bit more about the disease … diabetes. People told me you have to be careful because it is a dangerous disease and it will just kill you right there and ah, it ah, it ah, it … it doesn't just come and then you know kill you right away, it just slowly, little by little, it damages your, all your senses and the way you perform and the walking and everything.

The once assertive, self-assured, and at times intimidating young man who I often used to see stumbling around town in a half drunken stupor, always sporting his ubiquitous sun glasses and baseball cap, had been reduced at the time that he uttered these words to a skinny, glassy eyed, feeble man now facing the very real possibility of his own death. As he spoke these words to me, lying there on his hospital bed the day before he was to leave for Guam for treatment for his failing kidneys (Yap State Memorial Hospital has no dialysis machines), all of Chep's previous bravado and intensity seemed to have been drained from his being. As he explained to me, his diabetes had progressed to the point where his right leg had been amputated above the knee, his eyesight was steadily deteriorating, and his kidneys were failing. He also had a 'bad heart' and there were problems with his 'veins', which were not, as he put it, 'letting enough blood through'. As a result, he was suffering from shortness of breath. He could barely sit up in bed without feeling dizzy and faint. Standing up was simply out of the question.

As we spoke together in the poorly lit space of his hospital room, Chep knew that he did not have long to live, and tragically, he was right – he died a few months later in a much better lit hospital room in Guam (the better lighting and medical equipment unable to counter the damage already done to his frail and failing body).

> This disease is terrible … it is just a terrible disease … it doesn't … the one thing I don't like about it is that it doesn't just kill you right there. It slowly, you know … kills you little by little. One body part goes, then this, this, this, this … same … same … and that is worse … that is the pain … painful part of it. First they cut your leg and then they cut another leg and then they cut your hand and then your eyes, you lose your teeth, all those things, and then the last thing you die. But uh, I don't know, I don't know … just … I am going into a darkness. I don't know what is there … what is going to happen there. When I think about it maybe I have … I have ah … one of these days I know I am going to die but I don't know when. Sometimes when I get so … sick, you know I have to sleep all the time it doesn't really worry me … because I think … ah … I don't have to spend time worrying about myself or … so … that is the way it is … just the way it is. [I'm] Diabetic, that is that is just what it does to you.

Largely immobile, weak, at times disoriented, in constant pain and unsure of his future, Chep spent much of his last days contemplating the events and circumstances that led up to the onset of his illness. Unable to leave his hospital bed, his eyesight now too poor for him to read, he found himself regularly thinking through the various things he could have done differently to avoid his current fate. As it manifested most explicitly in the context of our interview together that day, Chep remarked,

> My diabetes I think it is definitely the … the lifestyle the way I used to have to uh … do things … I think … ah … alcohol is the one thing that is not good for that … and I had so much alcohol when I was growing up … and … like twenty years or the last twenty years when I started drinking before I stopped … it didn't bother me at the time. I didn't even feel anything. And I kept on doing it and people kept telling me hey you have to slow down your sick … 'Who said?' … um … I really, I really, I really don't know when … until I knew that I could not do it … I was so sick, I couldn't do it … so [it is only then that] I stopped.

His ongoing painful mooded attunement to the possibility that things could have been otherwise in his life was not, however, only disclosed in the context of his explicit reflections on regrets he had voiced over his own choices and decisions. They also extended to his critical evaluation of local orientations to illness that motivate deep-seated resistances to seeking out diagnosis and treatment. These orientations, as he came to realize only much too late, also played an important role in shaping his own actions (see Throop 2010). As he put it, sticking to a third-person description of such orientations,

> [Yapese people] don't want to know that they have this disease ... if they have it they don't want to know ... they don't want the doctor to tell them, 'Oh you have diabetes or you have already cancer or...' because that makes them so scared and worried about themselves. So they just ... you know ... if it happens it happens they don't want to be proven by the doctor that you have this, you are diabetic ... you are ... most of them are ... So that is why I think, that is why most of the people don't really go to the hospital ... it is no big deal ... I mean everybody wants to ... to take care of their body but they, nobody wants to be told your sick ... you can't eat that, you can't do that, you can't ... you have to stop doing that ... you are going to limit them from what they want to do.

Chep's mooded reflections thus not only opened opportunities for re-inhabiting past possibilities that were never at the time pursued but also enabled him to critically engage his own culturally instilled dispositions. This extended as well to his critical recognition of the many historical transformations that have led to a contemporary reliance upon foreign foods. In his estimation,

> the food that we are eating now days are not really good for our body. Sometimes, some of the food are good but we have to, you know, exercise and make your body work and you know get rid of the bad things but people in Yap are not doing that so, they don't really go to the taro patch or go fishing, you know ... in Yap ... in the old days ah ... going fishing is ... ah ... is a ... is an exercise ... you go fishing, you catch fish to eat while at the same time you are exercising ... and even going to the taro patch ... so that is how we ... so that is how people live on Yap ... uh ... in the past, they ... every morning, everyday they exercise because they have to go to the taro patch, to the garden, work, you know ... plant taro ... then they have to go fishing and catch fish while they are moving around ... so it, so it's a two-way street, you get the right kind food and you get exercise at the same time. But now days it like you ... you know ... you just go to work go to the store buy yourself a sack of rice and a couple of canned beefs and that is it.

For Chep, the 'best possible', as revealed in his mood inflected attunement to various dimensions of a life that could have been lived differently, was a mode of possibility that unfortunately could only be reclaimed from the past. Facing a future in which his own death was pressing on the most immediate of horizons, and a present in which his day-to-day existence was increasingly constricted by a painful deterioration of his existential viability, the space of his own ethical possibilities was only realizable in his ongoing re-inhabiting of what could have been otherwise in a mood of regret. Significantly, his abiding regretful mood also opened, and in so doing in part renewed, a critical engagement with those existential conditions into which he (and others in his community) have been thrown – namely a growing reliance on low-quality and overpriced foreign foods, a less active lifestyle, and an adherence to long-standing cultural orientations to the moral worth of enduring illness without complaint, each of which contribute to the conditions defining the dire situation that Yapese communities find themselves in. The extent to which this form of ethical generativity managed to impact the perspective of others in his community is admittedly, however, quite hard to say.

An Unfolding

While regret tethers us to the past, it is also potentially a mood that keeps that past alive – it opens and re-opens possibilities that did not transpire, the choices and consequences that were not realized, or the contexts that were avoided. It is in this respect, as the psychologist Landerman aptly phrases it, that regret can be understood to potentiate the very 'persistence of possibility'. Regret re-inhabits the past, literally re-enlivens a past to make it present again, and again, with the sense that we could have, and perhaps should have, done otherwise.[8] It is in this sense a repetition of the past. It is not however repetition as a dead weight. It is repetition as a singularized revisiting and re-opening of possibilities that were not in that moment pursued. In this capacity, regret sustains an engagement with a moral dilemma, situation, or failing in the mode of 'I could have acted otherwise', 'Things could have gone differently', 'What if we had or had not done this'. Regret, in this respect, is a mood that evokes not only the 'past perfect' in reference to the specific things I did or not did not do but also the imperfect past as a 'past' that is still potentially unfolding, with a renewed richness and diversity of aspects and dimensions, moral and otherwise, I may still yet uncover (see Schutz 1967; see also Wentzer 2014).

While such past possibilities were not pursued, and are never pursuable in precisely the same way again (that is, they are singular articulations arising in the midst of the ongoing flux of becoming that generates our being), as possibilities they open us up to an orientation to what might have been. The might have been, like the could yet still be, opens the past to modes of living through, living with, living again and living differently. In its retrospective modality at least, a regretful mood, as Steinbock argues for acts of memory more generally, '"liberates" the past from its otherwise fixed place; … [reaching] back to the past already accomplished, which is affectively significant in some way now, and accepting its pastness makes it present in a new way, emboldening it as a past in the present' (Steinbock 2014: 140). As such, what makes regret a distinctive type of moral mood is not only the fact that something specific went wrong or that we transgressed particular normative standards, our own or others, but instead that we find ourselves already presently dwelling in an attunement to the past that continually opens up the possibility, quite painful at times, that we could have done it differently, there might have been another way, that our history or fate could have been otherwise, that there could have been an alternative outcome to the trajectory and tonality of lives.

It is not only the past that is enlivened with such rays of possibility, however, for past possibilities feed constantly forward into ongoing and future concerns. Indeed, we might very well act differently if a similar situation happens to come about again. As attuned through a regretful mood to the horizon of our future actions, we hope that we will not react, feel, or do the same thing again. Next time, we would say something else, we would 'bite our tongue', we would wait and reflect more carefully before responding. We would not get upset or angered or act rashly. We would not miss another opportunity by hesitating or delaying. In this way, the opening up of possibilities of the past reconfigures our present concerns and our future goals, aspirations and hopes. To think of regretful moods in this way is to consider what it could it mean to live again, to have another chance, to get things right this time around, or to see anew the possibilities that were perhaps present in a now past moment that were either not then recognized as such or in the end never lived through. In the process we engage not only the ongoing flux of becoming that makes our particular modes of moral being possible, but also possibilities for the generative enlivening of the historical conditions we inhabit, and in so doing, may potentially transform.

While for Thiil the 'best possible' opened by such regretful mooded attunements may yet still indeed be possible for her, her family and the surrounding community, the singular possibilities opened by Chep's mooded attunements have now faded in the wake of his passing, although it is always still possible that they may yet generatively be taken up by others close enough to be touched by what was once disclosed by them.

Acknowledgements

I would like to thank Cheryl Mattingly, Maria Louw, Thomas Schwarz Wentzer and Rasmus Dyring for their editorial efforts and for their gracious invitation to participate in the Aarhus Institute of Advanced Studies conference 'Moral Engines: Exploring the Moral Drives of Human Life'. Their invitation to participate in the conference was the driving force that brought the possibility of this chapter into being. Thanks also to all the participants at the conference whose reflections, critiques and responses helped me to significantly refine and enhance my thinking on regret as a particular type of moral mood. Versions of this chapter were also presented at the Being, Presence, Ontology Colloquium Series, Department of Anthropology, Princeton University; the Departmental Colloquium Series, Department of Anthropology, UCSD; the Philosophy, Poetry and Religion Seminar Series, Mahindra Humanities Center, Harvard University; and the Worlds of Being Workshop on Culture and the

Self, Department of Psychology, Duquesne University. I would like to express my thanks to all of the organizers and participants for also greatly enhancing my engagement with the experience of regret. Finally, I would like to extend a heartfelt thanks to Zöe Wool who so generously shared a draft of her unpublished manuscript, a brilliant piece that provided an early and important pathway for me to better formulate my own thinking about the topic.

C. Jason Throop is Professor and Chair at the Department of Anthropology at UCLA. His books include *Suffering and Sentiment: Exploring the Vicissitudes of Experience and Pain in Yap* (University of California Press, 2010); *The Anthropology of Empathy: Experiencing the Lives of Others in Pacific Societies* (Berghahn, 2011, co-edited with Douglas Hollan); and *Toward an Anthropology of the Will* (Stanford University Press, 2010, co-edited with Keith M. Murphy).

Notes

1. More modestly, this would also include our efforts to simply keep going (Zigon 2007, 2011; cf. Badiou 2001).
2. These figures are taken from FSM Department of Health, Education and Social Affairs memo: http://www.epidemiology.pitt.edu/documents/internships/opps/DiabetesResearchinFSM07.pdf
3. According to 2013 figures on diabetes prevalence rates, the ten countries with the highest prevalence rates are: Tokelau (37.5%), Federated States of Micronesia (35%), Marshall Islands (34.9%), Kiribati (28.8%), Cook Islands (25.7%), Vanuatu (24%), Saudi Arabia (23.9%), Nauru (23.3%), Kuwait (23.1%) and Qatar (22.9%).
4. It is quite unfortunate that I only became aware of Teresa Kuan's article 'The Problem of Moral Luck, Anthropological Speaking' (2017) a few weeks prior to looking over the final page proofs for this chapter. Her discussion of 'agent-regret' and her resonate observation that anthropologist have paid scant attention to the topic, are of clear significance to the argument advanced here. I deeply regret (!) that a more thorough engagement with her work is not possible in the context of this chapter and will have to wait for another time and venue.
5. While my position is that regret – as a painful orientation to past possibilities that is attuned to how things could have been otherwise – is a core existential capacity (or in the language of this present volume a moral engine) that both patterns and drives moral experience. I am also very well aware of, and interested in, further thinking through the ways in which regret may be distinctively articulated in specific contexts (historical, cultural or otherwise) in which orientations to the fated unfolding of personal or historical trajectories are taken for granted. In such cases, experiences of regret would necessarily be inflected by assumptions that past actions, events and happenings are not open to any possibility of an 'otherwise', as the lives we have lived, the choices we have made, and the situations we have lived through, were always already fated to unfold the way that they did. And yet, whether our lives are deemed to be fated or not, I would still maintain that experiences of regret arise and are attuned to what Michael Jackson has characterized to be an underlying 'mystery of existential discontent – the question as to why human beings, regardless of the external circumstances, are haunted by a sense of insufficiency and loss' (2011: xi). Where Jackson works to further illuminate this mystery through his focus upon 'hope' as 'that sense that one may become other or more than one presently is or was fated to be' (ibid.), this present chapter thus looks instead to

　　regret as a mood that is responsive to the ways in which one could have 'become other or more' than one became or was 'fated to be'.

6. In this way, moral moods, while dispositional, should be distinguished from more deterministic renderings of moral dispositions found in some contemporary articulations of so-called 'third-person' virtue ethical theories (see Mattingly 2012, 2014). This is because a moral mood's indeterminacy may potentiate openings for change.

7. While I draw much inspiration from Steinbock's work on moral emotions (see Steinbock 2014), and in particular his distillation of Husserl's ethics of the "best possible' (see Steinbock 1995), I should note that I differ from his position in substantial ways in terms of my analysis of regret. For Steinbock, regret is deemed an all-too 'thin' and norm-bound orientation to have much existential weight morally speaking. Accordingly, he argues, it can be contrasted with the much 'deeper' and ethically salient emotions of remorse and repentance. Closely associated with a discernment of 'who I am' as a moral being, Steinbock argues that 'repentance is that [non-punctual] act, re-action that modifies the meaning of that past event or present self as it orients toward the future. It does so in relation to who I am now and to who I can become; it liberates me from the otherwise determining or motivating power of the past and the present' (2014: 140). In the case of remorse, Steinbock holds that 'While there is no positive orientation in remorse, it is nonetheless more affectively significant, "deeper", than, say being sorry [regretful]. In remorse, however, one dwells on or with the past, holds on to it, like a tenacious retention which is not restorative' (2014: 143). A key problem that I see with Steinbock's rather quick dismal of regret is that it again covers over the complex affective, emotional and mooded dimensions of the experience. As a result, Steinbock's rendering fails to disclose the significant ethical implications of regret.

8. In interesting to note in this respect that the temporal unfolding of regret seem to bear a family resemblance to Freud's classic account of melancholic moods (see Freud 1989). As David Eng and David Kazanjian maintain, 'we find in Freud's conception of melancholia's persistent struggle with its lost object not simply a "grasping" and "holding" on to a fixed notion of the past but rather a continuous engagement with loss and its remains. This engagement generates sites for memory and history, for the rewriting of the past as well as the reimagining of the future. While mourning abandons lost objects by laying their histories to rest, melancholia's continued and open relation to the past finally allows us to gain new perspectives and new understandings of lost objects' (2003: 4; cf. Garcia 2010: 74–76).

References

Ahmed, Sara. 2010. *The Promise of Happiness*. Durham, NC: Duke University Press.
———. 2014. 'Not in the Mood', *New Formations: A Journal of Culture/Theory/Politics* 82: 13–28.
Badiou, Alain. 2001. *Ethics: An Essay on the Understanding of Evil*. London: Verso.
Boss, Medard. 1979. *Existential Foundations of Medicine and Psychology*. Berkeley: University of California Press.
Daniel, Valentine. 2000. 'Mood, Moment, and Mind', in Veena Das, Arthur Kleinman, Mamphela Ramphele and Pamela Reynolds (eds), *Violence and Subjectivity*. Berkeley: University of California Press, pp. 333–66.
Egan, James A. 1998. 'Taro, Fish, and Funerals: Transformations in the Yapese Cultural Topography of Wealth'. Ph.D. Thesis, University of California Irvine.
Eng, David L. and David Kazanjian. 2003. 'Introduction: Mourning Remains', in David L. Eng and David Kazanjian (eds.), *Loss: The Politics of Mourning*. Berkeley: University of California Press, pp. 1–28.

Fassin, Didier. 2012. *Moral Anthropology*. Malden, MA: Wiley-Blackwell.
_____. 2013. 'On Resentment and Ressentiment: The Politics and Ethics of Moral Emotions', *Current Anthropology* 54(3): 249–67.
Faubion, James. 2011. *An Anthropology of Ethics*. Cambridge: Cambridge University Press.
Freud, Sigmund. 1989. Mourning and Melancholia, in Peter Gay, (ed.), *The Freud Reader*. New York: W.W. Norton.
Garcia, Angela. 2010. *The Pastoral Clinic: Addiction and Dispossession along the Rio Grande*. Berkeley: University of California Press.
Garro, Linda. 1995. 'Individual or Societal Responsibility? Explanations of Diabetes in an Anishinaabe (Ojibway) Community', *Social Science and Medicine* 40: 37–46.
_____. 1996. 'Intracultural Variation in Causal Accounts of Diabetes: A Comparison of Three Canadian Anishinaabe (Ojibway) Communities', *Culture, Medicine, and Psychiatry* 20(4): 381–420.
Geertz, Clifford. 1973. *The Interpretation of Cultures*. New York: Basic Books.
Gewertz, Deborah and Frederick Errington. 2010. *Cheap Meat: Flap Food Nations in the Pacific Islands*. Berkeley: University of California Press.
Guarigata, Leonor, et al. (eds). 2013. *IDF Diabetes Atlas, Sixth Edition*. Brussels: International Diabetes Federation.
Heidegger, Martin. 1962. *Being and Time*, trans. E. Macquarie and J. Robinson. Oxford. Blackwell Publishing.
Humphrey, Caroline and Altanhuu Hürelbaatar. 2005. 'Regret as a Political Intervention: An Essay in the Historical Anthropology of the Early Mongols', *Past and Present: A Journal of Historical Studies* 186(1): 3–45.
Husserl, Edmund. 1989. 'Fünf Aufsätze und Vorträge (1922–1937)', in Thomas Nenon and Hans Rainer Sepp (eds), *Husserliana*. Boston: Kluwer, vol. 27.
_____. 2001. *Analyses Concerning Passive and Active Synthesis*. Dordrecht: Kluwer Academic Press.
Ichiho, Henry, et al. 2013. 'An Assessment of Non-Communicable Diseases, Diabetes, and Related Risk Factors in the Federated States of Micronesia, State of Yap: A Systems Perspective', *Hawai'i Journal of Medicine & Public Health* 72(5 Suppl 1): 57–67.
Jackson, Michael. 2011. *Life Within Limits: Well-Being in a World of Want*. Durham, NC: Duke University Press.
Joe, Jennie R. and Robert S. Young (eds). 1993. *Diabetes as a Disease of Civilization: The Impact of Culture Change on Indigenous People*. Berlin: de Gruyter.
Kuan, Teresa. 2017. 'The Problem of Moral Luck, Anthropologically Speaking', *Anthropological Theory* 17(1): 30–59.
Labby, David. 1976. *The Demystification of Yap: Dialectics of Culture on a Micronesian Island*. Chicago: Chicago University Press.
Laidlaw, James. 2013. *The Subject of Virtue*. Cambridge: Cambridge University Press.
Lambek, Michael. 2010. *Ordinary Ethics: Anthropology, Language, and Action*. New York: Fordham University Press.
Landerman, Janet. 1993. *Regret: The Persistence of the Possible*. Oxford: Oxford University Press.
Lee, Nam-In. 1998. 'Edmund Husserl's Phenomenology of Mood', in Natalie Depraz and Dan Zahavi (eds), *Alterity and Facticity: New Perspectives on Husserl*. Dordrecht: Kluwer Academic Publishers, pp. 103–122.
Lingenfelter, Sherwood. 1979. 'Yap Eating Classes: A Study of Structure and Communitas', *Journal of the Polynesian Society* 88(4): 415–32.
Mattingly, Cheryl. 2012. 'Two Virtue Ethics and the Anthropology of Morality', *Anthropological Theory* 12(2): 161–84.

_____. 2014. *Moral Laboratories: Family Peril and the Struggle for a Good Life.* Berkeley: University of California Press.

McLennan, Amy and Stanley J. Ulijaszek. 2015. 'An Anthropological Insight into the Pacific Island Diabetes Crisis and its Clinical Implications', *Diabetes Management* 5(3): 143–45.

Peijnenburg, Jeanne. 2007. 'Regret and Retroaction', *Homo Oeconomicus* 24(2): 295–313.

Popkin, Barry M. 2015. 'Nutrition Transition and the Global Diabetes Epidemic', *Current Diabetes Reports* 15: 64.

Ram, Kalpana. 2015. 'Moods and Method: Heidegger and Merleau-Ponty on Emotion and Understanding', in *Phenomenology in Anthropology: A Sense of Perspective.* Bloomington: Indiana University Press, pp. 29–49.

Ratcliffe, Matthew. 2013. 'Why Mood Matters', in Mark A. Wrathall (ed.), *The Cambridge Companion to Being and Time.* Cambridge: Cambridge University Press, pp. 157–176.

_____. 2015. *Experiences of Depression: A Study in Phenomenology.* Oxford: Oxford University Press.

Robbins, Joel. 2004. *Becoming Sinners.* Berkeley: University of California Press.

Scheper-Hughes, Nancy. 2005. 'The Politics of Remorse', in Conerly Casey and Robert Edgerton (eds), *A Companion to Psychological Anthropology: Modernity and Psychocultural Change.* Oxford: Wiley-Blackwell, pp. 469–94.

Schutz, Alfred. 1967. *The Phenomenology of the Social World.* Evanston, IL: Northwestern University Press.

Steinbock, Anthony J. 1995. *Home and Beyond: Generative Phenomenology after Husserl.* Evanston, IL: Northwestern University Press.

_____. 2014. *Moral Emotions: Reclaiming the Evidence of the Heart.* Evanston, IL: Northwestern University Press.

Throop, C. Jason. 2003. 'Articulating Experience', *Anthropological Theory* 3(2): 219–41.

_____. 2009a. 'Interpretation and the Limits of Interpretability: On Rethinking Clifford Geertz' Semiotics of Religious Experience', *Journal of North African Studies* 14(3/4): 369–84.

_____. 2009b. 'Intermediary Varieties of Experience', *Ethnos* 74(4): 535–58.

_____. 2010. *Suffering and Sentiment: Exploring the Vicissitudes of Experience and Pain in Yap.* Berkeley: University of California Press.

_____. 2012. 'Moral Sentiments', in Didier Fassin (ed.), *A Companion to Moral Anthropology.* Oxford: Wiley-Blackwell, pp. 150–68.

_____. 2014. 'Moral Moods', *Ethos* 42(1): 65–83.

_____. 2015a. 'Ambivalent Happiness and Virtuous Suffering', *HAU: Journal of Ethnographic Theory* 5(3): 45–68.

_____. 2015b. 'Sacred Suffering: A Phenomenological Anthropological Perspective', in Chris Houston and Kalpana Ram (eds), *Phenomenology in Anthropology: A Sense of Perspective.* Bloomington: Indiana University Press, pp. 68–89.

_____. 2017. 'Despairing Moods: Worldly Attunements and Permeable Personhood in Yap', *Ethos* 45(2): 199–215.

Throop, C. Jason and Alessandro Duranti. 2015. 'Attention, Ritual Glitches, and Attentional Pull: The President and the Queen', *Phenomenology and Cognitive Sciences* 14(4): 1055–1082.

Wentzer, Thomas Schwarz. 2014. '"I have seen Königsberg burning": Philosophical Anthropology and the Responsiveness of Historical Experience', *Anthropological Theory* 14(1): 27–48.

Wikan, Unni. 2013. *Resonance: Beyond Words.* Chicago: University of Chicago Press.

Wilce, Jim. 2005. 'Traditional Laments and Postmodern Regrets: The Circulation of Discourse in a Metacultural Context', *Journal of Linguistic Anthropology* 15(1): 60–71.

Wool, Zöe. Under Review. 'War, Work, and the Edges of Regret: The American Moral Economy of Sacrifice and the Worthiness of Injured Soldiers'.

Zigon, Jarrett. 2007. 'Moral Breakdown and the Ethical Demand: A Theoretical Framework for the Anthropology of Moralities', *Anthropological Theory* 7(2): 131–50.

_____. 2011. *'HIV is God's Blessing': Rehabilitating Morality in Neoliberal Russia.* Berkeley: University of California Press.

_____. 2014. 'Attunement and Fidelity: Two Ontological Conditions for Morally Being-in-the-World', *Ethos* 42(1): 16–30.

Zigon, Jarrett and C. Jason Throop. 2014. 'Moral Experience: Introduction', *Ethos* 42(1): 1–15.

4

Haunting as Moral Engine
Ethical Striving and Moral Aporias among Sufis in Uzbekistan

Maria Louw

Do Not Think of a Polar Bear

I know a story: someone asked a *tabib* [traditional healer] if he could explain how to make a certain medicine for a certain disease. The *tabib* answered him, 'Take these things and cook them, and when you cook them you must not think of a polar bear!' The man could not make the medicine, because if you are told not to think of a polar bear you will think of it all the time. This is what Sufis experience. The Sufi knows that he should not do this or that. Before he did not know. Evil things were habits for him. When he thinks of them, evil things give him orders all the time.

This quote stems from an interview I conducted with Rustam,[1] a young Sufi in Bukhara, an ancient Silk Road oasis and centre for Islamic learning and mysticism, which is now part of Uzbekistan. Rustam was talking about his paradoxical experiences upon entering the Sufi path, feeling 'evil things' (Uzbek: *yomon narsalar*) as even stronger forces in his life the more he attempted to avoid them. Previously, for example, the fact that he enjoyed eyeing up some of the girls in the classes he took at university did not really bother him, but the fact that he was now more conscious of the morally reprehensible aspect of having improper thoughts about girls made these thoughts take up even more space in his mind, sometimes to the point where he could hardly concentrate on the lectures.

Rustam's reflections point to what is indeed often an inherent irony of moral experience: the more a person strives for ethical clarity and self-consistency, the more opaque and challenging the moral landscape may often seem (cf. Laidlaw 2014: 173). Rustam talked about the haunting of 'evil things'. Very often, however, as I will show in this chapter, when people find themselves amidst the multiple concerns characterizing everyday life, and are not, like Rustam, in an interview situation, trying to make sense of it all to an anthropologist interested in Sufism, they are less categorical in their judgments about good and evil (cf. Zigon and Throop 2014: 2). Still, the image of the polar bear which keeps haunting one exactly because one tries to ignore it is good as a starting point for what I have in mind here. In the following, I take as an ethnographic point of departure a group of Uzbeks who are formally initiated into the Naqshbandiyya Sufi way or merely following (some of) its principles, and who, through continuous work on the self, seek to approach God as well as to realize Sufism as this-worldly ethics, letting it guide their relations with others.[2] Drawing inspiration from thinkers who have highlighted what is often the ambiguous and undetermined character of moral life, and with the concept of haunting as my central analytical lens, I focus on the way in which Sufis, in their search for moral perfection, are frequently haunted by the moral choices they could have made, the moral acts they could have engaged in, the moral persons they could have become. This haunting, I argue, makes moral reflection and questioning a lingering presence in the background of everyday existence; a disturbing reminder of how the (moral) foundations on which a life is based may be shaky, and how every intersubjective encounter may be a moral 'engine' in the sense of having the potential to redirect one's care and concern, sometimes in unplanned and surprising ways. In Central Asia, among Sufis, but also among the population more generally, a certain degree of openness – the willingness and ability to (temporarily) stray away from one's chosen moral path, however right this path may, or merely to give emotional space to what one had to leave behind on the path, acknowledging life's insurmountable value conflicts – tends to be seen as essential for the virtuous human being.

Let me now turn to an example, which may also introduce the context.

Muazzam

Muazzam was a middle-aged woman who lived together with her parents in a small flat in Bukhara where I visited her for the first time back in 1999. Telling me about her growing engagement in 'spiritual' matters, she recounted how she had started to develop an interest in Islam already in 1983: back then, as she told it, she was sick and unable to do anything. Then she had a dream in which an old man came to her and scolded her for sitting passively at home. He said that she had to become Muslim and start healing people, using the techniques of her ancestors – which she did, although in a discreet way: this was back in the Soviet days when the practice of religion was strongly discouraged.[3] Then Gorbachev came to power, and things started to change.

The years surrounding the break-up of the Soviet Union and the independence of Uzbekistan were unsettling ones for the people who lived there: it was a time when the world as they knew it was replaced by something yet to come into being, and when all sorts of hopes and fears for the future proliferated. Many of these hopes and fears had to do with religion. There was a sense among large parts of the population that the seventy years of Soviet rule and attempts to do away with religion had made people forget what it meant to be Muslim and, correspondingly, there was widespread hope that people would soon be able to recover that lost knowledge, filling up what was perceived to be an ideological and moral vacuum and a cynical atmosphere in society. But people equally feared that the perceived ideological and moral vacuum would make a fertile soil for blind religious extremism. Religion, in short, was – and is still now – ambiguously conceived of as both a major source of morality, hope and sense of direction and, in its extreme or excessive forms, as a danger-ous opium which brainwashes people with ready-made answers to life's ques-tions, bereaving them of their normal sense of moral judgment (Louw 2007, 2013; Rasanayagam 2011).

Muazzam, like many others, found herself exploring what it meant to be Muslim around this time. She felt that there was something missing from her life, and that she needed a deeper understanding of the forces that made her able to heal others. She did many things wrong at that time, she recalled, and felt the need to improve her character. And in 1998, after having been intro-duced to it by a friend, she decided to become a follower of the Naqshbandiyya Sufi *tariqa*: one of the world's most widespread Sufi orders, which has strong historical roots in Central Asia,[4] and which – partly because its teaching has been promoted by governments there[5] – enjoys immense popularity in the region today, also among many 'ordinary' Muslims who may not have been formally initiated into it but still find inspiration in at least aspects of its teach-ing (Louw 2007).

Naqshbandiyya and Moral Perfectionism

When Muazzam told me about her engagement in Sufism, like other Bukhara Naqshbandis she emphasized the constant work on the self as its central feature. She strove to cultivate herself, and more particularly her senses, in order to perceive other, and deeper or more spiritual aspects of the world around her than the untrained senses are able to perceive, and thus to become able to live a life characterized by a religiously grounded ethics in a predomi-nantly secular society.

Talking about the moral and spiritual constitution of a human being, Bukhara Naqshbandis take as a point of departure the classical concepts of *qalb* (heart or soul), *ruh* (spirit), *aql* (intellect) and *nafs* (desire, ego or base instincts) which have provided the foundation for the development of theories of human psychology throughout the history of Sufism (cf. Schimmel 1975: 112, 191–93). In classical Sufi psychology the *nafs* is considered as the moral person's greatest enemy: not only does it encourage a person to act amorally, it also seeks to legitimize amoral acts. A Naqshbandi is encouraged to act contrary to the demands of the *nafs* in order to tame it and gain control of it. More extreme forms of *nafs-jihad* are rare in the Naqshbandiyya, which tends to consider excessive asceticism risky and incompatible with the modern world. Classical means for taming and training the *nafs* like fasting and sleeplessness, however, are practiced. Most importantly, however, the Sufi seeks to tame the *nafs* through the *dhikr*, i.e. the remembrance of recollection of God in the form of repetitive invocations of his names and various religious formulas.

The Naqshbandiyya is known for its inner or unspoken (*khufiyya*) *dhikr*. This *dhikr* is also referred to as the *dhikr* of the heart (Uzbek: *dhikr qalbi*). When the *dhikr* is focused in the heart – i.e. in the centre for the battle between good and evil in a human being – it is argued, the body will be cleansed, physically and spiritually, and the *nafs* will be tamed. Taming the *nafs*, a person will experience the opening of the 'eye of the heart' and the 'ear of the heart' (Uzbek: *qalb ko'zi, qalb quloqi*): a person whose heart's senses have been opened will start becoming more sensitive to God's demands as well as the demands of people around him or her, more able to feel people's inner lives, become more attuned to the ethical demands of the Other.

The ultimate goal is to make the *dhikr* a habit for the heart and in this way to dissolve the distinction between the worldly and the transcendent, to fill each act with the presence of God and make an ordinary life into a travel towards God. Central to the Naqshbandiyya is the idea that one should not turn one's back to the world, but combine spiritual development with a this-worldly engagement: 'The heart with God; the hand at work', as a saying goes which is attributed to Bahouddin Naqshband, patron saint of Bukhara and a central figure in the development of the teachings of the Naqshbandiyya. This idea has been interpreted in various ways through the history of the Naqshbandiyya: as a call for adaptation to society, as a call for jihad against society, and everything in between.[6] For the Naqshbandis I met in Bukhara it was a continuous source of reflection, and their very engagement in Sufism seemed to be characterized by a continuous effort to strike a balance between this-worldliness and transcendence; between attention to God's demands and the demands of people around them. Sometimes they criticized and tried to steer away from the evils they encountered in the surrounding society – the cynicism, greediness and materialism they found characteristic of it – and sometimes they emphasized the need to engage in it all and make a living, pointing out that entrepreneurial spirit and responsibility are central virtues in Islam, and in the Naqshbandiyya more particularly (Louw 2007). In short, rather than providing them with easy answers to questions about how they should lead their lives and a ready-made template for virtuous subject formation, their engagement in the Naqshbandiyya prompted them to continuously ask themselves such questions.

Virtuous Subject Formation: Saba Mahmood and her Critics

Recently, there have been quite a few studies focusing on self-cultivation through religious practice in Islam (see, for example, Hirschkind 2006; Mahmood 2005; Marsden 2005; Rasanayagam 2011), many of these taking as their point of departure virtue ethics in one variety or the other. Saba Mahmood (2005), notably, has been groundbreaking in her study of how women engaging in piety movements in Egypt cultivate virtuous dispositions through specific sets of techniques, providing important critiques of liberal assumptions about agency and correctives to the common idea that Muslim piety equals radicalism in the political sense and should by definition be seen as a threat to the secular order.

In a more general theoretical critique of what she terms a 'poststructuralist' virtue ethics in anthropology, Cheryl Mattingly has pointed out that a study like Mahmood's, focusing on how ethical subjectivity is formed by pre-existing moral codes and practices, tends to downplay the doubt, ambiguities and challenges people face in their everyday lives where they may move between different moral worlds with competing moral claims, and where it may quite often be difficult to discern what constitutes the most appropriate action and what kind of self one ought to become – and that they tend to overlook how the moral ordinary may offer resources for critique and transformation (Mattingly 2012, 2013 and 2014).

Based on his fieldwork among young Muslims in Egypt, Samuli Schielke, similarly, has formulated a general critique against the recent focus on self-cultivation in anthropology, which, he argues, has a tendency to assume that ethical subjects have consistent and clear dispositions, that they know what they want and what has the greatest value for them. Thus, they are often blind to the complexities and ambiguities which characterize everyday ethical practice, to the ways in which subjects most often have to navigate various and sometimes contradictory ideas about the good person, the good life and the good society (Schielke 2009; see also Deeb and Harb 2013: 16; and Laidlaw 2014: 167–73). Among the young Muslims Schielke focuses on, values related to the Islamic piety movements they engage in exist in a complex relationship with other values and ideals related to, for example, romantic love, family ties, success and self-realization – values and ideals which are often quite hard to balance. 'Moral reasoning', Schielke writes, therefore often becomes a matter of 'deciding, in a moment, who you want to be … these are always painful decisions, and they leave people remorseful in different ways' (ibid: 171). In a public climate strongly influenced by Salafi revivalist notions of piety, morality and religion, where value conflicts tend to be perceived as merely personal problems to be overcome, such remorse resulting from value conflicts is hard to articulate.

I sympathize greatly with these critics. Indeed, when one does not merely focus on what Sufis have to say about Sufism as it ought to be, but on how they actually live it, a picture emerges in which frustrations, remorse and pain – but also, occasionally, a humorous reconciliation with life's insurmountable value conflicts or a defiant determination to act in spite of them – takes centre stage. Contrary to the Salafis Schielke writes about, however, the value conflicts, the remorse, the pain, the defiance, the humour as well as other emotions, moods and attitudes involved in making difficult decisions of a moral nature, so it seems, should be articulated or brought forward in some other way if one wants to prove oneself as a good or morally mature person. Let us again return to Muazzam.

Haunting

'We are Sufis', Muazzam said, referring to the group of Naqshbandi women she met with regularly, 'but we are not like Sufis in the past. In Bahouddin Naqshband's time, they were very pure, very close to God. Their devotion to Islam was so big that they would not interrupt their prayers, even if a fire broke loose around them, or an invading army stood next to them. Today we have forgotten what real Sufism is'.

If there was a theme which permeated the way Naqshbandis in Bukhara talked about Sufism in the late 1990s and the beginning of the new millennium, it was oblivion and the loss of knowledge. People repeatedly emphasized that what they practiced was not real Sufism; it did not even come close. This idea – that 'real' Sufism is a past phenomenon – actually has a long history in Sufism[7] but was perhaps accentuated in a context like that of post-Soviet Uzbekistan which was characterized by a general ethos of post-colonial loss, where 'the 70 Soviet years' were regularly blamed for everything from economic chaos and political corruption to religious and moral ignorance and confusion (Louw 2007).

In her own self-understanding, then, Muazzam was not a real Sufi. However, since starting to practice Sufism, she had experienced some positive changes to her character: previously, she tended to fight and quarrel with her neighbours and to spread gossip, but now she had become more humble and calm. This newfound strength in her character, however, was accompanied by what she experienced as an increasing sensitivity or porousness, in particular in relation to things which are *haram*, i.e. forbidden according to Islam. She first experienced this when her brother got married. As it is common practice among relatives she had offered her help, but on the day of the wedding she fell ill, and no doctors were able to help her. She knew that it was because of the vodka and the pork sausages that were served at the wedding feast and the drunkenness, gossiping and improper behaviour of the people who attended it. The next time she experienced it was also on the occasion of a wedding, this time her sister's: she wanted to help, but she fell ill. Then she realized that she could no longer participate in such events.

When Muazzam started telling her story, it was meant to illustrate how her character had changed for the better, how she had become able to stay away from things, acts and events which are considered forbidden or inappropriate according to Islam, what it meant to have one's heart's eye and ears opened. But as she told me the story she increasingly seemed to be filled with sadness: she recounted how she cried because she was no longer able to help, in spite of the fact that she knew that she was not responsible – it was God who would not let her help – and how, one night, she had a very vivid dream in which her sister came to her, asking her for a cup of water. Muazzam did not grant her wish, but shut the door in her face.

Denying water to a person who asks for it is virtually unthinkable in Central Asia. Muazzam was not sure about the dream: she knew that it might be her *nafs* trying to trick her into indulging in what was *haram* – the *nafs* does indeed sometimes play tricks with a person's dreams, trying to make them seem like visionary dreams. But the very vividness of the dream and the way it kept haunting her after she woke up, although she wanted to shake it off – something which often distinguishes visionary dreams of divine origin from 'ordinary' dreams (which are seen as meaningless or stemming from unconscious desires) (Louw 2010, 2015) – made her doubt that what she was doing was right; it blurred the distinction between what was right and what was wrong, between which demands she should respond to and which she should ignore.

When Muazzam was not able to participate in the weddings of her brother and sister, she did not merely create distance between herself and beloved family members – who were all the more important to her as she had never married and started a family on her own – but also between herself and central local ideas about what it means to be Muslim. Events which mark important moments in the life of a Muslim – circumcision, marriage and death – involve the exchange of gifts and hospitality and are important contexts for the establishment and maintenance of social networks (cf. Werner 1999). Religious authorities often criticize them, pointing out that they are not sanctioned by scripture, and that the great expenses involved in throwing them is an unnecessary burden for many families to bear. Nonetheless, it is widely considered essential for a Muslim to participate in them, thus showing oneself to be a person who contributes to the cohesion of the community (cf. Borbieva 2012; Rasanayagam 2011). This 'participation', as it is called, is a central activity of Central Asian families, and in particular women: an activity, which creates important social networks, and which become increasingly important in times of stress and hardship. In other words, for Muazzam this was no simple conflict between 'religious' piety and 'social' norms, as living up to one's social obligations, in local understandings, is considered absolutely central to Muslimness. By avoiding what was *haram*, she acted in ways which were rather inappropriate in local understandings of what it means to be a good Muslim.

Muazzam switched back and forth between celebrating the person her engagement in Naqshbandiyya had helped her to become, and lamenting the other persons which were lost in the process. As psychoanalyst Adam Phillips writes in *Missing Out: In Praise of the Unlived Life*, large parts of our mental life are about the lives we are not living, the lives we could be leading but for some reason are not (Phillips 2012: xi).[8] Unlived lives also seemed to lurk in the background of Muazzam's experience. They were pushed to the background of experience and lived a ghostly life there, haunting her.

Haunting describes the seething presence of what appears not to be there, the ghost or apparition being a form through which something barely visible or lost makes itself known (Gordon 2008: 8; Frederiksen 2014; Navaro-Yashin 2012). Jacques Derrida used the concept in his book 'Specters of Marx', reflecting on the persistence of the concept of (utopian) revolution despite its apparent eradication from the scene of politics and history: the concept, he argued, had taken on a ghostly aspect, being present and yet not present at the same time (Derrida 1994). It has since been taken up by a number of anthropologists in order to elucidate how ghostly presences of various sorts – spectres of people, ideas and things which have disappeared – haunt the present (see, for example, Aretxaga 2005; Carsten 2007; Frederiksen 2014; Kwon 2006; Navaro-Yashin 2012). Here I use it to refer to the moral choices one did not make but could have made, the moral acts one did not engage in but could have engaged in, and the moral persons one did not become but could have become – in short, by the moral potential in all that which is discarded in the search for moral perfection and which continues to linger in the background of experience. What haunted Muazzam was not experienced as 'evil things' 'giving orders' as in Rustam's story about the polar bear. Rather, the 'lost persons', so to speak, who let themselves be heard in ghostly, if also quite visceral, ways, created fundamental doubt in her about who she was, what she had been, and what she should strive to become. At stake was her very existence as a moral being (cf. Throop 2014: 69).

The Fragility of Goodness

An important inspiration for me in trying to get at an understanding of situations such as Muazzam's – and the central significance of emotions and moods such as frustration, doubt and remorse in the moral lives of Sufis like her – has been Martha Nussbaum's reading of the Greek tragedy in *The Fragility of Goodness* (Nussbaum 2001 [1986]), and her discussion of the tension in moral life between what is within a person's control, and what is outside it; between what we strive for and what merely happens to us; and what is often the moral tragedy involved in trying to lead a good life. The tragic poets show us situations in which good people are ruined because of things that just happen to them; they show us situations where good people do bad things because of circumstances outside their control; and, most relevant here, they show us situations of tragic conflict where two central commitments come into conflict, where the character knows what he or she does, but where there is nothing he or she can do without doing wrong. In such situations, tragedy shows us, the solution is not merely to rank one's obligations, to use reason to decide what is to have most value. Although one attempts to do so, and although one is quite sure that one has made the right choice, a good person at least will nonetheless feel pain and regret: 'the only thing remotely like a solution here', Nussbaum writes, 'is in fact, to describe and see the conflict clearly and to acknowledge that there is no way out' (ibid.: 49–50).

Tragedy dwells upon such situations, exploring what goodness means in these cases. Aeschylus, for example, tells the story about Agamemnon, the great king, who is leading his troops against Troy, but who incurs the wrath of Artemis who prevents the army from setting off. Calchas, the prophet, declares that the only way he can appease Artemis is by sacrificing his daughter Iphigenia. If Agamemnon does not fulfil Artemis' condition, everyone, including Iphigenia, will die. Agamemnon does eventually sacrifice Iphigenia; her death appeases Artemis, and the Greek army sets out for Troy. This decision is probably the best one he could have made, but the chorus accuses him of being evil, not because of his decision as such, but because of his change of thought and passion, which accompanies the killing: Agamemnon shows no sign of remorse – he is able to dissociate himself from his commitment as father – and precisely because of this change in his emotions he proves himself less good (ibid.: 34–55).

The Moral Force of Emotions

The example of Muazzam, of course, is less dramatic and grandiose; it does not involve any killings and is not about the lives of heroes and kings, but it nonetheless exhibits the same kind of conflict as tragedies are made of. It shows that when a person cares deeply about more than one thing – which most people certainly do – the very course of life will lead that person to situations where he or she cannot honour all of their commitments. And it shows how a person's emotional responses to complicated moral dilemmas may be absolutely central to how his or her moral character is perceived.

While we sit there in Muazzam's home and talk about the pain and regret she felt when she was not able to attend her sister's wedding, the same sister who lives nearby with her family happens to arrive. They embrace, chat, and Muazzam introduces me and tells her about my work in Uzbekistan and my interest in Sufism more particularly. Her sister then tells me how proud they are of Muazzam, as she is such a source of moral inspiration for them all, that people in the neighbourhood always whisper 'look, there is a Naqshbandi' when she passes by, although she has not told them that she is a follower of the Naqshbandi way: there is just something in the way she talks and her character which stands out. Muazzam laughs, seeming a bit embarrassed and again emphasizes that she is not a 'real' Sufi, that she is still learning. 'How can you be a Sufi with a sister like me!', the sister says, and they both laugh.

Precisely because she 'fails' in her transformation, because she is not, and does not consider herself, a 'real' Sufi, I would argue, others consider her a good person and a good Muslim. What makes Muazzam virtuous in the eyes of others is exactly her doubt and remorse – the fact that following the right way does not feel wholly right for her, and that she is haunted by other moral persons she could have become but who were sacrificed along the way. Had she shown no remorse, she would have been perceived as emotionally, morally and intellectually immature in the eyes of others.

Acting in the 'right way' is less a matter of adhering to (more or less strictly defined) principles than it is a matter of coming to terms with conflicts of commitments and values, of finding some kind of (temporary) balance between them when it is possible, bending principles when it is possible, and of accepting and living with what may be the suffering that results when it is not possible (Deeb and Harb 2013: 18; Laidlaw 2014: 127–28). One of the most loathed characters in the imaginations of people in Central Asia is the person – the 'extremist' – who is so completely brainwashed by a set of ideas – however true these ideas may be – that any risk of conflict and tension is closed off. Most have stories to tell about people who turn their backs on their families and communities in their devotion to Islam because they are unable to combine their engagement in Islam with an ordinary life among family and community members who do not live up to their ideals, and who, in doing this, forget that love, loyalty and respect to those to whom one owes one's existence is indeed central to what Islam is all about.

The example of Muazzam, her ethical striving and remorse, also shows how emotions are morally charged and may affect relations with others no less than acts and explicit moral reflections do. It shows that when the possibilities for being a moral person, which are rejected but continue to haunt one, are performed through the expression of emotions – such as in Muazzam's remorse, for example, or in the humorous reconciliation with life's insurmountable moral challenges that found expression in her meeting with her sister – one may, in a sense, be more than one (moral) person at the same time; the ghostly is acknowledged and revealed.

While there has been a recent boom in studies of emotions and affect in anthropology and related disciplines (see, for example, Ahmed 2004; Beatty 2010, 2015; Brennan 2004; Frederiksen 2014; Martin 2013; Navaro-Yashin 2012; Svasek 2005; Thrift 2004), very few of these studies have touched upon the moral force of emotions. Likewise, the recent moral turn in anthropology has seen relatively little attention paid to emotions; just like in the history of philosophy, the emotions have most often been considered relatively irrelevant in accounts of ethical judgment (Nussbaum 2001). One of the few anthropologists who have paid particular attention to how sentiments, emotions, feelings and moods are made ethically significant is Jason Throop (see Throop

2010, 2012, 2014, and this volume). In his article 'Moral Moods' (2014), Throop focuses on the concept of 'mood', exploring how moods may carry moral concerns. Moods, he argues, are somewhere halfway between moments of explicit ethical reflection and habitual embodied forms of morality. The complex temporal expanse of moods, he contends, provides a way for moral problems to remain viscerally bound to one's being, 'while extending moments of transgression, worry, and/or concern into both past and possible future horizons of experience that stretch well beyond the confines of the present or even the particularities of an ongoing interaction or narrative' (ibid: 68). Furthermore, Throop argues, when we are 'in' a mood, the line between our subjective experience and the intersubjective world that surrounds us is often blurred, leaving undefined precisely who or what is to blame for a particular moral failing, concern or predicament. Moods therefore reveal moral concerns in flux and often inhabit an ambivalent existential expanse where the possible, the ideal and the actual coalesce in rather complicated ways, and where moods may allow us to hold ambivalent, unresolved or contradictory assessments of our moral life in a semi-reflective expanse that may or may not result in permanent transformations of our being (ibid.: 70–71).

The haunting experienced by Muazzam and others often took the form of shifting moods and emotions that seemed to have a life of their own, overwhelming them in ways that were beyond their control and understanding, complicating moral principles and decisions, and revealing moral concerns in flux. Furthermore, their example shows that the performance of such moods, or emotions, may play a larger role in moral life than has usually been acknowledged.

Let me provide another concrete example to further illustrate this point.

Feruza

We are sitting at Feruza's balcony,[9] enjoying a cup of tea and the cool evening, chatting about this and that. She keeps returning to the *tugh*, the pole, which marks the tombs of *avliyo*, Muslim 'saints': persons who, by the grace of God and because of their exemplary lives, hold a special relationship with God and possess *baraka*, blessing power. Placed on the top of the pole is an image of a hand. While some people say that the hand symbolizes the five pillars of Islam, in this part of the world it is much more common to link it to Alexander Makedonskiy, Alexander the Great, who is a great legendary figure in Central Asia, as in other parts of the world. The story goes that Alexander, when he sensed that his death was near, told people around him to bury him with an empty hand on his grave as a symbol that although he had conquered the world, he left it empty-handed, carrying nothing with him to the next life.

People forget about that, Feruza said. They forget that all that stays with them is their deeds in this world, whether these have been good or bad. Feruza was worried about her son, Tohir, who was recently sacked from his job in the state administration. According to Feruza, the reason was that Tohir had had a conflict with his boss due to the fact that he did not share his colleagues' taste for nightly visits to restaurants, bars and discotheques, and participating in various shady affairs, including the acceptance of bribes.

Losing his job was no small issue for Tohir. He was in his mid-twenties and expected to marry and start his own family soon, but his parents refused to arrange his marriage before he had found himself a job that would enable him to support his own family. Until then, he would remain dependent on his parents like a child. Thus, the stakes were his honour, status and identity as man and future family head. When people in the neighbourhood asked Tohir if he would soon start working, and if his wedding party would soon be held, he would answer in the affirmative, boasting that his wedding would be so spectacular that they had never seen the like. But as time went by, he became more and more apathetic and started barricading himself inside the family's apartment, spending most of the day sleeping and watching television and expressing bitterness towards his surroundings. Sometimes he blamed the whole society, the corruption of which made it impossible to reach any goals in life without being rich or knowing the right people. At other times he blamed his father for not being able to help him. Mahmud, his father, had also been unemployed for a while. In 1999, the family spent all their savings to send him to Vladivostok, where Feruza's brother lived, because they heard that it was fairly easy to get a job there. Mahmud went together with a friend, who quickly got a job. Mahmud, however, had to give up after two months, having spent all the money.

Feruza had not been formally initiated in the Naqshbandiyya Sufi order, but like many others she strove to live by at least some of its principles and engage in some of its practices, such as the silent *dhikr* which, as she pointed out, was quite practical for a hardworking person like her because it could be practiced at any time, in almost any context, while she commuted to and from work, for example (she was an engineer), or when she did her housework. This recollection of God, she pointed out, helped her to stay clear of the evils she felt surrounding her. Now sitting there at the balcony and pondering Tohir's situation, she kept returning to the *tugh*, pointing out that people nowadays were selfish and obsessed with money, that they forgot about each other and the life hereafter. The employees at her son's former place of work had been involved in the trafficking of women to Dubai; she was grateful that he had left the place in time, without getting involved in things like that. But it was also immensely painful for her to see her son – who had previously been cheerful and full of self-confidence – languishing on the sofa. 'This is no life for a young man', she repeatedly said, and also referred to the Bahouddin Naqshband 'motto' I quoted previously – 'The heart with God, the hand at work' – pointing out how important it was for a man to make his own living.

A couple of days after that evening on the balcony I learned that Feruza had persuaded Tohir to contact his former boss's superiors – people who worked abroad now and whom he used to consider as his patrons – for help. 'I have to help my son', she said. 'This is no life for a young man. What kind of mother would I be if I just let him lie there without doing anything?' In a desperate attempt to change the minds of Tohir's former bosses the family bought a fancy and very expensive cake and sent him off to his former place of work in his finest clothes. When Tohir returned home, he was still carrying the cake under his arm. His former superiors had refused to accept it. For a while it stood on the kitchen table – formerly a representation of hope, now one of humiliation – until Feruza cut through the thick atmosphere of shame and humiliation by declaring that if these crap-eating donkeys would not eat the cake, they would eat it themselves, and started cutting it into big pieces. Later that evening I found her immersed in the practice of the *dhikr*.

These glimpses of Feruza's life bring us even further from Rustam's polar bear story and the idea that 'evil things' give you orders when you try to ignore them. For Feruza there was no clear-cut answer to what was good and what was evil. The Naqshbandiyya's teachings – and the exemplary lives of *avliyo*, Muslim 'saints' – provided her with different moral models or exemplars (cf. Robbins, this volume; Laidlaw 2014: 82–87) that she emphasized at various times – the virtue of forsaking the striving for power and richness in this world, but also the virtue of acting, working hard to make a living, contributing to the prosperity of society. The moral person she was one day was always accompanied by another moral person she could have been; the concern that was at the forefront one day went into the background the next, in a constant attempt to reconcile being a good mother and being a good Muslim. These concerns sometimes seemed to overlap and sometimes seemed to drag her in separate directions; sometimes they made their appearance even when she seemed to ignore them, not only in the ways in which she chose to act and her explicit moral reflections, but also in the subtle shifts of emotion which accompanied the acts and the reflections. These emotions included the anger and frustration which seemed to accompany the point she repeatedly made about her gratitude for the fact that her son had left a place characterized by amoral and shady affairs, and what may perhaps best be described as the defiance which marked her efforts to nonetheless secure her son a job at this morally dubious place, a determination to act and find a way out of the misery that characterized the family's life.

Conclusion: Haunting and the Moral Nerve of the Everyday

The Naqshbandiyya's teaching rarely brings any definite answers to the Sufis I have come to know in Uzbekistan and their questions about how to lead their lives, but is, rather, a source of shifting and sometimes paradoxical moral reflections. But perhaps in this – fundamentally impossible – striving for the realization of the transcendent ideals of Sufism there was a moral drive which, in spite of all the frustrations, made the engagement in Sufism so meaningful: a conatus or will to be moral, which thrives by never really succeeding.

Some of this may be more or less specific to Sufism which – although one should be careful not to create a caricature of a historically very complex tradition – has always had a tendency to scepticism towards stiffened social and moral norms and pointed at the limits of intentional action, emphasizing that (moral) inspiration which may come out of the blue – in visions or inspirational dreams, for example – and change a person's life in a second, reminding one of the unpredictability of divine interventions and the contingency of life itself (cf. Mittermaier 2012) and the weight it has given to the paradoxical, providing epistemologies of uncertainty which, rather than bringing meaning and certainty to its practitioners, tend to shake the ground beneath their feet and reverse standard orientations.

But the example may also point at something more general: the more we seek 'closure' by ranking some concerns as more important than others, the more those concerns which are discarded tend to haunt us. This haunting makes the moral persons we could have become, but did not become, follow us like shadows in the stories we like to tell about ourselves and in the emotional depths of our being and gives everyday existence a moral 'nerve'. It makes the moral a seething presence in everyday life, continuously reminding us that the (moral) foundations on which a life is based may be shaky, and that every intersubjective encounter – whether it is a face-to-face encounter with another human being (say, one's son lying passively on the sofa or one's sister asking one to help on the occasion of her wedding) or, say, an encounter in what may be a visionary dream – may be a moral 'engine' in the sense of having the potential to redirect one's care and concern in directions which do not necessarily follow a larger masterplan.

Maria Louw is Associate Professor at the Department of Anthropology, Aarhus University. She is the author of *Everyday Islam in Post-Soviet Central Asia* (Routledge 2007) and a number of other publications focusing on religion, secularism, atheism and morality in Central Asia.

Notes

1. All names cited in this chapter are pseudonyms.
2. The chapter is based on thirteen months of fieldwork conducted in Bukhara, Uzbekistan in 1998–1999 and 2000, and two weeks of fieldwork conducted in 2011.
3. Religion was seen in Marxist terms as a form of false consciousness which inhibited people from acting on the real material world and realizing their true humanity; the Soviet period saw the dismantling of religious institutions and the placing of those which remained under strict control. The struggle against religion took many forms, ranging from the outright destruction of religious institutions and the liquidation or arrest of religious authorities to anti-religious propaganda and the more subtle mimicking of

'religious' forms in the creation of 'secular' rituals that acted as substitutes for religious ones (cf. Anderson 1994; Binns 1979; Ramet 1987).

4. On the history of the Naqshbandiyya Sufi *tariqa* in Central Asia, see Algar 1990a and 1990b.

5. In Uzbekistan, more particularly, Sufism and in particular the Naqshbandi tradition has been coopted by the post-Soviet government as a kind of Islam which is the bearer of the nation's humanist traditions and, moreover, is compatible with a modern, secular state and a counterweight to political Islam (Louw 2007; Paul 2002; Rasanayagam 2011; Peshkova 2014; Schubel 1999). This is quite ironic as Naqshbandiyya through history has been distinguished by its strong involvement in worldly affairs – including political affairs (Algar 1990b; Zarcone 1996: 64; Zelkina 2000: 81).

6. In Central Asia, more often than not, there has been a close relationship between the Naqshbandiyya and the ruling classes (Algar 1990a: 16; Algar 1990b: 126–27; Levin 1996: 106; Rashid 2002; Schubel 1999; Zelkina 2000: 81–3). However, the Naqshbandiyya has also provided organization and leadership for many conflicts, including jihad against Russian colonists in North Caucus in 1830–1859, against Russians and Soviets in parts of Turkestan in the nineteenth and twentieth centuries as well as rebellions against Chinese rule in Xinjiang (Bennigsen and Wimbush 1985: 3; Manz 1987; Olcott 1995: 35; Voll 1994: 65; Zarcone 1996; Zelkina 2000).

7. As reflected, for example, in the often quoted saying of Abu'l-Hasan Bushandi (d. 960): 'Sufism today is a name without reality, whereas once it was a reality without a name'.

8. I am grateful to Joel Robbins for bringing Phillips' book to my attention.

9. This story is a modified version of a case I previously addressed in Louw 2007.

References

Ahmed, S. 2004. *The Cultural Politics of Emotion*. Edinburgh: Edinburgh University Press.

Algar, Hamid. 1990a. 'A Brief History of the Naqshbandi Order', in M. Gaborieau, A. Popovic and T. Zarcone (eds), *Naqshbandis: cheminements et situation actuelle d'un ordre mystique musulman*. Istanbul/Paris: ISIS.

_____. 1990b. 'Political Aspects of Naqshbandi History', in M. Gaborieau, A. Popovic and T. Zarcone (eds), *Naqshbandis: cheminements et situation actuelle d'un ordre mystique musulman*. Istanbul/Paris: ISIS.

Anderson, John. 1994. *Religion, State and Politics in the Soviet Union and Successor States*. Cambridge: Cambridge University Press.

Aretxaga, Begoña. 2005. *States of Terror: Begoña Aretxaga's Essays*, ed. Joseba Zulaika. Reno: Center for Basque Studies.

Beatty, A. 2010. 'How Did It Feel for You? Emotion, Narrative, and the Limits of Ethnography', *American Anthropologist* 112(3): 430–43.

_____. 2015. Anthropology and Emotion, *Journal of the Royal Anthropological Institute (N.S.)* 20: 545–63.

Bennigsen, A. and S.E. Wimbush. 1985. *Mystics and Commissars: Sufism in the Soviet Union*. London: Hurst and Company.

Binns, Christopher A.P. 1979. 'The Changing Face of Power: Revolution and Accommodation in the Development of the Soviet Ceremonial System: Part I', *Man* 14: 585–606.

Borbieva, Noor O'Neill. 2012. 'Empowering Muslim Women: Independent Religious Fellowships in the Kyrgyz Republic', *Slavic Review* 71: 2.

Brennan, Theresa. 2004. *The Transmission of Affect*. Ithaca: Cornell University Press.

Carsten, Janet (ed.). 2007. *Ghosts of Memory: Essays on Remembrance and Relatedness.* Oxford: Blackwell.

Deeb, Lara and Mona Harb. 2013. *Leisurely Islam: Negotiating Geography and Morality in Shi'ite South Beirut.* Princeton: Princeton University Press.

Derrida, Jacques. 2004. *Specters of Marx: The State of Debt, the Work of Mourning, and the New International.* New York and London: Routledge.

Frederiksen, Martin D. 2014. *Young Men, Time, and Boredom in the Republic of Georgia.* Philadelphia: Temple University Press.

Gordon, Avery F. 2008. *Ghostly Matters: Haunting and the Sociological Imagination.* Minneapolis and London: University of Minnesota Press.

Hirschkind, Charles. 2006. *The Ethical Soundscape: Cassette Sermons and Islamic Counter-Publics in Egypt.* New York: Columbia University Press.

Kwon, Heonik. 2006. *After the Massacre: Commemoration and Consolation in Ha My and My Lai.* Berkeley: University of California Press.

Laidlaw, James. 2014. *The Subject of Virtue: An Anthropology of Ethics and Freedom.* Cambridge: Cambridge University Press.

Levin, T. 1996. *The Hundred Thousand Fools of God: Musical Travels in Central Asia.* Bloomington and Indianapolis: Indiana University Press.

Louw, Maria. 2007. *Everyday Islam in Post-Soviet Central Asia.* London and New York: Routledge.

——. 2010. 'Dreaming up Futures: Dream Omens and Magic in Bishkek', *History and Anthropology* 21(3): 277–92.

——. 2013. 'Even Honey May Become Bitter When There is Too Much of It: Islam as Threat and Source of Well-Being in Post- Soviet Kyrgyzstan', *Central Asian Survey* 32(4): 514–26.

——. 2015. 'The Art of Dealing with Things You Do Not Believe In: Dream Omens and Their Meanings in Post-Soviet Kyrgyzstan', in Vibeke Steffen, Kirsten Marie Raahauge and Steffen Jøhncke (eds), *On the Limits of Reason – New Perspectives in Anthropological Studies of Magic, Social Technology, and Uncertainty.* Chicago: University of Chicago Press.

Manz, B.F. 1987. 'Central Asian Uprisings in the Nineteenth Century': Ferghana under the Russians', *The Russian Review* 46: 267–81.

Marsden, Magnus. 2005. *Living Islam: Muslim Religious Experience in Pakistan's North-West Frontier.* Cambridge: Cambridge University Press.

Martin, E. 2013. 'The Potentiality of Ethnography and the Limits of Affect Theory', *Current Anthropology* 54(S7): 149–58.

Mattingly, Cheryl. 2012. 'Two Virtue Ethics and the Anthropology of Morality', *Anthropological Theory* 12(2) 161–84.

——. 2013. 'Moral Selves and Moral Scenes: Narrative Experiments in Everyday Life', *Ethnos* 78(3): 301–27.

——. 2014. *Moral Laboratories – Family Peril and the Struggle for a Good Life.* Oakland, CA: University of California Press.

Mahmood, Saba. 2005. *Politics of Piety: The Islamic Revival and the Feminist Subject.* Princeton and Oxford: Princeton University Press.

Mittermaier, Amira. 2012. 'Dreams from Elsewhere: Muslim Subjectivities Beyond the Trope of Self-cultivation', *Journal of the Royal Anthropological Institute* 18: 247–65.

Navaro-Yashin, Yael. 2012. *The Make-Believe Space: Affective Geography in a Postwar Polity.* Durham and London: Duke University Press.

Nussbaum, Martha. (2001 (1986). *The Fragility of Goodness: Luck and Ethics in Greek Tragedy and Philosophy*, revised edition. Cambridge: Cambridge University Press.

_____. 2001. *Upheavals of Thought: The Intelligence of Emotions*. Cambridge: Cambridge University Press.

Olcott, M.B. 1995. 'Islam and Fundamentalism in Independent Central Asia', in Y. Ro'I (ed.), *Muslim Eurasia: Conflicting Legacies*. London: Frank Cass: 21–40.

Paul, Jürgen. 2002. 'Contemporary Uzbek Hagiography and its Sources', *Hallsche Beiträge zur Orientwissenschaft* 32: 631–38.

Peshkova, Svetlana. 2014. *Women, Islam, and Identity: Public Life in Private Spaces in Uzbekistan*. Syracuse, NY: Syracuse University Press.

Phillips, Adam. 2012. *Missing Out: In Praise of the Unlived Life*. London: Penguin Books.

Ramet, Pedro. 1987. *Cross and Commissar: The Politics of Religion in Eastern Europe and the USSR*. Bloomington: Indiana University Press.

Rasanayagam, Johan. 2011. *Islam in Post-Soviet Uzbekistan: The Morality of Experience*. Cambridge: Cambridge University Press.

Rashid, Ahmed. 2002. *Jihad: The Rise of Militant Islam in Central Asia*. New Haven and London: Yale University Press.

Schielke, Samuli. 2009. 'Ambivalent Commitments: Troubles of Morality, Religiosity and Aspiration among Young Egyptians', *Journal of Religion in Africa* 39: 158–85.

Schimmel, A. 1975. *Mystical Dimensions of Islam*. Chapel Hill: The University of North Carolina Press.

Schubel, V. 1999. 'Post-Soviet Hagiography and the Reconstruction of the Naqshbandi Tradition in Contemporary Uzbekistan', in E. Özdalga (ed.), *Naqshbandis in Western and Central Asia: Change and Continuity*. Istanbul: Swedish Research Centre in Istanbul.

Svasek, Maruska. 2005. 'Introduction: Emotions in Anthropology', in Kay Milton and Maruska Svasek (eds), *Mixed Emotions, Anthropological Studies of Feeling*. Oxford: Berg: pp. 1–23.

Thrift, Nigel. 2004. 'Intensities of Feeling: Towards a Spatial Politics of Affect', *Geografiska Annaler* 86 B (1): 57–78.

Throop, Jason. 2010. *Suffering and Sentiment: Exploring the Vicissitudes of Experience and Pain in Yap*. Berkeley: University of California Press.

_____. 2012. 'Moral Sentiments', in Didier Fassin (ed.), *A Companion to Moral Anthropology*. Oxford: Wiley-Blackwell, pp. 150–68.

_____. 2014. 'Moral Moods', *Ethos* 42(1): 65–83.

Voll, J.O. 1994. 'Central Asia as Part of the Modern Islamic World', in B.F. Manz (ed.), *Central Asia in Historical Perspective*. Boulder, CO: Westview Press, pp. 62–81.

Werner, C.A. 1999. 'The Dynamics of Feasting and Gift Exchange in Rural Kazakstan', in I. Svanberg (ed.), *Contemporary Kazaks: Cultural and Social Perspectives*. New York: St Martin's Press, pp. 47–72.

Zarcone, Thierry. 1996. 'Sufi Movements: Search for Identity and Islamic Resurgence', in K. Warikoo (ed.), *Central Asia*. New Delhi: Har-anand Publications, pp. 63–79.

Zelkina, Anna. 2000. *In Quest for God and Freedom: The Sufi Response to the Russian Advance in the North Caucasus*. London: Hurst and Company.

Zigon, Jarrett and Jason Throop. 2014. 'Moral Experience: Introduction', *Ethos* 42(1): 1–15.

5

Every Day
Forgiving after War in Northern Uganda

Lotte Meinert

Introduction

The profoundness of every single day actions and words as moral engines of forgiveness and promise is remarkable after the war in northern Uganda. I have split the word everyday into the two parts 'every' and 'day', to emphasize the moral significance and possibility of single routine actions.[1] This is not the idea of morality as unreflective and embedded in the habitual in a Maussian sense. What I want is to highlight the importance of the ordinary, as others have done (Lambek 2010; Mattingly 2014), and give attention to every day actions and words rather than the extraordinary reconciliation rituals and trials that often draw the focus of the media in post-conflict situations in Africa. Trials and rituals are important parts of public and collective moral work after conflicts, but my focus in this chapter is on the renewed moral sense of every day actions that may normally, or under other circumstances, seem banal and ordinary, such as grinding your sesame seeds on your neighbours' grinding stone, cooking and sharing food with all family members, letting a friend look after your child, taking turns when fetching water, and having a casual conversation. These ordinary actions come to carry enormous moral weight in situations where 'wrongs' and forgiveness are being questioned. They become windows, so to speak, through which people continuously monitor how social processes are going.

A War of Social Torture

The 'wrongs' committed during the war in northern Uganda may be regarded as a form of moral breakdown (Zigon 2007) because many of the atrocities were carried out within intimate relationships where family members, and others who could usually trust each other, were forced to kill or harm each other. Yet, in the context of a twenty-year long war that constantly shakes people's moral standards through ongoing forms of what Chris Dolan has described as 'social torture', sustained by the government army and the donors who provided humanitarian aid (2009), practices, reflections and responses are so prolonged that they may extend beyond any definition of momentary breakdown. What I am particularly interested in here are local considerations and practices of responding to 'wrongs', and what a situation of apparently constant breakdown and repair may teach us about the moral domain – what is it to be picking up pieces of sociality that have fallen apart, when everyday relationships – such as parent-child relations, commonly taken for granted as good and caring in nature – fall apart, and what might be considered part of what Heidegger described as being-in-the-world (1996 [1953]). These relationships become present-at-hand when they fall apart, as Heidegger's famous hammer example taught us. When family members hurt, betray and sometimes even kill each other, the nature of family relations emerges as something problematic to reflect upon, and afterwards appears as something to practice more consciously and carefully in order to respond to and repair the breakdown. This is a continuous process that creates a heightened awareness of the fragility of social relations and there is very little, if any, sense of 'taken for granted morality'. It may not even make sense to think of morality as something that can be taken for granted in the first place. As Joel Robbins points out, referring to Fabion (2001): 'The ethical is a field of values, that actors are less obliged than encouraged to realize. Actors must feel the directive force of values, must recognize themselves as encouraged by them to be moral. The ethical field cannot be one governed by unconscious cultural compulsion' (2004: 315). And neither, obviously, is morality a phenomenon which is simply open to choice, as underlined by James Laidlaw (2002: 323). The dynamics of moral breakdown and repair in northern Uganda happen in the realm of the ordinary, yet this does not imply a descent into an ordinary unconscious state. What is going on appears more akin to a kind of societal-wide moral breakdown and repair awareness, as we see in Jonathan Lear's description of the Crow society (2006). This involves a renewed awareness of the morality of every single action; something gets strengthened in this process, and with it emerges a sense of the possibility of a new beginning.

Beginnings in the Aftermath

After peace was settled in northern Uganda in 2008 people began returning to their original homes from Internally Displaced Persons (IDP) camps. For more than twenty years the Ugandan military (UNDP) and the Lord's Resistance Army (LRA), the rebel group led by Joseph Kony, had locked the population in a brutal armed conflict that saw tens of thousands of people killed, around 2 million people displaced, and thousands abducted to join the rebel army. During the war both the rebels and the government forces committed atrocities against the population, which included making people commit crimes against each other (Finnström 2008; Dolan 2009). Those who were abducted were often forced to denounce, harm or even kill members of their families and communities, to prevent the abducted from escaping back home (Dolan 2009). This distorting of the line between victims and perpetrators obviously made homecoming complex. Many abductees escaped from the rebels during the war, sometimes because they had heard messages on the radio that they would be welcomed back home no matter what they had done to their families, no matter what the rebel leaders told them, and that they would be forgiven for the crimes they had been forced to commit. Yet returning home still presented not only political problems, but complicated social and personal challenges as well (Verma 2012). Relations between family members, neighbours and friends were made tense by feelings of mistrust and betrayal, and often people felt that they lived together as 'intimate enemies' (Baines 2010). Experiences of betrayal at interpersonal and political levels strongly marked the social atmosphere as one of 'tricky trust'; people emphasized that 'you could never know what is in another person's heart' (Meinert 2014).

During and after the war an abundance of NGOs, traditional and religious institutions got involved in reconciliation work, including the facilitation of traditional cleansing ceremonies, reconciliation rituals and reparation workshops (Akuni 2011; Finnegan 2010). Cleansing rituals for those who had committed crimes or been in contact with the dead and were affected by vengeful spirits of *cen* included the ceremony of stepping on eggs, *nyono tonggweno* and *ryemo cen* cleansing an area of evil spirits (Finnegan 2010; Harlacher et al. 2006) and the more elaborate *mat oput* ritual of 'drinking the bitter root', which involves material compensation. Some of these rituals were funded by international donors, such as the USAID (United States Agency for International Development)-funded Northern Uganda Transition Initiative which organized cleansing rituals before people moved back into their rural homes and started farming the land so that they would not be affected if they came upon the remains of unburied dead. Most initiatives aimed at collective and political levels and many promoted Christian and/or 'traditional Acholi' ethics of forgiveness as the 'good' and right way to overcome problems. Critical voices have pointed out how these endeavours tend to reify Acholi tradition (Allen 2006), with a 'turn to culture' (Branch 2011) as a way of fixing disorder, which takes the focus away from the problem as a national and international one. There have been debates among involved parties, as well as researchers, about what forms of retributive and restorative justice were appropriate in the aftermath of war: 'trial justice' through the International Criminal Court (ICC) and national courts or 'traditional justice' such as reconciliation rituals (Allen 2006; Finnegan 2010). When Dominique Ongwen, the second-in-command in the LRA, gave himself up in the Central African Republic in the beginning of 2015 and was taken to the ICC, the debate about justice was evoked again: should he be cleansed ritually and face 'traditional justice' and /or face 'trial justice' and be taken to national or international court? The justice question is an important political debate that also has ramifications for how people reflect upon wrongs they experience in their lives. Yet when listening to men and women's accounts of forgiveness it was striking that no one talked about forgiving the LRA rebels or the government army soldiers (UNDP). The emphasis in their accounts was on the personal and interpersonal processes of dealing with 'wrongs' and social 'invisible wounds' in everyday life (Whyte et al. 2015).

The Forgiveness Project

The accounts described here were part of a study of forgiveness in Acholi carried out as a collaboration between researchers at Gulu University in Uganda and Danish universities.[2] In this study we experimented with a combination of artistic and anthropological approaches to understand processes of forgiveness. Tove Nyholm, a Danish installation artist, came to work with researchers in Gulu district to collect oral accounts of forgiveness, and construct a sound installation where others could come and listen 'to voices from within', and record their own account if they wished to. The Danish artist had previously collected accounts and made installations on the themes of forgiveness and the sense of judgement in Denmark and in doing this she had been inspired by Hannah Arendt's writings. The intention of Nyholm's projects was to encourage reflection on forgiveness. The experiment was whether this would generate positive effects among those who heard it and whether they would be interested in forgiving others or asking for forgiveness. This moral potential in the project resonated well with Christian messages of forgiveness that are common in Acholi where the Roman Catholic and Anglican churches have been prominent for more than a century. The project also fit well with many of the ongoing political initiatives to promote reconciliation after the war. Yet when exploring the accounts further, we came to see how they were also about something more: they were windows onto the untangling of everyday wrongs in the shadow of much larger atrocities (Whyte et al. 2015).

Some of the 'wrongs' people experienced, and chose to talk about, were directly related to the war. Yet, most of the accounts included 'wrongs' that were not directly related to the war, but simply happened during the years of war as part of everyday camp life. What the lay people, who gave their accounts, regarded as most 'conciliatory' in the aftermath of war was the re-establishment of normal social relations – to be able to live as a family, visit friends and enjoy civility with their neighbours, which in this situation represent real hard-won accomplishments. The accounts we collected reflected the urge to mend these everyday relationships, sometimes by reflecting upon past experience, but more often by 'starting anew'. Acholi use the expression of 'keeping something in your heart', or 'holding someone in your heart' as a negative nagging feeling, as a cramped muscle, and they describe the relief of 'letting it go' and forgetting certain past experiences to give room for the flow of social life in the present and the future. The fact that people wanted to move on in everyday life, by what they describe as 'untying the knots' of interpersonal wrongs, did not automatically imply that they disregarded 'trial justice' as appropriate for other scales of war crimes, even though many had little trust in these systems of justice.

Our research group found people who were willing to share accounts of personal experience of forgiveness. The study and its purpose were explained to each of them and we sought their consent to share their accounts with others. Initially ten accounts, in Acholi or English, were recorded and each lasted between fifteen minutes and one hour. These accounts were carefully edited into clips of three to six minutes, capturing details of the situation, the wrong committed, the decision to forgive, the process and the impact of the act of forgiveness (Meinert et al. 2014). In one of the huts in the former camp for Internally Displaced People in Awach trading centre, the artist installed a sound system in a drum so that people could sit together, choose accounts to listen to, and afterwards discuss them. In a nearby hut those who were inspired to record their own account could do so with one of our research assistants. Three radio programmes in local FM stations broadcasted some of the accounts and invited leaders and others to discuss them on air. A mobile outreach unit took the sound system to eight different villages in Awach sub-county, where people were given a chance to listen to the accounts, record their own if they wanted to, and discuss ideas of forgiveness and 'letting go' as a tool for the attainment of peace. More than seven hundred people came to listen to the accounts and forty-eight people recorded their own accounts with the team. Apart from the artistic action project, we did a thematic analysis of thirty-five of the transcribed accounts and we carried out interviews with key informants about peace building and forgiveness. They included non-governmental organization representatives, local and religious leaders. Two focus group discussions were held with groups of elders in Awach sub-county and in Gulu town. These interviews and discussions focused on notions of forgiveness and reconciliation in northern Uganda. For the purpose of this chapter I focus on a few of the accounts.

Acan Sara

One of the accounts is from a young woman who we call Acan Sara, who was twenty-four years old when we talked to her in 2010. Below is an edited version of her long description and reflections.

I am a person who passed through the problem of abduction by the LRA. By the time I was taken, I was a girl of 12 years. ... I was forced to do things, which I did not want to do, like killing, which was not my wish, but because I was told to do it, I did. I was forced to have sex. Yet I did not have interest. Looting peoples' harvest I also didn't want to do, but I did. If you refused to do what they told you, they would beat you, or ask you to choose between death and doing what you were told to do. I was eating things, which I should not eat, like branches of trees, but I did, because I wanted to survive ... You drink any water which is not good for human beings, sometimes you even drink urine of your colleague, because you know you may not get water, so you drink anything.

My return [to the community] was not easy. I escaped during the exchange of fire between the LRA and the Government. I managed to escape and I footed up to home. When I returned home I found my father no more, only my mother with a baby that she got when I wasn't there. When I reached home, she welcomed me, because she knew it wasn't my wish to go to the bush. She knew it happened the way I did not want, she welcomed me, and I stayed with her very well.

I only got problems from neighbors and children of my age pointing fingers. They looked at me as if it was my wish to go to join the rebels, and also some neighbors, whose children were abducted and went to the bush, but died during the war, they looked at me as if I was the one who killed their children.

At the borehole people did not want me to pump water first, even when I came there first. They would say I am a rebel and wherever I moved, people would point at me saying I had *cen* – bad spirits – and that if anyone associated with me I could kill or burn their houses or harm them.

If any boy came to talk to me about love they would tell the boy that this lady has bad evil because she was abducted by the rebels and she has been killing people. If you fall in love with her, she can get up anytime at night and strangle you.

I have passed through many problems, which cannot make me have peace even if at home. ... I tried to go back to school ..., but life in school was not easy, because I could not ask for anything from other students, because they look at me as if I have evil spirits.

People I was with in the bush (former rebels) are here now. I have already forgiven them because I know it was not their intension to do those things. Like one lady with whom I shared a man. She was older and the one in-charge of distributing things. When I was hungry, I could not eat unless she gave me, but sometimes she would only look at me [and not give me], even if there was something to eat. I did everything for her, I washed her clothes, I was like her house girl, but we were sharing a man.

She was mistreating me, but now we are staying together, as I talk now, we work together.... I have forgiven her, because she was also mistreated there. So after we shared ideas among ourselves, as we talk now, we are okay, we share a lot, our children also love each other. Since their father is no longer there, we have to bring them up.

Who, What, Why Forgive?

There are several issues to consider in Acan's account and reflections, but let me highlight a few of those that are also significant in other accounts for our discussion of moral engines. These issues have to do with who and what is forgiven, and why.

Acan in this account forgives her co-wife. Even though the wrongs committed by the co-wife (denying food) may not compare to the exploitation by the commanders who forced her to kill, have sex and loot villages, it is still the co-wife she ends up talking about and whom she forgives. It is possible that Acan considered the abuses by the commanders beyond forgiveness, beyond the moral domain. Or perhaps it was still too dangerous to forgive those more serious crimes, because to forgive someone also involves making an accusation and taking the moral high ground, which can be a critical and thus vulnerable position. At the time when Acan gave her account (2010), many of the LRA commanders were still in the bush and there was ambiguity around the legal amnesty processes for those who had held higher ranks. Yet, what seems even more prominent in Acan's account, as well as in other accounts, is that the person who is experienced as relevant for forgiveness is always an intimate other, a person she lives with every day and a person she has a future with. The co-wife and Acan have children with the same man, the man has died, but as Acan said: we need to bring up the children.

In this sense – from Acan's perspective – forgiveness emerges as pertinent when it regards a person she interacts with every day. Perhaps forgiveness, in the sense of 'untying the knots', is most likely to take place in everyday interaction and words.[3]Acan does not interact with the commanders; they are not relevant in her present and future life and thus are unavailable for her forgiving actions or words.

Hannah Arendt saw forgiveness as a necessary element in social life, where people constantly transgress against one another. She writes: 'Trespassing is an everyday occurrence which … needs forgiving, dismissing, in order to make it possible for life to go on by constantly releasing men from what they have done unknowingly' (Arendt 1958: 240). I will get back to the discussion of the 'unknowingly' aspect, but for now I want to emphasize how Arendt distinguishes radical evil, which can neither be forgiven nor punished, from the common wrongdoings that are not even necessarily intentional. For her, forgiving is an eminently human and social disposition arising 'directly out of the will to live together with others in the mode of acting and speaking' (ibid.: 246).

People forgive because of a determination to go on living with the person who offended them: 'Forgiving and the relationship it establishes is always an eminently personal … affair in which *what* was done is forgiven for the sake of *who* did it' (ibid.: 241), writes Arendt.

In the accounts we collected it was significant that most of those who were forgiven were kin: blood relatives or in-laws (such as a father, mother, brother, co-wife, step-mother, son, brother's wife) or close relations (such as a friend, a room-mate or neighbour). In all of the accounts, the 'forgiver' (victim) and the wrongdoer had a personal relationship. Yet, these were never simple relationships between two single persons. Because the wrongdoer was nearly always someone in an existing relationship with the forgiver, other persons and family members were involved as well. The relations were never exclusively dyadic. In Acan's account there is the co-wife and the children to consider. The issue is not simply about two people's hurt feelings, but about a family and generations who need to live together; life has to go on.

What was forgiven – the wrongs people considered forgivable – were remarkably often some kind of betrayal or mis-recognition in intimate relationships. Sometimes there was a direct link to the war, but often the 'wrongs' comprised conflicts and discrimination that occurred before the war, or elsewhere in Uganda, for example a stepmother's neglect, a father's failure to pay school fees, physical assaults, jealousy between co-wives, money issues. What were forgiven were common problems that are endemic to social life with its kinship organization and competition over resources. Even though such conflicts seemed almost inevitable, there was a strong moral sense that solidarity, family unity and civility should prevail – also during times of war and displacement, despite the bad conditions people lived under. A prominent theme in the accounts was that of betrayal by kin or neighbours upon whom one should be able to depend. Greed, selfishness, neglect and envy that hurt others were not only seen as offences against individual persons, but also as failures of social values. It was not always easy to distinguish the offences connected to the war from the betrayals by kin and neighbours, for example when Amal Jane was identified to the LRA by a neighbour and the LRA beat her senseless, trying to extort information from her about the whereabouts of her father-in-law (her account is described later in the chapter). Another example was Santa who was convinced that she would not have been abducted by the LRA had her father supported her with school fees to go to school as he should have. In these cases the offences committed by the LRA were linked to what was considered to be failures on the part of family and neighbours. Even in cases where the wrong was committed by a member of the LRA, the offence became an issue when the victim and the offender had to resume a personal relationship during or after the war.

The wrongs which stood out from the many wrongs as relevant for forgiveness were cases when someone had expectations of the person who committed the wrong: when they 'thought they were together', would protect each other, and – somewhat different from what Arendt writes – also when they did something bad 'knowingly', such as when Acan's co-wife had food, but did not give Acan any, even though the co-wife knew she was starving; she only looked at Acan, acknowledging that she knew that she had made her suffer. Whether a person had violated others consciously or unconsciously was considered important for the relevance of forgiving. When George met his tormentor two years after he escaped from the rebel army, he first got upset and angry, but with time he realized that his bitterness was useless. 'I started to see ... maybe he didn't know what he was doing ... Me, what I saw, you know ... Kony was abducting people when they were still young'. Being with the rebels in the bush (*lum*), in the tall grass and in the dark where you cannot really see, was sometimes considered a mitigating factor and a reason for forgiveness. If someone had committed wrongs he or she did not know about at the time – or did not come to realize later, or was not willing to realize – this could also make forgiving either irrelevant or more complicated.

Otti Peter debates the issue of knowing in his account about his abductor. Peter was abducted when he was about seventeen years and spent around six months with the rebels. When he was wounded he was able to negotiate a release. Years later Peter was confronted with his abductor in a boarding school, where they were supposed to share a room. This man did not want to admit the wrongs he did, but wanted to continue staying together, as if nothing bad had really happened. Peter tried to inspire his abductor by telling him about his own process of forgiving himself for what he had done, by explaining how it was done in a state of 'bush' *lum* mentality, darkness, because they did not really know what they were doing. They just kept going 'unknowingly'. Peter's abductor did not want to stop and reflect and realize what he had been doing and Peter reckoned that this was because the abductor was possibly still involved in some kind of economic rebel activity.

For wrongs to be forgivable they had to be considered by the actors to be within the domain of the moral – immoral rather than amoral – and the wrongs had to be considered immoral by the person who committed them, at least at some point. Actions may have been happening in a state of amorality, what Peter described as 'in the bush' and 'in darkness', but later he realized that those actions were immoral – part of what human beings know we should not do to each other. Marilyn Strathern notes that in Papua New Guinea (1997: 142) when actions are undertaken unconsciously, such as when a person is driven to act by sorcery or having their minds twisted by magic, those actions are generally taken out of the moral domain and regarded as amoral rather than immoral. Peter tries to define 'what happened in the bush' as amoral rather than immoral. And many Acholi wonder about how the spirits of Joseph Kony were involved in twisting so many minds. When people are drawing lines around what happened in 'the bush' as amoral, we can see this as evoking the idea of bush as nature and wild, and the village as cultural and civilized, so well known in structural analyses of African cosmology. Yet, rather than definitive and structural, I see the act of drawing a line as a form of moral experimental work: for Peter talking to his abductor, it is a highly risky and uncertain endeavour to suggest that they were both very wrong 'in the bush', because he does not know how the man will react, and which side he is on now. Peter tries it out in the subjunctive mode: if we say that when we were in the bush we did horrible things, which we did not even realize – maybe some kind of evil spirit was involved – can we agree that at that time we did not know what we were doing, but by realizing now that it was wrong, we can be together, forgive each other? The abductor did not respond fully as Peter would have hoped by realizing that he had done wrong because he was in the bush, but now he was out of the bush. Peter took this as a sign that the man wanted to continue in an under-cover 'bush-mode', so Peter carefully backed off, but they promised each other to 'let go' of those memories of what they had done.

Jacques Derrida (2003) claims in his book on cosmopolitanism and forgiveness that that true forgiveness consists in forgiving the unforgivable. If forgiveness only forgave the forgivable, forgiveness would disappear, he argues. While the argument makes logical sense, and is an elegant historical analysis of the genealogy of concepts, the logic does not seem to hold entirely in relation to the experiences described in accounts in northern Uganda. What is true forgiveness? Does it make sense to measure this? And by logic? By experience? Derrida points to a tension in the concept between unconditioned, gracious, uneconomic forgiveness granted to the guilty as guilty, and conditioned forgiveness that is proportionate to recognition of fault and to repentance. This tension is always negotiated when forgiveness is in question, according to Derrida. This is a tension and negotiation recognizable in reconciliation rituals in northern Uganda. Some rituals, like the ceremony of stepping on eggs, *nyono tonggweno*, is unconditioned and uneconomic, while the *mat oput* ritual of 'drinking the bitter root' is highly conditioned upon recognition of fault and involves substantial material compensation. The character of the wrong committed is important for negotiating which ritual is needed and the decision is to some extent a political one, to be considered among elders. Yet when we turn away from the rituals to the accounts of interpersonal forgiveness, what was forgiven was not considered unforgivable. In fact, people often searched for reasons and conditions why the wrongs were forgivable and the actions were intelligible.

Now we will move on to the questions about why people take the trouble to forgive and how they do it. Clearly not all people forgive others for causing wrongs and we should keep in mind that the accounts I write about here are from a self-selected group of people who chose to forgive, and also decided to be explicit about it. In most accounts, the person forgiving mentions various kinds of 'mitigating circumstances' on the transgressor's side, as an important reason why they can forgive. Acan explains that others also mistreated her co-wife in the bush, and the co-wife did not 'want it to stop with her – she had to pay'. For Acan, the mitigating circumstance was the fact that the co-wife was being punished herself by others and wanted to pass this on, and this was a kind of logic Acan could grasp afterwards. In this way people could forgive when they were able to somehow explain and understand the actions and motivations of the other. Being able to understand the logic or dynamic behind certain actions was important, perhaps because one had been in a similar situation oneself. When Acan said 'I can understand her actions', there was probably also an implicit pledge and hope that others could and would understand and forgive Acan's actions.

Peter went to the extent of explaining some of the ambivalent pleasures of violence and abduction, which he had experienced himself, as a reason why he could forgive his abductor. He understood the attraction to 'bush life' himself and knew that it was also something you could leave and give up. In his account Peter also emphasized the pragmatics of staying together as a reason why it was possible and necessary to forgive:

> He [the abductor] had to understand, 'cause we were in the same room. We could take breakfast together, go to school together. [So] we promised each other. To let go of those memories. Whether bad or good. Because in the bush you were enjoying life, you looted things, you enjoyed, beating up people who tried to escape from the group. You enjoyed.

Peter explained how he dealt with the wrongs he himself had done:

> Of cause for me, I had already, even from my, from the bottom of my heart [let go]. I had even forgiven my own self, doing something wrong to some other person. Of cause you have to first forgive your self. You have done something. If you don't meditate it fully, you may not think you have done something wrong. I had to meditate it from within myself: I forgive my own self. Then I started also forgiving others.

The most prominent reason people mentioned for why they forgave was pragmatic – in a deep sense – like Peter's. He had to share a room with this man and wanted to do this in a way where he could feel safe and not terrified.

Listen to the words of Amal Jane, who was identified to the LRA by a neighbour; the LRA beat her senseless, to get information from her about her father-in-law. After about ten years of silence, living next to the neighbour in the camp, she said:

> I was annoyed with that man for a very long time. We stayed in the camp for almost ten years and we did not talk to each other. … Now we started talking, because we are in a group together, he also comes there. I found it really bad not to greet him, since they come in our place, and we also go to their place.
>
> …
>
> If you don't let go, you yourself will also feel difficulties in life, if you are staying in the same place with somebody having a bad relationship. That kind of living is not good. Even you yourself you'll feel bad. If you face wrongdoing by others, you should reduce your annoyance right from the heart.
>
> Someone can kill your dear ones – and you still talk to them.
> Water can also kill – and you still use water.
> Fire can also burn your child – and you use fire.
> What about human beings like you? You should talk to them, and forgive them.

There is a kind of practical moral wisdom in Jane's words, and a coming to terms with the fact that bad and evil cannot be rejected; it is all part of life: Even when people are evil they still need each other, if they hope to have a future. There is a strong sense in the accounts that people forgive because they long to begin again.

For Arendt, new beginnings are made possible through forgiveness because the constant mutual release makes human beings free to start over. Forgiveness is what Arendt describes as the epitome of natality, because forgiveness is an action that makes something new possible, creating new promises (1958: 237), rather than re-actions, such as revenge, which tend to produce more re-actions.

In Arendt's words, 'the possible redemption from the predicament of irreversibility – of being unable to undo what one has done though one did not, and could not, have known what he was doing – is the faculty of forgiving'. Arendt goes on to describe how the remedy for unpredictability, for the chaotic uncertainty of the future, is contained in the faculty to make and keep promises.

> The two faculties belong together insofar as one of them, forgiving, serves to undo the deeds of the past, ... and the other, binding oneself through promise, serves to set up in the ocean of uncertainty, which the future is by definition, islands of security without which not even continuity, let alone durability of any kind, would be possible in the relationships between men. Without being forgiven, released from the consequences of what we have done, our capacity to act would, as it were, be confined to one single deed from which we could never recover, we would remain victims of its consequences forever.

Forgiveness, in the accounts we heard in northern Uganda, is considered a virtue of everyday interaction, civility and mutuality. People emphasized the moral and social value of forgiving as well as the personal benefits they realized as individuals. In the accounts many underlined how they felt freed when the bitterness against a wrongdoer was released, enabling relationships with the offender to be smoothed out.

Likewise, 'the promise', in the sense Arendt writes about, is regarded as a fragile affair and considered contingent upon everyday action and words. So far the promises heard in northern Uganda have not been in big scale political rhetoric of 'Never Again', such as we have heard it recently about the Rwandan genocide. But there is a sense of promises that people try to keep alive by having everyday conversations and interactions with those in their vicinity, despite the fact that they have transgressed norms.

People sometimes discussed reconciliation rituals ('drinking the bitter root' and 'stepping on eggs' ceremonies), and political and religious speeches as inspiration for forgiveness processes; these were important in their own way, but the principal site of the work of forgiving was in everyday encounters. There was a sense in some of the political speeches that those words had very little to do with the social processes taking place on the ground. Veena Das has an apt description of this phenomenon when she writes 'Words when they lead lives outside the ordinary, become emptied of experience, lose touch with life – in Wittgenstein, it is the scene of language gone on a holiday' (2007: 6). Das, writing about the survivors of riots in India, notices that life was recovered 'not through some grand gestures in the realm of the transcendent but through a descent into the ordinary'. She argues that there is a mutual absorption of the violent and the ordinary (2007: 7). Das emphasizes how the ordinary sometimes becomes, in fact, something wondrous, an essential source of hope, what she calls a 'temporality of second chances' (2007: 101). This sense of a special time and emerging possibilities seems to characterize the fragile and wondrous beginnings after war in northern Uganda.

Words and Every Day Actions

In Acholi people say that you can forgive with the tongue, but that does not mean that you have forgiven in your heart (Kusk 2013). Words alone cannot be trusted – if anything can. If you really forgive, it is something you may explicate, but it is primarily something you demonstrate every day through your actions. Therefore forgiveness is not a final act but a continuing process. Yet, actions alone without any verbal communication are not enough either. One of the young women talks in her account about how, when she got back to her family after her abduction, she was allowed to live and be part of everyday life, but her father never really spoke to her, never said welcome, or had a conversation, so she was uncertain and did not really know if she was forgiven and truly welcome back.

The emphasis, however, and evidence – or rather constant evaluation – of forgiveness was most often put on apparently small, everyday actions and their instability. Did a neighbour use to share food when children ran to her compound, but recently sent them home without food? Did a co-wife start talking and chatting more than she used to? Did the children let Acan get her turn at the bore hole day after day? Forgiveness in this sense is not spectacular, dramatic or grandiose, but embedded in the ordinary. I borrow Lone Grøn's oxymoronic term 'significant routines' (2005) to grasp the profoundness of the small actions in forgiveness. The routines of fetching water, cooking food, getting fire from a neighbour, are not seen as simply mundane and 'getting on with it', but significant actions – each single time they are practiced – as a window through which forgiveness can be monitored.

The Moral Machine: The Grinding Stone

It is in this sense that I think of every single day as moral machinery to emphasize the strenuous continuous work implied in forgiving. It is not to be compared to an automatic, well-oiled and smooth running machine, where you simply push a button and it works, where you insert a 'wrong' all tangled up, it runs through the machinery and comes out 'righted' and straight. No, rather it is like the most commonly known machines in rural East Africa: the grinding mills and grinding stones where people transform their grain crops into edible food. Grinding mills, which run on the power of a small generator, are part of almost any small trading centre and are a place where people discuss and work, because they constantly break down or are out of fuel; people try to figure them out, constantly repair them, look for spare parts for them, and debate who should buy fuel for them to make them run, and when they don't work anyway (which is actually most of the time), people retreat to the grinding stone. The grinding stone is the most reliable 'machine' of the hand, that through hours and hours of muscle work transforms the hard grains and seeds of sesame, millet or maize into what it takes to make food, feed your family and sustain life. The grinding stone may not be what people in Uganda feel is 'the ideal machine' because it is old fashioned, whereas the modern and powered grinding mill is faster and much less work; but given that the latter is often broken, the grinding stone is frequently the best possibility available. Practically every homestead has a grinding stone, and if you don't have one you are dependent on borrowing your neighbour's.

These experiences with grinding machines serve as a comment to the title of this book – Moral Engines – reminding us that engines require work, they don't run by themselves without any attentions, they sometimes break down, and it is troublesome to repair them and understand them. It is wondrous when they do work, and when they don't, we try some other solution. Grinding by hand is a good metaphor for forgiveness work in northern Uganda; it is slow, it takes muscle power, you get better at it with experience and it is continuous work that has to be done every single day, not unlike moral work such as forgiving.

The Laboratory of 'How Can We Live Together?'

The work of forgiving in the post-conflict situation in northern Uganda finds great resonance with Cheryl Mattingly's concept of moral laboratories, because this notion emphasizes the experimental and experiential aspect of moral reflexive practice that happens in the midst of everyday life, which is a messy and unpredictable affair (2014). As Mattingly writes, the everyday lab does not have a well-defined *telos*, but foregrounds the human predicament of trying to live a life that one is somehow responsible for (ibid.: xx).

The moral attempts in the forgiveness accounts from northern Uganda are less about trying to reach a normative ideal, but more about trying out what is possible, given the situation, the past and the prospects. Mattingly emphasizes how turbulence and uncertainty are pervasive qualities in the everyday lab and how ordinary routines are not the daily expression of a habitual way of life culturally inherited, so much as a fragile achievement, a hard won moment of mundaneness. Under such circumstances, the ordinary carries a special moral weight and it can acquire an unexpected symbolic density (ibid.). This captures precisely what I am trying to point out about the profoundness of everyday actions in post-war Acholi.

An important aspect of the experimental work of forgiving had to do with working out how to deal with the fact that people knew – in some sense – when they wronged others. There were accounts about moral transgression that happened unknowingly, as Arendt describes, but often people knew they were doing wrong, and did it anyway.

The grinding work of forgiving afterwards involved, I would argue, a heightened sense of the fragility of the experiment to live together.

Lotte Meinert is a Professor of Anthropology at the Department of Culture and Society, Aarhus University, Denmark. She has been principal researcher and manager for Changing Human Security: Recovery after War in Northern Uganda (2008–2013) and is co-principal investigator and co-manager of the Center for Cultural Epidemics (EPICENTER). She is author and co-editor of multiple books, including *Hopes in Friction* (2008).

Notes

1. I am inspired here by Jane Guyer's ideas about possibility; Guyer, drawing upon Ernest Gellner, points to the continual temporal metamorphosis in human life: Another day is also An Other Day, another generation is also An Other Generation (Guyer, personal communication 2014). Everyday is also Every Day. In other words, the continuation and routine of every day carries possibilities that are beyond mere continuation and routine.
2. The Forgiveness *Timu Kica* project was part of a larger research collaboration between Gulu University in Uganda and Aarhus, Southern Denmark and Copenhagen Universities. The overall project was called 'Changing Human Security: Recovery after Armed Conflict in Northern Uganda' and was funded by the Danish research council for development research from 2008 to 2013. I would like to acknowledge all the collaborators and participants in the *Timu Kica* project, who have contributed in their various ways.
3. There are two examples in the accounts of persons forgiving someone who is not present. One is geographically distant, and the other one dead. Yet this is not the trend in the accounts.

References

Akuni, Job. 2011. *The Role of Traditional Rituals in Conflict Management*. N.p.: LAP Lambert Academic Publishing.

Allen, Tim. 2006. *Trial Justice: The International Criminal Court and the Lord's Resistance Army*. London, UK: Zed Books.

Arendt, Hannah. 1958 *The Human Condition*. Chicago: Chicago University Press.

Baines, Erin. 2010. 'Spirits and Social Reconstruction after Mass Violence: Rethinking Transitional Justice', *African Affairs* 109(436): 409–30.

Branch, Adam. 2011. *Displacing Human Rights: War and Intervention in Northern Uganda*. Oxford: Oxford University Press.

Das, Veena. 2007. *Life and Words: Violence and the Descent into the Ordinary*. Berkeley, Los Angeles and London: University of California Press.

Derrida, Jacques. 2003. *On Cosmopolitanism and Forgiveness*. New York and London: Routledge.

Dolan, Chris. 2009. *Social Torture: The Case of Northern Uganda*, 1986–2006. New York: Berghahn Books.

Fabion, James. 2001. 'Toward an Anthropology of Ethics: Foucault and the Pedagogies of Autopoiesis'. *Representations* 70 (1): 83–104.

Finnegan, Amy. 2010. 'Forging Forgiveness: Collective Efforts amidst War in Northern Uganda', *Sociological Inquiry* 80(3): 424–47.

Finström, Sverker. 2008. *Living with Bad Surroundings: War, History and Everyday Moments in Northern Uganda*. Durham, NC: Duke University Press.

Grøn, Lone. 2005. 'Winds of Change, Bodies of Persistence: Health Promotion and lifestyle change in institutional and everyday contexts'. Ph.D. thesis. Aarhus University.

Harlacher, Thomas. 2009. *Traditional Ways of Coping with Consequences of Traumatic Stress in Acholiland: Northern Ugandan Ethnography from a Western Psychological Perspective*. Freiburg: Department of Psychology, University of Freiburg, Switzerland.

Heidegger, Martin. 1996 [1953]. *Being and Time*. Albany: State University of New York Press.

Kusk, Mette Lind. 2013. 'At tilgive med hjertet eller med tungen?' [To forgive with heart or tongue?], *Jordens Folk* 48(2): 4–11.

Laidlaw, James. 2002. For an Anthropology of Ethics and Freedom. Journal of the Royal Anthropological Institute. 8(2): 311–332.

Lambek, Michael. 2010. 'Toward an Ethics of the Act', in Michael Lambek (ed.), Ordinary Ethics. New York: Fordham University Press.

Lear, Jonathan. 2006 *Radical Hope: Ethics in the Face of Cultural Devastation*. Cambridge, MA: Harvard University Press.

Mattingly, Cheryl. 2014. *Moral Laboratories: Family Peril and the Struggle for a Good Life*. Oakland: University of California Press.

Meinert, Lotte. 2014. 'Tricky Trust: Distrust as a Point of Departure and Trust as a Social Achievement in Uganda', in S. Lisberg, E. Pedersen and A.L. Dalsgård (eds), *Anthropology and Philosophy: Dialogues on Trust and Hope*. New York: Berghahn Books. 118–131.

Meinert, Lotte, Julaina Obika and Susan Reynolds Whyte. 2014. 'Crafting Forgiveness Accounts after War in Northern Uganda: Editing for Effect', *Anthropology Today* 30(4): 10–15.

Robins, Joel. 2004. Becoming Sinners. Christianity and Moral Torment in a Papua New Guinea Society. University of California Press.

Strathern, Marilyn. 1997. 'Prefigured Features: A View from the New Guinea Highlands'. *The Australian Journal of Anthropology* 8 (2): 89–103.

Verma, Cecilie Lanken. 2012. 'Truths out of Place: Homecoming, Intervention, and Story-making in War-torn Northern Uganda', *Children's Geographies* 10(4): 441–55.

Whyte, Susan Reynolds, Julaina Obika and Lotte Meinert. 2015. 'Untying Wrongs in Northern Uganda', in William Olsen and Walter E.A. Van Beek (eds), *Evil in Africa: Encounters with the Everyday*. Bloomington and Indianapolis: Indiana University Press.

Zigon, Jarett. 2007. 'Moral Breakdown and the Ethical Demand', *Anthropological Theory* 7(2): 131–50.

6

The Provocation of Freedom

Rasmus Dyring

There is no other task of thought, on the subject of freedom, than that which
consists in transforming its sense of a property held by a subject into the sense of a
condition or space in which alone something like a 'subject' can eventually come to
be born, and thus to be born (or to die) *to* freedom...

—Jean-Luc Nancy, *The Experience of Freedom*

Introduction

Recently anthropology has taken an interest in the ethical. But the question of
the ethical is not an innocent one and this turn in anthropology toward the
ethical is no innocent turn.

With the emphasis on such a conceptual prism as the ethical in the investigation of human social life, the basic drives that gather and bind us together in
communities and prompt social action are modified and appear in a new
modality. Leaving behind the more traditional sociological approach that
takes the question of the imperative quality in practical matters to be fundamentally reducible to the normativity inherent in a given social reality and the
more or less mechanistic reproduction of this social normativity by way of
enculturation and habitus, the basic drives in communitary life and their
inherent imperative quality are now, with this turn to the ethical, to be understood in connection with such concepts as the care of the self, practical
wisdom, the good, judgment, responsibility and freedom.

In terms of ontology, this shift in analytical focus seems to imply a drastic
reconfiguration in the modal hierarchy according to which social practice as
analytical unit is construed. At least, this would be one consequence of James
Laidlaw's famous – and, I believe, accurate – proclamation that 'an anthropology

of ethics will only be possible – will only be prevented from constantly collapsing into general questions of social regularity and social control – if we take seriously, as something requiring ethnographic description, the *possibilities of human freedom*' (2002: 315, emphasis added). That is to say, the tenability of the ethical turn in anthropology requires that ontological priority is shifted from the modal category of reality – from the 'moral facts', to put it in the positivist terminology of the often criticized Durkheimian sociology – to the category of possibility in order to clear a conceptual space for undetermined deliberation (Lambek 2010a, 2010b), moral experimentation (Mattingly 2013, 2014), cultural change (Robbins 2007) and a reflective stance (Laidlaw 2002, 2014; Zigon 2007).

If this is so – and this to be sure is still an open and largely unthematized question in the current theoretical debates – the possibility of an anthropology of ethics would seem to hinge not only on the ability to address in adequate methodological terms 'the possibilities of human freedom'; a corresponding fundamental shift toward an ontological prioritization of the modal category of possibility in the understanding of the existential conditions of human practice, of the human condition as such, would equally be a necessary requirement if the anthropological study of the ethical is to be properly different from the study of the reproduction of social normativity (I pursue this argument at length elsewhere; see Dyring under review).

That the notion of ethics urges us to recognize that the possible takes ontological precedence over the real in the realm of human affairs by no means implies that we have to accept a version of human freedom that stresses the radical independence from external forces of an autonomous individual. The ontological characterization in question does not even initially speak of properties ascribed to an individual human being or the faculty of the will, but more primordially to the way a world, *in casu* a moral world, is opened, and the way in which human beings find themselves emplaced in a world where the moral appears to matter. In the terminology of hermeneutical phenomenology, it expresses the point that a present reality only appears as it does within the horizon of an underdetermined future and hence in light of (still) unrealized projects, ideals, values, narrative trajectories, etc. That is to say, the present state of affairs only becomes what it is because it is always already transcended, from the ground up, toward a range of possibilities.

At this point two fundamental problems present themselves and both revolve around the ontological issue of the modal characteristics of social practice. First, if the present is disclosed in light of a range of possibilities that can be spelled out, for instance, in terms of future projects, values and ideals, would this not simply – with half a turn of the hermeneutic circle – once again reinstate the ontological priority of the given, the hegemony of the positivist metaphysics of reality? After all, are these projects, values and ideals not themselves grounded in the historico-cultural reality in which they are pursued? And secondly, if the category of possibility really takes priority in ethical life, how are we to conceive of the practical necessity with which ethical matters make themselves known in human life? In the Durkheimian picture it is the reality of 'attachment to group' and the disciplining, sanctioning power of society that constitute the 'moral engines' in social practice (Durkheim 1973; 2010: 43ff). But if it is possibility and not a given reality that takes onto-logical priority, how can 'possibility' be said to drive ethical life and necessitate ethics as an inexorable dimension of practical life?

Both of these problems involve questions of such magnitude and complex-ity that they each go well beyond what a single chapter can address satisfacto-rily, let alone exhaustively. All I can hope for here is to begin qualifying these problems and make a convincing case for a certain existential phenomenologi-cal approach to them. In what follows, I will hence present one path into the intricate web of questions they raise.

In the first section, I consider the notions of the real (or the actual) and the possible, and direct further investigations towards the idea that an anthropol-ogy of ethics should concern itself not only with 'the possibilities of human freedom', but equally with an experiential exploration and explication of the conditions of possibility of such possibilities. This line of argument will simul-taneously indicate an opening in the circularity that threatens to reinstate the hegemony of the metaphysics of reality as pointed to in the first problem out-lined above. In the second section, I will follow a clue from Kierkegaard's moral psychology as to the experiential domain in which the possible inter-sects and unsettles the real. Here I make the case that the advent of ethical possibility is to be explored in terms of moral experiences that are character-ized by the passivity of moods and pathic stirrings, rather than the active comportment of reflective agency. Throughout the final three sections, I will present an elaborate phenomenology of the moral experience that Marco Evaristti's art installation *Helena and El Pescador* (2000) elicits. By qualifying and pursuing the question of how the moral experience of possibility in and of itself institutes a dimension of practical necessity, I address the second problem raised above. Since the notion of freedom that emerges from these explorations more precisely relates to a fundamental feature of the human condition that calls forth and demands our practical engagement, rather than to free agency in the face of constraining structures, or the Kantian autono-mous subject, or the Foucauldian active exercise of freedom in the care of the self, I will term this phenomenon – which I take to be an originary existential moral engine – the provocation of freedom.

The Anthropology of Ethics and the Question of (its) Possibility

What is at stake – both in this chapter, in this book, and in general in the current debate – is how to understand the very possibility of the anthropology of the ethical. The word 'possibility' should here be heard in two senses; at stake is the possibility of developing a sound anthropological approach to the ethical. But such an approach relies heavily on figuring out what the term 'possibility' itself can even mean in the anthropology study of the ethical. The battle over the definitional power in this bourgeoning field of study is, hence, a battle that is to a large extend to be fought on the battlefield of modality, about the nature of the ontological relationship between possibility, reality and necessity.

This discussion and, in particular, the question of the meaning of possibility, might be illustratively framed in dialogue with Jonathan Lear's *Radical Hope* (2006), which deals with the coming to an end, i.e. the becoming impossible, of the traditional way of life of the Native American Nation of the Crow toward the end of the nineteenth century. In his methodological considerations in the beginning of the book, Lear writes of the difference between anthropology and philosophy that '[a] philosophical inquiry may rely on historical and anthropological accounts of how a traditional culture actually came to an end, but ultimately it wants to know not about actuality but about possibility' (Lear 2006: 9). And in a similar vein a couple of pages earlier, Lear writes of the work presented in *Radical Hope*, that it 'is a work of philosophical anthropology. Unlike an anthropological study, I am not primarily concerned with what actually happened to the tribe or any other group. I am concerned rather with the *field of possibilities* in which all human endeavors gain meaning' (Lear 2006: 7, emphasis added).

According to this view, then, a basic difference between a sociocultural anthropological and a philosophico-anthropological approach lies in the fact that the latter is concerned with possibility, while the former is concerned merely with actuality, with the positively given 'data': i.e. with culture understood as 'that complex whole which includes knowledge, belief, art, morals, law, custom, and any other capabilities and habits acquired by man as a member of society' (Tylor 1920: 1); or as 'the totality of the mental and physical reactions and activities that characterize the behavior of the individuals composing a social group collectively and individually in relation to their natural environment, to other groups, to members of the group itself and of each individual to himself' (Boas 1938: 159); or with the social facts understood as 'any way of acting, whether fixed or not, capable of exerting over the individual an external constraint' and which is 'general over the whole of a given society whilst having an *existence of its own, independent of its individual manifestations*' (Durkheim 1982: 59, emphasis in original; cf. 2010: 35); or with the 'the imponderabilia of actual life' observed 'in their full actuality' (Malinowski 1984: 18); or with the total social fact (Mauss 1990: 100ff); or with habitus as a 'socially constituted system of cognitive and motivating structures' (Bourdieu 2013: 76).

In spite of the testimony of these seminal voices from the anthropological tradition, I believe that Lear's wholesale characterization of anthropology as a study of the human being that is merely concerned with the givens of an actual reality misses the mark and, as a consequence, obscures a more important distinction to be drawn within the 'fields of possibilities' rather than between actuality and possibility. A first objection to this wholesale characterization might thus be that especially after the *Writing Culture* movement in the 1980s, it has been impossible to think of culture as an actually given homogenous 'complex whole' and of social reality as something ethnography can represent exhaustively. Instead, Culture, as a unitary whole, is something produced in the process of ethnographic writing. For such a postmodern anthropology, the division between what is actually the case and what might possibly by the case seems also to have been undercut (Clifford and Marcus 1986). A second objection, which brings us closer to the present considerations, is that a main concern in recent anthropological writing on the ethical has indeed been that of how to deal with the such notions as possibility, potentiality, indeterminacy and freedom within, and somewhat against the grain of a theoretical tradition that finds itself in the very long shadows of the so called social sciences of *unfreedom* (cf. Laidlaw 2014).

In these recent anthropological considerations of possibility and freedom there seems to be four recurring, although by no means universally accepted, traits. First of all, freedom, or undetermined possibility more generally, is not simply considered a fact of the state of nature, nor a fact of transcendental reason, but something actively exercised, something that takes place in acts and speech acts, practical experimentation etc. Secondly, the exercise of freedom takes place within a historically and culturally constituted field of possibilities, within value spheres or in relation to cultural discourses and institutional regimes. Thirdly, this exercise of freedom involves some aspect of character formation or work-of-self. And fourthly, this exercise of freedom and ethical work entails some degree of reflectivity, consciousness or deliberation (Laidlaw 2002, 2014; Lambek 2010a, 2010b; Mahmood 2005; Mattingly 2010, 2012, 2013; Robbins 2007; Zigon 2007, 2008, 2009. C. Jason Throop [2010, 2012, this volume] notably diverts from these activist schematics and emphasizes the more passive registers of moral life).

Yet, even, or perhaps especially, with this current theoretical development in mind, I would still like to press this issue of a distinction that turns on the ontological relationship between the actual and the possible. But here the point will not be to pit a science of the actual against a science of the possible, but rather to make a more delicate distinction between an approach to the ethical that grants ontological primacy to the real (e.g. cultural discourses and subject positions that reside on the level of the collective etc., cf. Mahmood 2005; Faubion 2011) and one that grants ontological primacy to possibility.

Let me start by calling to mind that the kind of possibility with which Lear's *Radical Hope* is concerned is not limited to an investigation of a historical field of possibilities within which ethical subjects can exercise their freedom, according to which a self can work on itself and 'subjectivate' itself, and according to which a virtuous character can take form – although this, to be sure, is also part and parcel of the picture painted of the traditional way of life of the Crow. Instead, the main aim of Lear's work is to inquire as to what it, on the one hand, means for singular human beings that such culturally framed fields of possibilities become impossible and, on the other, to explore the ethical, or, as it were, the existential dynamics involved in the becoming possible of new fields of possibilities. Hence, the distinction in levels of analysis that Lear's work foregrounds – *pace* Lear's own obstructively imprecise characterization of this point – is not that between a level of brute facts and a level of possibilities open for actualization. Rather, the distinction is, on closer inspection, to be draw between a level on which the ranges of possibilities open for actualization belong and a level on which such possibilities are constituted and repeated in their being-possible.

What is thus elucidative in this – at first sight, rather harsh and in some respects reductive – division between a study of actuality and a study of possibility is not that an anthropological approach is supposedly unable to deal with the subjunctive, with the fields of possibilities for action, with possible futures and the haunting of past possibilities, with the evaluation and choice of various courses of action (because it evidently is dealing with these matters), but that the radical inquiry into the very conditions of possibility of historically and culturally framed fields of possibilities is the heartland of philosophical inquiry. An anthropology of ethics that takes seriously 'the possibilities of human freedom' must venture into the philosophical anthropological borderland and investigate exactly the generative relationship between these levels of possibility.

Freedom, Anxiety and Moral Experience

Having briefly discussed various approaches to social practice and ethical life in terms of their modal configurations, and having found in the process an opening in the theoretical landscape for a philosophical anthropology of ethics, the task in the remainder of this chapter will be to elaborate on the question of the possibility of possibilities.

A primary concern in this respect must be that of where this kind of condition of possibility is to be sought out phenomenologically, when we are no longer speaking about fields of possibilities concretely afforded in specific historico-cultural contexts. Obviously, if this approach is to have any relevance in the anthropology of ethics, this cannot be a matter of conditions of possibility in the Kantian sense; i.e. those *a priori* conditions that make possible empirical experience, but that qua conditions of empirical experience, are not themselves open to empirical examination, but accessible only in transcendental deductions. The conditions of possibility of interest here will have to be open to phenomenological and ethnographic exploration and hence be accessible in ordinary experience. In order to approximate an understanding of what this means, let me briefly, once again, consult Lear and his account of how the Crow people manage to make possible a new horizon of possibilities.

The main protagonist in the story told by Lear is the last of the great Crow chiefs, Chief Plenty Coups. As a child, the chief-to-be had had a dream that would guide him the rest of life in his efforts to lead the Crow through the world shattering changes their way of life would experience in the face of the predicament imposed on them by their white colonizers. Here is not the place to account in detail for Plenty Coups' dream and Lear's analysis of it. Of importance in the present context is Lear's insistence on taking the dream seriously as a wellspring of ethical possibility.

Lear contends that Plenty Coups' dream amounts to more than the soaring, hallucinating fantasy of an exhausted, self-mutilated young boy (as was sometimes done on a vision quest to induce dreaming, Plenty Coups had cut off a joint on one of his fingers). Rather, Plenty Coups' dream was a creative response to the dire predicament of the Crow Nation; it should be seen as 'a response to a communal sense of anxiety' (2006: 77). And furthermore, it should be seen as a mode of responding to the pathos of anxiety that was able to transcend the limits of the accustomed fields of possibilities and the limits of ordinary ethical deliberation. As Lear puts it, 'It is not unreasonable to suppose that a sensitive nine-year-old was attuned to the anxiety in his community and that he was able to dream what he was not yet in a position to think' (2006: 77). But it was not merely because he was still a child that he was unable to arrive by way of reflective ethical deliberation at what the dream showed him. No Crow, however prudent, would have been able to.

The new possibility which the dream revealed – namely the possibility of building a Crow life around virtues of learning, instead of virtues of war – was not a matter 'that could be reasoned about in the preexisting terms of the good life.' (Lear 2006: 92) Only with Plenty Coups' dream – a dream that was grounded in a communitary pathos of anxiety shared by the Crow, the anxiety of a way-of-life, and thus a dream that Plenty Coups dreamed on behalf of the tribe – did it become possible to transcend *in practice* the traditionally afforded range of Crow possibilities for ethical being, because it immediately opened the possibility of a radically hopeful posture that surpassed any available traditional conception of the good Crow life and reached toward a possible future beyond the current comprehension of any Crow, Plenty Coups himself included.

Returning now to the question of locating a realm of experience in which to seek out the possibility of possibilities, Lear clearly directs the analysis away from the level of intentional, deliberative action and towards registers of existential pathos – in the present case the pathos of anxiety and the posture of hope assumed in the place opened and circumscribed by this anxiety. This is the clue that I wish to take from Lear.

Kierkegaard writes of the concept of anxiety that it 'is altogether different from fear and similar concepts that refer to something definite, whereas anxiety is freedom's actuality as the possibility of possibility' (Kierkegaard 1980: 42 [*SV* 6: 136]). Concluding this preparatory discussion of the ontological relationship between actuality and possibility – and in the effort of avoiding the misunderstanding that the philosophical-anthropological investigation of possibility dismisses any appeal to the actual, and thereby also the misunderstanding that the present chapter should be an argument against experience-near exploration and against the importance of fieldwork – it is worth noting that Kierkegaard intimately relates actuality and possibility in this characterization of the phenomenon of anxiety. Freedom is actual in anxiety, but not actual in the sense that freedom can be examined by treating anxiety as a neuro-physiological state that can be measured and subjected to the methods of the hard sciences. And, it is not actual in the same sense that the object of fear – for instance, the speeding car that suddenly makes an unexpected turn toward my son – is actual. The actuality of freedom that takes place in anxiety has no object, it is an experience that experiences no definite thing, no-thing, and as such it harbours an experiential disclosure of possibility as such. I will unpack this important characterization later in the chapter.

In the sections that follow, I will work out in more detail how this shift in analytical focus from ethical activity to registers of existential pathos may be fruitful in the anthropology of ethics. More specifically I will point to a phenomenon I shall call the provocation of freedom as a phenomenon that originarily calls forth and thus 'precedes' the more active exercise of freedom.[1] I will do this first by looking to a very special work of art, and secondly by consulting Kierkegaard's phenomenology of anxiety.

Helena and the Question of the Practical Necessity of Ethical Engagement

In the year 2000, the Chilean-Danish artist Marco Evaristti put on exhibition his work *Helena & El Pescador* at the Trapholt Museum in Kolding, Denmark. The work consisted of two parts. One part called *El Pescador* (the Fisherman) is a self-portrait of the artist which did not receive much attention. The other part – *Helena* – on the other hand caused quite a stir. Let me quote at length art historian Anna Karina Hofbauer's description of the work:

> Ten white Moulinex Optiblend 2000 Mixers stood on a perfectly normal table. Each blender was filled with water, and in these rather unusual aquariums orange-red swordtails were swimming around. The blenders were clearly connected to the power supply and could be activated, everything being arranged in full view to the public. There were no notices or directions attached to the equipment but as the power switches were in full view this was unnecessary. If anyone decided to press the yellow button, this would immediately kill the fish and turn the contents of the mixers into cold fish soup. In this way, the public was placed in the situation of being judges making life and death decisions. The absence of information about what should be done with the work on display in the exhibition did not leave *Helena* undisturbed for long. Soon after the exhibition opened a visitor pressed the button.

> Power was connected to the blenders for two days and over that period a total of 16 fish died. The power was then cut off by the police and the Director of the museum at the time, Peter S. Meyer, was charged with cruelty to animals. (Hofbauer 2013: 22)

As Hofbauer here describes it, the spectator confronting the work finds him- or herself in a situation that with a certain urgency calls for a decision of whether or not to take an innocent life. In that respect there is something in this situation that at first glance resembles those perplexity inducing thought experiments so often found in moral philosophy. Take for example Bernard Williams's well known thought experiment in which the botanist Jim acciden- tally finds himself in the midst of a counter-insurgency operation in a village somewhere in the South American jungle:

> Jim finds himself in the central square of a small South American town. Tied up against the wall are a row of twenty Indians... in front of them several armed men in uniform... [T]he captain in charge ... explains that the Indians are a random group of the inhabitants who, after recent acts of protest against the government, are just about to be killed to remind other possible protesters of the advantages of not protesting. However ... the captain is happy to offer him [Jim] a guest's privilege of killing one of the Indians himself. If Jim accepts, then as a special mark of the occasion, the other Indians will be let off. Of course, if Jim refuses, then there is no special occasion, and Pedro [a soldier] here will do what he was about to do when Jim arrived, and kill them all... What should he do? (Smart and Williams 1973: 98–99)

Indeed – what should he do? What should one do in such a situation? Despite this similarity between *Helena* and the 'Jim and the Jungle' thought experi- ment, that one is faced with the urgent decision of whether or not to take an innocent life, there is the obvious and all-decisive difference – a difference that will give a first pointer toward the provocative advent of freedom – that in Williams' scenario the ethical urgency and the subsequent ethical perplexity springs from the objective necessity inherent to the situation in which Jim at gun point must choose from a clearly delineated range of objective possibili- ties, whereas in *Helena* there is no such objective necessity that can account for the urgency felt by the spectator. So from where does this captive force spring that emplaces the spectator, as Hofbauer puts it, 'in a situation of making life and death decisions?' This question must be explored by examin- ing the manner in which the spectator engages actively with the work and how the confrontation with the work, more primordially, prompts the engagement of the spectator.

According to the artist, Marco Evaristti himself, the spectator, when con- fronted with *Helena*, engages actively with the work in one of three ways: as a sadist, who presses the blender button; as a voyeur, who watches those who press the button; or as a moralist, who protests, files complaints and alerts the authorities (Hofbauer 2013: 22). No matter which kind of engagement the spectator enacts, he or she is quite concretely interacting with the work, responding to it – most directly and most actively, of course, in the case of the one who in fact presses the button, thereby taking part in the work. But the way Evaristti describes it, those belonging to the other two groups are also actively involved with the work: whereas the one who presses the button is obviously active, those watching and those moralizing are reactive to the activity of the former (or the activity of the artist or that of the museum putting the work on display). Whether actively pressing the button or re-acting to others pressing the button – all the three types of engagement with the work proposed by Evaristti are understood as activist types of engagement, relying in their engagement on the fact, on the objective reality[2] of the act of pressing the button. Such an activist interpretation is also advanced by Hofbauer. In her words, '*Helena* would not have become a complete interactive work if the button had not been pressed. The total completion of the work occurred when an observer decided to press the button and take the opportunity to partici-pate' (Hofbauer 2013: 23). So, Hofbauer emphasizes the fact of the pressed button – here almost rendered as the result of an arbitrary decision, an act of *liberum arbitrium* – as that which originally realizes participation, as that which completes the work, as that which thereby institutes the ground of objective necessity upon which the subsequent play of reactions can unfold.

But is participation in the work really accomplished only and originarily in and through the direct and indirect interaction with the work based on an arbitrary, free choice? I quoted Hofbauer earlier as writing that when con-fronted with *Helena*, 'the public was placed in the situation of being judges making life and death decisions' (Hofbauer 2013: 22). But if participation in the work is only and originarily accomplished in the activity of, and the re-activity to, the pressing of the button, how can we account for the prior experi-ence of being emplaced in such a situation of being judges over life and death?

It seems that the work prior to affording the concrete ethical possibilities of being sadists, voyeurs and moralists has already somehow called the specta-tors into a shared space in which these concrete possibilities for action origi-narily are made possible not merely by virtue of the objective possibility that I in fact can, and possess the know-how to, press a button on this apparatus, but by virtue of an experienced urgency that I, exactly I, must decide whether or not to press the button. In other words, I am irrevocably put on the spot, and no one can decide in my place.

We can hence discern two moments in this experience that takes place between the work and the spectators, and that emplaces the spectators in an ethically engaging space before the spectator begins engaging actively of his or her own accord: there is, on the one hand, the moment in which the spectators engage with and respond quite concretely to the work, press the button or react to others pressing the button. And there is, on the other hand, a moment that in an ontological sense is prior to this – a moment I shall call proto-responsive – in which the work originarily engages the spectators and calls forth, and demands of them, their engagement. The concrete acts of the first moment are easily observable. In the case of *Helena* these concrete acts made it through the camera lenses and into the newspapers the next day. The proto-responsive moment, however, is most often covered over in day-to-day living in a haze of objective necessity, as it was also covered over with objective necessity in Williams's thought experiment.

Kierkegaard's Phenomenology of Responsive Engagement

In Kierkegaard's work we find some resources for thinking through more elaborately what is at play in this proto-responsive dimension of ethical engagement. In his analysis of the phenomenon of sin – in particular, Adam's original sin – in *The Concept of Anxiety*, Kierkegaard explores the existential forces at play before Adam's transgressive act brought about the fall of man into sin, i.e. into the ethical domain in which the difference between good and evil is posited. Dissatisfied with the traditional theological explanations of the transition from a state of absolute innocence to a state of sinfulness – explanations that rest on the notion of *concupiscentia*, that is, a desire for the forbidden – Kierkegaard suggests that this transition should be investigated instead with reference to the phenomenon of anxiety. Interestingly, both the explanation drawing on *concupiscentia* and the one drawing on anxiety find Adam's transgressive act to be grounded in a certain pathos and both take the confrontation with the prohibition not to eat from the tree of knowledge of good and evil to be that which awakens in Adam the pathic responses of desire or anxiety, respectively, and hence, that which modifies the pathically circumscribed manner in which Adam finds himself emplaced in the world into a mode of being-in-the-world in which the transgressive act first becomes possible.[3] But the way this dynamic between demand and response is understood is what radically sets apart the two explanations.

The doctrine of *concupiscentia* states that the prohibition stirred in Adam the desire to do the forbidden, which consequently caused Adam to act and eat from the tree of knowledge of good and evil. But, as Kierkegaard points out, how can a desire to transgress arise in he who is as yet absolutely ignorant of good and evil, when the very understanding of such categories as 'transgression', 'the forbidden', 'prohibition' entails the understanding that it is wrong, perhaps even evil, to transgress, to do the forbidden, to break the prohibition. This means that in the doctrine of *concupiscentia*, the knowledge of good and evil that Adam is supposed to have attained only after the transgressive act is presupposed in the explanation of the causal conditions of that very act, and by the same token, a chain of causality and necessity is introduced between the sphere of innocence and that of sinfulness. By introducing such a link, as Kierkegaard writes, '[t]he qualitative leap is enervated; the fall becomes something successive' (1980: 40 [*SV* 6: 135]).

By contrast, Kierkegaard's anxiety-based explanation of the transition refrains from giving any causes of the act that led to the fall. Yet, despite the absence of causal necessity, the transgressive act is performed neither into a pure, non-restrictive vacuum, nor is it arbitrary. Anxiety, in Kierkegaard's understanding, comes in as a liminal phenomenon between absolute innocence and fallen sinfulness. An analysis of this phenomenon of anxiety will hence bring our explanation of the transition right up to that outermost ledge whence Adam's qualitative leap is taken, without, on the one hand, introducing an instance of causal necessity from which the leap follows as an effect, and, on the other hand, leaving it an absolutely arbitrary deed.

Let me sketch the main points in Kierkegaard's account of the fall, before moving on to a discussion of some phenomenal similarities between Adam's situation and the situation in which the spectators of *Helena* find themselves. As Kierkegaard explains, Adam is initially innocent and innocence is ignorance – Adam does not know any better and is therefore exempt from responsibility. But with God's prohibition the state of innocence is modified: a modification that is in essence an experiential or phenomenological modification. As Kierkegaard writes of the events immediately surrounding the prohibition: 'Innocence still is, but only a word is required and the ignorance is concentrated. Innocence naturally cannot understand this word, but at that moment anxiety has, as it were, caught its first prey. Instead of nothing, it now has an *enigmatic word*' (1980: 44 [*SV* 6:138], emphasis added). Adam cannot understand what is said. The understanding of the semantic content of the prohibition qua prohibition, as we have already noted, relies on the not yet acquired knowledge of good and evil. But there is something indicative in the very saying of the prohibition that Adam can indeed 'understand', because this kind of 'understanding' requires only a pathic modification of his ignorance, not positive knowledge as such. The saying of the prohibition confronts Adam with a limit, but not a limit that outlines spheres of right and wrong conduct within his paradisiac world. The limit stands forth as a rift in the fabric of Adam's innocent world, a rift of concentrated, impenetrable ignorance, thematized nothingness, and as such the prohibition confronts Adam with a limit that enigmatically delimits his very world. It is, however, of crucial importance to note that this experience of the limit drawn in and through the prohibition does not close off Adam's world – it opens his world towards the enigma indicated in this experience of limit, because the enigmatic quality of the liminal experience overflows the experienced limit, thus assailing and drawing in the experiencing person. Because the prohibition says that Adam should not do this thing that he does not understand, it indicates that Adam is in fact able to do 'something' that, however, withdraws into the inexplicable and enigmatic. As Kierkegaard writes: 'The prohibition induces in him anxiety, for the prohibition awakens in him freedom's possibility... the anxious possibility of *being able*' (1980: 44-45 [*SV* 6: 138], emphasis in original). The experience of the limit drawn in the prohibition overflows with an experience of 'pure', enigmatic potency that comes over Adam in the unsettling pathos of anxiety: unsettling, because this experience of simply *being-able* immediately also entails the at once sweet and terrifying urge to throw oneself into the unknown and begin doing something, whatever it might turn out to be: 'The infinite possibility of being able', Kierkegaard writes, 'that was awakened by the prohibition now draws closer, because this possibility points to a possibility as its sequence' (1980: 45 [*SV* 6: 139]).

The experience of being-able is, hence, pointed towards the possibility of doing something inexplicable in the direction of that enigmatic 'beyond' indicated by the limit drawn by the prohibition. Standing anxiously on this ledge, drawn towards it by the enigmatic experience of this double possibility of simply being-able and of doing something inexplicable with this sensation of being-able, Adam's innocence is, as Kierkegaard puts it, 'brought to its uttermost [til sit Yderste]' (1980: 45 [*SV* 6: 139]). In conclusion, the pathos of anxiety emplaces Adam at that limit whence the qualitative leap leaps into the positively ethical domain in which good and evil are posited. This limit is the limit at which the concrete transgressive enaction of the concrete possibility of eating from the tree originarily is constituted as possible.

The Responsive Engagement in *Helena* and in Moral Experience in General

Having now followed Kierkegaard and Adam up to that point where the concrete acting begins, we have arrived again in that nexus we found also in the moral experience that arises in the confrontation with *Helena*: the nexus that is a point of transition between a proto-responsive engagement that originarily opens a situation for action and the more concrete responses to the possibilities that present themselves in this situation. So let me return again to *Helena* and the question of how we can account for that engagement with the work, which seemed to be in place prior to any active operation of the blender button; and, hence, how we can account for that manner in which the work engages the spectators and emplaces them, as art historian Hofbauer puts it, 'in the situation of being judges making life and death decisions' (Hofbauer 2013: 22).

Let me suggest first of all that what the work calls forth, what it provokes is a situation in which the spectators – before anyone pressed the button the first time, and simply by virtue of their being in the presence of what to a matter-of-fact assessment is nothing but quite normal blenders on a quite normal table containing quite normal fish – find themselves in an experience overflowing with a sense of being-able. This sensation crystallized in the observable fact that the artist and the director of the museum were asked by several spectators immediately after the opening of the exhibition and prior to the liquidation of the first fish if there indeed was power connected to the blenders. Both the director and the artist refused to answer the questions (Richter 2000).

Whether these questions took the concrete shape of worries, of shock or whether they fed off the shared atmosphere in the room, which was described by journalists as ecstatic and exhilarated, the grounding experience underlying them was an unsettling sense of being-able awoken in those present: a sense of being-able which was directed towards an enigmatic possibility of exercising this being-able – namely the enigmatic possibility of perhaps, perhaps not – depending on the unknown aspect of the connection to electric power – liquidating a fish. Finding themselves in this situation of being-able, the spectators were at once anxious and urged on, repulsed and attracted. They were, as Kierkegaard writes of anxiety, in a certain ambiguous state of pathos characterized as 'a sympathetic antipathy and an antipathetic sympathy' (1980: 42 [*SV* 6: 136]). As one of the first persons to liquidate a fish said: 'Almost all of us desire to do it, but refrain from doing it, because we are ethically educated not to do it' (Richter 2000, my translation).

Just as Adam, by way of the pathos of anxiety, was emplaced at that limit of possibility whence the qualitative leap leaps into the concrete enaction of a possibility, so too do we find here that the spectators are engaged by *Helena* and brought to the limit by a grounding experience of simply being-able and the indication of an enigmatic possibility that urges on this sensation of being-able to transition itself into concrete action; this action may now – only by virtue of this transition – be observed as the enaction of the concrete possibilities of one of those types of ethical character of which we earlier heard Evaristti speak: namely, the sadists, the voyeurs and the moralists.

Yet, there seems to be an important difference between the situation in which Adam finds himself and the situation of *Helena's* spectators: Adam is absolutely innocent qua ignorant as regards good and evil, whereas the spectators facing *Helena* – as I quoted the fish-blending person saying above – are 'ethically educated'. That is, the spectators find themselves in a world where the notions of good and evil are already effectively in play. However, towards its end Kierkegaard's explanation of the fall takes a quite surprising turn, which might also smooth out a bit this radical separation between a sphere of ignorance and a sphere of ethical knowledge of good and evil.

Where the notion of *concupiscentia* – the desire for the forbidden – relates causally the prohibition, this intermediary desire, and the consequent transgressive act, Kierkegaard's notion of anxiety, as I have already argued, makes the prohibition only an occasion that by virtue of its inexplicability awakens an experience of possibility in Adam. Kierkegaard has thus cleared of all substantive content the prohibition as it is experienced by Adam and made it a merely formal indicator. But Kierkegaard goes further in this direction and proposes that there need not even be an external party that forbids in order for the anxious experience of freedom to arise. As Kierkegaard writes:

> Innocence can indeed speak ... [and] in language it possesses the expression for everything spiritual. Accordingly, one need merely assume that Adam talked to himself... From the fact that Adam was able to talk, it does not follow in a deeper sense that he was able to understand what was said. This applies above all to the

difference between good and evil, which indeed can be expressed in language but nevertheless *is* only for freedom… (1980: 45–46 [*SV* 6: 139])

So the prohibition only reifies something that already looms in language itself – in the clear world of meaningfulness itself, we might even say – as a perpetual source of anxiety. One only has to stumble across it and anxiety, and with it, the experience of freedom, is awoken. So qua language-beings, who are always already emplaced in linguistic contexts, we have the conceptual distinction between good and evil *in potentia* without necessarily understanding it but it is only when freedom is awoken that we truly come to understand this distinction in its actuality. But what is it that we understand? It is not good and evil in the sense of substantive accounts of what is good and what is evil. What we understand qua free beings is the difference between good and evil qua difference. As free beings we understand that the difference between good and evil matters, but that we at same time cannot account once and for all for what the good is. Abstracting from this the Christological terminology of good and evil, what is indicated with this elusive difference is a realm of practical indeterminacy, a being-in-the-difference of existential indeterminacy, that qua its enigmatic, anxiety-inducing character discloses in practical life a poignantly felt imperative, practically necessitating quality.

The anxious experience of freedom arises here not because we as ethically educated people know with certainty that we should not blend fish, but because we do not know. *Helena* hence shows us that we are in a fundamental state of ignorance as to what in an absolute sense counts as good and evil, but that we are free beings for whom the difference between good and evil is nonetheless absolute and absolutely a matter to be reckoned with.

Conclusion

Judging by aesthetic standards, *Helena* is certainly not in the same league as Michelangelo's *David*. It is more than anything a provocative gesture. But its provocation does not consist in simply going against the grain of moral or legal conventions like the provocative acts of civil disobedience or political activism actively does. To be exact, the provocative force arising in the experience of *Helena* does not come from the work itself, it does not have an objective source, but resides in the very experience of the work and in the experience of this enigmatic, elusive difference between good and evil. The work, then, like the prohibition in the tale of Adam, is merely an occasion for something to expressly come to the fore within experience: namely, as Kierkegaard puts it, freedom's actuality as the possibility of possibility. The provocative, imperative, engaging force, then, is really the force of freedom making itself known. Hence, *Helena* is a window onto the moral engine that is the provocation of freedom.

Acknowledgements

I would like to thank the participants at the Moral Engines conference for their great questions. In particular, I would like to thank Michael D. Jackson for opening a very stimulating line of thought. Finally, I would like to thank Line Ryberg Ingerslev, Kasper Lysemose and Thomas Schwarz Wentzer from the 'Existential Anthropology – Inquiring Human Responsiveness' research project for their helpful comments. The work presented in this chapter is supported by a grant from the Danish Research Council (FKK), 11-104778.

Rasmus Dyring is Assistant Professor at the Department of Philosophy and History of Ideas, Aarhus University. In dialogue with the anthropology of ethics, Dyring's research aims at foregrounding the existential dimensions of ethical life. He has published several articles on this subject, for instance, 'A Spectacle of Disappearance' (*Tropos*, 2015).

Notes

1. Elsewhere I have undertaken a longer analysis of Kierkegaard's philosophical anthropology and its analytical potential in the context of a philosophical anthropology of the ethical (Dyring 2015b).
2. The same goes for the imagined fact of having pressed the button, and the registration of one's reaction to this imagined fact.
3. It would be natural to extend this discussion of the relationship between interdiction and the experience of freedom to the terrain of traditional anthropological issues such as that of the taboo. I would like to thank Michael D. Jackson for raising this point – and in particular the question of the relationship between the incest prohibition and human freedom – in the discussion of the conference version of this chapter. *Prima facie*, it would seem odd to insist that this kind of prohibition also carries that formally indicative force I am here calling the provocation of freedom. However, two things might be said in this respect. First, the provocation of freedom explored here is not to be equated with the liberty from structural constraints experienced in moments of actual transgression. And furthermore, the argument would not be that freedom follows from the 'sin' of incest. Secondly, it might be wise to follow Bataille on this matter, when he acknowledges the universal adherence to this taboo throughout the world, but nonetheless finds it reducible it to a general taboo on sexuality; i.e. on the natural violence that lurks in the human being (Bataille 1986: 50-51). Bataille argues that the taboos – both the taboo on death and the taboo on sexuality – respond to the pathos of anguish before the violence of our natural being that at any moment threatens to break into our ordinary, regulated 'world of work'. Hence, the taboo erects a barrier against such excessive, anxiety provoking phenomena. However, just as Kierkegaard observed in his treatment of the responsive relationship between prohibition and anxiety, Bataille writes that '[i]t is always a temptation to knock down a barrier; the forbidden action takes on a significance it lacks before fear widens the gap between us and it and invests it with an aura of excitement' (Bataille 1986: 48). And as is the case in Kierkegaard, it should be noted that in Bataille's rendition it is not the prohibition itself that tempts: the operative term is rather the fear, or better yet, the sweet anguish before the excess of our natural being.

References

Bataille, G. 1986. *Erotism: Death and Sensuality*, trans. Mary Dalwood. San Francisco: City Light Books.
Boas, F. 1938. *The Mind of Primitive Man*. New York: The MacMillan Company.
Bourdieu, P. 2013. *Outline of a Theory of Practice*. Cambridge: Cambridge University Press.
Clifford, J. and G. Marcus (eds). 1986. *Writing Culture: the Poetics and Politics of Ethnography*. Berkeley: University of California Press.
Durkheim, E. 2010. *Sociology and Philosophy*, trans. D.F. Pocock. New York: Routledge.
_____. 1973. *Moral Education: A Study in the Theory and Application of the Sociology of Education*, trans. Everett K. Wilson and Herman Schnurer. New York: The Free Press.
_____. 1982. *The Rules of Sociological Method and Selected Texts on Sociology and its Method*, trans. W.D. Halls. New York: The Free Press.
Dyring, R. 2015a. 'A Spectacle of Disappearance: On the Aesthetics and Anthropology of Emancipation', *Tropos* 8(1): 11–33.
_____. 2015b. 'The Pathos and Postures of Freedom: Kierkegaardian Clues to a Philosophical Anthropology of the Ethical', *Danish Yearbook of Philosophy* 47: 41–63.
_____. under review. 'From Moral Facts to Ethical Facticity: On the Problem of Freedom in the Anthropology of Ethics', *HAU: Journal of Ethnographic Theory*. Special Issue: 'The Human Condition – Reinventing Philosophical Anthropology', ed. Cheryl Mattingly and Thomas Schwarz Wentzer.
Faubion, James D. 2011. *An Anthropology of Ethics*. Cambridge: Cambridge University Press.
Hofbauer, A.K. 2013. 'The Participation of the Observer as an Experiment in the Art of Marco Evaristti', in Malou Erritzøe (ed.), *Marco Evarristi*, published in connection with the exhibition *Marco Evaristti*. Kolding: Kunstmuseet Trapholt.
Kierkegaard, S. 1980. *The Concept of Anxiety: Kierkegaard's Writings, VIII*, trans. Reidar Thomte. Princeton: Princeton University Press.
_____. 1995. *Samlede Værker bd. 6* (SV6). Haslev: Gyldendals Bogklubber.
Laidlaw, J. 2002. 'For an Anthropology of Ethics and Freedom', *Journal of the Royal Anthropological Institute* 8(2): 311–32.
_____. 2014. *The Subject of Virtue: An Anthropology of Ethics and Freedom*. Cambridge: Cambridge University Press.
Lambek, Michael. 2010a. 'Introduction', in Michael Lambek (ed.), *Ordinary Ethics: Anthropology, Language and Action*. New York: Fordham University Press, pp. 1–38.
_____. 2010b. 'Toward an Ethics of the Act', in Michael Lambek (ed.), *Ordinary Ethics: Anthropology, Language and Action*. New York: Fordham University Press, 2010, pp. 39–63.
Lear, J. 2006. *Radical Hope: Ethics in the Face Cultural Devastation*. Cambridge: Harvard University Press.
Mahmood, S. 2005. *The Politics of Piety: The Islamic Revival and the Feminist Subject*. Princeton: Princeton University Press
Malinowski, B. 1984. *Argonauts of the Western Pacific*. Long Grove: Waveland Press, Inc.
Mattingly, C. 2010. *The Paradox of Hope: Journeys through a Clinical Borderland*. Berkeley: University of California Press.

_____. 2012. 'Two Virtue Ethics and the Anthropology of Morality', *Anthropological Theory* 12(2): 161–84.

_____. 2013. 'Moral Selves and Moral Scenes: Narrative Experiments in Everyday Life', *Ethnos: Journal of Anthropology* 78(3): 301–27.

_____. 2014. *Moral Laboratories: Family Life and the Struggle for a Good Life.* Oakland: University of California Press.

Mauss, M. 1990. *The Gift*, trans. W.D. Halls. New York: Routledge.

Nancy, J.-L. 1993. *The Experience of Freedom*, trans. Bridget McDonald. Stanford: Stanford University Press.

Richter, L. 2000. 'Jeg kunne ikke holde fingerne væk', *Ekstra Bladet* (12 February), Side 4, Artikel-id: Z5518886.

Robbins, J. 2007. 'Between Reproduction and Freedom: Morality, Value, and Radical Cultural Change', *Ethnos: Journal of Anthropology* 72(3): 293–314.

Smart, J.J.C. and B. Williams. 1973. *Utilitarianism: For and Against.* Cambridge: Cambridge University Press.

Throop, C.J. 2010. *Suffering and Sentiment: Exploring the Vicissitudes of Experience and Pain in Yap.* Berkeley: University of California Press.

_____. 2012. 'Moral Sentiments', in D. Fassin (ed.), *A Companion to Moral Anthropology.* Oxford: Wiley-Blackwell, pp. 150–68.

Tylor, E. 1920. *Primitive Culture.* New York: J. P. Putnam's Sons.

Zigon, J. 2007. 'Moral Breakdown and Ethical Demand', *Anthropological Theory* 7(2): 131–50.

_____. 2008. *Morality: An Anthropological Perspective.* London: Berg.

_____. 2009. 'Within a Range of Possibilities: Morality and Ethics in Social Life', *Ethnos: Journal of Anthropology* 74(2): 251–76.

PART II

Moral Engines and 'Moral Facts'

7

On the Immanence of Ethics

Michael Lambek

Ethics is a complex topic on which it would be impossible to construct a model that was at once fully comprehensive, consistent and true to life. Indeed, that very inability itself serves as a subject of some ethical thought. Hence, I invite you to read my chapter as just one among many possible ways to think about the ethical in human life. I begin by reflecting on some of the words in the title and introduction to this volume and continue by presenting my perspective on ethics, an argument that will unfold in two movements and a coda on irony. The first movement elaborates an Aristotelian conception of practical judgment while the second draws from the philosophy of language for an understanding of action.[1]

Moral Engines or Moral Tracks?

When I think of engines, the first image that comes to mind is a steaming locomotive. Engines are big and powerful beasts; they pull mysterious loads of freight, nose into the Gard du Nord and out of Paddington, or steam across the Ganges Plain with masses of people sprouting from them. With respect to ethics I find the concept of engines too powerful, too mechanical, and, all in all, rather frightening. Made by human hands and human design, they too readily take on an inhuman force and autonomy.

Engines are doubly engineered, both designed and driven. Hence talk about moral engines is likely to move from description to prescription. Some would say that this is precisely the ethical, engaged thing to do. Others would consider it an invitation to the sins of moralizing or hubris. We do know that moral engineering can be a very dangerous business.

The introduction speaks also of 'striving', as if ethics did not come easily or naturally. I do not think this is quite right. While the acts and issues we describe specifically as ethical are often marked by their difficulty, this has to do less with the presence or absence, strength or weakness of any force either external or intrinsic to something we could call 'ethics' or 'morality' (words that I use interchangeably), but rather to the situation of our being in the world, and the complexity of our social commitments and concerns. Two widely prevalent sources of difficulty are conflict among prior commitments and the incommensurability of criteria. We cannot care equally for everyone or for every goal or challenge that life offers and we are forced to think about these matters. But again, terms like 'driving' and 'striving' exaggerate the effort.

I don't think engines drive ethics and I am not enough of a post-humanist to think that engines can be moral. I would say rather that morality – or ethics – is in one sense a human capacity (Macpherson 1973), like musicality, but more evenly distributed. The questions then, are what is needed to bring out this capacity, to cultivate it, and what conditions are necessary for people to exercise and realize their capacity, or conversely, what conditions inhibit its exercise. You cannot readily exercise the capacity to make music without voice, instruments or compositions. What counts in making music is less an engine than, so to speak, a track.

For engines to move trains, there must be tracks. Tracks are humble, unobtrusive, ordinary. Tracks are fundamental in these respects: they are enabling, providing a surface that facilitates movement against the friction of rougher ground; they are part of broader landscapes; and they run in specific directions, they lead somewhere, somewhere in particular, not everywhere at once. They provide direction and continuity: horizons but also limits. I evoke this metaphor to think about the criteria and means necessary for moral thought and action and to reframe the question from one of force to quality.

Approaching the Ethical

If the idea of ethical relativism makes many people uneasy, meta-ethical relativism or perspectivism is a perfectly reasonable conclusion to draw from the history of philosophical accounts. Kantians, Aristotelians and Nietzscheans each have interesting things to say. To go even further, maybe there is no single discrete field of ethics or morality to isolate and think about, no single, let alone pair, of elephants, for blind scholars to touch from different sides. The point here is analogous to the one Talal Asad (2003) makes about religion, namely that ethics as a demarcated field is a social objectification, not a natural kind (cf. Hacking 1999). That said, what I think Asad missed out with respect to religion, and what I claim for ethics is that it names something intrinsic to social life. To draw on a term from religion, ethics is immanent to human sociality. The problem is how to perceive this immanence without destroying it through acts of rationalization or objectification.

I see ethics as neither a discrete object nor a distinctive force. And while not discounting it as a distinctive human capacity, I write about it more as a property, quality or function[2] of human action, or a perspective on action, hence of or on actors, and cumulatively of or on character and lives. I take ethics to be found at the conjunction of practical judgment and performative action. By 'immanent' I signal that the ethical is a constitutive dimension of social life, neither transcendent of it nor a detachable part of it. Indeed, I think it as much a category mistake to attempt to distinguish ethics from action as it is mind from body.

This position is close to Durkheim on the moral, but where Durkheim saw morality as a function of rules or structure and linked it to the obligatory, I see it as a function of action and criteria and link it rather to obligation. Ethics is less static, less determined and less mechanical than a simplistic picture of Durkheim would have it, but it is no less immanent to the social.

I acknowledge two strands of thought about ethics, one of which sees the ethical path in the correct and deliberate following of rules and the other in the courage or insight to ignore, subvert, reinvent or transcend rules. But I think there is a middle path, which is exactly the theory of the middle path, namely the Aristotelian attention to practical judgment and the wisdom or character to judge well. From this perspective, there *are* no absolute rules and every circumstance opens its own challenges. Correctness of judgment is subject to debate and the ethical subsists as much in serious engagement in that debate as it does in following any one path. Morality must always be open to the challenge that it is mistaken. Hence any account of moral engines, judgment or rules must also think about the affordance of voice and of plurality of voice. Insofar as recognizing and ensuring the plurality of voice is politics or the political, so too is the ethical also at once political. But there is more to voice than volubility or being heard and more to ethics than mere politics.[3]

Without ignoring the compelling questions about whether politics governs ethics or how ethics should or could govern politics, or where matters of ethics transcend those of religious practice, or indeed who can and should decide where the boundaries among ethics, law and religion lie, I am after something deeper and perhaps prior. I attend to the relatively pre-objectified ethical dimensions of everyday life and ordinary action, perhaps the infra-ethical. My approach also attempts to escape or transcend issues raised by cultural difference and relativism without resorting to a universalism grounded directly in either abstract reason or human biology. Instead I ground ethics in human sociality and language. We cannot and do not live without it. Ethics is ordinary before it is extraordinary.

Ethical Practice: Judgment, Acknowledgement and Justification

Some thinkers distinguish between ethics and morality, according to whether people conceive of the good as a matter of following convention or as having the freedom, need, courage or imagination to break free of it. Such distinctions objectify from the start what must be part of the ongoing work of ethics and evade some of the most challenging questions.[4] One of the lessons of social theory has been that the distinction between convention and freedom is a false or limited opposition. Precipitous existential freedom is rarely encountered in ordinary life; we are always already committed to some identity, relationship or course of action. Hence, there is an inextricable connection, or productive tension, between freedom and obligation in practice, a relationship that is easier to see when we approach the subject ethnographically than by means of reified abstractions.

Ethnographically, it is also evident that people both collectively and individually often freely and deliberately engage in specific kinds of discipline in order to cultivate an ethical disposition in themselves or their children, as though the ordinary social rules or conventional cultural ends were not enough, but equally as though sheer freedom was at least as dangerous an alternative.[5] We cannot think how to live in the absence of postulated ends and instantiated criteria and we cannot live in the abstract or only in our minds.

The relation between freedom and rule or convention is evident also in the mundane fact that people are regularly faced with deciding among several competing or incommensurable commitments. As a trivial example, we may feel relatively obligated to spend Christmas with family but relatively free to decide whether to spend it with our own parents or those of our partner, and free even to rationalize the fact that we've decided to stay at home this year, go to Mexico, or convert to Islam instead. This entails practical judgment, which is a more realistic concept than either freedom or rule, especially when the latter are understood as mutually exclusive alternatives or distinct provinces of social life or moments of social history. In other words, we are not free to live outside any rules or obligations, but we are both free and obliged to distinguish among them. Rather than speak of rules that we follow or break, it is more precise to talk about criteria, commitments and incommensurable values. And rather than speaking of choosing between them, I think it is clearer to say that we exercise some kind of judgment among and with respect to them.[6]

In distinguishing judgment as the central feature of ethical action I refer not primarily to the acts of courts of law or divine beings, nor to what is always explicit, handed down as *a* judgment. Another word might be discernment. The concept of practical reason or judgment (Aristotelian *phronesis*) begins with the idea that the good or right thing to do in a given set of circumstances, or how to do it, is not always obvious. We may learn to exercise judgment such that it goes smoothly, almost without saying, as a matter of virtuous character, but that does not make it simple. For Aristotle it is a matter of finding the right balance to fit the circumstances. Not only are circumstances always changing, but in social life there are always diverse calls upon our attention, competing or incommensurable criteria, obligations, values, desires, interests, relationships, etc. Our initial judgment is often poor and wisdom is not readily achieved.

Some qualifications of common depictions of Aristotle are in order. In contrast to some virtue theorists, I do not think that in any given circumstance the right thing to do is always obvious to the person of good character, or that the virtues to apply are necessarily consistent with one another. For example, the tension between justice and compassion might remain irresolvable; *phronesis* can be seen precisely as the meta-virtue of balancing among the virtues. Practical judgement likewise entails adjusting between incommensurable values, that is, values that do not meet fully along a single dimension or criterion, as for example, between devotion to one's job or calling and to one's children. This is one reason we say we cannot put a price on them; to do so would render them falsely commensurate. That is exactly why judgment is called for and why it is often neither evident nor easy, nor likely to produce common agreement. Hence also why it changes according to circumstances.

A further qualification to some renderings of Aristotle's depiction of virtuous judgment lies in the observation that there are often disruptions. This is a point developed in a variety of ways by Jonathan Lear (2000, 2011) in his confrontation of Greek thought with psychoanalysis. Such disruptions, characterized perhaps by bad judgment, incontinence, doubt, self-reflection, indecision or retraction, can produce real disorientation, vertigo, but also, as Lear insists, renewed enthusiasm, aspiration and commitment. Indeed, Lear says, 'It is constitutive of our life with the concepts with which we understand ourselves that they are subject to ironic disruption' (2011: 22). So if ethics is immanent to society or sociality, this does not mean that virtuous practice goes without saying; Cheryl Mattingly (2012) and James Laidlaw (2014) have each lucidly addressed this point.

Indeed, for Aristotle wise judgment entails reflection and feeling.[7] Reflection can occur before, during and after the act. Put another way, and anticipating a different tradition that I am coming to, ethical practice entails acknowledgement of what one is about to do, is doing or has done. If judgement is a defining feature of the ethical dimension of practice, so acknowledgement is the quintessential ethical act, a point developed in the work of Stanley Cavell. At certain moments, as he says, we owe people an acknowledgement and often we owe it to ourselves.

Of course, simple acknowledgement rapidly expands into justification.[8] We can explore the reasons people give for what they do; how they describe acts of commission or omission, as committed by themselves or others; how they explain giving more attention to one set of parents than another; how they live with the fact that there are homeless and hungry people down the street or across town; how they justify killing in warfare or infanticide; how they, or we, live with a moral queasiness about the state of the world and turn that into programmes and projects from religious piety to existentialism or humanitarianism, or from social or political activism (of various stripes) to critique or academic anthropology, or how people justify withholding engagement entirely; if religious, how they live with passionate investment in redemption while recognizing the ultimate inadequacy of any human return for divine gifts; and how they abstract and objectify all these justifications into and with respect to the discursive fields and professional codes that some people take to be the actual substance of ethics.

But ethics does not enter the picture only with such rationalized objectifications as professional codes or programmes, or with respect to big ticket items or exceptional circumstances like abortion or warfare; it inflects our practice all the time. Nothing could be more ordinary than ethical judgment, as ordinary as hailing someone by name or kinship term or saying good morning; greetings themselves are forms of practical acknowledgment. As Jack Sidnell (2010) has shown by means of conversational analysis, judgment occurs by the microsecond.

A lesson from taking practice seriously is that the connection between freedom and convention, no less than that between ambiguity and certainty, has an intrinsically temporal dimension.[9] Action and disruption take place in time and, obviously, the degree to which judgment is rendered explicit or coalesces into a narrative is a function of time. For the duration of this chapter I will juxtapose two features of temporality, namely the continuity inherent in the stream of practice and the discontinuity occasioned by discrete, consequential acts. Ongoing judgment and specific acknowledgments are expressions of this dichotomy.

Practice and Performance

I have suggested that judgment is intrinsic to practice and I called such practical judgment ethical. Practical judgment transcends any simple distinction between freedom and rule or convention; it describes the shifting balance of interest and disinterest (selfishness and unselfishness, but also attention and complacency) in our lives; and it describes what happens when incommensurable values or virtues meet. However, in and of itself it cannot redress ambivalence and uncertainty. For example, what is to say that a given judgment is right or that it will not be immediately overturned?

How is judgment possible in the first place? Whence come the criteria on the basis of which to exercise judgement, render justifications or authorize the judgments and justifications made? Whence come the criteria appropriate for a given situation, including the criteria that define a situation as such in the first place? I suggest that the source of criteria lies in the act of speaking itself. This is the next step of my argument for the immanence of the ethical.

It is an entailment of the focus on judgment that ethics and the ethical in my terminology describe not just the right and the good, or actually doing what is right or good, but the possibility – and indeed the necessity – for discriminating between right and wrong, just and unjust, for conceptualizing, discerning and acknowledging what is right and good, and for acknowledging the means at hand for constituting practice as right and good, for reflecting on the right and good, and for orienting human beings towards them. Ethics depends on the availability of criteria. I make no assumptions that reasoning will inevitably reach the same conclusions about what *is* right and good; the point is rather how specific criteria move in and out of relevance. Nowhere do I say that good behaviour or wise judgments are themselves immanent. What I do say is that the possibilities for acting (well) and judging (wisely) are immanent.

One way that criteria emerge is through illocutionary action. Once I perform the act of marriage, the criteria that apply to me and to my subsequent behaviour change. My behaviour itself may not change but it is subject to different evaluation. Marriage is an obvious example but the effects are equivalent for any *rite de passage* and indeed any ritual, or even such ostensibly trivial matters as making an appointment. Among Azande both the accusation of witchcraft and the apology for it put the protagonists and their relationships under particular descriptions (as philosophers say) and with respect to new or renewed criteria. Performativity establishes who we are in relation to one another, to ourselves and the world, that is to say, it establishes the criteria by which our relational practice – as a marital partner, citizen, Christian, Muslim, Hindu, Jew or Azande, but also as a parent or child, friend, man or woman, or simple human being – ought to be carried out and can be evaluated. It does not determine practice, but it establishes the relevance of specific criteria for practice and the nature of our commitments to persons and projects.

In his monumental work on ritual and religion, Roy Rappaport (1999) begins by arguing that ritual serves to offset the uncertainty made available by language, namely the fact that we can use language both to lie and to imagine alternative worlds and courses of action. Hence we may be sceptical of what others say to us and be ambivalent, inconsistent or untrustworthy ourselves. Ritual offsets or overcomes these effects by offering public enactments of commitment to particular statements, relationships and courses of action as well as acceptance of the very means that establish such things, thus, not only to *this* marriage, but to weddings and the institution of marriage. Following from Rappaport, I have been implicitly suggesting two reasons, uncertainty and ambivalence, as to why ethics cannot be a purely subjective matter, and hence a matter of either pure freedom or biology, but subsists in reference and relation to public conventional formulations, acts and utterances that are precisely certain and unambiguous.[10] Such public acts provide criteria that enhance clarity or reduce uncertainty, not just with respect to specific judgments, but also to specific commitments, and indeed to who we are.

Whereas Rappaport saw ritual as redressing certain effects of language and hence as a necessary complement to language as a constitutive element of human society or the human condition, it is more precise and truer to his source in J.L. Austin to say that if language in its semantic or locutionary dimensions generates alternatives and uncertainty, in the senses Rappaport explicates, language simultaneously generates certainty or at least commit-ment in its pragmatic or illocutionary dimensions.[11] This is more in line with the reading of Austin offered by Cavell in which every utterance may carry the illocutionary entailment of meaning what we say (1976) and equally imposes the requirement of an acknowledgement on the part of the addressee. Even to say 'yes' or 'I know' are performative acts. As Cavell himself says, they are '*similar* to "I promise" *in a specific respect ...* namely, that *you give others your word*'. Cavell continues, '*this* connection (this inner connection...) between claiming to know and making a promise ... reveals human speech to be radi-cally, in each uttered word, ethical. Speaking, or failing to speak, to another is as subject to responsibility, say to further response, as touching, or failing to touch, another' (2010: 320–21).

Rappaport can be read to argue that what ritual does is to extend and elabo-rate this function of language, to shore it up against what also concerns Cavell, namely scepticism and the recognition that ordinary language is 'founded on nothing but itself' (Laugier 2005: 87). Cavell's response is to situate the pre-cariousness of the ordinary. 'One struggle is between criteria (i.e., the ordi-nary) and scepticism (the desire for the empty, freedom from myself); another is between the ordinary and the aphoristic (the desire for the transcendental, for a satisfaction out of the ordinary that is not provided by the provision of language games...)' (Cavell 2005: 170). The ordinary is precarious insofar as criteria are not 'the means by which the existence of something is established with certainty'. Cavell's is a kind of intellectual post-religious stance and one might note in comparison how ritual in Rappaport's argument is meant to offset scepticism and to provide at least moments of certainty or a glimpse of what certainty might be, as well as how it is religion that offers the aphoristic or transcendental.

As Maurice Bloch has argued (2004), ritual shifts the weight or balance from the locutionary to the illocutionary function or force of ordinary speak-ing such that the latter comes to outweigh the former and moreover is wit-nessed or authorized by more than merely a single speaker and addressee. This is especially evident with respect to what Rappaport (1999) called ultimate sacred postulates, which are in effect semantically empty ('informationless') utterances, and hence devoid of locutionary function or referential meaning, that are charged with illocutionary force. As parts of liturgical orders each sacred postulate also carries the weight of multiple invocations within the imagined past and present community. Established and reiterated in ritual, ultimate sacred postulates offer sanctification to more mundane utterances, as in blessings, curses or oaths.

Performance includes a spectrum from fundamental and profoundly real-ized but highly formalized and specific ritual acts like the transubstantiation and ingestion of Christ, through those practices we refer to as simple eti-quette, to the illocutionary force of any and every utterance. One can be put under a description as a god or a fellow human being, an invited dinner guest or unwelcome neighbour, dignified or shamed. Performativity can transform tacit processes or understandings into explicit descriptions,[12] acts into facts, or the inchoate into structure. It consigns to the background the range of what is possible but unsaid or undone while foregrounding the specificity of what is said or done and must now be acknowledged as said and done. Within any given social field, the divisions can become more elaborate and the criteria more specific, producing various modes of refinement, the sorts of distinctions made evident in J.L. Austin's (1979) wonderful discussion of excuses or in Jane Austen's ironic attunement to social form.

Where I conducted fieldwork, from 1975 onwards in the western Indian Ocean island of Mayotte, exchanges of acts of Muslim prayer over and on behalf of one another were very common. But performativity is not uniformly positive. In Mayotte sorcery was sometimes described by lurid details of dancing naked on a new grave or bribing a spirit with a bloody sacrifice to do one's bidding. But in the end, it was understood as someone proactively taking responsibility for, and satisfaction from, the misfortunes of others, through a performative act (Lambek 1993: 262). An act of sorcery is a kind of decisive acknowledgement to oneself before the fact that, should so-and-so fall ill, I am happy to consider this my doing. This is a deliberate act, but it is an act, as philosophers say, of placing something under a description. As in Zande witchcraft, the act of sorcery in Mayotte is understood as distinct from the direct material causes of the misfortune, whether understood as operating through nature, termites, amoral spirits or God. However, the performative act is at one level of abstraction from material causality beyond what the Zande and Evans-Pritchard (1937) call witchcraft; it is not spontaneous or unrecognized by the agent, not discernible in the bowels of the sorcerer. Moreover, its direct effects lie only in the ethical, not the material realm; it does not produce the misfortune, only the accountability for it. In Mayotte, to take on the responsibility or satisfaction for another's misfortune is a deliberate act of judgment or acknowledgment instantiated by means of a specific kind of utterance. And, no doubt, as a deliberate act it occurs with far less frequency than certain other performative acts, namely diagnoses or accusations of sorcery, would suppose. Given the possibility of Schadenfreude, there is room for ambiguity as to what one might have liked to do, but unlike the Azande, who cannot be sure whether the accusation against them is unjustified, persons in Mayotte know whether they committed sorcery, that is, whether they committed themselves *to* sorcery. The catch is that in the face of accusation they have no means to prove their innocence.

I have been giving pre-eminence to ritual rather than to bureaucratic regimes of ethics and hence putting aside the question of the sort of historical break marked by Weber, Foucault or Asad. My 'framework of "ordinary ethics" … suggests that action is best [or first] understood in terms of the performative criteria which authorize it rather than in terms of an external body of thought which legitimates it' (Alex Beliaev, personal communication, 2012).

In sum, my argument for the immanence of ethics rests on the relationship between practice and performative acts. Practice and performance in my usage are not discrete phenomena but different modalities of action and different analytic lenses on it. While practice is conceptualized as relatively continuous and open, performance in the sense I use it here refers to acts that can be conceptualized as discrete, finite, precise, and as completed in the doing (though this does not preclude their repetition).[13] Muslim practice is constituted through performative utterances like the *b'ismillah*, which confer criteria on the segments of practice they initiate, whether starting a prayer, journey or meal. To borrow for one sentence from the language of cybernetics, performance is practice divided and marked digitally, practice is performance extended analogically. Hence the relationship of practice to performance is one of the continuous to the discontinuous, the open to the finite, the free to the determined, the uncertain to the certain, or the ambiguous to the definitive. By means of the performativity found in proclamations, people like uncertain bridegrooms or Azande accused of witchcraft no longer need to wonder about their actions but receive conclusive attribution and hence also a relatively clear framework with which to guide or interpret their subsequent practice.

I have been articulating practice, especially practical judgment, from the Aristotelian tradition, with a concept of performance, or rather performativeness, in Austin's sense. Performative acts provide the means or criteria according to which practical judgment is executed and distinct intentions or commitments are specified and clarified (Lambek 2010a). The utterance of a promise, say to show up for an event, is different from vague hopes that one will, and it can be further strengthened by swearing an oath. Promise and oath set up new relations between the parties involved, casting forward a moral space such that the relations between the parties are constituted by expectations and criteria through which subsequent practice will be articulated and evaluated, both by themselves and by others. It doesn't mean that the promise will be kept but it does mean that not keeping it will be judged as a more or less spectacular failure of some kind. Discrete performances emerge from and are marked within the stream of practice; simultaneously, they articulate the practice that follows from them (and sometimes retroactively what led up to them), putting people and relationships under a particular description and providing their practice with the criteria through which it may be ascertained, defined, appreciated and evaluated.[14]

The proclaimed marriage of Aristotle and Austin may appear a somewhat unusual performative event, though hopefully not an infelicitous one. My argument does not contradict the initial concern with virtuous practice or practical judgment but rather moves beyond mere description of judgment to grasp how the criteria that constitute specific practices are established and instantiated, that is, to grasp the conditions or criteria that make practical judgment possible in the first place and that shape particular stretches of practice. However, if performances articulate practice and make judgment possible and necessary, it is equally the case that new performances can only arise from the stream of practice, as products of practical judgment, for example, whether to address someone by a particular kin term or consult the oracle, how to acknowledge a gift or respond to a verbal address, when to perform an ancestral sacrifice, and so forth. In many instances, of course, access to authoritative consequential performance may be contested and constrained.

Social acts occur under a description or set of descriptions and initiate new descriptions, and we all operate with a set of criteria by which we can – or must – describe our own conduct, as well as that of others. One could distinguish relatively standard acts from contested and limited ones, as well as from surprising disruptions or contingent events – things like the arrival of Captain Cook, for example – that have no description to begin with or whose description may be fought over retroactively, even centuries later. The criteria that define acts as such or that are put into play in consequence of them are not universally shared, categorical (absolute) or entirely obvious; culture, history, religious traditions, public institutions, retroactive narrative and the relative power of distinct voices and interests articulate with whatever mental structures, forces and dispositions we have.

Many questions remain, for example the availability and specificity of distinct performative acts and the very large matter of the relationship of acting or doing to being, in both ordinary and exceptional forms of life. There is the perennial Jewish question of whether one is a Jew by virtue of birth, practice or interpellation; that is to say, which are the performative acts – or the orders or registers of such acts – that count? The same holds for hyphenated-Americans (and others) of all kinds and, in some conversations, for gender and sexuality, no less than for the matter of simple dignity. There is also the question of radically original acts and how beginnings are retroactively inscribed.[15]

Preliminary Conclusion

To sum up, before we can talk about moral engines, we need to know how we recognize what is good and distinguish it from what is not good, or less good. In order to do so we need criteria. So the question is, where do criteria for action and judgment – or for thinking about action and judgment – come from and how are they activated or put into play? I am less interested in whether they are given or constructed, universal or particular, derived from nature or from nurture, than in how they become foregrounded, relevant at particular times, places, events and circumstances. Insofar as the ethical depends on the establishment of specific criteria and commitment to them, it is intrinsic to registers of personhood, hence in the first instance kinship, and established by means of ritual, especially in what is constituted through liturgical orders and hierarchies of sanctity, hence of religion, and of contract and precedent, hence of law and citizenship. These overlapping fields, registers and orders of personhood and relationality provide the tracks along which moral engines can run. Ethics is not an autonomous realm but is always part of a broader landscape.

One track along which criteria and commitments emerge is the culturally constituted life cycle, the ways in which infants are socialized, biological beings come to be committed to one another in the relationships we call kinship, young people are initiated into various kinds of community membership, and adults, elders and ancestors are tasked with responsibility or granted deference. Such a perspective does not force us to distinguish the natural from the cultural but rather encourages us to look at how life unfolds by means of performative acts, from spontaneous responses between mother and child through the explicit and elaborated ones we call ritual. Ethics is simply an aspect of ordinary life, emerging in and through ordinary acts and shaping further acts. The ethical is intrinsic to the conjunction of language and action that constitutes ordinary human worlds, as inseparable from social action as mind is from body.

Harder questions include the following. Assuming that criteria do not remain stable and constant, what accounts for the presence, kind and differentiation of criteria? What enables or authorizes the performative acts that put criteria into play? And how is it that when criteria conflict or are incommensurable, some become more relevant or salient than others? Can we talk about contexts – social fields, cultures, historical periods, religious traditions or movements – in which there are more or fewer criteria in play? Can there be too few criteria, or too many? If criteria form a condition for moral thought and action, can they also inhibit or constrain it, in certain circumstances their very number or clutter getting in the way of moral insight? I am thinking here of the ways in which criteria constitute and elaborate social hierarchy, inhibit social mobility and produce shame or complacency as well as excellence.

Conversely, what disables performative acts or reduces their availability or consistency, such that there is a diminishment in the kinds and coherence of acts and the forms of fine ethical discrimination they provide, hence fewer criteria by which to orient and evaluate practice, exercise judgment or acknowledge one's own actions, commitments and relationships as well as those of others? The result would be not so much a rise in unethical or immoral behaviour (except possibly from an external perspective) as a loss of precision, a thinning or flattening of the ethical terrain, not Auschwitz but anomie. A broader question is what are the right sorts of criteria? Criteria need to articulate with one another and with the world. We might argue, for example, that there needs to be an attunement between available criteria and the sorts of tasks Erik Erikson (1950) attributed to the various phases of the life cycle, suitably calibrated to cultural differences.

Ethics then is not something found or generated entirely within us, spontaneous urges, needs or desires to care for the self or care for others, nor some force that comes from the outside like fear of punishment or social shaming, nor yet is it described by some intersection or fusion of the internal and external, like guilt or conscience. These models each place culture and social action at some distance from the individual. I begin instead with a kind of Weberian or Geertzian understanding that human being is itself always already culturally constituted and that meaning and meaningfulness are critical to existence, and further, and more specifically, that what Geertz calls models of the world and models for living in it must reasonably coincide. Meanings and models are not simply in the air, not purely ideal; rather, they are enacted and re-enacted in performative acts, through illocutionary force. Hence to move to another (mixed) set of predecessors, like Durkheim and Wittgenstein, I see ritual as intrinsic to society and to human being in the world with others.

Coda on Irony

The final reason I speak of the immanence of the ethical is the human recognition of the limits to, or the limitations of, what I have said about the conjunction of performance and practice. Human beings acknowledge the inevitability of difficulty, lapses, competing obligations, incommensurable, imposed and arbitrary criteria, and sometimes the inadequacy or sheer absence of any criteria with which to face a given situation. These matters have been the subject of much tragedy, both written and lived. A poignant modern instance is *Sophie's Choice*,[16] in which a mother has no criteria for selecting which of her children will die and no criteria for justifying her choice, hence an act she is unable to acknowledge.

Thus, if the subject of ethics, qua philosophical, poetic or religious discourse, must account first for the possibility and necessity in the human situation for discriminating what to do, it must also explore the void or tragedy of the exhaustion or absence of criteria with which to make judgments and our scepticism concerning them. Making criteria available is part of the work of culture (or social life) and a feature of action. Conversely and concomitantly, recognition of the limits of criteria and of the impossibility of ever being completely or consistently ethical (and, paradoxically, sometimes failing in its own recognition of impossibility) is part of the work of philosophy, that is, of ethical reflection, and of therapy. In both making criteria available, unquestionable and authoritative and in reflecting on their limits, religion – or the kinds of practices and reflections we now place under the name of religion – has played a central role. The human condition is not a simple state of nature and it is not a state of innocence. In this respect, the expulsion from the Garden of Eden offers a more sophisticated account than most evolutionary psychology.

At the threshold of necessity and impossibility, ethical recognition is not only tragic but ironic.[17] Witchcraft, in Evans-Pritchard's famous argument, is supposed to explain unfortunate events. But it also raises a good deal of uncertainty. One cannot know before the fact who the witch is, or where and when a witch will strike next. One cannot even know whether one may be accused of being a witch oneself, or even whether the accusation might be correct. In fact, the presumption or diagnosis of witchcraft raises more questions than it answers. Who was the witch responsible for this event? Who are the witches among us? Why, really, do they act as they do? What, actually, am *I* capable of doing? (Lambek 2003: 7). The accused responds by acknowledging the possibility that he is a witch. The ethical scene here affords a kind of irony that is not merely the irony that we cannot know the intentions of others or that as we plan our life projects and programmes, they are being undermined by other forces. Rather, it is the recognition that we cannot fully know our own intentions. This is of course not restricted to the Azande or to witchcraft. As Paul Antze has aptly put it,

> If it is true, as Freud says, that much of our life is driven by impulses lying outside of consciousness, and that the unconscious consists precisely in what is *opposed* or *contrary*, what is 'incompatible with the ego,' then it becomes much harder to be sure what our actions mean or even who is acting. To what extent are we the authors of anything we do? Can we ever know our own intentions? Does knowing make a difference? (Antze 2003: 104, emphasis in original)

Or, as I have put it (after Alexander Nehamas), '*What irony frequently throws into question is intentionality itself*' (Lambek 2003: 10, emphasis in original). Whatever the status we ascribe to the unconscious, there is the question of how we find ourselves in the language games we do and how we face or transcend the arbitrariness of the claims we have made as to who we are (Lear 2011). For Lear this can be aspirational rather than tragic.[18] No account of the ethical would be complete without recognizing these matters. The questions are how ethical subjects recognize them, how discursive forms, rituals and therapeutic or disciplinary practices enable or conceal them, and how claims of moral effectiveness or fulfilment may contain their own undoing.

Here is a final illustration of a limit to the arguments I have made so far. In a recent essay, Didier Fassin (2014) takes up a documentary film about a Palestinian mother whose child, suffering from a life-threatening illness, is taken to an Israeli hospital.[19] The mother thanks the doctors, wishing for her son to be cured so that he can grow up to become a suicide bomber. Fassin reads her statement as performative, but equally thinks that it is unclear *what kind of performative* is being enacted. There is a level of irony in the sense that the mother herself may not know what she wants or means, at least not consistently, or that she is saying different things to different audiences, perhaps in different voices. While a clear performative act can establish criteria, an ambiguous one can hardly do the same. The example illustrates how one and the same utterance can look different depending on whether it is understood in reference to pre-existing criteria, thus as on-going practice, in my sense, or as establishing new criteria, as performative, but to what effect. This returns us to Rappaport's gradation between ordinary acts and the more elaborate constructions we call ritual and liturgical orders and why significant performatives are embedded within the latter – both to abstract them more conclusively from the stream of practice and so that participants and witnesses can know precisely what kind of performative acts they are jointly engaged in and whether the felicity conditions are met.

The ambivalence of the Palestinian woman adds a final point. If I have tried to articulate a connection between Aristotle on practice and Austin on action, the third figure lurking in this chapter has been Freud.[20] I cannot articulate the relationship between Aristotle or Kierkegaard and Freud as lucidly as Lear, nor the relationship between Austin and Freud as subtly as Cavell, but like Cavell and Lear I want to articulate philosophy with psychoanalysis (and both with anthropology), in a way that doesn't mistake mind and emotion for finally clear-cut cognitive, social, neurological or genetic forces or mechanisms. Instead, 'The pervasive irony of the human condition [lies in] the unfathomability of the sources of our judgment and action' (Lambek 2010b: 722).

Michael Lambek is professor of anthropology and Canada Research Chair at the University of Toronto Scarborough. In 2016–2017 he was a fellow at the Wissenschaftskolleg zu Berlin, and interim editor of *Hau*. Relevant publications include *The Weight of the Past* (Palgrave Macmillan, 2002), *The Ethical Condition* (Chicago, 2015), *Four Lectures on Ethics* (with Veena Das, Webb Keane and Didier Fassin, Hau Books, 2015), and *Ordinary Ethics* (ed. Fordham 2010).

Notes

I dedicate this chapter to Saba Mahmood, a brilliant, forceful thinker and pioneer in the anthropology of ethics, politics, and religion.

1. My work is supported by the Social Sciences and Humanities Research Council of Canada and the Canada Research Chairs programme. Earlier versions were presented at the Institute for Advanced Study, Princeton; the Department of Anthropology, Berkeley; and the Institute on Culture, Religion, and World Affairs, Boston University. My thanks go to Didier Fassin, Nancy Scheper-Hughes and Bob Hefner, respectively, as well as to very attentive audiences. Since the Aarhus conference, much of the material in this chapter has been considerably extended and developed as 'The Ethical Condition', Chapter One of my book, *The Ethical Condition: Essays on Action, Person, and Value* (Chicago: University of Chicago Press, 2015). Many passages here are similar or reproduced verbatim, with permission of the University of Chicago Press.
2. I mean of course function in the mathematical sense, not the organic or Radcliffe-Brownian one.
3. Veena Das (2007) draws a perceptive distinction between voice and volubility, a point I have been reminded of by Anna Kruglova (2015), who is putting it to excellent use. My ideas about ethics have developed in conjunction with a continuing interpretation of a body of ethnographic material from fieldwork conducted in the western Indian Ocean: in a village on the island of Mayotte since 1975; and in the city of Majunga in northwest

Madagascar since the early 1990's. Attention to Malagasy spirit possession has privileged in my thinking questions of voice and action, that is, of ethics, first, because possession is itself a kind of meta-commentary, at once serious and ironic, about personhood and ethical life; second, because it is an intensified form of living with others; and third, because it sets up the challenge of showing how even speech and action conducted in a state of dissociation and as someone other than oneself is nonetheless deeply ethically informed. For one thing, it heightens questions of the relationship of action to passion that I take to be central to ethics but do not take up here.

4. Moreover, there is no consistent application of the terms ethics and morality, some writers applying them in more or less directly opposite senses from other writers.

5. It could therefore be said that adherents of piety movements like those described by Mahmood (2005) act like good Durkheimians.

6. For further discussion of practice and incommensurability, see Lambek 1993, and on the distinction between choice and judgment, Lambek 2008.

7. *Phronesis* entails a conjunction of doing the right thing, feeling the right way about it and doing it for the right reasons; action, intention and feelings should be aligned. My thanks to Simon Lambek (personal communication) for phrasing it so succinctly for me.

8. Where Keane (2010) places justification – the giving of reasons – as the distinguishing feature of ethics, I see it as secondary to judgment.

9. The temporality of practice is a lesson learned from Bourdieu (1977), after Mauss.

10. However, to follow from Weber, if performative acts like those of the Zande oracle reduce uncertainty or produce certainty, that is not to say they alleviate anxiety or that their very existence may not produce or enhance it. Anticipating the results of the oracle would certainly not be a matter of equanimity for anyone whose name might be invoked.

11. I leave aside the perlocutionary; however, the opposition or tension might be compared with Plato's conflict between philosophy and poetry (locutionary and perlocutionary).

12. Maurice Bloch (personal communication, 24 August 2013) challenges this point insofar as 'The whole point about performatives is that they create something that does not exist before the performance. So they can't possibly make explicit something which exists elsewhere'. But I am saying that rendering the tacit into the explicit is precisely a matter of creating something new.

13. Elsewhere I speak of taboos as 'continuous performatives' and such a usage might be closer to Butler on gender or Goffman on everyday life. These usages are still closer to my depiction of performance than of practice in the current chapter. In Lear's terms (2011) they are all 'pretending'.

14. In a somewhat different, possibly confusing, but not contradictory usage, 'performances' could be individual occurrences or instances of particular practices, where a 'practice' signifies such genres of acts as naming, thanking, accusing, blessing, marrying, initiating, terminating and so forth. Thus Harvey Sacks (1985) can write of 'doing "being ordinary"'.

15. See Faubion (2011) on radical acts, Arendt (1998) on narration, and Lambek (2007) on sacrifice as beginning.

16. In the book by William Styron and subsequently the film, directed by Alan J. Pakula, a mother must decide which of her two children to save and which to give up to the murderers at a Nazi death camp.

17. On the irony of ethics or the ethics of irony, Kierkegaard is no doubt the master. Like spirit mediums or a good novelist, he makes his points through an ironic play of voices. For a recent foray into this terrain, see Lear (2011) and also Nehamas (1998), whose otherwise excellent philosophical account of irony largely omits Kierkegaard.

18. Lear writes of irony as 'pretense-transcending aspiring' (2011: 20) and as 'a peculiar form of *committed* reflection' (21, his emphasis).

19. Shlomi Eldar, *Precious Life*.

20. Arendt on action is also buried here.

References

Antze, Paul. 2003. 'Illness as Irony in Psychoanalysis', in Michael Lambek and Paul Antze (eds), *Illness and Irony: On the Ambiguity of Suffering in Culture*. New York: Berghahn Books, pp. 102–21.

Arendt, Hannah. 1998 [1958]. *The Human Condition*. Chicago: University of Chicago Press.

Asad, Talal. 2003. *Formations of the Secular: Christianity, Islam, Modernity*. Stanford: Stanford University Press.

Austin, J.L. 1976. *How To Do Things with Words*. Oxford: Oxford University Press.

_____. 1979. 'A Plea for Excuses', in O. Urmson and G.J. Warnock (eds), *Philosophical Papers*. New York: Oxford University Press, pp. 175–204.

Bloch, Maurice. 2004. *Ritual History and Power*. New York: Berg.

Bourdieu, Pierre. 1977. *Outline of a Theory of Practice*. Cambridge: Cambridge University Press.

Cavell, Stanley. 1976. *Must We Mean What We Say?* Cambridge: Cambridge University Press.

_____. 2005. 'Responses', in Russell Goodman (ed.), *Contending with Stanley Cavell*. Oxford: Oxford University Press, pp. 157–76.

_____. 2010. *Little Did I Know*. Stanford: Stanford University Press.

Das, Veena. 2007. *Violence and the Descent into the Ordinary*. Berkeley: University of California Press.

Durkheim, Emile. 1973. *Emile Durkheim on Morality and Society*, ed. R. Bellah. Chicago: University of Chicago Press.

Erikson, Erik. 1950. *Childhood and Society*. New York: Norton.

Evans-Pritchard, E.E. 1937. *Witchcraft, Oracles and Magic among the Azande*. Oxford: Clarendon.

Fassin, Didier. 2014. 'In Praise of Treason: The Parallel Lives of Philosophy and Anthropology', in Veena Das, Michael D. Jackson, Arthur Kleinman, Bhrigupati Singh (eds.), *The Ground Between: Anthropologists Engage Philosophy*. Durham, NC: Duke University Press.

Faubion, James. 2011. *An Anthropology of Ethics*. Cambridge: Cambridge University Press.

Hacking, Ian. 1999. *The Social Construction of What?* Cambridge, MA: Harvard University Press.

Keane, Webb. 2010. 'Minds, Surfaces, and Reasons in the Anthropology of Ethics', in M. Lambek (ed.), *Ordinary Ethics: Anthropology, Language, and Action*. New York: Fordham University Press, pp. 64–83.

Kruglova, Anna. 2015. 'Anything Can Happen: Everyday Morality and Social Theory in Russia'. Ph.D. thesis, University of Toronto.

Laidlaw, James. 2014. *The Subject of Virtue: An Anthropology of Ethics and Freedom*. Cambridge: Cambridge University Press.

Lambek, M. 1993. *Knowledge and Practice in Mayotte: Local Discourses of Islam, Sorcery, and Spirit Possession*. Toronto: University of Toronto Press.

_____. 2003. 'Introduction', in Michael Lambek and Paul Antze (ed.), *Illness and Irony: On the Ambiguity of Suffering in Culture*. New York: Berghahn Books, pp. 1–19.

_____. 2007. 'Sacrifice and the Problem of Beginning: Reflections from Sakalava Mythopraxis', *Journal of the Royal Anthropological Institute* 13(1): 19–38.

_____. 2008. 'Virtue and Value', *Anthropological Theory* 8(2): 133–57.

_____. 2010a. 'Towards an Ethics of the Act', in Michael Lambek (ed.), *Ordinary Ethics: Anthropology, Language, and Action*. New York: Fordham University Press, pp. 39–63.

_____. 2010b. 'How To Make Up One's Mind: Reason, Passion, and Ethics in Spirit Possession', *University of Toronto Quarterly* 79(2), Special issue on *Models of Mind*, ed. Marlene Goldman and Jill Matus, pp. 720–41.

_____. 2015. 'The Ethical Condition', in Michael Lambek (ed.), *The Ethical Condition: Essays on Action, Person, and Value*. Chicago: University of Chicago Press, pp. 1–39.

Laugier, Sandra. 2005. 'Rethinking the Ordinary: Austin after Cavell', in Russell Goodman (ed.), *Contending with Stanley Cavell*. Oxford: Oxford University Press, pp. 82–99.

Lear, Jonathan. 2000. *Happiness, Death, and the Remainder of Life*. Cambridge, MA: Harvard University Press.

_____. 2011. *A Case for Irony*. Cambridge, MA: Harvard University Press.

Macpherson, C.B. 1973. *Democratic Theory: Essays in Retrieval*. Oxford: Clarendon.

Mahmood, Saba. 2005. *Politics of Piety*. Princeton: Princeton University Press.

Mattingly, Cheryl. 2012. 'Two Virtue Ethics and the Anthropology of Morality', *Anthropological Theory* 12: 161–84.

Nehamas, Alexander. 1998. *The Art of Living*. Berkeley: University of California Press.

Rappaport, Roy. 1999. *Ritual and Religion in the Making of Humanity*. Cambridge: Cambridge University Press.

Sacks, Harvey. 1985. 'On Doing "Being Ordinary"', in *Structures of Social Action*. Cambridge: Cambridge University Press, pp. 413–29.

Sidnell, Jack. 2010. 'The Ordinary Ethics of Everyday Talk', in M. Lambek (ed.), *Ordinary Ethics: Anthropology, Language, and Action*. New York: Fordham University Press, pp. 123–39.

8

Where in the World are Values?
Exemplarity and Moral Motivation

Joel Robbins

As will quickly become apparent, this is a chapter about values. It is concerned with providing a socially and psychologically realistic answer to the question of where people find values in the world. I also mean it to be a contribution to the rapidly growing anthropological discussion of morality. With a few notable exceptions, anthropologists only began to discuss morality and ethics systematically in the last decade or so, but they have quickly made up for lost time and are currently producing a large number of studies in this area (for a wide-ranging recent account, see Laidlaw 2013; for a partial review of some important issues in the emerging literature, see Robbins 2012a). In general terms, I want to suggest that the topic of values should be central to this developing discussion (Robbins 2012b). In the course of writing this chapter, however, I have found that in working out the problem of where in the world people find values, I have had little space to explicitly discuss the link between values and morality. Given this, I thought I might mention here at the outset that I follow Durkheim (1974) in defining moral facts as ones that awaken in people a combined sense of both duty and desire. It is values, I think, that account, at least in part, for the desire part of that mixture – the desire we have to do what is good or, put otherwise, our moral motivation. What people actually do will depend not only on how they balance the competing desires different values awaken within them, but on how they balance these desires with the feelings of duty different moral facts also arouse. For this reason, the relationship between what people value and what they do by way of carrying out moral actions is very complex. But in the background of the chapter that follows is the notion that there is some relationship between values, desires and moral actions that is worth investigating, and the linked idea that for this reason values are, in the terms of this collection, important moral engines that have the ability to act as drivers of people's moral behaviours.

This is an absurdly compressed and rough sketch of the moral social psychology that underlies this chapter. It is a moral social psychology that gives an important place to values, and in order to be both psychologically and socially realistic as a whole, this moral psychology needs to include a psychologically and socially realistic account of how people come to experience values as engines of moral force. This kind of account is what I am working towards in the current chapter. Up until several decades ago, anthropologists and many sociologists felt they had a secure answer to the questions of where values exist in the world and where people encounter them. This answer asserted that human beings are cultural animals, values are part of culture, and people receive their values by being socialized into cultures. But the recent loss of confidence in the culture concept has rendered this answer less persuasive than it once was. I begin, then, by discussing the social scientific loss of faith in the notion of culture and the problem this raises of how to talk about where values exist in the world. Having started there, I will not from that point on say much about morality, but I hope I have said enough to indicate that it is the horizon towards which my arguments here are ultimately heading.

If one looks around anthropology today, it is hard to miss that we are in the midst of what one might call a strongly anti-cultural moment. If the study of culture is about observing and explaining repeated patterns of behaviour and the recurring complexes of meaning or understanding that shape them, then an anthropology that is all about emergence, novelty and ever-shifting assemblages or networks of people, things and ideas cannot but reject the notion. Similarly, if we hold that the world is created anew every moment, culture is too slow, too heavy, too plodding to be of much analytic use. Better to approach our object of study by developing models of process and becoming if we want to account for a world we assume is much more fluid than the world of culture ever was, or was ever meant to be.

I realize this is a very hurried account of what is at most only one part of the contemporary anthropological zeitgeist. By way of fleshing it out, I will later try to give a slightly more developed account of one route anthropology followed in arriving at this anti-cultural point. But I want to allude to this aspect of the zeitgeist briefly at the outset because the fact that this anti-cultural emphasis is gaining momentum at present – that it appears to be attracting a lot of anthropology's best theoretical energies these days – provides an important frame for the argument I want to make here. Indeed, this argument arises from the fact that while I find myself still relatively happy with the concept of culture – especially with that version of the concept in which a cultural anthropological appreciation of its more idealist aspects is complemented by the tools linguistic anthropology affords us for paying greater attention to how it is realized and reproduced in interaction – I also recognize that culture is a harder and harder sell these days. Given that I lean in this contrary or even old fashioned cultural direction, I have to ask myself what someone with these inclinations can productively say now.

I have had two different impulses concerning how to respond to this question. One would be to launch a full-fledged defence of the concept of culture, working along the way to call into question the importance if not the existence of the emergent and fluid aspects of the world by stressing, among other things, the massively structured aspects of the lives we do in fact mostly live. In my quieter moments, I realize that mounting a full-scale defence of the culture concept along these lines would be a big job, perhaps taking up so much time that the moment at which it makes sense to offer it would have passed by the time I was ready to put it in play. Moreover, it may in any case be too early to undertake such a defence. Better perhaps to wait until anti-cultural anthropology has matured enough that its strongest arguments have risen to the surface and can be fully identified and directly taken on. And finally, I have a nagging sense that perhaps it would be best not to move immediately to defending the notion of culture against these attacks, but rather to begin by asking what new things one might learn about culture by exploring some of the issues they raise.

Mindful of these concerns, and intrigued in particular by the possibility that one might learn something new about culture by giving recent anti-cultural criticisms their due, my second, more modest impulse has won out. This one points to the project of asking how, assuming that culture may not be quite as powerful a force in shaping social life as anthropologists once thought, we might be able to account in new ways for the existence of some of the most important cultural things we were once so adept at using the culture concept to identify and analyse. Some years ago, I wrote an essay in this vein asking how we might still think about ritual in Durkheimian terms from the point of view of theoretical frameworks that hold that there is no such thing as society (Robbins 2010). Here I want to take on another classic object of cultural study – values – and ask if we might discover where in social life they exist. This becomes a pressing question once we set aside, at least for the purposes of argument, the claim that they exist within an enduring, routinely reproduced phenomenon called culture.

As it happens, the question of where values might be said to exist is not a new one; it arose well before our current anti-cultural debates, emerging at roughly the same time in fact as some of the ideas that eventually contributed to forming the now contested modern notion of culture. At the risk of remaining a bit longer at a relatively abstract level of argument, I want to review some of the history of this question of where values exist as a way of moving into my main argument.

It is important to recognize at the outset that the use of the term value with which we are familiar is not ancient.[1] It first takes off in the middle of the nineteenth century, when philosophers pick it up from political economists (Schnädelbach 1984: 161). From that point on, discussions about the nature of values play a key role in German philosophy in particular, and in the emerging social sciences as well, until the 1920s, after which they largely fade from the social scientific scene outside of their original home in economics. For our purposes, it is important to note that values became a preoccupation in the late nineteenth century just as the scientific-materialist worldview finally entrenched itself as the dominant modern understanding of the nature of existence. In that worldview, all that exists is matter, and matter is in itself devoid of meaning or purpose. What exists is not good or bad, beautiful or ugly, true or false (the classic triumvirate of value dimensions) – it simply is. In this worldview, as we all know, there is no intellectually legitimate way to move from 'is' to 'ought' – from fact to value. This way of construing matters left philosophers with a key question – what is the mode of existence of values? If the good, or the beautiful, or the true by definition cannot exist, since what exists is matter and matter is meaningless or without value in itself, then what is their mode of being in the world? It is this question that gets the philosophy of value off the ground.

As social scientists, we are most familiar with this set of problems from Weber, who was steeped in some of the German debates about the nature of value I alluded to above. He bequeathed to the social sciences the enormously influential view, one that comes out of this philosophical problematic (and ultimately out of Protestantism, but that is another story – see Albrow 1990; Scheler 1973: 67), that the world (including human existence) considered in material terms is a chaotic flux which only acquires meaningful shape when human beings impose their values upon it. In this view, values exist in human thought and are expressed in human action, and such action in turn orders the world in ways humans can comprehend. The claim that values are ideas that motivate action is thus one answer to the question of the mode of being of values. But as an answer to the question of how values exist that aims to explain why human beings do not live in chaotic, meaningless worlds, it leaves one problem unresolved. This is the problem of why it is that each human being does not impose his/her own unique set of values on the world, leading social life to take the form of a cacophony of opposed projects each based on wholly singular meaningful structurings of the chaos of material existence. This would only lead to another kind of unformed meaninglessness – a human war of all against all over whose meaningful orderings will rule the day. The anthropological notion of culture is a solution to this second problem of how values as ideas that motivate action can create an orderly world, for it suggests that values are shared between members of a society. People who share values will, on this model, all impose order on the chaos of existence in similar ways, thus allowing them to live relatively orderly lives together.

Various versions of this cultural solution to the problem of how values exist in the world and order it in meaningful ways served anthropology well for much of the twentieth century (which is perhaps why the issue of values has not of late been a central concern in the discipline). But in the last twenty-five years or so this cultural solution has in many quarters been abandoned. For a large number of contemporary anthropologists, the proximate cause of this abandonment has been the postmodern turn – a phrase which I realize now cannot but sound somewhat quaint, almost nostalgic, but which does usefully name an intellectual movement the effects of which still mark the intellectual scene today, at least in anthropology.

It was the postmodern turn which made notions of shared culture seem too deterministic, too disrespectful of the reality of chaos and the true individuality of persons, each of whom many anthropologists came to believe does have his or her own individual position in and perspective on the world. In a longer view, one that is just now coming into focus, it may well prove to be the case that the abandonment of notions of shared culture was in fact the result of another strong turn of the screw of the scientific worldview and its denial of the meaningfulness of what exists, a turn to which the postmodern critique of meaning and structure unwittingly lent a hand and which is evidenced, for example, in the contemporary ascendency of scientizing models across the social sciences and humanities, including in many of the anti-cultural theoretical positions with which I began. But regardless of the reasons for our current situation, it is certainly true that these days many anthropologists are not inclined to see the idea of shared culture as a good answer to the question of how values exist in the world, and are in anti-cultural terms more interested in documenting the world's chaotic or emergent aspects than its orderly and predictable ones. What I want to propose here is that if we accept that this is the case – that values are not likely to be as fully shared as anthropologists once supposed because we can no longer assume they are part of an enduring shared phenomenon called culture – then we will need to face anew the question of where in the world values exist. In providing a fresh answer to this question, I want to suggest that values exist in the first instance in what I am going to call exemplars or examples, or at least that people first encounter them in the world in this form.

What, then, is an example? I ultimately want to suggest that examples are concretely existing realizations of single values in their fullest forms. Having offered this definition, I realize that it is going to take some argumentative work to make it convincing, or even comprehensible, so let me start a bit further back in my chain of reasoning. A good place to turn at the outset is the work of the Italian philosopher Alessandro Ferrara (2008). In a book entitled *The Force of the Example*, Ferrara argues that we easily recognize two kinds of forces in the world. There is the force of what exists, or what he calls the force of things (1). And there is also, at least for human beings, the force of 'what ought to be the case – the force of ideas' (2, emphasis removed). These two forces, Ferarra recognizes, align with the modern dichotomy between fact and value, or the real and the ideal (ix). But as we have seen, this leaves us with the problem of the nature of the existence of values, for if the ideal or values are defined precisely by not existing as material things in the world, then where do they exist? And if they exist only in people's minds, why is the world not a chaotic mess of persons each pursuing wholly unrelated projects? Though

Ferrara's questions are close to these, he does not pose them in precisely this way. But he nonetheless does offer us some help in answering them when he proposes that the two sides of the dichotomy between what is and what should be needs to be supplemented by a middle term – 'the force of what is as it should be or the force of the example' (2–3, emphasis removed). '[T]he force of the example', he goes on to assert, 'is the force of what exerts appeal on us … by virtue of the singular and exceptional congruence that what is exemplary realizes and exhibits between the order of its own reality and the order of the normativity to which it responds' (3). To put this in the terms I will use from now on, an example is a realization of a value in the world, and it solicits our attention for precisely this reason.

When I claim that an example is the realization of a value in the world, I mean this in a somewhat special sense. In some respects, all human action realizes, or at least aims to realize, something the actor defines as valuable in the context in which the actor undertakes it. This is a very common view of human motivation and I do not intend to counter it here. Given this view, is it also right to say that every action, as the realization of a value in the world, is exemplary? If this is true, then I cannot be saying anything very useful about examples.

As a way around this problem, I want to sketch much too briefly an account of how values operate in action that suggests that most actions, even if motivated by values, do not fully realize any one of them and are thus not exemplary. Let me start by asserting that in any social milieu there are numerous values in play. I am going to take this claim about the plurality of values in any given society for granted here, rather than argue for it (as I have done elsewhere – Robbins 2013), and I hope that readers find it plausible enough on the basis of what they know about social life to let it stand for the purposes of my present argument. Now, given that in every society there exist a number of values, we can go on to note that some of these values work together such that realizing one value helps you to realize another one you count as even higher and so on, in what Nancy Munn (1986) refers to as chains of value transformation. For example, on Gawa Island, Papua New Guinea – a society in which people participate in the system of Kula exchange made famous by Malinowski – if you are a man you plant taro and yam gardens to give over to the family of the husband of one of your female relatives so that this family can eventually give you a Kula valuable and a canoe that you can further exchange along Kula paths in order to increase your range of spatio-temporal control and thus bolster your fame (Munn 1986: 123–29). At each step you are acting in terms of a value, though the ultimate purpose of the whole chain is only given by the final transformation that increases your fame, an outcome which realizes the chain's overall value. Much of the time, you are realizing only lower level values in actions that will have been of limited import if the chain is never completed.

By contrast with sets of values that link up in chains of value transformation, there are also values that do not work together in this way, but rather conflict, such that realizing one precludes realizing the other. Among some

Papua New Guinea groups, for example, giving the gift of a whole pig to one's affines so that they will reciprocate with a gift of access to a particular piece of land precludes giving that same pig to one's clan-mates to secure support in disputes. When faced with an exclusive choice between values of this kind, people often hedge, giving some smaller gifts of pork in each direction, realizing both values partially but neither one of them fully.

In both of these kinds of value relationship – that of value chains and that of value conflicts – values are often, perhaps usually, compromised in action. Most actions either do not realize a value that is in itself of great importance, but only one that is a link in a chain oriented toward realizing another value, or they are driven by a mix of partial value considerations. This is why not every action is exemplary, even if all actions are motivated by values.[2]

Against the background of this argument that most actions do not realize peoples' most important values, or realize them only in limited ways, I want to suggest that some actions stand out for accomplishing the opposite. There are some actions or products of action that realize important values in their fullest forms, or at least come close to this. It is these actions and their products that become exemplary and that have, as Ferrara puts it, a 'force' that solicits a special kind of attention or demand for appreciation from people. Examples, on this account, are social forms that realize a value to such a full extent. It is as embodied in examples in this way that values most forcefully or tangibly exist in social life.

Up to this point I have been discussing the tie between examples and values in relation to exemplary actions taken as a general phenomenon. But to render this argument realistic, we have to acknowledge that the appearance of examples is not random throughout social life. They do not occur, or at least people do not tend to encounter them, just anywhere and as performed by just anyone. In any given society there are specific people – living or historical – who are well known for having cultivated the ability to realize one or other value, and who thus stand as exemplary in relation to it. So one way people encounter examples in social life is in the form of exemplary persons. I also want to argue that perfected realizations of value can exist in certain kinds of institutions. Such value-perfected institutions most often take the form, I think, of rituals. Exemplifications of value probably also find more or less routine existence elsewhere in social life, for example in myth (Scheler 1987: 146). But for present purposes, I will focus on exemplary people and rituals by way of trying to sketch in ethnographic terms where both we as analysts and the people we study find values existing in social life.

I will start with exemplary persons. In thinking about such people, we can draw on the work of Max Scheler, one of the most important of the late nineteenth- to early twentieth-century philosophers and sociologists of value. In his essay 'Exemplars of Person and Leaders', Scheler defines exemplars, much as we have here, as the coming together of an idea of a value and a person (134), or, as he also expresses his point, as 'the *cast of a value formed by personhood*, using 'cast' here in the sense of a mould into which personhood must be fit in order to realize itself as valuable (139, emphasis in original). 'We consider our exemplars', Scheler further explains, 'as something good, perfect, and something which ought to be' (133). Moreover, we relate to exemplars most importantly on the basis of our 'faith' in them. This is not a religious faith, Scheler is quick to add, but faith 'in the sense of a well-founded, evidential and true love, and of the full understanding of the knowledge of the exemplar and his value' (144). Scheler's reference to love here is not casual, for he famously developed a phenomenology of value perception in which the emotions, and love and hate most prominently among them, are the 'organs' that perceive values in the world. But I refer to Scheler's claim that we love our exemplars not as an opening to a discussion of its elaborate theoretical grounding, but rather to connect it with Ferrara's claim that the exemplary exerts a force, that it draws us in and solicits a response. I will try to convince you that this holds up ethnographically in a moment. But to conclude laying out Scheler's ideas, let me just add that it is on the basis of the connections such love forges and the motivations it provides that people come to strive to realize values in themselves. '[I]t is as if', Scheler puts it, 'human beings pull *themselves* up by such *interhuman* exemplary strings' (143, emphasis in original). This is why for Scheler, 'What has a forming and grafting effect on our souls is not an abstract, universal moral rule but always, and only, a clear and intuitive grasp of the exemplarity of the person' (134).

The approach to examining the existence and force of values in social life that Scheler has helped me to lay out encourages us to look ethnographically at which persons people in the societies we study treat as exemplary and at the values they realize. Where I did fieldwork, among the Urapmin of Papua New Guinea, the cast of exemplary characters is not in broad outlines hard to identify; there are some people the Urapmin talk about far more than others, report dreams about with great frequency, and clearly orient to in thinking about the possibilities life presents to them. Because the Urapmin as a rule do not casually gossip, the fact that they regularly discuss the doings of this relatively small group of people is strong evidence of how important they are to them. Before looking at the exemplary quality of these characters in some detail, however, it will be useful for me to briefly introduce Urapmin society and the most general values that give it shape.

Finding Values among the Urapmin of Papua New Guinea

Urapmin is a community of approximately 390 people located in Papua New Guinea's West Sepik Province. I have elsewhere described the primary traditional value that Urapmin people orient to as that of relationalism – a value that defines the creation and maintenance of relationships as the most important things people do (Robbins 2004). While one can argue that relationalism is common throughout Melanesia – as evidenced, for example, by the strong tendency for people living in the region to find relation-making and maintaining exchanges the most worthwhile of social activities – its preeminence is perhaps even more to the fore in societies like the Urapmin which are cognatic, a form of social organization that renders people constantly aware of their need to create relations of residence, realized kinship, work, and the like, none of which are constituted by structural rules that might cause them to appear of their own accord. Households, villages, work groups, soccer teams, churches and all other relational assemblages shift composition regularly in Urapmin, and everyone recognizes that it takes relational work to put them together and keep them going. For this reason, relationships are what the Urapmin are working to produce most of the time.

Just beneath relationalism in the traditional Urapmin value hierarchy are two values that can, when realized in particular ways, support people's relational efforts. These are values that the Urapmin refer to as those of 'wilfulness' and 'lawfulness'. One's will (*san*) is the desiring part of the person, and it is the part that 'pushes' people to try to bring others into relationships and to keep them oriented to those relationships. It is a father's wilfulness, for example, that leads him to push his son and his son's new wife to live with him, rather than with her family, and then continues to push the new couple to garden with his family most days, rather than with the wife's relatives. In contrast to such wilfulness, which aims to create new relationships or enforce the maintenance of existing relationships against the claims of competing ones, lawfulness consists in honouring the hold each already existing relationship has over one's energy: a hold each relationship expresses by its demand that the legitimate expectations it establishes – most generally expectations for reciprocity and equivalent investment of attention – be met before any other relationship is attended to or any new relationship is established.

In order to fully serve the value of relationalism, people have to temper the full realization of the values of wilfulness and lawfulness. Developed to its furthest extent, the value of wilfulness constantly creates new relationships, letting older ones flame out as neglect and dispute take their toll. Lawfulness, for its part, when expressed most fully, meets only the demands of existing relationships and produces nothing new – an outcome that is equally untenable in a cognatic world where no relations can be assumed and none of necessity will last, and thus all have to be wilfully made in the first instance. Given that an excess of either wilfulness and lawfulness is ultimately counter-productive in relation to the paramount value of relationalism, the trick for most Urapmin is to learn to temper the full expression of either of these two subordinate values, balancing the exercise of will in creating relationships with a commitment to lawfulness in maintaining them.

What I have presented in a nutshell is a basic sketch of three of the key values traditionally recognized by the Urapmin, and I have laid out the hierarchy that holds between them, such that wilfulness and lawfulness, though each valued in itself to some extent, are ultimately subordinated to relationalism and usually only partially realized in the course of social life. But the argument about the mode of existence of values that this chapter has been laying out suggests that for people to come to know wilfulness and lawfulness as values, they need to encounter them in fully developed form as embodied in exemplars somewhere in their social worlds. People who exemplify these values in this sense, I want to suggest, are some of the ones that Urapmin people talk and dream about all the time.

Take Semis, for example. Semis is a man for whom many Urapmin feel great affection. He is most of the time a paragon of lawfulness. In 1977 the Urapmin converted themselves without the aid of missionaries to a vigorous version of charismatic Christianity that came to them in a revival movement that swept through Papua New Guinea. I cannot here tell the story of how the Urapmin became in their own understanding a completely Christian community at that time. But to understand how Semis lives his life and the bond many people feel to him as an exemplar, it helps to know that he was one of the leading figures in the revival, bravely helping to carry out the difficult and dangerous work of disposing of the powerful bones of the ancestors that had been at the centre of traditional Urapmin religion. Since the revival, he has gone on to serve for many years as one of the main pastors in the community.

The Urapmin Christianity Semis preaches and that his congregation seeks to practice promotes lawful behaviour while wholly condemning displays of wilfulness, and Semis comes closer than most people to living out its dictates. He displays his lawful character in many different ways. He does not, for example, push others to meet his relational demands. As a result of this, he has remained for many years a widower, raising his sole daughter to young adulthood and forming with her the smallest, least relationally complex household one can imagine in Urapmin, where one needs at least one man and one woman to carry out the work required to keep a family alive. Semis also works hard to control feelings of anger that 'arise' when his relational expectations are violated. This means he is sometimes taken advantage of in exchange relations, as when over time he accepted without any attempt at redress that his gift of a bow to establish a trade friendship with an important visitor to his house was destined to go unreciprocated, despite his many visits to the recipient's house in an effort to elicit the appropriate return. His success in keeping his anger at bay has given him a reputation as someone with an 'easy' heart, thought to be the ultimate cause of his lawful demeanour.

There are other people in Urapmin as committed to lawfulness as Semis, but most of them come close to falling into the role of what Urapmin call 'rubbish men'. Rubbish men are those so lacking in will that they are virtually without relationships. The Urapmin pity such people, rather than condemn them, but at the same time they do not hold them to be exemplary. Poor in the material resources one needs relationships to be able to produce in Urapmin, if rubbish men do not actively violate the law, they hardly fulfil it either. To fully realize lawfulness, one must both have relationships and meet the demands they put in place for reciprocal treatment, even as one does not push to expand into new relational territory. Semis manages to lawfully meet his relational obligations without any need for wilful expansion of them by virtue of his role as pastor – a position people support by sometimes giving him garden produce and by helping him to make and manage his own gardens. They do this for him more or less spontaneously (though he often wishes they would do more), and thus he does not need to push others in order to procure the resources he needs to lawfully relate to them. This makes him a paragon of robustly lived lawfulness – a kind of fully realized lawfulness that does not lead to social marginalization. Virtually no other Urapmin person can live like this, for they generally have to temper their realization of the value of lawfulness by putting their wills into play. But many of them admire Semis greatly. They go to him for advice, talk warmly about him in his absence, and fairly often they have dreams where they see Jesus take him to heaven.

It was not difficult during fieldwork to determine that people held Semis to be an exemplar. So many people made their regard for him clear in our conversations that his status was obvious to me almost from the start. Things were otherwise with the primary exemplar of wilfulness in the community. Kinimnok, a fifty-year-old man, is loud, domineering, energetic and extravagant in all sorts of ways, and he is clearly the most ostentatiously wilful Urapmin adult. One can observe the shape of fully realized wilfulness by looking at almost any area of Kinimnok's behaviour and personality. He is, for example, an almost obsessive hunter. Hunting is a prestigious activity for Urapmin men, and hunting success provides men with the prestige-food resources to make wilfully expansive, high-profile, relation-creating gifts. But there is also a general recognition that hunting is no substitute for responsible garden work when it comes to feeding a household and meeting the lawful demands of a normal relational network. A good man will put some energy into hunting, the Urapmin say, but only as a sideline to his more serious and steady gardening work.

The point that men should not be overly involved in hunting, despite its occasionally great rewards, is expressed in myths and folktales in which men obsessed with hunting fare poorly in the end by comparison with their more garden-focused cross-cousins. It is also complexly embedded in people's belief in the existence of a figure known as the *Nuk Wanang* or Marsupial Woman. The Marsupial Woman is a spirit guardian of the marsupials that humans hunt and eat. Sometimes she involves herself with men who hunt frequently. As a Marsupial Woman begins to have sexual relations with such a man and eventually marries him, she also gives him dreams telling him where to find game. This man then becomes a spectacularly successful hunter. But there is a downside to this arrangement, for eventually the Marsupial Woman becomes jealous of the hunter's human spouse and begins to feel that she is giving up too many of her marsupial wards in return for too little from the hunter. At this point, she begins to send notice of her dissatisfaction to him, causing him to have accidents while hunting and eventually killing him.

I knew several Urapmin men who, as they began to develop careers as successful hunters, came to suspect that the Marsupial Woman was making overtures to them by giving them so much game. As soon as they had even a close brush with an accidental fall in the bush they stopped hunting regularly to avoid contracting a marriage with her. But this is not the case with Kinimnok. He has long been an extraordinarily successful hunter, and he openly proclaims that he owes his success in part to his marriage to the Marsupial Woman. One often sees him publicly clutching his chest in pain and announcing that the Marsupial Woman is trying to kill him, but he has made no effort to break off his relationship with her by ceasing to hunt. Moreover, he has never foregone hunting in the face of the gardening difficulties his over-commitment to the bush have caused him and his family. Once during my fieldwork, things got so bad for Kinimnok in terms of staple garden foods that he was forced to buy a ripening taro garden from someone else in the community, a kind of purchase the Urapmin regard as very shameful. In his indulgent obsession with hunting, his acceptance of his marriage to the Marsupial Woman, and his failure to attend to the demands of routine subsistence chores, Kinimnok models what unbridled wilfulness looks like.

And that is just hunting. Kinimnok's wilful streak is also attested to by his conjugal life, for his marriage to the Nuk Wanang is not his only irregular union. At a time when Christianity has called polygamy into question, and when very few men try it and even fewer succeed, Kinimnok has for many years maintained plural marriages with a changing array of women. His current connubial arrangement is particularly shocking to Urapmin sensibilities. The Urapmin do all they can to erase any distinctions between natal children and step or adopted children, and growing up in a family for any reason confers all the rights of birth. Hence, when Kinimnok married the woman who is currently his senior wife and she brought with her a very young daughter, Kinimnok raised this daughter as his own. But when she reached puberty, he married her. Now he is married both to her and to her mother. The Urapmin recognize this arrangement as uncomfortably close to father-daughter incest and at best a very wilful act on Kinimnok's part in relation to his senior wife.

Kinimnok's overall personality is also marked by the regular display of wilfulness in interpersonal interaction. Particularly striking is how Kinimnok is quick to anger and to utter threats of physical violence, something other Urapmin rarely do. Some of Kinimnok's truculence stems from his belief that other men are always attempting to seduce his wives. It is also fuelled by his (largely unfounded in my experience) worry that others are slandering him behind his back or threatening to fight with him. His fears of encroachment are so highly pitched, and his short fuse so easily ignited, that he cannot even live in a normal Urapmin village. Instead, he lives in his own homestead a short walk from a village where many of his closest associates live, keeping a safe distance from others who might incite his wilful jealousy and rage.

There is a deep irony to Kinimnok's residential situation, however, and it points us towards his status as an exemplar of the value of wilfulness in its most fully realized form. This irony stems from the fact that although he resides outside of the village nearest to his house, Kinimnok is the person the village residents have elected to serve as their 'alderman' (Komiti) in the introduced structure of formal government in contemporary Urapmin. In this role, he represents them to the leading state government figure in the community – the Councillor – and acts as the mediator of first resort for their disputes.

As his status as alderman demonstrates, the fact that most Urapmin find Kinimnok's behaviour to exemplify wilfulness does not preclude their developing positive sentiments towards him. Indeed, most Urapmin feel some fondness and even admiration for Kinimnok, something I found quite shocking at first, since I had initially thought of him as a bully and buffoon. At one point when his anger had become particularly extreme, and when many people had heard him utter threats to murder an important Urapmin big man, there was talk of taking him to the District Court at the government office some six hours walk to the east of Urapmin. People were convinced that the magistrate at the district court would jail Kinimnok for a long time for his threatening behaviour. After the fear that Kinimnok's fate would include years of confinement away from the community became widespread, I began to hear from people how much they would miss him. He is so funny, he makes us laugh, they said. And they pointed out what a great hunter he was, and how generous he always was with food when one visited his house. I wondered at that point if perhaps I was just catching the positive commemorative mood that wells up when people anticipate an imminent death (albeit in this case a social one). So, long after this event had blown over without Kinimnok having to go to jail, I occasionally probed peoples' feelings about him only to find that they were in fact privately very positive, even if publicly they sometimes condemned his behaviour. I once asked a young man who his favourite Urapmin person was. 'Kinimnok', he answered without hesitation: 'He is funny, a great story teller, a skilful hunter and generous'. As is the case with Semis and his embodiment of an ideal of lawfulness lived out without compromise to the demands of wilfulness, so it was with Kinimnok and his untempered wilfulness: no one else managed to live like him. But they talked regularly about him, and in many respects they loved him in the way Scheler says exemplars must be loved. Through him, they learned by observation what wilfulness as a value looks like when it is realized to its fullest extent.

Up to this point, I have identified where the values of wilfulness and lawfulness exist in fully realized form in the landscape of Urapmin social life. It is through such exemplary figures as Semis and Kinimnok that the Urapmin encounter these values and learn to think about their own lives in terms of them. But what about the preeminent value of relationalism, the value in the service of which people usually temper their realization of lawfulness and wilfulness? Where do people find this value? They find it, I would suggest, in their big men.

I have written about Urapmin big men before in a manner that is quite compatible with my argument here, so I'm going to discuss them rather quickly (Robbins 2007). There are four big men in Urapmin. There is no disagreement about who qualifies for this role, and no suggestion that anyone but these four big men deserves this status. People talk about big men, and they dream about them, all the time. They are often frustrated with their own big men, the ones they personally follow, who can be quite wilfully pushy and themselves acknowledge that in terms of the law they are often 'bad' men. But at the same time, people also recognize that big men, who use their wills to build villages, push people to work together, and defend their followers' rights against infringement by the followers of other big men; they also treat them much of the time in the kinds of reciprocal ways that show their respect for the law. By balancing wilfulness and lawfulness in the most relationally productive way, the big men create the social contexts that allow their followers to live out their own relational lives productively as a compromise between these two values. This is why so much of people's sense of their own security, their sense that they can live their own lives productively, is bound up with their ties to their big men, such that people routinely express marked disquiet when the big man who lives closest to them leaves the community on an extended sojourn to visit friends and relatives elsewhere.

I do not want to say much more about big men here, except to note that at first their existence in Urapmin was a puzzle to me. Many of the culturally similar groups that live near the Urapmin do not feature prominent big men as part of their social organization. And in terms of relations of production and exchange, Urapmin social arrangements, like those of their neighbours, take the form generally understood to produce diversified, 'great man' styles of leadership instead of the more concentrated, multifunctional style of Urapmin big-manship. Given this, I am inclined to argue, and have argued more thoroughly elsewhere, that the Urapmin invest so heavily in their big men, and lend them such authority, not because they need them to operate their social lives in pragmatic terms, but because they need them as exemplars who demonstrate how the value of relationalism can be fully realized as a synthesis of partial realizations of the values of lawfulness and wilfulness that Semis and Kinimnok so fully represent (Robbins 2007). It is by encountering and pondering exemplars of the three values of relationalism, lawfulness, and wilfulness that the Urapmin identify the interhuman strings by which they can pull themselves up through their own social lives, and in this set the big men, who exemplify the realization of the preeminent value of relationalism, provide the sturdiest ropes.

Having to this point discussed in some detail how people encounter fully expressed values in the form of exemplary persons, I would like quickly to indicate how this analysis might be expanded by showing that people can also experience them through participation in institutions, and particularly through participation in some rituals (Robbins 2015 presents a fuller development of this argument about ritual and values). That rituals at least sometimes enact an idealized picture of the world is not a new insight. Jonathan Z. Smith (1982: 63) long ago defined ritual as 'a means of performing the way things ought to be in conscious tension to the way things are in such a way that this ritualized perfection is recollected in the ordinary, uncontrolled course of things'. Kapferer (2006: 673), more recently, has argued for a view of ritual as constituting a space of virtuality which 'allows people to break free from the constraints or determinations of everyday life' not in order to leave everyday life and its concerns behind, but to slow 'down its flux and speed' (676) so they can examine and perhaps transform its elements. In keeping with Kapferer's and Smith's analyses, I want to argue that some rituals accomplish this process of slowing down the production and perfecting the shape of representations precisely for values. They allow people to suspend the complex relations between values and action that usually holds in daily life – the kind of complex relations I explored earlier by pointing out that most of the time people are only making limited progress through the middle stretches of long chains of value transformation or are acting in ways the realize a number of values at once but only in compromised forms – and to thereby experience what it is like to realize one value fully. Such a value is realized in a space that has been in some respects simplified, but its ritual accomplishment nonetheless also remains in play in the rushed flux of everyday life because each ritual performance provides a brush with exemplarity that will henceforward solicit some of each ritual participants' energy toward the further realization of the value involved in more quotidian contexts of action.

To illustrate this approach to analysing ritual as affording an experience of fully realized value, I will briefly discuss the Urapmin Christian ritual of the Spirit dance or what they call the 'Spirit disco'. To understand the work the Spirit disco does in modelling a fully realized value, one needs to know that Urapmin Christianity largely disregards the traditional Urapmin value of relationalism in favour of its own promotion of the value of individualism. In the terms of their Christianity, the Urapmin recognize that they must save themselves as individuals, and that in their pursuit of such salvation their relationships will not help them. As one man told me, 'my wife cannot break off part of her belief and give it to me'. When it comes to belief, everyone has to have his or her own. And the way belief is displayed is through a constant commitment to lawfulness, for it is the will that leads to sin. This is why Urapmin Christianity only recognizes the value of lawfulness, and does not promote wilfulness in any situations, even when it contributes to realizing relational goals. It is because Semis, who we met earlier, lives by this Christian code that he stands for other Urapmin as an exemplar of lawful behaviour.

People can appreciate the shape of uncompromised lawfulness by observing Semis. But they can also come to experience it in their own practice through the Spirit disco, a setting in which lawfulness also helps to realize the preeminent Christian value of individualism in the fullest form it ever takes in Urapmin life. Spirit discos are circular dances performed at night inside the church. During the dance, some of the dancers become possessed by the Holy Spirit. Once this happens, they begin to flail wildly and will be 'controlled' by other dancers who hold them and do their best to prevent them from hurting themselves or others. During a successful dance, several people will become possessed in this way for up to an hour. At the height of the rite, the scene inside the church can be chaotic, with all of the possessed people careening unpredictably around the room as others struggle to keep up the circular pattern of the dance. Eventually, the Spirit will leave the possessed dancers one by one. When the Spirit leaves a dancer, he/she collapses on the floor, completely limp, effectively unconscious, and, as the Urapmin see it, at peace. After possession, people will lie on the church floor in this state for some time as the dancers slow down and eventually stop. Participants remain in church until those who were once possessed regain normal consciousness. Then everyone will pray together and the ritual ends.

In Urapmin understanding, the violence of possession during the Spirit disco is due to a battle within the possessed person's heart between the Holy Spirit and his/her sins. It is also noteworthy that it leads to exceptionally wilful behaviour, as the dancers lash out violently without regard to those around them. The conclusion of possession happens when the Spirit finally succeeds in 'throwing' the person's sins out of his/her body and the person is left in a peaceful, 'easy' state. Before commencing the Spirit disco, everyone must confess their sins to a pastor or deacon who will pray over them and tell God that the sins have been given to Him. But it is only during Spirit disco possession that the sins are finally removed from the body. This leaves the person ready for salvation. As the Urapmin see it, the previously possessed person lying still and alone on the Church floor represents the full realization of a lawful person, their slack bodies undisturbed by any wilful strivings. The person in post-possession repose, lying alone and unattended to on the church floor, also represents the fullest realization of the saved individual possible before Jesus' return. Since, as one person crystallized the general Urapmin understanding for me, 'once people leave the church building they will start sinning again', it is only at this moment at the end of the rite that one can be sure of one's own or someone else's salvation. It is thus the only time in Urapmin social life that the value of becoming a wholly lawful individual worthy of salvation is fully visible. The Spirit disco provides, then, an exemplary image of the value of Urapmin Christian individualism worked out in its fullest form.

Conclusion

Having considered the question of exemplarity and the existence of values from several ethnographic angles, I want to turn to a brief conclusion.

Louis Dumont (1980: xxxix), arguably the most important anthropological theorist of values, once wrote that 'If one concentrates no more on function but on meaning, then each sort of representation must be grasped where it is fully accentuated and elaborated, where it rises to predominance and not where it is kept, by the prevalence of other representations, in a rudimentary or residual state' (Dumont 1980: xxxix). The 'one' doing the grasping in Dumont's comment is clearly the analyst. But I have argued here that the people we study also need to grasp representations – at least representations of values – where they are 'fully accentuated and elaborated'. It is in grasping such fully elaborated representations that people experience the existence of values and come to feel their force as engines of moral action. That values come to exist in this way has been the burden of my argument.

Central to that argument has been the claim that people encounter fully elaborated versions of values not so much by being presented with abstract cultural definitions of them, but by coming into contact with people and institutions that exemplify them. For almost everyone, everyday life is in fact not marked by the realization of key values, but rather by the performance of actions aimed at achieving much lower level values or at realizing a number of values in compromised form. This is why exemplary persons and institutions are so important in social life: they present us with values in a way our routine experiences rarely do. I would in the end want to go further than this to suggest that it is our encounters with key values embodied in exemplary people and institutions that lend our lives a sense of moral purpose and of investment in the future, the pitched-forward quality of moving toward the good that is so crucial to our will to keep going and that the notion of moral engine that is at the centre of this collection aims to capture. And it is when such exemplary people and institutions are hard to find in the midst of our social lives that the moral investment in the future is most likely to falter. But that is an argument about what values do, not about where in the world they are, and so I'll leave it for another day.

All that remains then is for me to close what I referred to at the outset as one of the key frames around my argument – the one that has to do with our current anti-cultural moment and how we can rescue from its forceful critique some of the key figures of cultural analysis we might not want to lose. Having defined values as one of those figures worth holding on to, I have tried to give an account of how people might come to find themselves attached to values not because they have been bequeathed them from on high by an enduring, shared culture, but because they sometimes encounter them in the form of really existing exemplars. Such exemplars, when encountered, display a force that helps people think about what kinds of things they might really be after in the course of lives that do not at every moment appear to be directed toward much beyond momentary goals. If I have made my argument successfully, I hope to have conveyed that we can think about this value-directed, morally-informed, forward-looking aspect of human life without relying on older notions of culture, even as I would not want to preclude returning to such notions at some other time.

Joel Robbins is Sigrid Rausing Professor of Social Anthropology at the University of Cambridge. He is the author of *Becoming Sinners: Christianity and Moral Torment in a Papua New Guinea Society* (University of California Press, 2004), which was awarded the J.I. Staley Prize by the School for Advanced Research.

Notes

1. From this point through the next section of this chapter, the text that appears here also appears in similar form in a forthcoming volume to be published by Cambridge University Press entitled 'Recovering the Human Subject', edited by B. Bodenhorn et al. I thank the editors and publisher for allowing me to use this material here.
2. I would also note in passing that the fact that there are always numerous values in play, combined with the fact that most actions do not fully realize the values people find most important, is what gives social life the kind of complexity that leads so many anthropologists to abandon notions of order and culture. But this complexity is not proof of the absence of values, but rather follows from their existence.

References

Albrow, Martin. 1990. *Max Weber's Construction of Social Theory*. New York: St. Martin's Press.

Dumont, Louis. 1980. *Homo Hierarchicus: The Caste System and its Implications*, trans. M. Sainsbury, L. Dumont and B. Gulati. Chicago: University of Chicago Press.

Durkheim, Emile. 1974. *Sociology and Philosophy*, trans. D.F. Pocock. New York: Free Press.

Ferrara, Alessandro. 2008. *The Force of the Example: Explorations in the Paradigm of Judgement*. New York: Columbia University Press.

Kapferer, Bruce. 2006. 'Virtuality', in J. Kreinath, J. Snoek and M. Stausberg (eds), *Theorizing Rituals: Classical Topics, Theoretical Approaches, Analytical Concepts*. Leiden: Brill, pp. 671–84.

Laidlaw, James. 2013. *The Subject of Virtue: An Anthropology of Ethics and Freedom*. Cambridge: Cambridge University Press.

Munn, Nancy M. 1986. *The Fame of Gawa: A Symbolic Study of Value Transformation in a Massim (Papua New Guinea) Society*. New York: Cambridge University Press.

Robbins, Joel. 2004. *Becoming Sinners: Christianity and Moral Torment in a Papua New Guinea Society*. Berkeley: University of California Press.

_____. 2007. 'Morality, Politics and the Melanesian Big Man: On "The Melanesian Manager" and the Transformation of Political Anthropology', in J. Barker (ed.), *The Anthropology of Morality in Melanesia and Beyond*. Aldershot: Ashgate, pp. 25–37.

_____. 2010. 'If There is No Such Thing as Society, Is Ritual Still Special? On Using *The Elementary Forms* after Tarde', in M. Candea (ed.), *The Social after Gabriel Tarde: Debates and Assessments*. London: Routledge, pp. 93–101.

_____. 2012a. On Becoming Ethical Subjects: Freedom, Constraint, and the Anthropology of Morality. Anthropology of This Century 5. Available at http://aotcpress.com/articles/ethical-subjects-freedom-constraint-anthropology-morality/.

_____. 2012b. 'Cultural Values', in D. Fassin (ed.), *A Companion to Moral Anthropology*. Malden, MA: Wiley-Blackwell, pp. 117–32.

_____. 2013. 'Monism, Pluralism and the Structure of Value Relations: A Dumontian Contribution to the Contemporary Study of Value', *Hau: Journal of Ethnographic Theory* 3(1): 99–115.

_____. 2015. 'Ritual, Value, and Example: On the Perfection of Cultural of Cultural Representations', *Journal of the Royal Anthropological Institute* 21(S1): 18–29. (Special Issue: The Power of Example).

Scheler, Max. 1973. *Formalism in Ethics and a Non-Formal Ethics of Values: A New Attempt toward the Foundation of an Ethical Personalism*. Evanston, IL: Northwestern University Press.

_____. 1987. *Person and Self-Value: Three Essays*, trans. M.S. Frings. Dordrecht: Martinus Nijhoff.

Schnädelbach, Herbert. 1984. *Philosophy in Germany 1831–1933*. Cambridge: Cambridge University Press.

Smith, Jonathan Z. 1982. *Imagining Religion: From Babylon to Jonestown*. Chicago: University of Chicago Press.

9

Fault Lines in the Anthropology of Ethics

James Laidlaw

In May 2001, in that year's Malinowski Memorial Lecture at the London School of Economics, I said that there did not yet exist an anthropology of ethics (Laidlaw 2002). I tried to be clear that by this I did not mean that anthropologists did not write about morality. They have always done so, through the whole history of the discipline; indeed, it has always been central to their concerns. There being no 'anthropology of ethics' was a matter, rather, of the absence of debate among anthropologists as to the ethical dimension of human social life: its bases, its character, its extent and consequence, or what the editors of this volume are calling 'moral engines'. Anthropologists had not been arguing, explicitly and as such, about ethics or morality in the way they did argue about the nature of religion, the economy, politics and kinship, or about sacrifice, animism, prayer, development, gift-giving, money, dispute settlement, charisma, marriage, parenthood or naming. There were, that is to say, no focused debates on the nature of ethical life, no contending positions or rival schools of thought about it, and very little writing that took morality or ethics overtly as its object of inquiry and theoretical reflection.

About a decade and a half on, that situation has changed markedly. The volume of literature describing itself as contributing to the anthropology of ethics or morality is now large, and growing at what still seems to be a gathering pace. It is also still changing as it grows, but it is already clear that what is taking shape is not a unified movement, or anything so unidirectional or unbalancing as a 'turn', although I have seen the idea that we are going through an 'ethical turn' floated on occasion. Instead, I think we can begin to see emerging a set of questions and areas of inquiry, and in some cases, beginning to take shape, some moderately well formed debates. There are some questions that seem foundational enough to divide people and to start to define positions, even if it is not (yet) the case that the answers to these various questions correlate with each other so that people line up to form camps or schools.

In this chapter, I should like briefly to set out what seem to me to be the most fundamental questions that anthropologists interested in ethics/morality are in the process of taking positions about. Fittingly, they concern the very foundations of the ethical dimension of social life: again, what our editors refer to as the engines that drive moral life. The exercise is worth doing, I think, not just for the information of anyone coming more or less new to the literature, and not merely as an occasion for indicating and defending my own positions, but as an attempt to direct everyone's attention – and participants' argumentative focus – to where I think genuine and consequential debate and disagreement lie. Perhaps because it is a new and still rather inchoate field, it is, I observe, not at all uncommon to find that works currently being published present themselves rhetorically as refutations or critiques of positions or claims that, to the best of my knowledge, no one has ever put forward: straw men are being set alight and the resulting smoke is obscuring the shape of the field, so we are in danger of walking round in circles. My hope then is to help us to see a bit more clearly what we do and don't disagree about, and what might be at stake in those disagreements.

The following questions all overlap with each other, but just how they relate differs depending on how one answers each of them, so I shall treat them here as independent points of entry into the field. What is ethical agency and what range of entities in the world act as ethical subjects? Is ethics immanent and pervasive in all human life, or is it expressed in particular in certain circumstances, or in certain institutions or practices? Is freedom a necessary component of ethical life? If so, of what kind, and what, if any, relation does that freedom have to various ideas of political freedom?

What is an Ethical Subject?

One question that seems to me to be a matter of concern, and a useful diagnostic of different anthropological approaches to the ethical, is 'what is an ethical subject?' What is included among the things in the world that do or have ethics? This question, it is important to insist, is at least potentially and at least in part responsive to empirical ethnographic description, analysis and comparison, and therefore different in kind from the irremediably normative questions that concern the appropriate objects of one's ethical concern. To put the matter rather crudely: it is quite possible to think, and not a few people do say, that 'the planet' ought to be a central ethical concern and that 'we', as ethical subjects, should all be worried about it; rather fewer people think that 'the planet' is itself an ethical subject and that it should be worried about us. The question of what is our proper range of ethical concern is clearly distinguishable from the question of whom that 'our' – the class of agents to whom appeal might be made on ethical grounds – in fact encompasses. Who or what, as a matter of fact, has ethical concerns and values, and does ethics?

Let us take, as instances of how anthropologists are thinking about these questions, two contrasting comments on my recent book, *The Subject of Virtue* (2014a). Eduardo Kohn (2014) complains that I appear to conceive of ethical life in a way that restricts it too much to humans, which ignores the ways in which, in radically other ontologies such as those in Amazonia, other animal species, spirits and indeed the forest itself are recognized as being ethical agents. Cheryl Mattingly (2014a; also 2014b) meanwhile expresses the opposite worry, namely that in order to take account fully of everyday moral perplexity, a rich conception of specifically human moral agency is required, one that encompasses and integrates complex moral emotions, creativity and narrative self-understanding. So do we decide to extend ethical agency, as Kohn wants us to do, 'beyond the human', or do we resist the reduction this must entail in the name of a fulsome humanism? I think it is possible to agree with some of what both these authors say, so long as we approach the question of what is an ethical subject in strictly operational terms – who and what does ethics, when and where and in what ways? – and carefully not muddle that with the question of whether, as ethical subjects, we (including Amazonians) do or should care about nonhumans. Kohn's way of putting things – 'what role might nonhumans play in an ethical life?' – unfortunately invites just that confusion.

In this way, what we recognize as an ethical subject becomes obviously and directly related to the question of what we take ethical life to consist in. So, on the one hand, how we characterize ethics needs to be adequate to the complexities and subtleties of human experience as we encounter and describe them in diverse cultural settings, including the activities and processes Mattingly points to; on the other, we should recognize as instances of 'ethics' everywhere we find those processes and activities instantiated, including by entities other than human individuals. As it happens (see Laidlaw 2014b), I do not think Kohn actually provides evidence of animal species or spirits acting as ethical agents, even in an Amazonian ontology, but I do not rule out that such evidence could be provided, if not of the fully rounded and complex agency Mattingly rightly says is characteristic of human persons, then at least of some of the component processes or activities. We might decide that not every instance of every one of these, but only some set of them in complex interrelation, usefully counts as 'ethical agency', but that is a judgement that should come if at all as a result of, rather than being a premise of, our enquiries.

One of the things we have in mind when we take it as obvious that, generally speaking, human beings are ethical subjects, is that we are, as Charles Taylor puts it, 'self-interpreting animals' (1985). We do not merely do things, but as we do things – and indeed as a constitutive part of how we do things – we routinely form and hold descriptions of what we are doing. We know as we do it that we are 'cooking', 'typing', 'relaxing', 'telling a lie', 'sparing her feelings', or whatever. And we also evaluate those self-descriptions. This we do implicitly all the time, since our self-descriptions are not and cannot be always value neutral, and they are always subject also to conscious, reflective evaluation from time to time. This reflective self-evaluation, and the ways in which we adjust and shape our conduct in light of it, means that to some extent we shape and form ourselves, in the process of living a reflective life. It is obvious, and obviously central to what we mean when we say that human beings are ethical subjects, that ordinary human life is a life of continuous and routine self-description, self-evaluation and incremental self-constitution in this sense.

But is all this true of all humans, in all circumstances? It is not difficult to think of cases where the question is at least worth asking, people whom we hesitate to hold ethically responsible for things that they do: infants, people with severe learning disabilities, those suffering from dementia or in the grip of a psychotic illness. If we focus on questions not of who or what is of ethical value, but of who or what does ethical valuing and acts in light of that valuing (who or what engages in ethical reflection and judgement) and of who or what is socially recognized as doing so, then it seems reasonable to suggest that not all humans are ethical subjects, at least not in all respects or all of the time.

And might this question be open also to historical change and cultural variability? Jonathan Lear (2006, 2015) has forcefully argued that unjust societies systematically disable the ethical thought of those who live within them: both those who suffer and those who ostensibly benefit from injustice. If this is true, might one say that the more unjust a society, the more stunted and constricted would be the ethical life of its members? It does not seem plausible to suggest there could be a society in which people didn't describe and evaluate their actions to themselves at all, but it might make sense to say, for instance of the privileged in a monstrously unjust society, that no accurate self-description would be endurable, and that this fact would so effectively discourage conscious reflection that the higher orders at least of ethical life, in conscious and deliberate self-fashioning, would be lost to them. Foucault approached a parallel conclusion when he asked us to consider a slave so effectively and totally subject to physical coercion (what he referred to as 'capacity' rather than 'power', the latter being always to some degree reciprocal: Foucault 2000: 342) that he or she could do nothing other than to carry out the will of his or her master. He asserted that such a person would have no ethics (Foucault 1997: 286). What he seems to have meant by this is not merely that it would be unjust to hold the slave responsible for what he or she does under this kind of compulsion and duress, but further that such a situation would leave the slave no space for the kind of reflection that Foucault took to be diagnostic of ethical practice. So according to this view of ethics, perhaps social *milieux* differ, among other things, in the degree to which they allow people to function as ethical subjects.

Another possible limit to the apparently obvious idea that all humans are ethical subjects might lie in the fact that some projects of self-fashioning, while they begin in reflective self-interpretation and self-formation, progressively eliminate those capacities as they proceed. Ascetic regimes of ethical self-cultivation, including in some of the major world religions such as Christianity, Islam, Buddhism and Jainism (see, for example, Lester 2005; Hirschkind 2006; Mahmood 2005; Cook 2010; Laidlaw 1995, 2005), follow a dynamic that necessarily begins with the exercise of reflective self-interpretation, and the freedom to adjust one's conduct in light of self-evaluation, but lead people progressively to relinquish such capacities as they seek to conform to externally imposed criteria and norms, and ultimately to do so in ways that are not just habitual but actually involuntary: to make oneself literally unable to do other than conform to an ideal such as humility, obedience to God or non-attachment. Might we say that these are ethical projects that are in some respects at least self-negating, in that they lead one out of the ethical domain – out of what is seen in these religious traditions as merely worldly ethics – and into a realm of transcendent values and escape from the ordinary human condition (see discussion in Laidlaw 2014a; Faubion 2014b; Laidlaw 2014b)?

James Faubion (2014a) further points out that many religious and quasi-religious traditions valorize, and provide means for striving towards, a condition – sometimes called mystical – that involves the renunciation or self-transcendence of the self, to the point of the ontological negation of the subject as such. This kind of *telos* is indeed paradoxical: as Faubion puts it, the outcome is 'a subject that is not one'. And while embodying, in some respects and from particular points of view, the highest ethical ideals of their respective traditions, those who come closest to realizing these conditions are always also ethically eccentric and marginal figures, declaring themselves beyond the rules of right conduct that apply to everyone else, and therefore always in an at-best ambiguous relationship with established moral authority. In this respect, the mystic resembles more muscular figures of charismatic authority such as prophetic leaders in being at the same time central to the ethical field, in some ways indeed creative of the very possibility of specific forms of ethical life, yet also standing outside any such definite form of life: refusing the routinization that would follow from recognizing obligations to or value in either ordinary followers or everyday life, resolutely non-relational and, although being a law unto others, subject to no law themselves. So we have then a range of figures – ascetic renouncers, mystics, prophets – who seem to some extent to transcend the ethical condition.

But in addition to the question of whether some human individuals are excluded or act to absent themselves from the company of ethical subjects, we might ask whether human entities other than individuals engage in ethical thought and practice. There seems no reason *a priori* to exclude this idea, and several good anthropological ones for making as much sense of it as we can. It is surely a very serious testing ground, for instance, for the idea that persons in some social contexts are dividuals rather than individuals. Can we make sense of the idea that a dividual might be the locus of ethical self-fashioning?

More straightforward, I think, is the point that various groups of people and institutions – families, clubs and associations, corporations – engage in processes of self-description and evaluation, and seek more or less concertedly to shape themselves in the light of their ideals and values. And insofar as they do this – as a joint family seeks to contract a marriage or collectively manage its reputation, or as a political party seeks to 'return to its core values', or whatever – they exercise ethical agency. A good deal of the anthropology of kinship might be re-read, in light of the recent anthropology of ethics, as showing how collectivities and not just individuals are ethical subjects.

An interesting variant on this, and the most systematic exercise in the recent literature in the anthropology of ethics, describing how something more inclusive than an individual might properly be regarded as an ethical subject, is Faubion's (2011: 302–67) compelling account of the relationship between himself, as ethnographer, and his principal interlocutor in his research on Christian millennialism in Texas. Faubion argues persuasively that the relational entity that was himself-and-his-interlocutor engaged in an extended process of reflective self-formation.

So far we have considered the question of whether all humans are ethical subjects, and whether they are such only as individuals or also in some other groups or formations. But some anthropologists (Kohn, already mentioned, among them) have suggested that entities wholly other than humans ought also to be considered as ethical subjects. This is no surprise, given the energy currently being expended across a range of disciplines in the social sciences and beyond, advancing avowedly anti- or post-humanist agendas. These agendas have typically involved one of two strategies. The first is to downplay altogether attributes that might be thought to be distinctively human. This might involve for instance denying that ethics is more than a superficial or fundamentally fraudulent aspect of human life: those self-descriptions are never more than pleasing delusional fantasies; our genes make us act in their interests, or our animal emotions impel us to evolutionarily selected behaviour patterns, whatever we tell ourselves. That is one kind of anti-humanist agenda. The second involves re-imagining or redefining those supposedly specifically human attributes – reason, agency, reflection, freedom, ethics – so as to make them fit for non-human purposes.

A version of this second strategy seems to be emerging in the work of Jarrett Zigon, whose recent writings on drug rehabilitation (2014a, 2014b, this volume) include an argument for locating the agency required for ethical action and change not in human subjects but in what he calls 'assembled and situated worlds' of practices and policies. Zigon presents his argument as opposed to 'metaphysical humanism', and draws on a range of vitalist and phenomenological sources of inspiration that are common currency in the burgeoning 'post-human' literature to suggest that ethical life does not rely on any intrinsic characteristics or capacities of humans. Indeed, his is a determinedly externalist perspective: to live ethically is to live in 'attunement' with the life-world you inhabit. On this account, the features of the distinctively human that are at the forefront of Mattingly's 'first-person virtue ethics' (individual creativity, and the narrative continuity given to a human life by temporally extended projects and by enduring relations of intimate care) are replaced wholesale by a picture in which agency and care (or their absence) reside instead in the complex of institutions and practices which the individual inhabits, and morality consists in the individual being receptively in tune and affectively at one with that environment, so that he or she inhabits it in a state of 'existential comfort'.

This certainly has the effect of 'democratizing' ethical life well beyond the human, but it comes at a cost. Notice that instead of identifying the ethical, as I have been suggesting here, with a set of processes, such as reflection and self-evaluation, through which people may conceive, develop, embrace, pursue, question, revise and overhaul their various conceptions of the good and of how they should live, Zigon instead identifies moral life with a specific and singular ideal – what he describes in unambiguously affirmative terms as 'living sanely' in a state of what he calls 'existential comfort' – and he defines ethics as whatever conduces to the maintenance or restoration of that state. And the cost of this arises not only if this conception of sane moral living can be shown to be flawed or objectionable; it arises on account merely of the fact that it is corrigible. So while some may no doubt share Zigon's positive view of the condition of attunement, others might, for example, find this ideal unappealingly passive and conformist, or might be worried by its implicit authoritarianism (a danger, I myself would suggest, for which we might want generally to be on the lookout, wherever ideas are borrowed heavily from Heidegger). But the important point is that whatever we ourselves might variously think of these different judgements of this particular ideal, an anthropology of ethics, if it is to be of any interest whatsoever, necessarily requires a conception of the ethical that recognizes the historical and cultural variety of forms of ethical life, and recognizes also the variety of ideals and values and conceptions of human flourishing that have animated them. And for this, it is surely necessary that we do not assume that we already know what ethics looks like, or that only values we share and forms of life we approve are 'ethical'. Thus we must equip ourselves with concepts that do not pre-emptively commit us exclusively to our already-favoured vision of the good life. And whereas a focus on processes of reflection and self-formation does not do this, since these processes might be deployed in diverse ways and towards radically (if not quite infinitely) divergent ends, to identify the ethical exclusively with achieving and maintaining a state of 'attunement' plainly does pre-emptively so commit us.

Now my claim is emphatically not – to revert again to Mattingly's concern – that self-interpretation and reflective self-formation exhaust what we should mean by ethical agency. I would however wish to claim that these, if anything is, must be part of what we mean by ethics. So I have taken this as my starting point in addressing the question of what is the range of entities we might identify as ethical subjects. But recognizing that there are other activities and processes that might make up ethical agency, and also wishing, in response to Kohn and others, to be open to the question of whether ethical agency is restricted to humans, another line of enquiry suggests itself.

One of the interesting themes in recent ethnographies of human-animal relations is the idea that animals behave differently and exhibit more or fewer of the features of a mental life (they become more intelligent, etc.) depending on how they are treated by the humans with whom they are in relations. The claim is that important characteristics we might think of as distinguishing different species – such as intelligence – are not in fact rigidly species-specific and determined biologically, but are at least in part performative and interactive. To put it very crudely, animals become more intelligent if you treat them as if they are (e.g. Crist 1999; Despret 2004). Insofar as there might be merit in this argument, we could then similarly ask whether some of what Mattingly identifies as specifically human moral agency – for example the expression of moral emotions such as guilt, shame, anger or compassion – might be similar. Some species might be able to come to express such emotions, in the right kinds of social relations.

This possibility is interesting, from my point of view, however, not principally in relation to this question of non-human ethics – I doubt that anything we will learn about ethical agency among animals will radically change our understanding of human ethical life – but because the general argument about the interactive origins of moral emotions is an extremely plausible one, and is of the first interest, whether non-humans are part of our enquiry or not. How do we become ethical subjects, with the capacities of self-description and evaluation, already discussed, and expressing moral emotions? Are these capacities that are somehow inherent, or do they emerge and develop only through social interaction? I find the case for the latter thesis – one of the most eloquent and sophisticated expressions of which remains Adam Smith's *The Theory of Moral Sentiments* (1976 [1790]) – generally very persuasive. If it is the case, as Smith insists, that being 'in society' is the essential medium through which we develop our sense of self, our capacity for reflection and self-evaluation, and the expression of our moral sentiments, this would certainly help to explain why these same effects might be observable, if only to a limited degree, in animals that are incorporated closely into our social life. So I would see attempts to show that forests think or that dogs can show compassion as interesting not so much for any anti-humanist agenda with which they might be associated, as for the light they throw on some of the constituent features of the ethical dimension of human life.

I would add that insofar as one takes this broadly Smithian view of the ethical subject as necessarily constituted relationally, then the tension some authors feel there must somehow be between ethics conceived as care of the self and ethics conceived as care for others is revealed as the mirage that it is. They can only ever be two sides of the same coin.

Is Ethics 'Ordinary'?

Who or whatever we decide are ethical subjects, a related question is: are they ethical all of the time? In the recent anthropological literature, some have wanted to say that the ethical is woven pervasively into everyday life in such a way that human conduct is always necessarily ethical; others have wanted to identify ethics as something that happens occasionally, in distinct episodes and specific situations. The disagreements that are emerging around this matter are clearly strongly felt, but perhaps not yet clearly delineated.

One position holds that ethics is 'ordinary', in the sense not just that it is normal and everyday for human action to be ethical, but further that to be ethical is an immanent and essential feature, by definition present in all human action everywhere. This position has been developed and articulated by Michael Lambek over a number of years (e.g. 2000, 2008, 2010, 2015b, this volume). For Lambek, it is a category mistake to distinguish ethics from action in general, so in his terms even asking the question of whether all action is ethical makes no sense. Because human action is always subject to criteria of evaluation, it cannot be other than ethical. Therefore, the ethical dimension is an immanent aspect of all human action as such.

Another rendering of this position is given by Veena Das (2007, 2010a, 2010b, 2012, 2014, 2015), using very similar vocabulary and invoking a similar series of intellectual reference points. Like Lambek, Das strenuously resists locating 'the ethical' anywhere other than in what she refers to as the everyday or ordinary. This means in particular that the ethical is not to be found precisely where it is most often and most insistently claimed in practice: by religious or political leaders or movements aiming at a transcendent good (Das 2015). Lambek is perhaps less determined than Das to exclude all figures of religious authority from the ethical, although even he prefers to find it in marginal or eccentric rather than powerful figures (e.g. Lambek 2002). Das's ethnographic essays do invite us to recognize exemplary moral wisdom, but always in instances of un-dramatic actions by apparently unremarkable people in modest circumstances: the undemonstrative gestures whereby the afflictions wrought on ordinary people – very commonly by precisely the people and institutions who set themselves up as 'ethical' – are ameliorated, and an endurable ordinary life together pieced together and sustained. And Das is reluctant to describe the work people do to bring this about – characteristically, in her accounts, in almost imperceptible modifications of gesture or conduct – as resulting from anything as explicitly deliberative or conscious as a 'decision'. The thinking that inhabits everyday conduct, in Das's accounts, is characteristically tacit.

For both Lambek and Das, then, the ethical is pervasively immanent in everyday human life – not in thought more than action, not in religion more than in getting a livelihood, not in this day more than that, and especially not in organized or explicit striving for the good more than in habitual getting along.

Perhaps the most directly contrasting position is Zigon's (2007, 2014a, 2014b). Zigon characterizes moral life in ways that superficially resemble those of Das and Lambek (why this should be is an interesting question, but one which I shall not address here), with an emphasis on habit and routine (alongside, in his case, formal institutions and public discourse) as one important location of everyday morality. But his conception of everyday practice is really crucially different from theirs. While Lambek emphasizes that human action pervasively requires the exercise of practical reason, and Das similarly insists that the habitual and everyday are where ethical thinking is most importantly located, the absence of thought is precisely what for Zigon characterizes moral life in a state of equilibrium: everyday morality on his account is the unconscious following of rules, and conforming to standards and expectations without even being aware that this is what one is doing, so that morality is 'a kind of habitus or an unreflective and unreflexive disposition of everyday social life' (2008: 17). Ethics, thus, is the process that occurs when this equilibrium breaks down, following a change in the environment or circumstances meaning that established unconscious routine may no longer be followed. In terms of the vocabulary Zigon introduces in his more recent writings, ethics is the recuperative process that occurs when a state of attunement is disrupted. In response to this external shock, conscious thought and reflection may become necessary, and as a result changes occur in the agent's conduct and dispositions, so that a new equilibrium, a new state of attunement with a changed life-world, becomes possible. Or, as we have seen, the processes that restore attunement may have their origins largely outside the individual, in the assemblage of institutions and relations he or she dwells within. Either way ethics, in Zigon's account, is episodic, and sane everyday moral life is what we find outside and after the successful completion of those episodes. So in addition to an argument for locating ethical agency very substantially outside the human individual, in the institutions and practices of the life-world, Zigon also argues for restricting that agency temporally, to outside the ordinary, where Das and Lambek by contrast want to insist that it exclusively resides.

A third position, which is not exactly located between these two because it is much more nearly compatible with the first than with the second, has been articulated by Webb Keane (2010, 2014a, 2014b, 2016), and (in relation to this question) is also roughly my own. On this account, ethics is certainly woven pervasively into everyday life, and it is not an accidental but an intrinsic feature of human social life that this is generally so. Ethical life is non-contingently built on basic facts about human action. But this does not mean that it is always and everywhere the same, or always equally to the fore. As Keane observes, sometimes we are very much in the midst of what is going on, and the ethical dimension is largely tacit – though this does not mean that it is unavailable to consciousness; the habitual, again, is not 'unthinking' – but sometimes we stand back to some extent from what we are doing and the situation we are in, and experience some kind of reflective distance. On this account, both these states of affairs (or rather, the infinite subtle gradations between the poles that mark them) are part of ethics. And because the factors that provoke and enable reflective distance – most conspicuously the institutions, practices and relationships explicitly associated with encouraging and enabling ethical self-fashioning – have histories, so too does ethics. It is part of the work of an anthropology of ethics to describe the historical changes, the changing kinds of institutions and practices, that explain the greater and lesser degrees to which, as well as the differing ways in which, people at varying historical junctures have become taken up with ethical reflection and the formulation and following of explicit, more or less rationalized, ethical doctrines.

Ethical reflection is more concerted in some settings and institutions (such as those dedicated to ethical pedagogy) than in others, and it is subject at times to intensification, such as in periods of reforming (religious or political) zeal. The idea that there are institutionalized settings that frame explicit projects of ethical self-fashioning – and that make ethical reflection a more or less full-time or especially intensive matter – follows directly from my description above of humans as self-interpreting animals. We are all the time necessarily involved in describing to ourselves what we are doing, and those descriptions are always at least implicitly evaluative. And this necessarily means that in the midst of our everyday going on, we incrementally and over time fashion ourselves, as the usually unintended outcome of the everyday decisions and actions we take, in light of those changing descriptions and evaluations. This, expressed in slightly different language, is roughly what Lambek and Das mean by ordinary ethics (and differs from either attunement or moral breakdown as Zigon's envisages them). But there are many situations in which people do go beyond this. They quite deliberately set out on a concerted project of re-fashioning themselves, in light of a set of values or doctrines to which they consciously subscribe, or of modelling their conduct on that of chosen exemplars. Sometimes this occurs in response to the kind of external shock Zigon calls a 'moral breakdown', and this might help to explain why some people join a piety movement, a revolutionary cell, a monastery, a therapeutic programme or a self-improvement scheme. But conscious ethical self-formation of this more-than-ordinary kind is also a routinely available set of options, present in valued exemplars, in ritual, in specific roles and institutions, in all societies and civilizations.

In insisting on the ordinariness of ethics, Das highlights the incontestable fact that projects directed towards achieving a transcendent ideal or ultimate good very often motivate people to behave in highly destructive ways, on occasions for instance to set aside the subtle attentiveness and responsiveness to others that enable them to maintain decent lives together, and instead to follow remorselessly a single, perhaps decontextualized set of criteria of judgement so that they become cruel and brutal in the name of an ultimate good. This is all obviously true and important to remember. But not all projects of self-improvement have these features to an equal degree. In addition, some also obviously lead people to heightened sensitivity or enlarged sympathy or motivate them much more strenuously to try to do good. And most importantly, to say that these efforts to achieve an ideal, however liberal or intolerant their effects might be, are ethical projects is not to approve of them (any more than saying as I did above that some religious and political projects lead their participants out of the ethical domain is to deprecate them). Such projects are massively various, and directed towards mutually conflicting ends and ideals. It would be impossible coherently to approve of them all. There is nothing paradoxical in saying that a cause, a movement, or a course of action is ethical and also making a negative judgement on it.

Das and Lambek make an important point when they insist that such projects are not – even if their proponents often claim this – either all there is to ethics or where it essentially lies. And they are right too to point out that sometimes they are actively hostile to or act to undermine the delicate fabric of everyday ethical life, especially as that is experienced by poor or otherwise disadvantaged people. The rationalization, systematization and institutionalization that separates these projects of self-cultivation from the same processes of self-description, reflection and evaluation in 'everyday' or 'ordinary' life have varied and complex effects. Believing that sometimes, or even typically, those effects are on the whole negative, which, I take it, is the basis for these authors' antipathy to un-ordinary ethics, is not a good reason to deny the continuities that exist between them and 'ordinary' ethics, or to deny the term 'ethical' to them.

But if this is conceded, and we enlarge the field of ethics to include much that is not in Das's or Lambek's terms 'ordinary', a distinction drawn within that field is nevertheless, I think, helpful. Keane adopts from the philosopher Bernard Williams (1985; see also Laidlaw 2002, 2014a: 110–19) a distinction between ethics and morality that is very different from that described above from Zigon. 'Ethics' here designates what happens whenever and wherever and to whatever extent people address Socrates's question: 'How ought one to live?' So it encompasses both reflective everyday evaluation and concerted self-cultivation, the ordinary and the aspirational. 'Morality' or 'the morality system' on the other hand is used to refer to a subset of answers to that general ethical question. In Williams, it refers to the most influential moral philosophies in the West since Kant, which include both deontological and consequentialist theories, all of which have been profoundly shaped by a Christian inheritance, and all of which share distinctive features in their formulation, including the notion of specifically moral obligations that are supposed to trump all other kinds of values, duties or injunctions. Keane broadens this conception beyond the modern West, and beyond some of those specific features Williams thought central to 'the morality system', and uses the expression 'morality systems' to include all formulations of ethical rules, values and practices that have been subject to deliberate, self-conscious systematization, typically through the agency of a specialist clerisy, of some form or other.

Now, Keane's own discussion of what he calls 'morality systems' does depend heavily on an account of the consequences of monotheism. Since there are systems that share the general features Keane ascribes to 'morality systems' (but not those of Williams's 'morality system' – this being a reason why Keane's coinage might confuse as much as it clarifies) but which are not monotheistic – not only those such as Marxist Communism, which might plausibly be argued to have inherited those features at one remove, but also forms of Buddhism, Jainism and Hinduism, which do without a monotheistic theology – it might be necessary to amend some features of his account in light of a wider set of historical comparisons. But it is certainly helpful to be able to focus on the question of what happens to ethical life when it is subjected to self-conscious and institutionalized reflexive systematization.

The three positions identified here on the ordinariness of ethics imply divergent research programmes for anthropology. For those who maintain the immanence of ethics in ordinary life, the priority seems to be to deepen our understanding of the irreducibly ethical dimension of the human condition, to maintain resistance to the claims to transcendence of that condition in overtly self-proclaimed 'ethical' or 'moral' institutions and projects, and to celebrate the ways in which the ordinary reasserts itself in the face of such aspirationally transcendent institutions and practices. The facts of cultural difference and historical change are largely incidental to these concerns; engagement is with very general if not actually universal or invariant features of the human condition (see the exchange between Lempert (2013, 2015) and Lambek (2015a)). This would suggest an affinity with much of the literature in the anthropology of suffering, which as Robbins (2013) has recently argued tends to emphasize both the commonalities among states of affliction irrespective of social and cultural diversity, and the ability of the ethnographer's innate human sympathy to establish understanding, irrespective of social and cultural distance, based on those affective commonalities, obviating the need, apparently, for systematic social or cultural analysis. These observations point to where both the appeal and the limitations of this programme might lie for anthropology.

With respect to Zigon's ideas, two research programmes suggest themselves. One would be to try to specify the causes and courses of 'moral breakdown' and the relation (somewhat obscure, it seems to me, so far, in Zigon's writings) between the micro-dynamics of individual psychology and macro-historical change. Can the apparently intuitive idea that the breakdown of Soviet socialism was somehow causally related to widespread moral crises among Russians be substantiated in detail? How do we tell the difference between the effects of the breakdown of that system, and the effects of 'breakdown' attributable to the system itself? The other would be to test claims to non-human ethical agency (on the part of 'life-worlds' or non-humans, for example). Do such claims bring into view hitherto unappreciated aspects of ethical life? Or do they require, in order to include the non-human, a hollowing out of the content of ethics to the point where it cannot begin to capture the complexities of what the ordinary ethicists describe?

The third position, which I have summarized here mostly from Keane, would assign a much less central importance than in Zigon's approach to questions of non-human ethical agency, but equally, by contrast with 'ordinary ethics', would directly imply a commitment to historical and comparative analysis. Foucault (1986) was embarking on a project to describe the differences between historically produced moral systems when he distinguished those focused on ethical projects from those focused on moral codes. What kinds of historical circumstances give rise to Keane's 'morality systems' and empower them in relation to each other and to less systematized versions of ethical life? How do they differ from each other in their constitution – how important are codified rules, exemplars, narratives, distinctive moods or emotions? – and how does significant change happen?

Does Ethics Require Freedom?

How, if at all, does ethical life differ from or exceed the observation of generally accepted social conventions? Kenneth Read asked this question in his seminal 1955 paper, 'Morality and the Concept of the Person among the Guhuku-Gama', and it was such a profound challenge to an assumption held in common by the dominant schools of anthropology in the mid-twentieth century that it seems hardly to have registered. For British structural-functionalists, the thing to be explained about morality was 'how custom binds' (Fortes 1977). Morality was assumed to be a matter of following custom; the question was by what mechanisms people are brought to do so. Equally, for Boasian cultural anthropology, morality was, in Ruth Benedict's chilling phrase, 'a convenient term for socially approved habits' (1934: 73). Against all this, and against the cultural relativism with respect to morality that both stances inevitably seemed to underpin, Read protested that ethics surely also includes the possibility of critical reflection on the familiar or generally accepted, and that ethical ideals and values inevitably imply the possibility of the perception of a gap between how things are and how they ideally ought to be, and therefore at least open up the possibility of a desire and motivation to close such a gap. So ethics cannot consist only of conformity with 'socially accepted habits'. Conventional anthropological descriptions of morality, Read protested, were simply bypassing all that is most interesting and puzzling about their declared subject matter.

His own proposal was to focus on the ontological assumptions underlying culturally various conceptions of the moral person: in the moral psychologies prevalent in different societies, what capacities (reason? will? conscience? heart? friends?) do people need to possess in order to live ethically? What are the culturally variable ways in which people are something more than merely

followers of custom? In this programmatic essay, Read did not get very far –
and as far as he did get, he was going, I think, in the wrong direction (Laidlaw
2014a: 214–16) – in answering this question, but it remains clearly an indispensable one to ask. And I agree with Read that while – to put it in my terms
rather than his – the ethical subject is differently constituted in different social
relations, morality systems and ethical projects, anything recognizable as
ethical life will presuppose subjects being able to exercise something like what
I have called reflective freedom (Laidlaw 2014a: 147–49): the capacity reflectively to evaluate in the light of values and ideals.

The proponents of ordinary ethics seem content to bypass this matter of
freedom. Lambek, for instance, prefers to avoid reference to freedom in favour
of the observation that people's conduct is 'undetermined' (2015b). Although
it is part of their account of everyday conduct that it involves the exercise of
reason and judgement, and that habit is not unthinking, there is resistance to
the implication, undoubtedly present in the idea of reflective freedom, of
standing back or self-distancing, perhaps because it suggests that there could
be a continuity between a reflective or critical dimension of everyday ethical
life and ethical projects that claim or aim at transcendence. Since self-distancing reflection is often where commitment to projects of self-transformation
begins, acknowledging such reflection as an essential part of ethical life might
seem to ordinary ethicists to come perilously close to legitimizing such tran-
scendence-oriented projects, and so by extension the churches, states and
other powerful institutions that propagate or impose them. But logically I do
not think any of that follows: again, if we accept that recognizing something as
an aspect or instance of ethics is not the same thing as approving of it.

In the formulation I set out above, ethics is founded on the pervasive fact
of self-interpretation and on the fact that the self-descriptions this process
gives rise to are necessarily evaluative. Not all of this, of course, is conscious
or reflective. Much of it is routine, habitual and taken-for-granted. But we
would be left, I think, with a significantly truncated picture of human life if we
allowed that fact to deflect us from acknowledging our capacity for reflection,
however intermittently it might be exercised. If we did not develop such
capacities – and as I have said already, I see them as the outcome of the inescapable inter-subjective, relational nature of social life – we simply would not
be, in Taylor's terms, self-interpreting animals. We do not have to be exercising this capacity continuously, or indeed at any specific time, for it to make a
difference to the quality of our conduct. To put it very baldly, if we were not at
times capable of conscious reflection, or if we never in our lives exercised that
capacity, our everyday and habitual conduct would not be pervasively saturated with meaning, as the ordinary ethicists rightly insist that it is.

A key element in Taylor's (1985) account of self-interpretation is his
concept of 'strong evaluation', which refers to the fact that we do not merely
have, for instance, this or that wish or desire, on the basis of which we act and
of which we might become conscious. We also evaluate those wishes and

desires. There are some we approve, identify with, and commit ourselves to; there are others about which we are ambivalent; others still that we deprecate, regret or struggle against. Taylor is not the only author to have thought that this is central to human agency. Harry Frankfurt (1988) sees the existence of what he calls 'second-order desires' as the basis for such form and degree of 'freedom of the will' as is required to make sense of moral agency. This 'freedom of the will' is plainly not possible without – again, at least intermittent – conscious reflection, and it is a prerequisite for any of the narrative consistency and self-identity through time on which Mattingly rightly insists as a feature of ethical life. As Adam Smith asserted, this capacity for reflection on the self is developed as a result of our inter-personal interactions and social relations. And without the capacity for strong evaluation and reflection on the self – which is impossible to imagine without self-consciousness – I do not see that it would make much sense to say that we even had an ethical life: the term would be redundant.

Therefore, I think Kenneth Read was on the right track in claiming that some kind of reflective evaluation is what marks ethics from the mere following of custom. It is clear, however, that there is deeply felt resistance among some anthropologists (though by no means all) to this line of thought, and in particular to the inescapable conclusion from it that something that it would be eccentric not to call freedom is therefore at the heart of ethics.

Much of this resistance derives, I think, from the concern that 'freedom' as a value inevitably carries specifically Western cultural baggage. Some have claimed that freedom has never been much valued or emphasized except in the modern West – and indeed the modern, secularist, liberal, capitalist West – and although that is demonstrably untrue (Laidlaw 2014a: 138–78), freedom has certainly been a matter of very extensive and developed concern in the West; for this reason, and also because specific ideas and representations about freedom have featured prominently in and been exported as part of colonial and neo-colonial projects, it has come to be thus associated (positively or negatively) for many people in many parts of the world. Furthermore, and perhaps most pertinently, contending ideas of political freedom, and their conflicts with other values such as equality, have been and remain diagnostic of the major ideological cleavages within those roughly modern, secularist, liberal, capitalist, 'Western' polities. These are ideas about which it is impossible to be neutral, certainly if you live in one of these polities. But two things need saying to counter this concern.

First, the idea of reflective freedom that is necessary to get any concept of ethics off the ground is just not the same idea as any of those of political liberty that have been central to our ideological battles, whether it is the liberal idea of 'negative liberty', or the 'positive liberty' that has been so often opposed to it (Berlin 2002), or competing non-liberal ideas such as republican freedom (Skinner 1998). It differs also from ideas about political liberty in persistently non-liberal polities, such as Russia (Humphrey 2007).

On the other hand, although these are importantly different and distinct ideas, the possibility that there might be causal connections between them is of the first importance for a serious anthropological engagement with ethics. To return to a point made earlier, as Jonathan Lear eloquently points out, people's capacity for reflective freedom and therefore their capacity for ethical life may be curtailed in some political and social systems and encouraged and developed in others, and we should surely see it as part of the anthropological project to discover which is which. It would be strange indeed if the presence or absence of different forms of political liberty were irrelevant to those dynamic processes of development or suppression of human capacities.

It has become a commonplace piety that however else it might develop, the anthropology of ethics or morality should not become cut off from the anthropology of politics (e.g. Fassin 2014). And many have rightly called for connections between them to be established or clarified. Well, here is the clearest and most direct connection possible: a framing for ethnographic enquiry into the forms, constraints and possibilities of ethical life under diverse political regimes and circumstances, and the basis for a project of systematic comparison of political orders in terms of the possibilities of ethical life they respectively promote and inhibit. Of course, as I have said already, to say that something is ethical is not necessarily to approve of it – one can imagine a movement, a party or even a society of highly ethical monsters – but the question of the extent to which a political form enables or inhibits ethical life is unlikely to be irrelevant to its evaluation. And although it obviously involves a risk that political doctrines or regimes one personally subscribes to or has some kind of vicarious sympathy for might not come out entirely well from being examined and compared in these terms, that risk should surely not impel us to shy away from an exercise of such clear and substantial anthropological value.

James Laidlaw is William Wyse Professor of Social Anthropology, and a Fellow of King's College, in the University of Cambridge. His publications include *The Subject of Virtue* (2014), *Religion, Anthropology, and Cognitive Science* (2007), *Ritual and Memory* (2004), *The Essential Edmund Leach* (2000), *Riches and Renunciation* (1995) and *The Archetypal Actions of Ritual* (1994).

References

Benedict, Ruth. 1934. 'Anthropology and the Abnormal', *Journal of General Psychology* 10: 59–79.
Berlin, Isaiah. 2002. *Liberty*, ed. Henry Hardy. Oxford: Oxford University Press.
Cook, Joanna. 2010. *Meditation in Modern Buddhism: Renunciation and Change in Thai Monastic Life*. Cambridge: Cambridge University Press.
Crist, Eileen. 1999. *Images of Animals: Anthropomorphism and Animal Mind*. Philadelphia: Temple University Press.

Das, Veena. 2007. *Life and Words: Violence and Descent into the Ordinary*. Berkeley: University of California Press.

———. 2010a. 'Moral and Spiritual Striving in the Everyday: To Be a Muslim in Contemporary India', in Anand Pandian and Daud Ali (eds), *Ethical Life in South Asia*. Bloomington: Indiana University Press, pp. 232–52.

———. 2010b. 'Engaging the Life of the Other: Love and Everyday Life', in Michael Lambek (ed.), *Ordinary Ethics: Anthropology, Language, and Action*. New York: Fordham University Press, pp. 376–99.

———. 2012. 'Ordinary Ethics', in Didier Fassin (ed.), *A Companion to Moral Anthropology*. Oxford: Wiley-Blackwell, pp. 133–49.

———. 2014. 'Ethics, the Householder's Dilemma, and the Difficulty of Reality', *HAU: Journal of Ethnographic Theory* 4: 487–95.

———. 2015. 'Everyday Life and its Moderate Amorality', in 'There is No Such Thing as the Good: The 2013 Meeting of the Group for Debates in Anthropological Theory', ed. Soumhya Venkatesan, *Critique of Anthropology* 35: 433–40.

Despret, Vinciane. 2004. 'The Body We Care for: Figures of Anthropo-zoo-genesis', *Body & Society* 10: 111–34.

Fassin, Didier. 2014. 'The Ethical Turn in Anthropology: Promises and Uncertainties', *HAU: Journal of Ethnographic Theory* 4: 429–35.

Faubion, James D. 2011. *An Anthropology of Ethics*. Cambridge: Cambridge University Press.

———. 2014a. 'The Subject that is Not One: On the Ethics of Mysticism', *Anthropological Theory* 13: 287–307.

———. 2014b. 'Anthropologies of Ethics: Where We've Been, Where We Are, Where We Might Go', *HAU: Journal of Ethnographic Theory* 4: 437–42.

Fortes, Meyer. 1977. 'Custom and Conscience in Anthropological Perspective', *International Review of Psychoanalysis* 4: 127–54.

Foucault, Michel. 1986 (1984). *The Use of Pleasure: The History of Sexuality*, Volume 2. London: Viking.

———. 1997. *Ethics, Subjectivity, and Truth: Essential Works of Foucault 1954–1980*, Volume 1, ed. Paul Rabinow. New York: New Press.

———. 2000. *Power: Essential Works of Foucault 1954–1980*, Volume 3, ed. James D. Faubion. New York: New Press.

Frankfurt, Harry G. 1988. *The Importance of What We Care About: Philosophical Essays*. Cambridge: Cambridge University Press.

Hirschkind, Charles. 2006. *The Ethical Soundscape: Cassette Sermons and Islamic Counter-Publics in Egypt*. New York: Columbia University Press.

Humphrey, Caroline. 2007. 'Alternative Freedoms', *Proceedings of the American Philosophical Society* 151: 1–10.

Keane, Webb. 2010. 'Minds, Surfaces, and Reasons in the Anthropology of Ethics', in Michael Lambek (ed.), *Ordinary Ethics: Anthropology, Language, and Action*. New York: Fordham University Press, pp. 64–83.

———. 2014a. 'Affordances and Reflexivity in Ethical Life: An Ethnographic Stance', *Anthropological Theory* 14: 3–26.

———. 2014b. 'Freedom, Reflexivity, and the Sheer Everydayness of Ethics', *HAU: Journal of Ethnographic Theory* 4: 433–57.

———. 2016. *Ethical Life: Its Natural and Social Histories*. Princeton: Princeton University Press.

Kohn, Eduardo. 2014. 'Toward an Ethical Practice in the Anthropocene', *HAU: Journal of Ethnographic Theory* 4: 459–64.

Laidlaw, James. 1995. *Riches and Renunciation: Religion, Economy, and Society among the Jains*. Oxford: Clarendon Press.

_____. 2002. 'For an Anthropology of Ethics and Freedom', *Journal of the Royal Anthropological Institute* 8: 311–32.

_____. 2005. 'A Life Worth Leaving: Fasting to Death as Telos of a Jain Religious Life', *Economy and Society* 34: 178–99.

_____. 2014a. *The Subject of Virtue: An Anthropology of Ethics and Freedom*. Cambridge: Cambridge University Press.

_____. 2014b. 'Significant Differences: Response to HAU Book Symposium on Laidlaw, James. 2014. *The subject of virtue: An anthropology of ethics and freedom*. Cambridge: Cambridge University Press', *HAU: Journal of Ethnographic Theory* 4: 497–506.

Lambek, Michael. 2000. 'The Anthropology of Religion and the Quarrel between Poetry and Philosophy', *Current Anthropology* 41: 309–20.

_____. 2002. 'Nuriaty, the Saint, and the Sultan: Virtuous Subject and Subjective Virtuoso of the Postmodern Colony', in Richard Werbner (ed.), *Postcolonial Subjectivities in Africa*. London: Zed Books. Available at https://www.sss.ias.edu/files/Nuriaty,%20the%20Saint%20and%20the%20Sultan.pdf.

_____. 2008. 'Value and Virtue', *Anthropological Theory* 8: 133–57.

_____. 2010. 'Toward an Ethics of the Act', in *Ordinary Ethics: Anthropology, Language, and Action*. New York: Fordham University Press, pp. 39–63.

_____. 2015a. 'On the Immanence of the Ethical: A Response to Lempert's "No Ordinary Ethics"', *Anthropological Theory* 15: 128–32.

_____. 2015b. *The Ethical Condition: Essays on Action, Person, and Value*. Chicago: University of Chicago Press.

Lear, Jonathan. 2006. *Radical Hope: Ethics in the Face of Cultural Destruction*. Cambridge, MA: Harvard University Press.

_____. 2015. 'Waiting with Coetzee', *Raritan* 34(4): 1–26.

Lempert, Michael. 2013. 'No Ordinary Ethics', *Anthropological Theory* 13: 370–93.

_____. 2015. 'Ethics Without Immanence: A Reply to Michael Lambek', *Anthropological Theory* 15: 133–40.

Lester, Rebecca J. 2005. *Jesus in Our Wombs: Embodying Modernity in a Mexican Convent*. Berkeley: University of California Press.

Mahmood, Saba. 2005. *Politics of Piety: The Islamic Revival and the Feminist Subject*. Princeton: Princeton University Press.

Mattingly, Cheryl. 2014a. 'Moral Deliberation and the Agentive Self in Laidlaw's Ethics', *HAU: Journal of Ethnographic Theory* 4: 473–86.

_____. 2014b. *Moral Laboratories: Family Peril and the Struggle for a Good Life*. Princeton: Princeton University Press.

Read, Kenneth E. 1955. 'Morality and the Concept of the Person among the Gahuku-Gama', *Oceania* 23: 233–82.

Robbins, Joel. 2013. 'Beyond the Suffering Subject: Toward an Anthropology of the Good', *Journal of the Royal Anthropological Institute* 19: 447–62.

Skinner, Quentin. 1998. *Liberty Before Liberalism*. Cambridge: Cambridge University Press.

Smith, Adam. 1976 [1790]. *The Theory of Moral Sentiments*, ed. D.D. Rafael and A.L. Macfie. Oxford: Oxford University Press.

Taylor, Charles. 1985. 'Self-Interpreting Animals', in *Human Agency and Language: Philosophical Papers*, Volume 1. Cambridge: Cambridge University Press, pp. 45–76.

Williams, Bernard. 1985. *Ethics and the Limits of Philosophy*. London: Collins.

Zigon, Jarrett. 2007. 'Moral Breakdown and Ethical Demand: A Theoretical Framework for an Anthropology of Moralities', *Anthropological Theory* 7: 131–50.
_____. 2008. *Morality: An Anthropological Perspective*. Oxford: Berg.
_____. 2014a. 'Attunement and Fidelity: Two Ontological Conditions for Morally Being-in-the-World', *Ethos* 42: 16–30.
_____. 2014b. 'An Ethics of Dwelling and a Politics of World-Building: A Critical Response to Ordinary Ethics', *Journal of the Royal Anthropological Institute* 20: 746–64.

Part III

Moral Engines and the Human Condition

10

An Ethics of Dwelling and a Politics of Worldbuilding
Responding to the Demands of the Drug War

Jarrett Zigon

As this volume attests, analyses of morality and ethics have become central to the work of many anthropologists. Indeed, the disciplinary scene has certainly changed since the early 2000s when I was writing my dissertation and desperately searched for explicit anthropological work on the topic. Since that time there has been a wave of anthropological work on moralities and ethics, the most noteworthy of which, I would argue, is the specifically programmatic or theoretically-analytic questioning of what counts as morality and ethics (e.g., Robbins 2004; Zigon 2007, 2011, 2012, 2013, 2017; Lambek 2010; Throop 2010; Faubion 2011; Mattingly 2014). This work has made at least three significant contributions: firstly, the avoidance of simply equating morality or ethics with normative social behaviour; secondly, the avoidance of analysing ethnographic data through the lens of our own moral assumptions, traditions and concepts; and thirdly, the avoidance of falling into moralizing analysis motivated by the urge, for example, to reveal the injustices uncovered through fieldwork.

This is an approach to the study of moralities and ethics that takes them seriously as social phenomena, and recognizes them not as distal aspects of primary social practices such as politics or religion but as distinct and significant factors in shaping these. Perhaps what is most significant about this approach is the possibility it allows for questioning and rethinking some of the most basic assumptions and concepts generally associated with morality. For a critical anthropological study of moralities is perfectly situated not only to disclose the genealogy of moral concepts and reveal their potentially (not so) hidden political-economic implications, but also to offer new concepts that better articulate the moral experiences of our ethnographic subjects (Zigon 2014a, 2014b, 2017).

In this chapter I will do just this by addressing the central question of this volume – indeed, perhaps the central question of human existence – that is, how to understand ethical motivation or the ethical drives of human life. To do this I take up an ethnographic example of anti-drug war political activism that shows how critical hermeneutics provides a framework for recognizing the emergence of ethical demands from a world. The first step of such hermeneutics is the recognition that although many of our informants may utilize the dominant moral vocabulary available today, ethical imperatives may exceed that which is intended or meant by this vocabulary. As a result, it behoves us to consider that when our informants use a familiar moral concept, it may be because it is the only concept historically available to try to articulate something about being-in-the-world that exceeds what it is that concept has come to represent, indicate or mean; and, as such, we may recognize this concept as a marker of the problematic of ethics – a place from which our analysis can begin – but not as the end or aim of ethics. In so doing, critical hermeneutics, furthermore, seeks to counter the deep moralism that has to a great extent saturated much of our social, analytic and political lives, and as a result attempts to rethink the link between ethics and politics. Thus, I argue that a critical hermeneutics of moralities provides a theoretic-analytic for rethinking a moral tradition characterized by metaphysical humanism, as well as the social and political worlds in which the concepts and assumptions of this tradition are mobilized (see Zigon 2017).

Drug War

The war on drugs was first declared by Richard Nixon and since the early 1980s has become a highly militarized, punitive, highly expensive international 'war on people', as many anti-drug war activists put it, waged to some extent by nearly every country on the globe. It is difficult to conclude that the drug war has been anything but a disastrous failure no matter how one looks at it. From the mass incarceration of a significant proportion of a generation of African-American men in the United States, to the street battles, assassinations and 'collateral damage' that has led to over 70,000 deaths in Mexico since 2006, to the torturous rehabilitation conditions found throughout Russia, to the extrajudicial killings in 2003 of at least 2,275 suspected drug 'offenders' in Thailand by the military and police, to the preventable health risks users and non-users are exposed to everywhere as the result of stigmatization and lack of harm reduction programmes, the drug war seemingly has resulted in little more than the death, suffering and stigmatization of millions of users and non-users alike. Meanwhile, drug cartels continue to accumulate wealth and power that in some instances far surpasses that of sovereign nations, and states increasingly tighten security and surveillance that impacts the lives of entire populations.[1]

It is precisely this situation that anti-drug war activists around the globe are mobilizing against (Zigon 2015). Like nearly every political movement on the contemporary political scene, the anti-drug war movement regularly mixes moral language with its political agenda and in this sense could be seen as an example of the political moralism that Wendy Brown (2001) argues character-izes contemporary politics. Thus, dignity, rights, respect and justice are some of the moral key words that the spokespersons for this movement will regu-larly invoke. For example, once while interviewing a regional director of one of the most influential international drug policy reform organizations, I was told that one of the goals of the organization, as well as her personal view on the matter, is that all drug users should be treated with dignity. Indeed, this was not surprising as dignity is a moral concept that is regularly used by anti-drug war political activists in their struggle against prohibition and the negative effects of what they call 'a war on people' – drug users and non-drug users alike. I asked her what she meant by 'dignity' and she replied:

> Well, I mean our health policies, our criminal justice policies. None of them really treat an individual who is struggling with drugs, whether it's drug possession, drug use, drug selling, with dignity. They don't recognize the fact that an individual's life may have been challenging and so the decisions that they've had to make, that have brought them to this place in their life, may not be decisions that we think are good, but maybe the best decision out of a range of decisions and options that were avail-able at the time those decisions were made. And, I think a lot of the local healthcare collaboratives that have sprung up over the last couple of decades like syringe exchange programs and things like that, are some of the only places where there actually is dignity for people who are using drugs and who are struggling in life.

It seems, then, that according to this leading advocate of drug policy reform, dignity is not about an inherent essence or capacity of the natural human as it is so often glossed in human rights discourse. Rather, dignity here is primarily conceived as the outcome of a particular social configuration of non-prohibi-tionist policies and services that begin not with judgment but with quality care and an understanding of how certain life trajectories may provide limited pos-sibilities for being-in-the-world. In fact, in the director's utterance she locates dignity only once and it is not in, on or as a part of an individual person, but rather she locates it in a socio-politically configured space she calls local healthcare collaboratives. It is in particularly assembled and situated worlds of certain practices, policies, ideas and aims, 'where there actually is dignity for people'. When persons become a part of such assemblages they too take on such dignity not because it was a latent aspect of their natural essence, but because this particular assemblage provides certain conditions within which they can dwell. As a result, and as will become clear below, new possibilities arise for them that may allow them to become something that previously would not have been possible. It is this being-at-home in the world and the openness to possibilities that this form of being allows that the director articu-lates when she uses the word 'dignity' but that I will refer to as dwelling.

In the rest of this section I will try to show that what this director refers to as 'dignity' may in fact be better conceived as dwelling, and that an anthropological study of moralities/ethics[2] is most productive when it does not assume that we already know how to recognize these. Rather, we may be analytically better off accepting that although oftentimes our informants will use the moral vocabulary of dominant moral discourses, they may use this vocabulary to indicate an ethical imperative that exceeds that which the former can articulate. Is this, after all, really very surprising? Is it unreasonable to consider the possibility that a very particular set of moral concepts that have a very particular history would not entirely or even adequately cover the range of possible moral/ethical concerns, problems, anxieties or ways of being-in-the-world? For the director's use of dignity in this utterance clearly seems to be intending some other state of affairs that exceeds what the 'ordinary' or dominant use of 'dignity' would entail. Her use of dignity seems to be pointing to a moral aim that is not covered under the ordinary use of the concept but she uses it nevertheless.

Perhaps this is so because there is not yet another moral concept available for her to use. It is the gap of this 'not yet' that critical hermeneutics attempts to fill. And this is the case because hermeneutic analysis assumes that we humans are always ahead of ourselves, constantly engaged in an existentially interpretive process to catch up to our being, a being that can never be completely met. Because of this assumption critical hermeneutics cannot take concepts to literally mean what they are 'supposed' to mean, but, rather, by doing ethnographic analysis as a form of the phenomenological epoché (Throop 2012), critical hermeneutics asks what the use of the concept points us towards. In so doing, a central task of critical hermeneutics is to offer possibilities for thinking, doing and becoming morally and politically otherwise, rather than reproducing the moral vocabulary that clearly no longer resonates with what it is like to be-in-this-world today (Zigon 2017).

But the director did use 'dignity' and when I pushed her a little bit on just this point she responded that she is trying to talk 'about the way the social context has impacted this individual's life and how that all goes together to create the current circumstances. Regardless of what those current circumstances are, everyone should be treated with dignity'. And here again we see that in response to my slight pushing she more or less repeats – in a much abbreviated form – what she had told me above but this time seems to put more emphasis on the dignity of individuals rather than how singular assemblages in the world are places of 'dignity'. It is in the anthropologist's push for clarification, I suggest, in the forced reflection upon the use of language, that the director returns to the dominant use of dignity as that which is a characteristic of individuals; that individuals should be treated as dignified beings. In this reflection, return and reliance upon a dominant moral discourse the director shifts her articulation of 'dignity' from that of a description of an assembled world, as a part of which one can dwell, to that of the dominant notion of an adjectival being standing over and against the world and already pre-known in its moral totality. This shift is not surprising since our contemporary dominant moral discourses and their attendant political discourses – those that utilize the language of rights, dignity, responsibility, good, evil and so on – begin from the ontological condition of *a priori* totalized subjects standing over and against the world they happen to live in, and stand there as the basis and source of morality/ethics.

Ethics of Dwelling – NYC

The police in New York City already 'know' the being-in-the-world of a young black man when they (not so) randomly stop and frisk him on the street. Stop and Frisk has been a key police tactic in the war on drugs used in New York City. In 2012, for example, 532,911 individuals were stopped and frisked in New York City, 55 per cent of whom were African American and 32 per cent of whom were Latino. Perhaps most disturbing about this form of surveillance is that 89 per cent of all of those stopped and frisked in 2012 were deemed 'innocent', that is, the search they were exposed to turned up nothing. The highest number of arrests (more than 5,000) were carried out for possessing personal-use quantities of marijuana, which under New York City law is not an offence unless it is shown in public, which is exactly what it is when a police officer asks you to empty your pockets. Overwhelmingly, those stopped, frisked and arrested are young African-American and Latino men, and this tactic is predominantly carried out in the neighbourhoods where these men live.[3] It has created a situation in which one's neighbourhood, one's street, one's own front stoop is no longer a place where one can dwell. It is just this inability to dwell in their world that has led many African-American and Latin-American people in New York City who do and do not use drugs to politically mobilize against this and other tactics of the war on drugs.

Consider, for example, Terrance, who is a fifty-year-old African-American man from the Bronx, a former crack user who has been incarcerated twice; now, as a leader of the city's users' union, he regularly meets with New York State and City politicians and officials in an attempt to end prohibitionist laws and policies. Terrance once told me:

> I kind of think that what really put me, or what really motivated me was uhm, was seeing the harassment that, you know, people in our community are going through on a daily basis trying to struggle, trying to make ends meet, you know. I mean, it's not fair that you would come to my community, and you don't live there and you can tell me where I can stand, you can tell me that because I live here I can't stand in front of my building, I can't stand on this corner, I can't congregate with individuals in my social setting in front of my building. You know, I'm trespassing in my own neighbourhood. Come on! You know, then uhm, and all these unnecessary, all these arrests that were taking place that were just, I can't even find the words to describe

it, you know what I'm saying, but it was unorthodox, you know, to a point where if I'm coming out of my building, like I been many times, and stopped and frisked because I'm a person of colour and I don't have my sneakers tied or I'm wearing, you know, or I have clothes on that are related to gangsters or whatever, which are the clothings that a lot of people in the neighbourhood wear, you know, and I'm going to work and I'm still being stopped. You're not giving me no freedom to walk in my own neighbourhood, but if I was in another neighbourhood, another colour, you wouldn't be stopping me. So why am I, at this point right here, being profiled? So, profiling was something that really irritated me ... So that was my motivation for, you know, starting to come to [the union] and getting involved.

The director of the drug policy organization might characterize the situation Terrance describes as one in which Terrance and his neighbours are treated without dignity. Those who protest against Stop and Frisk policies in front of City Hall often hold signs that call for justice. But Terrance finds no use for what Hannah Arendt called 'bannisters' to articulate the moral breakdown that motivates him to struggle politically against the drug war. Rather, for Terrance it all comes done to the fact that the drug war situation has rendered him a stranger in his world: a person who in his total being is assumed from the beginning to be untrustworthy, dangerous, potential evil waiting to manifest. Terrance's motivation for becoming and remaining politically active is not moral outrage erupting from an internal sense of dignity, but is better considered, I suggest, as a moral breakdown that stems from the fact that the drug war situation has resulted in him experiencing himself as if 'You know, I'm trespassing in my own neighbourhood'.

This moral breakdown, however, is not simply about Terrance and his neighbours not being able to live normally and go about their everyday lives, although it is also about that. But this unsettledness points to a deeper and more existential and ontological demand to be in the world in a certain way. For not only is Terrance unable to live the everyday in his world, neither can he dwell in his world. And this is an important distinction for the purpose of this chapter as it provides a line of flight along which we can reconceive morality/ethics, as well as politics. For dwelling is not simply being able to live one's everydayness. Humans have an incredible capacity to adapt to all kinds of conditions in which they can live. The innumerable stories of mundane everydayness lived out in extreme contexts of poverty or war attest to this. In contrast, to dwell is to be-in-the-world in such a way that one's being is not reduced to such a degree that being-in-the-world becomes something like trapped in a world. The everydayness that Terrance and his neighbours are forced to live because of the situation of the drug war is more akin to being trapped in a world than dwelling.

This distinction can be seen, for example, in Heidegger's conception of dwelling as both building and care (1975b). In considering the phrase 'poetically man dwells' found in one of Hölderlin's poems, Heidegger (1975a) interprets dwelling as ongoing *poiesis*, or as creative building that allows for continued poetic dwelling. Such poetic or creative dwelling is being-in-the-world in such a way that as part of that world one is intimately intertwined with and concerned for it and its constituent parts. Furthermore, to dwell is also to be in a world in such a way that one's being is never pre-limited within a pre-assumed totality, but, rather, that possibilities for becoming otherwise remain open. Becoming otherwise, then, is a process of poetic dwelling, of building and maintaining a world in which such dwelling always remains possible (cf. Heidegger 1975b; Ingold 2011; Povinelli 2011). This is an ethic of dwelling as a politics of worldbuilding.

Terrance is struggling to dwell in a world that has made it nearly impossible for him and his neighbours to do so. And yet he keeps going. Despite having a prison record that is a direct result of drug war surveillance – a record that has taken away his ability, for example, to vote, receive student and other kinds of loans, to travel abroad, and to be hired for many jobs – Terrance struggles to find a way to dwell, to be in the world in such a way that both feels, as it were, right, and provides possibilities for becoming otherwise. A significant part of his ethical struggle to dwell has been his political activity with the users' union, but perhaps more important for Terrance is his work at the syringe exchange programme in his Bronx neighbourhood. Just as the director of the drug policy reform organization articulated syringe exchanges and other such collaborative health programmes as a place where 'dignity' is located, Terrance sees his neighbourhood programme as one of the few places where people who use drugs can dwell. Terrance, of course, does not put it quite like this, but he does describe it as a place where people who use can feel safe, not judged or stigmatized, where they can just 'hang out' and socialize with others; he describes it as a place where many of their needs can be met, and they can learn how to satisfy their own needs. The programme is also a place where – through a project run by Terrance – people who use can be trained to become outreach workers, learn skills and become educated in certain ways that translate into other kinds of jobs, and, significantly, become trained to participate in the political activity of the users' union. All of this – the being and feeling at home, the sociality, and the openness of possibilities to become otherwise – is what I am trying to get at by using the term dwelling not only as a moral concept but as an ethical imperative for human existence.

What is an ethical imperative for human existence and how does it differ from the metaphysical humanism that is characteristic of much moral philosophy and, as I have argued elsewhere (2014a), increasingly anthropological studies of ethics and moralities as well? Both dwelling as an existential imperative and metaphysical humanist conceptions such as dignity make claims about the essential 'nature' of being human. To make a claim that all humans share some essence in and of itself is not a problem. How, after all, could it be said that we study humans and not chimpanzees, dogs, trees or starfish if we do not acknowledge that there is something essential about what it is to be any one of these particular existents? The problem of metaphysical humanism is that it assumes an *a priori*, predefined human with very specific characteristics and capacities – such as Reason and Morality, along with the latter's assumed qualities of dignity, rights and autonomy – that are held to be the case prior to any actual intertwining with any particular world. The only question that remains is if these characteristics and capacities will be allowed to manifest and flourish in a particular social and political world. Luckily, built into this perspective is the answer to the question of what the social and political world ought to be like in order to support this flourishing: it just so happens to be a world that very much resembles our own.

To claim that dwelling is an ethical imperative for human existence, on the other hand, does not assert any predefined characteristics or capacities of humanness. Rather, it is simply to claim that to be human is to be intimately intertwined with a world for which one is concerned and which is concerned, in turn, for it.[4] And, it should be noted that this concern makes no normative claim beyond maintaining the ability to dwell in that world. Because of this mutual concern between oneself and a world, an openness always remains such that both oneself and that world can become otherwise so as to maintain this mutual concern. To speak of dwelling as an ethical imperative, then, does not predefine how or what a human becomes, nor does it predefine what kind of world this human must become a part of. Rather, it is simply to acknowledge that to be human is always to be concernedly intertwined in a world with others, and this being-together always manifests differently. Dwelling, then, is that existential imperative of humanness that allows for the very differences of ways of being-in-the-world, ethically acting and valuing, and socially and politically inter- and intra-acting that anthropologists tend to focus on. Thus, while it is certainly the case that I assume an existential essence of the being we call human, this is a minimal essence that provides the open ground for becoming in diverse and differing ways. In contrast, metaphysical humanism assumes a predefined and closed conception of humanness whereby to be human is always and only to be defined by Reason and Morality and their concomitant attributes such as dignity or responsibility. Thus, while metaphysical humanism simply repeats and projects a certain predefined conception of humanness, dwelling offers an ontological starting point for understanding how differences manifest because of an essential sharedness, as well as offering a link between this ontological starting point, ethical motivation and political practice.

This is so because when worlds breakdown, dwelling is no longer possible. When this occurs the demand of an ethics of dwelling is felt and some respond to this demand. Thus, Terrance is not alone in his struggle to enact an ethics of dwelling in New York City. There is also, for example, Martin, an African-American man in his mid-forties, who formerly used heroin but now only occasionally uses cocaine. Like Terrance, Martin also works at a syringe exchange programme in his neighbourhood and is one of the leaders of the New York City users' union and one of the union's most publicly outspoken members. Once when we were talking about how he got involved with the union and what his involvement has done for him, he told me that for him it was an 'awakening'. As he put it: 'I guess you could say it was more of an awakening once I saw what [the union] was actually about. And that's the way I like to look at it now, as basically an awakening'. I asked him what he meant by an awakening and he continued:

> When I say an awakening, meaning that for so long being a user and just not having the understanding that there are opportunities for people like myself to actually meet with our legislators and actually talk to them about things that are needed in our community, actually being able to have an influence and getting new legislation passed, you know what I'm saying, and moving, and possibly moving policy. To me, that's an awakening as far as being, as far as being able to be made aware that, yeah, these things are possible. So that's what I mean by saying that's an awakening ... It was a whole new world that basically opened up and it's a challenge, it's an everyday challenge to try and let others know that they have the same opportunities that I had as far as gaining that awakening.

Martin describes his participation in anti-drug war politics as an awakening, as the opening of 'a whole new world' in which he could do, think and be in ways that he never imagined were possible for him before. As he told me later that day, participating in the union and working as an advocacy liaison at the exchange programme have given him the possibility of becoming an entirely different person than he was before. Martin's motivations for joining the union, like Terrance's, did not stem from moral outrage but instead from the experience of having his mother, who was also an injecting drug user, die in his arms from complications related to the HIV/AIDS she contracted as a user who had no access to syringe exchange. The moral breakdown that resulted from this experience brought about for Martin a deep-seated awareness that for drug users it had become impossible to dwell in a world in which the war on drugs is waged on people like his mother, himself and his friends. Of course those who did not die could survive within the limiting conditions allowed by this war. But Martin felt that he and his loved ones could not dwell; he felt that they had their open possibilities for being-in-the-world closed simply because they put a substance in their body that the state prohibits.

Martin eventually discovered that the ethics of dwelling as a politics of worldbuilding that he enacts opens new possibilities, new worlds for him and others. He discovered that this ethics of dwelling awakened him. Motivated by this awakening, he now seeks to provide this to those users who are still trapped in what he calls the 'void' that most people who use drugs are trapped in as a result of prohibitionist policies that, among other things, limit users' being-in-the-world to the stigmatized identity of an immoral and irresponsible addict who is certainly untrustworthy and potentially dangerous. As of yet Martin and Terrance's activities are limited to building what we might call new 'subjective worlds'. But in the next section I will briefly consider a politics of worldbuilding that is in the process of building an entirely new and parallel world in the midst of another North American city.

Politics of Worldbuilding – Vancouver

Terrance's experience in parts of the Bronx shows us that prohibitionist policies render entire neighbourhoods zones of uninhabitability. Another such zone of uninhabitability emerged in the Downtown Eastside of Vancouver, Canada, as a result of the drug war situation in that city. A hundred years ago the Downtown Eastside was a centre of business, commerce and government in Vancouver, but by the late twentieth century it had become the frontline of the drug war in the city. Businesses and government offices had moved out to be replaced with single room occupancy (SRO) hotels and abandoned spaces. It was not uncommon for commuters who had no other option than to take a bus through this part of town to look out the window and see dead bodies from overdose lying on the sidewalks. The back alleyways that run throughout the neighbourhood had become heroin shooting galleries, places of business for sex workers, a place to sleep and congregate and buy and sell drugs, and yet another place to die from overdose. Hundreds of people a year, in fact, would die of overdose in this neighbourhood alone. It was, as one eventual protest by drug users would call it, 'the killing fields'.

This neighbourhood had become a world in which the people who lived there – a great number of whom were drug users – could no longer dwell. This world had become uninhabitable and unbearable. Those who lived there were reduced to objects that metaphorically and quite literally became just another 'piece of trash' on the sidewalk or in the alley. Eventually many of these users, their neighbours and some of the organizations already working in the neighbourhood – mostly SRO organizations – mobilized to address the fact of the unbearableness of this world. Here is an example of how from the breakdown of a world, out of its unbearableness, a demand for another kind of ethics emerges; this is an ethics of dwelling, which we can also call politics – that is, politics as a process of worldbuilding.

Such an ethics of dwelling as a politics of worldbuilding is underway in Vancouver, and anti-drug war activists around the globe look to it as a model for their own activities. In addition to similar kinds of harm reduction practices and activism to that done by Terrance and Martin in New York, activists in Vancouver were also able to create the only legally sanctioned safe injection site (Insite) in North America. But while the establishment of Insite is a central aspect of the new world that has emerged out of the breakdown of the Downtown Eastside, it is just one aspect of this new world, within which it is now possible for drug users to dwell. This new world consists of, among other things, art galleries and studios, a bank, a grocery store, a dentist office, a community centre, a medical centre, and a network of social enterprises, where users can be trained for employment and work, and which includes two coffee shops/cafes and various stores.

This is a new world attuned to itself and its inhabitants, and as such remains open to possibilities for it and them becoming otherwise (see Zigon 2017).

Consider the following example. One October morning I was standing outside one of the social enterprise cafes talking with its manager and the director of the first nations programme of one of the neighbourhood organizations. The director was telling me that unlike most service programmes around the globe, Vancouver's is unique in that they have built what he called a structure but I will call a world, in which any one of the programmes or businesses within this world serves as an entry point for the others. The director went on to draw a distinction. As he put it, normally if one is seeking some services then one must and can only find these at a particular location run by a particular organization that is generally disconnected from other kinds of programmes and services. The director called this common way of providing and finding services linear because there is only one entry point and it provides only one kind of service. Vancouver's Downtown Eastside, on the other hand, is a world of networked services and social enterprises into which one can enter at any point and be referred to, learn about, and take advantage of any number of other available possibilities within this world.

The director continued and gave me the following example of how this emergence of possibilities happens. The bank, he said as he pointed to it across the street and which is a part of this networked world, can be an entry point for a range of possibilities. The bank is a space where tellers come to know local customers quite well as they all tend to be people from the neighbourhood. Over time they hear their stories, see them in the streets and in the cafes, or in the community centre, and thus a relationship is built over time. It is not uncommon, then, that someone might confide in a teller about some difficulties she might be experiencing, or the teller might simply be able to see that she is acting differently than usual, and thus the teller can suggest she go across the street to the detox centre, for example, or to the dentist, or suggest she seek employment at one of the social enterprises within the neighbourhood. The bank, then, becomes an entry point into a range of possibilities that emerges from a world that is attuned to the ways of being and becoming of itself. It is a space or clearing from which a world opens itself to one of its inhabitants who dwells within it.

The bank is not simply a place to keep one's money so that the bank can make profit; it is also a clearing in a world specifically attuned to those beings that dwell there. Thus, not only are the tellers and customers attuned to these possibilities, but so too is the architectural space and technology of the bank. The lobby, for example, unlike in other banks, is not simply a place to fill out deposit slips or wait to meet a teller or service representative, it is also a space for people in the neighbourhood to hang out, drink the free coffee, and use computers and the internet provided to anyone free of charge. The bank lobby is a clearing where it is possible to learn about what is happening elsewhere in the neighbourhood – for example, political rallies, concerts, yoga sessions or art exhibitions – by talking with others or reading the announcements posted there. It is also a clearing opening onto the globe as one can interact with others anywhere or learn about anything via the internet. The bank lobby, then, is a clearing out of which possibilities of learning, acting and becoming are opened. And just in case this is not enough, the lobby is also a space where anyone can go and get a safe crack pipe from a vending machine, probably the only bank anywhere that offers a crack pipe vending machine. This bank, then, is a space of opening possibilities that is just one part of a new world that has emerged in the Downtown Eastside as a result of the politics of worldbuilding enacted as a result of the demands of an ethics of dwelling.

This is a brief example, then, of how unlike much political activity in North America and other parts of the globe that is driven by a political moralism that shouts out platitudes of moral outrage, activists in Vancouver are enacting another kind of politics because it evokes another kind of morality. They are not holding on to bannisters in their attempt to build a world in which they and others can once again dwell. Rather, they are responding with an ethics that has emerged from the demand that as a human being-in-the-world it is existentially necessary to be able to do so, that is, dwell.

Some Closing Words

In this chapter I have tried to show that anthropological studies of moralities and ethics are best served by not restricting their analyses to the already well-established moral concepts and frameworks of Western moral philosophy. As an illustration, I have provided a critical hermeneutics that discloses how ethical imperatives may exceed familiar moral concepts despite the fact that the latter are utilized in ordinary everyday language because they are the only moral concepts currently available. I have argued that familiar moral concepts ought not be considered as moral aims, but rather as pointing to or indicating an ethical problem or imperative that cannot yet be neatly conceptualized but nevertheless motivates action in the world. It is the analysis of these ethical problems or imperatives that I have been arguing critical hermeneutics is suited to do.

'Dignity' is one of those familiar moral concepts that anti-drug war political activists regularly utilize. I have tried to show that how at least one major player in the international drug policy reform world uses this concept is better conceived as pointing to the existential inability for many people around the world to dwell in worlds conditioned by the war on drugs. Terrance and Martin made this particularly clear in their articulation of why they were motivated to become politically active in the users' union, and further described to me how they conceive of this work as providing spaces within which users and non-users can dwell and as such become open to new possibilities for being-in-the-world. Martin described this experience of dwelling as an 'awakening'. Both Terrance and Martin, like many other activists around the globe, look to the new world being created 'on the ground' in Vancouver as an example of the kind of politics of worldbuilding they are trying to enact in response to the ethical demand they have felt.

The dominant meaning of the concept 'dignity' captures none of this, and yet this is precisely what the director, Terrance, Martin, activists in Vancouver, and many others have talked to me about and shown me they are doing in their political activism. They are attempting to transform worlds so that those who have found themselves in them no longer have their way of being-in-the-world limited to such a degree that in a very real sense they may be better described as trapped in a world than as dwelling in a world. In other words, by looking to see what the familiar concept of 'dignity' points to, rather than taking it as the aim or end of moral activity, we discover that in this instance 'dignity' points to an ethical imperative that has ontological and political implications. That is to say, the ethics of dwelling that drives the anti-drug war political movement is an ethical motivation for doing a kind of politics that seeks to change the ontological conditions of worlds because those conditions that are currently enacted through the war on drugs have become existentially unbearable. In this sense, moralities and ethics, and the politics they may demand, emerge from the ontological conditions we happen to find ourselves in for being-in-the-world.

Jarrett Zigon is the William and Linda Porterfield Professor of Biomedical Ethics and Professor of Anthropology at the University of Virginia. His most recent book, *Disappointment: Toward a Critical Hermeneutics of Worldbuilding*, addresses the question of political motivation and disappointment in our contemporary world through a rethinking of the relation between ethics, politics and ontologies.

Notes

1. Significantly revised versions of this chapter have been published in *Journal of the Royal Anthropological Institute* as 'An Ethics of Dwelling and a Politics of World-Building: a Critical Response to Ordinary Ethics' (Zigon 2014a), and in *Disappointment: Toward a Critical Hermeneutics of Worldbuilding* (Zigon 2017). For more information see, for example, www.drugpolicy.org and www.opensocietyfoundations.org.
2. I use the shorthand morality/ethics or ethics/morality when discussing anthropological studies and approaches since as of yet there is no agreement by anthropologists as to what either concept means, or which is more useful; both are thus often used interchangeably or one is simply chosen rather than the other. This conceptual situation is reflected in this volume.
3. For this and other information, see http://www.nyclu.org/content/stop-and-frisk-data and http://www.nyclu.org/news/ analysis-finds-racial-disparities-ineffectiveness-nypd-stop-and-frisk-program-links-tactic-soar.
4. Here I want to go beyond the Heideggerian notion of concern (*Besorgen*) as Dasein's concern for things and practices of the world, and even beyond the late Heidegger's extension of care and concern to that of Being in general, and suggest that an ethics of

dwelling ultimately entails a mutual concern between all of those existents that become intertwined within a world. Dwelling entails a mutual responsivity of all existents of proximity; this mutual responsivity can be called attunement.

References

Brown, Wendy. 2001. *Politics Out of History*. Princeton: Princeton University Press.
Faubion, James D. 2011. *An Anthropology of Ethics*. Cambridge: Cambridge University Press.
Heidegger, Martin. 1975a. '...Poetically Man Dwells ...', in *Poetry, Language, Thought*. New York: Harper Colophon Books, pp. 211–29.
_____. 1975b. 'Building Dwelling Thinking', in *Poetry, Language, Thought*. New York: Harper Colophon Books, pp. 143–61.
Ingold, Tim. 2011. *The Perception of the Environment: Essays on Livelihood, Dwelling and Skill*. London: Routledge.
Lambek, Michael. 2010. *Ordinary Ethics: Anthropology, Language, and Action*. New York: Fordham University Press.
Mattingly, Cheryl. 2014. *Moral Laboratories: Family Peril and the Struggle for a Good Life*. Berkeley: University of California Press.
Povinelli, Elizabeth A. 2011. *Economies of Abandonment: Social Belonging and Endurance in Late Liberalism*. Durham, NC: Duke University Press.
Robbins, Joel. 2004. *Becoming Sinners: Christianity and Moral Torment in a Papua New Guinea Society*. Berkeley: University of California Press.
Throop, C. Jason. 2010. *Suffering and Sentiment: Exploring the Vicissitudes of Experience and Pain in Yap*. Berkeley: University of California Press.
_____. 2012. 'On Inaccessibility and Vulnerability: Some Horizons of Compatibility between Phenomenology and Psychoanalysis', *Ethos* 40(1): 75–96.
Zigon, Jarrett. 2007. 'Moral Breakdown and the Ethical Demand: A Theoretical Framework for an Anthropology of Moralities', *Anthropological Theory* 7(2): 131–50.
_____. 2011. *HIV Is God's Blessing: Rehabilitating Morality in Neoliberal Russia*. Berkeley: University of California Press.
_____. 2012. 'Narratives', in Didier Fassin (ed.), *A Companion to Moral Anthropology*. Malden, MA: Wiley-Blackwell, pp. 204–20.
_____. 2013. 'On Love: Remaking Moral Subjectivity in Postrehabilitation Russia', *American Ethnologist* 40(1): 201–15.
_____. 2014a. 'An Ethics of Dwelling and a Politics of World-Building: A Critical Response to Ordinary Ethics', *Journal of the Royal Anthropological Institute* (N.S.) 20: 746–64.
_____. 2014b. 'Attunement and Fidelity: Two Ontological Conditions for Morally Being-in-the-World', *Ethos* 42(1): 16–30.
_____. 2015. 'What is a Situation? An Assemblic Ethnography of the Drug War', *Cultural Anthropology* 30(3): 501–24.
_____. 2017. *Disappointment: Toward a Critical Hermeneutics of Worldbuilding*. New York: Fordham University Press.

11

Human, the Responding Being
Considerations Towards a Philosophical Anthropology of Responsiveness

Thomas Schwarz Wentzer

This chapter makes a case for a way to deal with ethics from an angle that is rather unusual in recent philosophy as well as in anthropology. I take the question concerning 'moral engines' to be a matter of philosophical anthropology. The concept of responsiveness qualifies this perspective by pursuing a phenomenological approach; hence I take human responsiveness to be the existential condition that helps us to understand the roots – rather than the engine – of ethics and human agency.

It might be helpful to begin this chapter by adding some introductory remarks to the drift of the argument and the aforementioned notions. The term 'philosophical anthropology' means something different than merely the philosophical reflection of ethnographic fieldwork, its ontologies, epistemologies or methodologies. It refers to the legacy of a tradition in the first half of twentieth-century German thinking, which attempted to deal with the human in a way that avoids both naturalistic reductionisms and idealist shortcomings, while defending a philosophical take on the human (a comprehending analysis is provided by Fischer 2008; for an informative characterization see Solies 2010; Wulf 2013). The representatives of this tradition – one might mention books by, among others, Paul Alsberg (1975 [1922]), Max Scheler (2009 [1928]), Helmuth Plessner (1975 [1928]), Arnold Gehlen (1986 [1940]), Erich Rothacker (2008 [1944]), Adolf Portmann (1969 [1944]), but also Ernst Cassirer (1992 [1944]), Hannah Arendt (1958) and even Martin Heidegger (1962 [1927]) could be said to belong to its scope – all tried to pursue the question 'what is the human being?' in contrast to traditional religious and metaphysical conceptions and in contact to recent findings in both social and natural sciences. They took Scheler's lament as their vantage point; a century ago in an essay entitled 'Towards the

Idea of Man' (1915) Scheler observed what he maintained to be the paradox of his age, according to which there never had been a time that knew so much about the human being and that yet lacked an approach apt to encompass the findings of the various disciplines in science and the humanities into a suitable conception of human nature (Scheler 1955).

Although a philosophical undertaking, the protagonists of philosophical anthropology thus draw heavily on biology, psychology, ethology, sociology, linguistics, history or palaeoanthropology. They shared the conviction that philosophy can no longer claim the authority to deal with the human condition in a mere conceptual analysis *a priori*. Akin to Wittgenstein, whose slogan 'Back to the rough ground' articulated the need to account for the disturbances, anomalies and frictions that real life poses to all too smooth philosophical conceptualizations (Wittgenstein 1958: 107; on the impact of Wittgenstein to anthropologists, see for instance Geertz 2000: xii ff.), the different approaches all provide accounts which highlight the cosmopolitan or mundane openness of human existence as the flipside of its dispersed nature that necessarily disseminates humanity into an infinite number of sociocultural lifeforms. The myth of the tower of Babel provides an early version of the anthropological conundrum involved with the question of human nature. Examining the (rough) ground of the historical truth that it entails – the dispersion of human nature expressed as the dissemination of human sociocultural life – means to partake in the discourse of philosophical anthropology.

Traditional (metaphysical) anthropology from Plato through Pico della Mirandola to Kant had tried to locate the question 'what is the human being?' on a vertical axis, locating humanity somewhere between the beast (or pure nature) and the divine (or spirit viz. pure reason). On this axis one might place the discourse concerning the human-animal distinction (Agamben 2004) and its critical revision in various forms of evolutionary theory and adjacent forms of naturalism (with developmental cognitive science as a recent prominent approach; Baron-Cohen et al. 2000; Tomasello 2008). Modern and postmodern (social and cultural) anthropologies counter this set-up by insisting on the horizontal axis. In the aftermath of historicist criticism, they deliver studies based on ethnographic material to encompass the empirical manifold of the diversity of human living in its historical social reality. Philosophical anthropology tries to place the facticity of human existence in the crossing of the vertical and the horizontal, claiming some functional equivalent to human nature that precisely lets us understand why the human species is not bound to a particular niche or determinate life form, but why it instead is released into the openness of a global existence in history.[1]

Given the recent interest in the interface between ethnography and philosophy (Das et al. 2014; Ingold 2011), it seems odd that the tradition of philosophical anthropology does not enjoy more general interest both within and beyond philosophy; it remained by and large without any resonance in Anglo-American philosophy nor in cultural and social anthropology. It could be interesting to dig into the reasons for this unrealized reception that ultimately left philosophical anthropology to be a German affair. But this cannot be done in this chapter.

The reason why I nonetheless believe that we might gain a lot from this forgotten tradition lies in its efforts to conceptualize what may be called the 'immanent transcendence' (Tugendhat 2007: 19) of the human. The fact that any attempt to determine something like human nature or human essence obviously has failed due to the irreducible manifold of human lifeforms, its dynamicity and wealth of cultural values and societies in history, gives striking evidence of the need for a corresponding philosophical discourse. The anti-metaphysical impulse of cultural relativism and the corresponding debates in twentieth-century anthropology bear witness to the necessity to reflect this fact. The subject matter – the human being – seems to transcend or to exceed any effort of its conceptual determination. Philosophical anthropology acknowledges this peculiar situation, presuming that it is due to the way humans are that they transcend their essence. It is worth recalling that philosophical anthropology from the very start endorses the substantial truth of Scheler's aforementioned paradox. Hence, we need to develop a conception of the human that reflects the essential impossibility of any positive account of a human essence. As Scheler wrote, 'precisely the indefinability belongs to the essence of man' (Scheler 1955: 186); it seems to be part of human nature to transcend its nature. The human way of being is characterized by this immanent transcendence; and philosophical anthropology could be the name for an agenda that elaborates on this crucial aspect of the human condition.

In what sense then does a plea for philosophical anthropology help in order to deal with the question concerning 'moral engines'? In my view ethics or the ethical is characterized by a familiar state of immanent transcendence. On the one hand the ethical does not refer to a domain alongside, say, religion or economy. Morality does not only enter into the picture when one acts according to moral norms, or when one claims the authority of such norms for one's actions over and against laws or traditional social rules of an allegedly lower moral value. The ethical penetrates human social existence to a degree that literally every action of ours can possibly be subjected to ethical evaluation. Hence, I agree with what has recently been phrased as the 'immanence of the ethical' (Lambek 2015); human life is ethical in nature, which obviously does not imply that human acting always or mostly could be qualified as morally good. But on the other hand it is precisely the possible ubiquity of the ethical that exceeds the limits of norms and values. It might well be that philosophical ethics can basically be rendered by the single question 'how should one live?' as Plato's Socrates reveals to Thrasymachos as to the real issue of their argument on the nature of justice (Plato, Resp. 352 d). But as Bernard Williams convincingly has shown, performing the very question implies pressing philosophy to its limits (Williams 1985). Put in other words, the ethical perspective – which can be put on every action – leaves human agency in a situation, which seems to establish an asymmetry between the question and its ethical demand ('how should one live?') on the one hand and our available answers on the other. Or even worse, we lack criteria that could qualify our responses to provide valid answers to this question in the first place. We may fall back on norms that have proven to be socially acceptable or to customs that use to satisfy, say, religious needs and requests. But the ethical perspective implies a certain dynamic that exceeds the positivity of a given norm and its measurable fulfilment in a particular action. As every father or every teacher knows only too well, the trouble is that doing our best is not the same as providing the good (Lear 2011). There will always remain more to be said, to be said appropriately, as there is more to know, to know completely and more to be done, to be done well, rather than well enough.

Hence the ethical is characterized by a dynamic similar to what was said above about human nature. Its power – whether captured as 'moral engine' or in a non-mechanistic metaphor – lies within the immanent urge to transcend any given option towards its presumably better state or alternative. It too is characterized by its immanent transcendence. And I believe that there is a certain explanatory relation between the essential indefinability of the human and the immanent transcendence of the ethical; it is due to the human condition that humans have to lead a life instead of just living it. The essential indeterminacy of our human condition urges us to live a life in light of ethics and ethical evaluation. Hence the roots of ethics have to be found in human nature, but, as indicated, neither ethics nor human nature depict determinable conceptual elements that would represent available fixed entities or features.

Although this chapter, due to the profession of its author, does not draw on ethnographic fieldwork, I nonetheless believe I have a case in claiming that the agenda that might follow from my considerations so far is not unfamiliar to other ('real') people dealing with their life in everydayness. What I have loosely outlined so far might come along rather theoretically, presupposing philosophical terms, traditions and disciplines, authorships and maybe even classics in philosophy. The intention behind this setting, however, is to understand what I take to be an existential condition for human agency as such and from a first-person perspective. Plato's and William's question – 'how should one live?' – does not gain its significance from being located in a noble philosophical discourse among the experts in the ivory tower, but from its universal relevance to everybody struggling with the burdens of living a human life. This is not to say that everybody actually asks or should ask this particular question in its literal phrase. But I presume that everybody has probably undergone situations in which she experienced the overwhelming force of a demand and the insufficiency of her response in return. One does the best one can, but one does not know to what degree one is able to achieve what really would have been appropriate. One still has to act. This situation adds a dimension to pragmatism that due to the normativist or rule-based set-up of its available positions to my knowledge has not found its adequate treatment yet. I feel that human agency cannot sufficiently be dealt with by describing agency in terms of following rules or norms, of taking initiatives or deliberative actions, but, rather, in terms of responsiveness (Waldenfels 1994). The ethical dimension is not a perspective that an agent is free to choose or to dismiss. It is not based upon moral norms, principles or maxims alone, but precedes as well as exceeds the scope of our normative commitments towards something I would like to call an existential commitment. One experiences oneself as being exposed to a demand that remains transcendent, even when it comes from within, from what one takes to be one's own moral obligations. A moral agent in that sense is somebody who responds to an ethical demand; hence my suggestion is to think of the human as the responsive being.

This leaves us with three claims I want to elaborate upon in the rest of the chapter. First, philosophical anthropology pursues the question concerning the nature of the human being by acknowledging the essential indeterminacy of the human. Second, the ethical is characterized by its immanent transcendence, experienced in claims and requests that exceed what we can positively account for. Its essence is to be the counterfactual that perforates the pure facticity of the given. Third, such a set-up calls for its analysis from the point of view of phenomenology, from the first-person perspective, illuminating what it is like to be in a state of ontological indeterminacy and ethical overload. Humans are responsive beings, responding to the demands of existence.

A World of Difference: Human Indeterminacy, World-Openness and Philosophical Anthropology

What is the human being? Some readers will suspect that this question is hopelessly outdated, as it is said to presuppose metaphysical essentialism or to favour humanity to the disadvantage of other species; and in both cases it seems to ignore the immeasurable diversity of human life on Earth. Recent approaches commonly referred to as post- or transhumanism dismiss this question for reasons of its alleged commitment to (Christian) humanism, which apparently falls short of describing the continuity of organic life, or for its incapacity to give a timely account of the significance of technology and its bio-cultural potential for the future to come (Ferrando 2013; Braidotti 2011).

A thinker commonly held to be unsuspicious of either of these worries is Friedrich Nietzsche, whose diagnosis of modern nihilism famously culminates in the claim concerning the 'death of God'. Nietzsche unmistakably espouses a future 'philosophy of the Earth' as his kind of naturalism that nonetheless supports the idea of an 'enhancement [Erhöhung] of the type *"Man"'* (Nietzsche 2002, sec. 257). In his *Thus spoke Zarathustra*, Nietzsche recommends a stance known as the doctrine of the Übermensch, according to which one must overcome oneself in order to become oneself. Setting aside Nietzsche's aristocratism with its problematic heroic undertones, he does nevertheless try to capture what has been referred to as immanent transcendence above, namely the drive to push the limits of human life and to reanimate its petrified structures, overcoming their traditional values in the name of the dynamics of life itself. Nietzsche's vitriolic criticism of Christian morality and his genealogical approach accordingly rebut unhistorical, *a priori* thinking that Western humanism had been based upon. It therefore does not surprise that Nietzsche's thinking and some of his motives have gained entrance into posthumanist discussions. However, Nietzsche does not dismiss the problem of the human; these motives do not preclude him from addressing and exploring human nature, on the contrary. It is because of the lack of a metaphysical essence, of a divine moral authority and transcendent eternal values that the question 'what is the human being?' becomes all the more striking. Nietzsche's texts are documents in favour of the project called philosophical anthropology, based on the fundamental immanence and the naturalism (which is not the same as physicalism) of his thinking (on Nietzsche and the succeeding tradition of philosophical anthropology see Schacht 2015).

Nietzsche characterizes the peculiar human condition by referring to man as 'the not yet determined animal' (Nietzsche 2002, sec. 62). The human is an animal species, but it differs from the rest of the animal realm with regard to the indeterminacy of its nature. It has an issue with limits and boundaries, with the shape and the form of its living, transgressing and overcoming itself in the course of its self-preservation. Whereas we are used to thinking of animals as being determined by the evolutionary process of genetic mutation and environmental pressure of selection, which made a species specialize to a determinate life form, apt to a biological niche, humans epitomize a species without proper specialization. Gehlen (1986: 33), commenting on Nietzsche and drawing on Herder's initial notion of man as the 'deficient being' (*Mängelwesen*), characterizes the human as being distinct from its primate ancestors and other living creatures by its lack of instincts and corresponding morphological dispositions, by the poverty of bodily abilities and suitable physiological equipment that all seem to guarantee the success of a species in the animal kingdom. Whereas all other species survive due to phylogenetic specialization, *homo sapiens* became a species of versatile generalists. Humans do not adapt to their environment via specific instincts and senso-motoric refinements of the body, but adjust to the world in all sorts of milieus, developing registers of flexible responses in social interaction via processes of communication, learning and knowledge exchange, mediated in language. Human infants are 'physiological premature neonates' (Portmann 1969: 45), who compensate for their natural poverty and their enduring neoteny by cultural processes, establishing technologies and social institutions; their nature is culture as 'the human world' (Gehlen 1986: 36ff.).

To what degree one is inclined to share or to object to Gehlen's *homo pauper* thesis in detail seems to be of minor importance (a prominent criticism is provided by Sloterdijk 2004: 701ff.); what is important is its result

– human's natural assignment to its being-in-the-world that adds human history and historicity to the registers of human evolution. The global consequence of the process of an entanglement of evolution and human history, which in fact undermines the ontological distinction of nature and culture, might be seen in what has recently been suggested under the name of the Anthropocene (Zalasiewicz 2013; Steffen et al. 2011). I believe that we have not yet understood the historical momentousness of the Anthropocene; we are in need of a corresponding conception of the human.

Hence humans entertain mediated relations to their world, transgressing the immediate functional circle of environmental metabolism towards a symbolic mediated and technologically facilitated mundanity. Alsberg (1975 had coined the notion and the principle of the 'elimination of the body' (*Körperausschaltung*), suggesting an understanding of hominid evolution based on a process of increasing distance to and remoteness from physical nature (on Alsberg see the illuminative contribution by Lysemose 2012). Alsberg saw the ability of early hominids to throw stones at natural enemies as the possibility to establish a boundary as a kind of virtual wall, suggesting that the human hand – the universal organon according to Aristotle – gains its virtuous versatility due to the ability to slip and let go, allowing the individual to distance itself from the world notwithstanding the lack of bodily strength or velocity. It is as if biological evolution led to a species that was bound to its nature by overcoming its natural boundaries, developing reflective and technological distance to its nature as its natural strategy to survive. According to Plessner, 'Due to its open drive structure and due to language appropriate to it, man is released from biological unambiguity – that the animals throughout reveal – to biological ambiguity. ... In a twofold distance to his own body, i.e., even distinct from his being-himself in his center, his inner life, man is placed in a *world*' (Plessner 1975: xviii, 293). Human evolution supports the species to survive in the stance of an 'eccentric positionality' (ibid.), with which notion Plessner – maybe too technically – captures his take on human embodiment in the double bind of being one's body and having one's body (in the delicate unity as lived body [*Leib*] *and* physical body [*Körper*]). The human being lives in 'mediated immediacy' (321ff.) and 'natural artificiality' (309ff.), being part of nature only via techniques of mediation that transcend the confines of nature. In short, we are not bound to a particular environment; our nature releases us towards a world.

Hence the discourse that Nietzsche inaugurates, ironically 'defining' the human as the not yet determined animal, leads to an insight that the leading representatives of philosophical anthropology in different versions and via diverging methodologies jointly endorse. *In-der-Welt-sein* ('Being-in-the-world'; Heidegger 1962: 78ff.), *Weltbildung* ('world-formation'; Heidegger 2008: 274ff.) and *Weltoffenheit* ('world-openness'; Scheler 2009) characterize the key feature of a being that remains naturally indeterminate and enacts its living in world-open existence.

This claim obviously entails elements about human agency and freedom. But note that philosophical anthropology does not address the issue of freedom by maintaining the possession of reason, consciousness or language as metaphysical features that establish a dualistic ontology (such as mind vs. matter or culture vs. nature), as Western rationalism since Descartes in various forms tends to presume. Philosophical anthropology approaches freedom in terms of human indeterminacy (or underdeterminism; Lambek 2015: 2), trying to give an account of the human condition that explains the peculiarity of its subject in a holistic approach and in contact with science without drawing on metaphysical or theological axioms.

Under Pressure: Locating the Ethical

The aforementioned notice according to the agenda of philosophical anthropology leaves us with an ontological result, claiming humans to be world-open creatures that are not bound to an environment but released to the world. I will at least give a sort of illustration of what 'world', 'world-openness' or 'being-in-the-world' in our context might mean. But I will do so by giving this argument a twist that adds an ethical dimension.

Nietzsche's phrase – the human as the not yet determined animal – entails not only a description of human biological indeterminacy as the condition of the possibility for an unrestricted engagement with and within the natural and social world. It also implies an implicit individual assignment, according to which we have to live up to its meaning by taking its content as a task to be fulfilled. Hence it is only a small step from Nietzsche's naturalistic to Heidegger's existential anthropology, according to which 'the "essence" of Dasein lies in its existence', urged by the facticity of its having to be (Heidegger 1962: 67). Due to its essential indeterminacy, the human being is concerned with its being, and this concern characterizes its existence in the most fundamental way. Humans are entities who 'in their Being, comport themselves towards their Being ... which is an issue for every such entity' (ibid.). I take it to be of pivotal importance to note that this claim introduces an existential dimension to what was until now only an academic or classificatory problem. The need for ethical orientation does not arise, because intellectuals with sociological, theological or philosophical training diagnose a certain decline of moral standards in postmodern societies in the age of globalized capitalism, even if such a verdict may actually be of some factual evidence. The need for ethical orientation is located on the level of the individual human in the pursuit of its daily living. It is not Nietzsche whose sentence prescribes moral behaviour as an ethical maxim; his sentence rather echoes the existential urge that is experienced by any member of the species independent of and prior to any 'recommendation' by moralists or ethical analytics. To understand Nietzsche's verdict means to feel the unease of the truth of its sentence: we have to lead a life instead of just living it (Gehlen 1986: 17).

I see in the work of recent anthropologists, for instance Cheryl Mattingly (2010, 2014), Michael Lambek (2003, 2015), Jarrett Zigon (2007, 2008) and notably Michael Jackson (2005, 2011, 2012, 2013, 2016, Jackson and Piette 2015), a kindred approach towards existential anthropology, delivering issues of universal human significance from ethnographic studies of particular life stories. Maybe one may say that existential anthropology actually indicates the intersection between philosophical anthropology and ethnography, approachable from both ends, with the first-person perspective and a sensitivity for the universal relevance of lived experience with its ethical quandaries as its vantage point.

Approaching from philosophy, I sense a similar drift already in Kant, who typically has to serve as the prime example of an armchair philosopher, far away from real life. But I think the argument in favour of philosophical anthropology pursued as existential anthropology actually accords with what Kant terms the 'cosmopolitism' of philosophy, i.e. the kind of question that every human qua being human presumably is interested in.

Kant famously divided the task of philosophy into three questions that in totum would cover the scope of human questioning: 'What can I know? What shall I do? What may I hope?' This interrogative threefold, Kant continues, can be expressed in one single question: 'What is the human being?' (Kant 2000: 25). Kant thus claims that the question regarding the nature of human beings is the ultimate subject of any philosophical concern. As such, all philosophical problems lead to this question about the human being. In doing so, Kant not only promoted philosophical anthropology to be the true successor of former metaphysical thinking (Tugendhat 2007), he did so using the first-person perspective as his starting point (this tends to be overlooked). The question regarding human nature is stated as the triple query posed to an 'I' or to 'me'. Thus, it cannot be dealt with in objective, observational discourse alone, but must recognize the authority of the questioning person too. Hence, the question 'what is the human being?' refers back to the question 'what kind of being am I / are we?' In this way the philosophical problem regarding the human becomes a matter of existential quality. The interrogator is forced to acknowledge the impossibility of a neutral stance towards the particular subject matter, experiencing herself as called upon to respond to the issue in her own name. The result of this reasoning inaugurated by Kant is this: the most universal question concerning humanity proves to be in requirement of an answer with a very special kind of individual dedication. It leaves no room for an evasive move that would allow individual commitment and responsibility to be avoided, as I myself am what I take human beings to be. That is to say, philosophical anthropology must be conceived as existential anthropology.

In fact Saint Augustine already sincerely expressed the existential pressure of human indeterminacy, thus responding to the question 'what am I?' by confessing the course of his life: 'What am I then, O my God? What nature am I? A life various and manifold, and exceeding immense' (Augustine 2008: book 10, chap. 17, verse 26). I take an episode of his as an example that might illustrate the claim concerning human world-openness with regard to ethical evaluation and judgment.

Thus, in the first autobiography of European literature, the *Confessions*, Augustine tells the following episode (Augustine 2008: 2. 4.9–10.18). He was a young man, sixteen years of age, and together with his friends he took pears from a tree in somebody's garden. The ruffians were not caught and had a good time. But decades later, Augustine, now the bishop of Hippo, has to acknowledge that it was a misdeed, indeed a moral mistake. Why did he do it? He could have been hungry. But as a matter of fact, it was neither hunger nor the prospect of delicious fruits that motivated this action. The gang threw most of their prey straight to the pigs. Maybe, Augustine ponders, he stole those pears because of a certain social dynamic that tends to tempt him to do things that he alone would not be capable of. Being in a pack alters things, so it might have been the struggle for social recognition that made him commit his crime. But then again, maybe the deed is the result of an even more complex psychological disposition. Augustine scrutinizes himself: what if the prospect of doing something illegal gave him a thrill and triggered him to commit the deed? But if that was the case, the motive cannot be localized between an agent's subjective desire and its intended object at all, but must be linked to his behaviour, to the normative systems that frame and sanction his actions. Hence Augustine has to confess that his desire was directed towards a violation of those norms in legal, moral and religious perspective. In this scenario, the motive of the action is a rather complex second order desire, to which Augustine has a certain evaluative predicate: sin, since the crime at the same time both acknowledges and wilfully violates the norm concerning the prohibition of theft, which is a divine commandment, after all. Augustine identifies this violation itself as lust provoking and as the true motive of the crime. In violating the law, he for a moment imitated the divine legislator, as if he was the autonomous creator of his life, not the creature of the Almighty. To feel this power was the true motivation for his deed, Augustine confesses; and while Nietzsche will praise the 'will to power' as the principle of life per se and the person able to affirm this truth as the Übermensch, Augustine exposes his desire as evil, blaming himself and his juvenile attitude. Why did he do it? He did so because he had the power to do so.

It might seem trivial, but let me point out that this power does not refer to a physical faculty. It is not that young Augustine can pick a pear from a tree. His power is not displayed by the ability to cope with the laws of gravitation, but by the possibility of violating the norms of social behaviour and moral conduct. He proves himself to be addressed by, but not subjected to, the commands of the normative systems that used to rule his life. It is hence the experience of not being bound by norms that lies at the bottom of ethical reasoning, the experience of freedom transcending the limits of socially sanctioned behaviour and moral conduct, or, in the idiom of Freud, of 'ego' to disobey the commands of 'super-ego' (Freud 2000: 273–330). The experience that Augustine describes seems to me as valid as ever, notwithstanding the religious agenda in which the episode is embedded. The true problem of ethics does not consist in the modern discourse about how to defend a universal moral law (Kant) or moral principle (utilitarianism) that determine moral goodness, but in the challenge to deal with the indeterminacy of human living. It is not a philosophical problem of how to legitimate norms and values, but an existential problem of how to respond to the excessive demand of performing human being.

To Augustine, a series of possible contexts with different norms and values enter the picture so that each could be taken to explain young Augustine's deed. The point here is not that Augustine or we are to find the 'true' motive behind his action. It is simply to recognize the fact of a plurality of possible economies of drives and desires that each belong to a corresponding normative system, altogether part of his world. Augustine can place his experience of stealing pears in different contexts, including the problem of his own possible freedom, which becomes manifest in his reflections. He is not only able to shift between those contexts, which each would lead to different interpretations and possibly to divergent ethical evaluations; he also reflects on the context dependence of human agency as such, arguing from a second-order interpretation, when he evaluates the various attempts of his interpretations. Hence Augustine experiences his world-openness and the ethical pressure linked to this existential condition. A creature adapted to its environment would behave in the context of a certain motivational system; Augustine must navigate between different possible contexts and normative systems that in their entirety belong to the world of his living. Ethics then is the expression and the discourse of the human need for orientation in their being-in-the-world.

I grant that my 'case' – the stolen pears, an autobiographic episode retold by the church father Saint Augustine – surely serves the catholic agenda of his author, who lets his ethical journey begin with the primordial sin of stealing the pear, not the apple, from the forbidden tree, ultimately finding the guiding thread for ethical orientation in the narrative confession of his faith to his God. The incident as such – the theft – seems moreover to be of minor ethical significance, compared to experiences of severe remorse in light of one's inhumanity (depicted for instance in Kleinman 2006: 27ff.), of fighting for one's family members against the odds of structural discrimination (Mattingly 2014: 35ff.), of everyday violence against women (Das 2007) or of life in the face and the aftermath of civil war (Jackson 2005: 53ff.). But, nevertheless, I take this case as an illustration for the claim I want to pursue, which maintains the essential indeterminacy of human existence experienced as the immanent transcendence of the ethical.

From a Phenomenological Point of View:
Human, the Responding Being

For these reasons, I believe that there is an immense and not yet exploited potential in the phenomenological tradition that is waiting for existential anthropology, both in its ethnographic as well its philosophical version Heidegger's phenomenology of Dasein in both its earlier (Heidegger 1962) and its later version (Heidegger 1947), Gadamer's philosophical hermeneutics (Gadamer 1986), Levinas' ontology of the ethical Other (Levinas 1969), Derrida's ethics of deconstruction (Derrida 1995, 1996), most recently Jean-Luc Nancy's social ontology (Nancy 2000, 2003) and notably Bernhard Waldenfels' phenomenology of alienness and alterity (Waldenfels 1994, 2011, 2015) all provide conceptual resources that might help us to understand what it means to live a life in light of the ethical. As mentioned above, Gehlen's phylogenetic approach characterizes the human by strategies of individual and collective compensations, which in turn deal with the species' residual instinct structure while being exposed to sensory overload and an excess of impulse. This third-person description can be rendered phenomenologically as the hiatus between demand and response. People do not notice the human condition in acts of cognitive acquisition, as if there was an specific universal character that they individually happen to instantiate as being just another token of a human type. They meet their lot in modes of lived experience, individually assigned to them; and phenomenology provides means to conceptualize these modes in accord with their givenness in first-person perspective (a corresponding anthropological approach as 'first-person virtue ethics' is outlined and pursued in Mattingly 2012 and 2014). In the following I will argue that the hiatus between demand and response characterizes the human condition from a phenomenological point of view. Responsiveness is the name for a way to cope with one's fragile and finite existence that captures our being called upon to act anyway.

This responsivist approach draws heavily on the phenomenology of Bernhard Waldenfels. In a programmatic passage, we find the following claim:

> Responding that comes to meet the alien call is not restricted to spoken utterances. … Responding embodies an ethos of the senses that extends from greeting rituals down to lovers' playing. In the end, the ancient definition 'The human being is an animal which has speech or reason' can be reformulated as follows: 'The human being is an animal which responds'. (Waldenfels 2011: 38)

The 'alien call' refers to the demand that calls upon our responsive strategies, which it both precedes as well as exceeds. Its alienness is due to its originating somewhere else, beyond the control of an agent's mastering, who nonetheless has to deal with its request. Responding thusly cannot erase the alienness of this origin, which remains an incommensurable moment that withdraws itself from its integration into the regulatory circuit of understanding. It is of pivotal importance not to misunderstand the phenomenology of responsiveness as a renewal of classical behaviorism and its stimulus-response model. Rather, we might think of a dialogical frame of questions and answers – hence a certain family resemblance to Gadamer's hermeneutic on the one and Austin's ordinary language philosophy on the other hand, which the responsivist approach nevertheless is distancing itself from – that provides a model to the responsivist account of experience and agency, thus without restricting the scope of this model to our linguistic capacities or communication in language. Responsiveness is not limited to communicative rationality; it is at stake already in our bodily existence as Leibwesen and our erotic existence, in aesthetic experiences, in our listening to memories and the voices of our past (for a responsivist account of historical experience, see Wentzer 2014). It characterizes our experiential existence in every direction: 'We conceive of responsiveness as the principal feature of all our discursive activity, practical doings and bodily comportment, which all become accessible from there' (Waldenfels 1994: 336).

The idea is that we deal with the situational affordances in our daily routines as well as in adventurous challenges during the course of our life, as if we were addressed and called upon (what late Heidegger rather dramatically phrases as 'the call of Being', 'der Anspruch des Seins'; Heidegger 1947); we respond when we act. In this view, human agency is neither causally determined (as in classical behaviorism) nor the spontaneous initiative of an autonomous subject (as modern philosophy often wants to make us believe).

The paradigm of responsiveness opens up a third way to the all too rigid dichotomy between 'passive' causal determinism and 'active' intentional freedom. Responding means to only have the second word, not to be in the position to initiate one's doings, but having to answer the requests that come from elsewhere or from somebody else, from a place that notoriously withdraws itself into the blind spots of our intentional awareness as well as of our normative entitlements (for the following, see Waldenfels 1994: 178, 327ff.). Whereas hermeneutics tend to integrate alterity – which urges the task of understanding to begin with – into the horizon of shared meaning, pragmatism in its various forms (including speech-act theory) usually finds norms of evaluable behaviour that deprives what is experienced from its unique singularity for the sake of general rules and their social structures. In both approaches, otherness is only dealt with within the safe harbour of intentional or normative comprehensibility. The irreducible event of our being-called-upon as such that urges the response is skipped over. Both accounts ignore what might be called the 'responsive difference' (Waldenfels 1994: 193ff., 344), the unbridgeable hiatus between the whereupon (the occasional event) of our responding and the what (the content) of our answer (for a similar interpretation, with a strong emphasis on the religious implications of this line of thinking, see Chrétien 2004).

An indication of this hiatus can be found in the difference between answer and reply, the two types of the response in our linguistic practices. I might reply to a tourist that I don't know the way to the station, but in doing so I do not answer her question. I nevertheless acknowledge her demand in replying, even if I am not able to fulfil the intention of her questioning. It is not that 'replying' in that sense was on the same scale as 'answering', only less exact or with a minor degree of epistemic evidence. Both types refer to two different and irreducible aspects of every demand, acknowledging the event of a request (raised for instance by a person's questioning) in replying and addressing the intention (what was asked in a corresponding question) in the answering statement. In situations like these we can easily distinguish between the speech act of replying and the propositional content that would satisfy the requirements of being a both correct and truthful answer to the question. Exactly the inability to answer however reveals the event as such and of having to respond anyway, as we grant that the demand deserves to be heard and responded to, even if we cannot fulfil what we take to be the questioner's intention. One might say that the demand expressed in a question entails an illocutionary force of otherness that escapes from its fulfilment in the content of its answer. Needless to say, we respond even if we refuse to reply, as not replying is a response too, correspondingly sanctioned in social intercourse.

As the use of the term 'illocutionary force' above indicates, Waldenfels' phenomenology and his account on responsiveness draw to some extent on Searle's theory of speech acts and especially on Austin's philosophy of ordinary language (see the discussion of both in Waldenfels 1994: 49ff.). However, both accounts are developed from the perspective of a speaker, intending to do something, not of a listener or respondent, being exposed to an alien demand. From the point of view of phenomenology, the 'force' is given as an 'illocutionary affection' or simply as pathos, which is not the passive counterpart or receiver to the active cause, but the affective illocution that a person finds herself delivered to in case of a demand that she meets. Pragmatism and ordinary language philosophy hence presuppose a set of rules or a system of norms that are already in play in order for the speech act analysis to start. By contrast, the paradigm of responsiveness does not just aim at a phenomenological (instead of pragmatist) reconstruction of those rules and norms. It is not that we inverse the order of normative behaviour, focusing on the respondent instead of the questioner, or on the listener instead of the speaker in their dialogical or pragmatic interaction. The phenomenon at stake – indeterminable otherness that requests my response – displays a pre-normative obligation that anchors the space of normative behaviour in the first place on the grounds of my factical existence. It reveals an existential commitment that precedes intentionality and its accounts on intentional subjects as well as (neo-)pragmatism and its approaches on competent speakers.[2] In contrast to these important theories in recent philosophy, Waldenfels aims at saving the unruly and unintentionable otherness that we meet as a potentially infinite demand. We give something in return; hence we re-act.

It might be helpful to add that the term existential commitment corresponds to what Michael Jackson's existential anthropology (2005, 2016) alludes to as existential imperative. It addresses the phenomenon from its other side, highlighting a person's or an agent's being addressed by such an imperative. Maintaining an existential imperative prior to moral (categorical) imperatives or social norms makes sense because one understands its imperative force without further ado. Being human simply means finding oneself committed to the task of this very being; being under the command of the existential imperative just is what this life form is about. The peculiarity of this kind of commitment relies in the fact that one cannot represent the content of the imperative without endorsing its imperative force.

Hence responsiveness is characterized by a certain pathos or pathic disposition of our responsive experiences. Pathos literally means the event of being affected; it is the event that happens to somebody in the dative clause of being the addressee of this happening (Waldenfels 2011: 27). Phenomena like attention or awareness are pathic in the sense that they rely on something that we are subjected to respond to, independent of or logically prior to our conscious or intentional directedness. We can be surprised or surprise ourselves; we can be hit by anxiety or joy; we fall in love or have to discover having been abandoned. In every one of those instances we find ourselves confronted with an event that happens to us; and this being exposed to something from beyond remains the irreducible source of the dynamics of human life and ethical orientation. Like ideas that happen to strike our minds or memories that all of a sudden come to the surface from their oblivion, we find ourselves struck by a request the moment we feel the urge to respond. From a third-person perspective one might be tempted to describe the relation of pathos and response following the timeline of successive moments, as if the antecedence of the pathos effected the consequence of its response. But this causal description misspells the phenomenological evidence of our lived experience, as

> pathos and response do not follow one after the other like two events; they are not even two distinct events, but one and the same experience, shifted in relation to itself: a genuine time lag. ... For this reason, we initially do not encounter pathos as *something* which we mean, understand, judge, reject or affirm; rather, it forms the time-place *from which* we do all this by responding to it. Everything which happens to me and to which I respond does not have a sense as such and does not obey a rule. (Waldenfels 2011: 50).

This passage contains Waldenfels' phenomenological account on what I have captured above as the 'existential commitment'. The very fact of our pathic being-affected has to be taken as the indication of a most individual position, as our disposition, as our spot, our *Dasein* or being-there (Heidegger 1962; Dyring 2015 speaks similarly of our 'emplacement'). The time-place of our existence becomes the stance from which we enter into the discourses of understanding and rule following; but as such this place withdraws itself from every possible intentional or pragmatist reconstruction. Like the eye that cannot see itself, pathos reminds us of the irreducible event character of the whereupon of our responding that refrains from its normative or semantic reconstruction. That is to say, one cannot explain away the facticity of an event by merely understanding it, regardless of whether this understanding follows the hermeneutics of meaning interpretation or the pragmatism of social normative commitments and entitlements. One has to respond anyway – and this puts a responsive agent into the position to take responsibility to her responses (for a thouroughgoing monograph on this point, see Raffoul 2010). I am the addressee of the demand that an event might raise to me, and as occupying this address or individual Dasein I experience myself as responsible for my responses.

We are now in a position to evaluate the claim concerning the human as the responding being, and to ask to what degree this claim might contribute to the guiding question concerning 'moral engines' or the 'roots of ethics'. The ethical, I would maintain, is bound to human responsiveness. The concept of responsiveness qualifies the facticity (Heidegger 1999) of human life, the fact that we always already find ourselves in particular situations that we did not initiate or design, without ever being capable of reaching the origin of these demands. To think of human existence in terms of responsiveness means acknowledging its internal remoteness and intrinsic alterity. Hence a phenomenology based on responsiveness reinterprets human living in light of the perspective of a person that experiences her existence as a demand she responds to in every sequence of her course of life. This means acknowledging our existential commitment as an ethical demand, i.e. as the task of leading one's life instead of living it. Responsiveness captures the thrownness of our existence in terms of qualified and yet insufficient and finite behaviour. We are responding to the fact of our historically situated existence in being who and what we are, responding in the conversation that we are

Thomas Schwarz Wentzer is associate professor and chair in the Department of Philosophy and History of Ideas, Aarhus University. He is author of *Bewahrung der Geschichte: Die hermeneutische Philosophie Walter Benjamins* (Philo-Verlag, 2002), and co-editor of *Finite but Unbounded: New Approaches in Philosophical Anthropology* (DeGruyter, 2017). He has published numerous articles on Heidegger, phenomenology, hermeneutics and philosophical anthropology.

Notes

1. The distinction of a vertical and a horizontal axis is inspired by Plessner 1975: 32 and Krüger 2009: 146 ff. The version rendered here is rather superficial and very sketchy. See Marquard 1971 and Zammito 2002, whose studies support the implicit historical argument of this claim.
2. The term 'existential commitment' is borrowed from John Haugeland (1998: 2). I agree with Haugeland that this term marks a claim against 'traditional' theories of intentionality, critically engaging with pragmatism and its followers in recent philosophy (such as Brandom 1994 and McDowell 1994).

References

Agamben, Giorgio. 2004. *The Open: Man and Animal*. Stanford, CA: Stanford University Press.

Alsberg, Paul. 1975 [1922]. *Das Menschheitsrätsel: Versuch einer prinzipiellen Lösung*. Dresden: Focus.

Arendt, Hannah. 1958. *The Human Condition*. Chicago: Chicago University Press.

Augustine. 2008. *Confessions, Oxford World's Classics*. Oxford: Oxford University Press.

Baron-Cohen, Simon, Helen Tager-Flusberg and Donald J. Cohen. 2000. *Understanding Other Minds: Perspectives from Developmental Cognitive Neuroscience*, 2nd edn. Oxford and New York: Oxford University Press.

Braidotti, Rosi. 2011. *The Posthuman*. Cambridge: Polity.

Brandom, Robert. 1994. *Making it Explicit: Reasoning, Representing and Discursive Commitment*. Cambridge: Harvard University Press.

Cassirer, Ernst. 1992 [1944]. *An Essay on Man: An Introduction to a Philosophy of Human Culture*. New Haven: Yale University Press.

Chrétien, Jean-Luc. 2004. *The Call and the Response*. New York: Fordham University Press.

Das, Veena. 2007. *Life and Words: Violence and the Descent into the Ordinary*. Berkeley: University of California Press.

Das, Veena, Michael D. Jackson, Arthur Kleinman and Bhrigupati Singh. 2014. *The Ground Between: Anthropologists Engage Philosophy*. Durham: Duke University Press.

Derrida, Jacques. 1995. *On the Name*, ed. Thomas Dutoit. Stanford: Stanford University Press.

_____. 1996. *The Gift of Death*, ed. David Wills. Chicago: Chicago University Press.

Dyring, Rasmus. 2015. 'Mood and Method: Where does Ethnographic Experience Truly Take Place?', in Dorthe Jørgensen, Gaetano Chiurazzi and Søren Tinning (eds), *Truth and Experience: Between Phenomenology and Hermeneutics*. Newcastle: Cambridge Scholars Publishing, pp. 293–317.

Ferrando, Francesca. 2013. 'Posthumanism, Transhumanism, Metahumanism and New Materialsm: Differences and Relations', *Existenz. An International Journal in Philosophy, Religion and Arts* 8(2): 26–32.

Fischer, Joachim. 2008. *Philosophische Anthropologie: Eine Denkrichtung des 20. Jahrhunderts*. Freiburg: Alber.

Freud, Sigmund. 2000. *Psychologie des Unbewussten: Studienausgabe*, ed. Alexander Richards, Angela Mitscherlich and James Strachey. Vol. 3. Frankfurt am Main: Fischer.

Gadamer, Hans-Georg. 1986. *Hermeneutik Wahrheit und Methode, Gesammelte Werke 1*. Tübingen: Mohr.

Geertz, Clifford. 2000. *Available Light: Anthropological Reflections on Philosophical Topics*. Princeton: Oxford: Princeton University Press.

Gehlen, Arnold. 1986. *Der Mensch: Seine Natur und seine Stellung in der Welt. 13. Aufl., Studienausgabe der Hauptwerke / Arnold Gehlen*. Wiesbaden: AULA-Verlag.

Haugeland, John. 1998. *Having Thought Essays in the Metaphysics of Mind*. Cambridge, MA: Harvard University Press.

Heidegger, Martin. 1947. *Platons Lehre von der Wahrheit mit einem Brief über den 'Humanismus'*. Bern: Francke.

_____. 1962. *Being and Time*, trans. John McQuarrie and Edward Robinson. New York: Harper and Brothers.

_____. 1999. *Ontology: the Hermeneutics of Facticity*. Bloomington, IN: Indiana University Press.

_____. 2008. *The Fundamental Concepts of Metaphysics: World, Finitude, Solitude*. Trans. William McNeill, Nicholas Walker. Bloomington, IN: Indiana University Press,

Ingold, Tim. 2011. *The Perception of the Environment Essays on Livelihood, Dwelling and Skill*, reissued with a new pref. ed. London: Routledge.

Jackson, Michael. 2005. *Existential Anthropology: Events, Exigencies and Effects, Methodology and History in Anthropology*. New York: Berghahn Books.

_____. 2011. *Life Within Limits: Well-being in a World of Want*. Durham, NC: Duke University Press.

_____. 2012. *Between One and One Another*. Berkeley: University of California Press.

_____. 2013. *Lifeworlds: Essays in Existential Anthropology*. Chicago and London: The University of Chicago Press.

_____. 2016. *As Wide as the World is Wise: Reinventing Philosophical Anthropology*. New York: Columbia University Press.

Jackson, Michael and Albert Piette. 2015. *What is Existential Anthropology*. New York: Berghahn Books.

Kant, Immanuel. 2000. *Schriften zur Logik, Physische Geographie, Pädagogik*. Unveränd. photomechanischer Abdr. des Textes der von der Preussischen Akademie der Wissenschaften 1902 begonnenen Ausg. von Kants gesammelten Schriften ed. 10 Bände vols. Vol. 9, *Kants Werke. Akademie Textausgabe*. Berlin: de Gruyter.

Kleinman, Arthur. 2006. *What Really Matters: Living a Moral Life Amidst Uncertainty and Danger*. New York: Oxford University Press.

Krüger, Hans-Peter. 2009. 'Philosophische Anthropologie als Lebenspolitik', *Deutsche Zeitschrift für Philosophie (Sonderband)*: 146–62.

Lambek, Michael. 2003. *The Weight of the Past: Living with History in Mahajanga, Madagascar, Contemporary Anthropology of Religion*. Basingstoke: Palgrave Macmillan.

_____. 2015. *The Ethical Condition Essays on Action, Person, and Value*. Chicago: University of Chicago Press.

Lear, Jonathan. 2011. *A Case for Irony, The Tanner Lectures on Human Values*. Cambridge, MA: Harvard University Press.

Levinas, Emmanuel. 1969. *Totality and Infinity. An Essay on Exteriority*, trans. Alphonso Lingis. Pittsburgh: Duquesne University Press.

Lysemose, Kasper. 2012. 'The Being, the Origin and the Becoming of Man: A Presentation of Philosophical Anthropogenealogy and Some Ensuing Methodological Considerations', *Human Studies* 35(1): 115–30.

Marquard, Odo. 1971. 'Anthropologie', in Joachim Ritter (ed.), *Historisches Wörterbuch der Philosophie*. Basel: Schwabe, 362–74.

Mattingly, Cheryl. 2010. *The Paradox of Hope: Journeys Through a Clinical Borderland*. Berkeley, CA: University of California Press.

_____. 2012. 'Two Virtue Ethics and the Anthropology of Morality', *Anthropological Theory* 12(2): 161–84.

_____. 2014. *Moral Laboratories: Family Peril and the Struggle for a Good Life*. Berkeley: University of California Press.

McDowell, John Henry. 1994. *Mind and World*. Cambridge, MA: Harvard University Press.

Nancy, Jean-Luc. 2000. *Being Singular Plural, Meridian, Crossing Aesthetics*. Stanford, CA: Stanford University Press.

_____. 2003. *A Finite Thinking, Cultural Memory in the Present*. Stanford, CA: Stanford University Press.

Nietzsche, Friedrich. 2002. *Beyond Good and Evil: Prelude to a Philosophy of the Future*. Cambridge and New York: Cambridge University Press.

Plessner, Helmuth. 1975. *Die Stufen des Organischen und der Mensch. Einleitung in die philosophische Anthropologie*. 3 ed, *Sammlung Göschen*. Berlin: de Gruyter.

Portmann, Adolf. 1969. *Biologische Fragmente zu einer Lehre vom Menschen*. 3., erw. Aufl. Basel, Stuttgart: Schwabe.

Raffoul, François. 2010. *The Origins of Responsibility*. Bloomington, IN: Indiana University Press.

Rothacker, Erich. 2008. *Probleme der Kulturanthropologie*. 3. Aufl. Bonn: Bouvier.

Schacht, Richard. 2015. 'Gehlen, Nietzsche and the Project of a Philosophical Anthropology', in Phillip Honenberger (ed.), *Naturalism and Philosophical Anthropology: Nature, Life, and the Human between Transcendental and Empirical Perspectives*. Basingstoke: Palgrave Macmillan, pp. 49–65.

Scheler, Max. 1955 [1915]. 'Zur Idee des Menschen', in Maria Scheler (ed.), *Vom Umsturz der Werte Abhandlungen und Aufsätze. Gesammelte Werke*. Bern: Francke, pp. 171–195

_____. 2009. *The Human Place in the Cosmos, Northwestern University Studies in Phenomenology and Existential Philosophy*. Evanston, IL: Northwestern University Press.

Sloterdijk, Peter. 2004. *Schäume*. Vol. 3, *Sphären. Plurale Sphärologie*. Frankfurt a. M.: Suhrkamp.

Solies, Dirk. 2010. 'German Anthropology', in H. James Birx (ed.), *21st Century Anthropology. A reference handbook*, Online-Ressource. Los Angeles: SAGE.

Steffen, Will, Jacques Grinevald, Paul Crutzen and John McNeill. 2011. 'The Anthropocene: Conceptual and Historical Perspectives', *Philosophical Transactions of the Royal Society A* (369): 842–67.

Tomasello, Michael. 2008. *Origins of Human Communication, The Jean Nicod Lectures*. Cambridge, MA: MIT Press.

Tugendhat, Ernst. 2007. *Anthropologie statt Metaphysik*. Munich: Beck.

Waldenfels, Bernhard. 1994. *Antwortregister*. Frankfurt am Main: Suhrkamp.

_____. 2011. *Phenomenology of the Alien: Basic Concepts*. Northwestern University studies in phenomenology and existential philosophy. Evanston, IL: Northwestern University Press.

_____. 2015. *Sozialität und Alterität: Modi sozialer Erfahrung*. Berlin: Suhrkamp.

Wentzer, Thomas Schwarz. 2014. '"I have seen Königsberg burning": Philosophical Anthropology and the Responsiveness of Historical Experience', *Anthropological Theory* 14(1): 27–48.

Williams, Bernard. 1985. *Ethics and the Limits of Philosophy*. Cambridge, MA: Harvard University Press.

Wittgenstein, Ludwig. 1958. *Philosophical Investigations*, 2nd edn. Oxford: Blackwell.

Wulf, Christoph. 2013. *Anthropology: a Continental Perspective*. Chicago: University of Chicago Press.

Zalasiewicz, Jan. 2013. 'The Epoch of Humans', *Nature Geoscience* 6, 8–9.

Zammito, John H. 2002. *Kant, Herder, and the Birth of Anthropology*. Chicago, IL: University of Chicago Press.

Zigon, Jarrett. 2007. 'Moral Breakdown and Ethical Demand', *Anthropological Theory* 7(2): 131–50.

_____. 2008. *Morality: An Anthropological Perspective*. New York: Berg.

12

The History of Responsibility

François Raffoul

The Question of Responsibility

When engaging with the question of 'moral engines' or 'moral drives' in human life, the first task is to rethink ethics and responsibility in light of the human condition, as a feature of human life, approached phenomenologically so as to remain faithful to its constitution. It will appear that responsibility, once reengaged phenomenologically, is to be taken as responsiveness to a call, rather than as the traditional accountability of the willful and powerful subject or agent. The aim of my recent work on responsibility (Raffoul 2010) was indeed to reengage the question of responsibility as it was elaborated in post-Nietzschean continental thought, and to explore its post-metaphysical, phenomenological and onto-logical senses, away from its traditional metaphysical understanding as accountability of the free autonomous subject. Returning through a historical genealogy to 'the origins of responsibility', following the 'long history of the origins of responsibility' of which Nietzsche speaks in the second essay of his *Genealogy of Morals*[1] (1967), I sought to reveal the emergence of post-meta-physical senses of responsibility in the works in Sartre, Levinas, Heidegger and Derrida. Despite what a certain *doxa* claims, ethics has not only been a constant concern of contemporary continental thought but has been in fact problema-tized anew and understood less as a normative body of moral rules and even less as an applied discipline, and more in terms of a philosophical reflection on the meaning of ethics as such, on the ethicality of ethics. Responsibility itself has been rethought in such a context, in a novel and original way, that is, away from an ideology of subjectivity, free will and power.

This project might seem paradoxical in several respects. Nietzsche's cri-tique of morality, for instance, has often been described as a nihilistic enterprise of the destruction of values leading to the impossibility of ethics, as if questioning ethics amounted to an attack on it, an assumption mocked by Merleau-Ponty when he wrote that 'From the simple fact that I make of morality a problem, you conclude that I deny it' (Merleau-Ponty 1964). One can also ascertain that Nietzsche's genealogy is not the simple dismissal of ethics as such, but rather an attack on a certain way of understanding ethics: Nietzsche targeted what he termed 'life-denying' philosophies, which he saw in Christianity, and of course Platonism, both of which posit another world beyond this world in a projection of ideals in opposition to life. In *The Will to Power*, in the section entitled 'Critique of Morality' (paragraph 254), Nietzsche explains that 'The inquiry into the origin of our evaluations and tables of the good is absolutely no way identical with a critique of them, as if often believed'. Further, he clarifies that such inquiry seeks instead to evaluate the value of morality for life: 'What are our evaluations and moral tables worth? What is the outcome of their rule? For whom? In relation to what? – Answer: for life' (Nietzsche 1968: 148).[2] By 'critique', Nietzsche does not mean a negative enterprise, nor an attack against morality, but rather an inquiry into the history of the origins of morality. Through the deconstruction of the tradition of responsibility (as we will see, essentially a critique of the identification of responsibility with accountability), Nietzsche undertakes a genealogy of responsibility and its fundamental concepts (causality, agency, will, subjectivity), thereby opening the way for a reelaboration of its phenomenological senses.

A clarification may then be helpful at the outset. Continental philosophies of ethics, which are in their very basis post-Nietzschean thoughts, have often been accused of moral relativism and nihilism. It is often alleged that post-Nietzschean continental thought has little to offer in terms of an ethical theory, or worse, that it actually develops an un-ethical posture, exemplified in the works of Heidegger, or the deconstructive work of Jacques Derrida. However, deconstruction needs to be taken in its positive sense, following Derrida who defined it as an affirmative gesture, as an opening of new possibilities, as the very reopening of the open. Derrida has stressed that ethical questions have always been present in his writings, even when they were not explicitly raised. To those who, as Derrida puts it, 'believe themselves to have found in Deconstruction [*'la' Déconstruction*] – as if there were one, and only one – a modern form of immorality, of amorality, or of irresponsibility', he replies by mentioning a number of his texts that 'testify to a permanent, extreme, direct, or oblique, in any event, increasingly intense attention, to those things which one could identify under the fine names of "ethics", "morality", "responsibility", "subject", etc.' (Derrida 1995).[3] There is an ethics of deconstruction, as such, before anything is said explicitly on ethics. Further, Derrida clarifies that his more explicit works on ethics (whether on justice, law and right, responsibility, moral decision, forgiveness, the gift, the secret, hospitality, etc.) do not constitute a system of moral norms, a normative ethics in the established sense of the term. In fact, one may ask whether it is the role of philosophy to prescribe norms of ethics, to establish a 'morality', to posit norms or values. Jean-Luc Nancy for instance considers that 'no philosophy either provides or is by itself a "morality" in this sense. Philosophy is not charged with prescribing norms or values' (Nancy 2002b).[4] Rather, the task of philosophy is to question the ethicality of ethics, to engage a philosophical reflection on the meaning of ethics, on what puts us 'in the position of having to choose norms or values' (HPP, 66). Philosophy does not indicate a choice, but articulates the situation of being 'in the position of making a choice'. A philosophical inquiry would then not so much propose a moral system as inquire into the meaning of ethics, the 'ethicality' of ethics. In an interview given a few months before his death, on 28 January 2004, to the daily communist newspaper *l'Humanité*, Derrida readily conceded that 'if by ethics one understands a system of rules, of moral norms, then no, I do not propose an ethics' (Derrida 2004).[5] In this respect, to understand ethics as an applied discipline forecloses the possibility of raising the indispensable prior question of the ethicality of ethics. The notion of application indeed assumes a ground for ethical rules. But it may be the case that ethical judgment, as Heidegger, Sartre, Levinas or Derrida would show, takes place in an un-grounded way, indeed, becomes only possible from such groundlessness: for Heidegger, being happens without a ground and the call of conscience has no author and no foundation. For Sartre, responsibility arises out of the groundlessness of existence, and ethics has no 'a priori Good' to rely upon. For Levinas, ethics arises out of a concern for an infinite other, and not from a rational basis. As for Derrida, responsible decision takes place as a leap and absolute risk beyond knowledge in an abysmal experience of the undecidable.[6] Applied ethics is thus the name of an ethics whose meaning is not reflected upon and which is inappropriately understood in terms of the theory-praxis, model-application schemas. At stake is a philosophical reflection on the meaning of responsibility, too often covered over by a problematic of accountability.

The motif of responsibility is central in contemporary continental philosophies of ethics, but it is reconceptualized from the ground up, in the wake of Nietzsche's genealogical deconstruction of morality and accountability. For instance, with Sartre the ethical is not a body of norms but instead a characteristic of existence. Ethics arises out of his phenomenological ontology because even though ontology is unable to formulate ethical imperatives, it nonetheless allows us to glimpse the existential situation of ethics. Existence for Sartre is identified with responsibility itself. Sartre posits human existence as absolute responsibility based on the withdrawal of essence and situates the origin of ethics and responsibility in the disappearance of a theological foundation for values. Human existence is identified with an absolute responsibility for itself based on the surge and self-invention of a groundless freedom. To that extent, there is an intrinsic ethicality of existence in Sartre's phenomenological ontology. This strongly suggests that if ontology cannot provide a morality or an ethics per se, it nevertheless articulates what one may call here the ethicality of ethics, the very possibility of ethics. When Heidegger was asked in his 'Letter on Humanism' why he did not write an ethics to supplement his fundamental ontology, he replied famously that the thinking of being was an originary ethics. The first gesture by Heidegger is thus to no longer separate ethics from ontology, as if they constituted separate independent spheres. Ethics cannot be approached except in terms of the event of being. In a sense, for Heidegger ethics is ontology itself. There is no need to 'add' an ethics as an applied discipline to an ontology that would then have been presupposed as unethical. Heidegger rethinks our being-responsible in terms of our answering the call of being and the ethical by way of a critique of the metaphysical tradition of ethics and a meditation on human beings' sojourn on the earth as *ethos*. He understands Dasein as an ethical notion and our relation to being as one of responsible engagement. Levinas defines the self as a responsibility for the other human, and breaks with Kantian universalism by situating ethics in the encounter with the singular other. Derrida understands deconstruction as responsiveness that engages – aporetically – a responsible decision. Responsibility itself is engaged as an experience of the impossible. We see the notion of responsibility articulated in terms of phenomenological responsiveness rather than in terms of the autonomy of the subject. It is clear that in such a context, responsibility itself is entirely rethought, in a novel and original way, that is, away from an ideology of subjectivity, will and power. Whether explicitly or implicitly, those continental thinkers allow for a rethinking of ethical responsibility as they take issue with traditional models, that is, with the model of accountability.

Indeed, the concept of responsibility has traditionally been associated, if not identified, with accountability, under the authority of a philosophy of free will and causality, itself resting upon a subject-based metaphysics. Responsibility is conceived in terms of causality as ground of the act or of the event. Accordingly, one is accountable as a subject who is the cause of his or her actions through the freedom of the will. Accountability, as a concept, thus assumes the position of a subject-cause, an agent or an author who can be displayed as a *subjectum* for its actions. Such is, for instance, Kant's definition of accountability or imputability (*Imputabilität*) in the third antinomy in the *Critique of Pure Reason*,[7] which he situates in the 'transcendental freedom' of the subject, capable of absolutely and spontaneously beginning a new series of causes. Identified with the concept of accountability, responsibility thus designates the capacity by an agent to be the cause and the ground of its acts. The unceasing calls for responsibility in our contemporary culture are always calls to such agency, to the position of a subject-cause – an insistence which as such deserves scrutiny. One might ask at the outset: what concept of responsibility does it seek to reinforce? What lack does it aim at supplementing? What shortcoming is it trying to compensate? What irresponsibility is it trying to suppress, exclude or negate? From what danger does it aim at protecting it? These questions already take us to the heart of the matter. This is necessarily accompanied by a system of control and punishment: a 'ready-made' guiding metaphysical interpretation of the concept of responsibility – namely accountability as indication of the power of a masterful and wilful subject – is thus left to rule exhaustively the hermeneutic domain of responsibility. Ironically, this predominant 'ideology of responsibility' is often accompanied by a singular absence of genuine reflection on the senses of responsibility, on what it means to be responsible – an ironic situation to be sure, as it is quite irresponsible not to know what responsibility means while one is calling for it! In the words of Jacques Derrida: 'not knowing, having neither a sufficient knowledge or consciousness of what being responsible *means*, is of itself a lack of responsibility. In order to be responsible it is necessary to respond to or answer to what being responsible means' (Derrida 1996: 25).[8]

In *Beyond Good and Evil*, Nietzsche took issue with the so-called 'science of morals' in which there is always something lacking, 'strange as it may sound: the problem of morality itself; what was lacking was any suspicion that there was something problematic there' (Nietzsche 1989: 98).[9] In paragraph 345 of *The Gay Science* (Book V), under the title of 'Morality as a problem', Nietzsche also suggests quite plainly that it is a matter of problematizing morality and its value, that is, of questioning it, as opposed to taking it for granted and leaving it unquestioned. For even

> if a morality has grown out of an error, the realization of this fact would not as much as touch the problem of its value. Thus nobody up to now has examined the value of that most famous of all medicines which is called morality; and the first step would be – for once to question it. Well then, precisely this is our task. (Nietzsche 1974: 285).

Insisting on the necessity and urgency of raising anew the question of the ethical, of making it problematic, indeed aporetic, Derrida thus writes: 'All this, therefore, still remains open, suspended, undecided, questionable even beyond the question, indeed, to make use of another figure, absolutely aporetic. What is the ethicality of ethics? The morality of morality? What is responsibility? What is the "What is?" in this case? Etc. These questions are always urgent' (P, 16). This questioning, however, proves to be historical.

The History of Responsibility

No concept is atemporal or a-historical. Nietzsche challenges this characteristic of philosophy to approach philosophical problems in an a-historical or dehistoricized way, and in particular those so-called historians of morality who lack 'historical spirit'. Nietzsche claims that 'the thinking of all of them is *by nature* unhistorical' (GM, 25). Such would be the 'common failing' of philosophers: they do not take account of the historicity of their object, and think of man as an '*aeterna veritas*'. Nietzsche accounts for this a-historicity in reference to what he calls the fetishism of language, i.e., our belief in grammar, and in paragraph 11 of volume I of *Human, All Too Human*, he explains that 'man has for long ages believed in the concept and names of things as in *aeternae veritates*', and that 'he really thought that in language he possessed knowledge of the world' (Nietzsche 1986: 16).[10] Lack of historical sense is therefore 'the family failing of all philosophers' (HH, 13); this is what is 'idiosyncratic' about them: 'their lack of a sense of history, their hatred for the very notion of becoming' (Nietzsche 1997: 18). They produce nothing but 'conceptual mummies'. Challenging the same a-historical approach to the question of responsibility, Derrida states that it 'is often thought, on the basis of an analysis of the very concepts of responsibility, freedom, or decision, that to be responsible, free, or capable of deciding cannot be something that is acquired, something conditioned or conditional' (GD, 5). However, as Nietzsche writes, 'everything has become: there are no eternal facts, just as there are no absolute truths. Consequently, what is needed from now on is historical philosophizing, and with it the virtue of modesty' (HH, 13). Responsibility would need to be resituated in its proper historicity.[11] An authentic philosophizing on responsibility would engage the history of the concept of responsibility, and would seek to ask: 'What would responsibility be if it were motivated, conditioned, made possible by a history?' (GD, 5).

The first task of such an enterprise will consist in undertaking a deconstructive genealogy of the concept of responsibility, which will reveal how responsibility has been constructed in such a way as to be progressively identified with accountability under the authority of a philosophy of will and subjectivity. Exposing this construction already entails undertaking its deconstruction. In fact, responsibility, the concept of accountability, might already be, in and of itself, in a state of self-deconstruction, according to the 'general law of construction' identified by Jean-Luc Nancy, who writes that a construction, 'like any construction, according to the general law of constructions, exposes itself, constitutively and in itself, to its deconstruction' (Nancy 2008: 48). This self-deconstruction of responsibility allows us to understand how the position of an accountable subject is always accompanied by an unavoidable double-bind: such a subject will be both in a position of mastery and the possible seat of accusation and punishment. The more it establishes its position of power as subject, the more it proposes itself as the potential recipient of an accusation or a persecution. In short, the more it asserts its power, the more the 'responsible subject' also undermines itself and deepens the abyss beneath it: the position of the power of the subject of imputation undermines itself in the very moment of its position, which also helps us to understand how Levinas is able to reverse the subject from the nominative of the tradition to the accusative of the hostage of the other, and how the 'subject' becomes 'the subjected'. Responsibility deconstructs itself. This is also why, no doubt, one is never responsible enough: responsibility actually engenders irresponsibility from within itself, it produces irresponsibility all the while reengaging efforts to suppress it. Irresponsibility will always be an integral and irreducible part of a fuller concept of responsibility.

In fact, one may discern the irreducible presence of a certain irresponsibility at the heart of responsible engagement: each time in different ways in Nietzsche, Heidegger, Sartre, Levinas or Derrida, one notes that responsibility seems rooted in an originary experience of irresponsibility, with responsibility arising out of it. Nietzsche speaks of the radical unaccountability of all things, negating responsibility and proclaiming the radical innocence of life and becoming. There is no intention, no design, no author, no cause, no responsibility, no agent: life eventuates in a tragic and innocent play, without a goal, not directed by a divine will. It is thus irresponsibility (as the unaccountability of all things) that is affirmed by Nietzsche! And yet, it is out of this very innocence and unaccountability of all things that a certain responsibility arises, as the affirmation of that very groundlessness and the recognition of a self-legislating humanity. One becomes responsible for a Godless existence, engaged in the creation of an existence that unfolds out of an absence of essence. In Heidegger's work, being happens without reason (the rose has no why, it grows because it grows, states *The Principle of Reason*), and there is no author of being. Yet one has to respond to this authorless call, and be responsible for one's thrown existence. For Sartre, even though he claims that we are responsible for everything and for all men, it is also the case that we have not chosen to be responsible, that we are not free to be free. We are 'condemned to be free', and this expression designates both the irresponsibility of our facticity and the unavoidability of our responsibility: one should almost speak here of the irresponsibility of responsibility. Derrida, for his part, seeks to return to the an-ethical origins of ethics. There is an irreducible irresponsibility at the origin of responsibility, so that we could be said to be irresponsibly responsible.

The two-fold aspect mentioned above of the prevailing metaphysical sense of responsibility – establishment of a power and accusation of a subject, supposition of a subject and undermining of the subject – in other words, the intimate connection between power and persecution, appears clearly, not only in Levinas's work (where responsibility is actually defined as persecution), but also in any genealogy of the concept of responsibility. As Nietzsche has shown decisively, at the root of responsibility as accountability we find the need to posit an agent-cause, that is, someone who can be held accountable and punished. A post-metaphysical sense of responsibility will certainly have to be distinguished from a problematics of punishment, just as it will also have to be differentiated from accountability. Responsibility will become less about the establishment of a sphere of control and power, less about the establishment of a sovereign subject, and more about an exposure to an event that does not come from us and yet calls us. The issue is to explore these senses so as to rethink the concept of responsibility from the ground up.

In this respect, one needs to question the classical opposition between free will and determinism, which has enframed traditional accounts of responsibility and continues to structure a large number of discussions on responsibility, and which may prove inadequate to an exploration of the phenomenological senses of responsibility. A questioning on the being of responsibility will necessarily undercut the classic opposition between free will and determinism, which ultimately remains an ontical distinction. One also needs to question the identification of responsibility with imputation or accountability. Imputability, or accountability, itself rests upon and presupposes a certain conception of the human being, as subject. A philosophical enterprise would thus need to distinguish responsibility – whose etymological roots, from the Latin *respondere*, mobilize the domain of answerability or responsiveness – with the accountability of a subject, that is, within a metaphysics of the free autonomous subject. What does 'to be responsible' mean, if no longer referred to the subject? This question requires a historical genealogy which allows us to dissociate the senses of responsibility from its enframing in a metaphysics of subjectivity, power and will. Might there not be other ways to think of responsibility, once the categories just mentioned are questioned or challenged with and after Nietzsche's genealogy of responsibility? What would responsibility mean if not thought as the consequence of free will? If it no longer designates the capacity of a subject to 'own' its thoughts and acts? If the category of causality is no longer operative or at least problematized?

Is the concept, indeed the experience, of responsibility exhausted by the sense of accountability? Should responsibility be conceived exclusively in terms of the causality of the will? On the basis of the voluntary, or conscious intention? As the subjectivity or ground of the act? Should responsibility be identified with the position of a power, of a sovereign agency? Can responsibility be enframed exclusively within a philosophy of accountability, in the context of a metaphysics of subjectivity and free will? In fact, it may well be the case that in such an enframing, the phenomenological and ontological sources of what is called 'responsibility' have remained obscure and neglected. It will thus be a matter of dissociating the concept of responsibility from its metaphysical interpretation, and freeing it from the dominance of the motifs of subjectivity and power so as to retrieve its phenomenological provenance.

In the course of a historical deconstructive genealogy of responsibility, four motifs that govern the traditional interpretation of responsibility – what we could call the four 'fundamental concepts' of the traditional account of responsibility – appear.

First, the belief that the human being is an agent or a subject, i.e., the reliance on subjectivity (*subjectum* in its logical or grammatical sense of foundation) as ground of imputation. A critique of such a subject, whether Nietzschean in inspiration, phenomenological or deconstructive, will radically transform our understanding of what it means to be responsible. A reconsideration of responsibility away from the dominance of the motif of the subject will imply a reconsideration of what it means to be human.

Second, the notion that the subject is a voluntary agent, i.e., the reliance on the voluntary and so-called 'free will'. A phenomenological critique to the notion of free will, whether Nietzschean (free will is a fiction), Heideggerian (free will does not capture the essence of freedom, of what it means to be free) or Levinassian in inspiration (responsibility takes place before the freedom of the self, pre-assigned passively to the other), would radically transform our understanding of responsibility. It would in any case reveal responsibility not as the position of the power of the subject, but as a relation to and assumption of a certain passivity, that of our finitude as mortal beings and of our exposure to the inappropriable alterity that calls us.

Third, the reliance on causality. To be the 'cause of' and to be 'responsible for' are conflated. However, this in itself is problematic: does the category of cause apply to the human being's relation to itself and others? Does it apply to what happens in its eventfulness? Is an event, as event, 'caused'? Is it caused by a 'will'? Does the very eventfulness of the event not precisely point to a certain excess with respect to the enframing of causality? Can an event worthy of its name be even conditioned by a causality? Or should one not assume, as Jean-Luc Marion invites us to do, a certain excess of the event with respect to causality? Marion writes of 'the character and the dignity of an event – that is, an event or a phenomenon that is unforeseeable (on the basis of the past), not exhaustively comprehensible (on the basis of the present), not reproducible (on the basis of the future), in short, absolute, unique, happening. We will therefore call it a *pure event*' (Marion 2000: 204).[12] Further, does causality capture the original sense of responsibility as responsiveness?

Fourth, the assumption that the responsible subject is a rational subject, that the basis for ethical responsibility is rational agency. Nietzsche stated that traditional moral philosophers 'wanted to supply a rational foundation for morality … Morality itself, however, was accepted as "given". … What was lacking was any suspicion that there was something problematic here' (BGE, 98). What would happen to the concept of responsibility if it were dissociated, as is the case with Levinas, but also with Heidegger or Derrida, from the predominance of reason, of giving reasons (principle of sufficient reason) or providing an account of oneself? Should responsibility be placed under the authority of the principle of sufficient reason? Under the request or demand for a ground or justification (accountability), characteristic of rationalist metaphysical thought? Derrida understands responsibility as a response to the event of the other, an event that is always unpredictable, incalculable, one that thereby always breaks the demand for sufficient reason. 'The coming of the other, the arriving of the arriving one (*l'arrivée de l'arrivant*), is (what) who arrives as an unpredictable event', Derrida explains, an event that can only challenge the demand for reasons, the principle of sufficient reason 'insofar as reason is limited to "giving an account" (*reddere rationem, logon didonai*)'. The issue is not of complying with the demands of such reason rendering, but instead of 'not simply denying or ignoring this unforeseeable and incalculable coming of the other' (Derrida and Roudinesco 2004: 50).

The Being of Responsibility

Once a certain subjectivist bias or assumption has been abandoned, a conceptual work on the very sense of being responsible, on what it means to be responsible, becomes both possible and necessary. A genealogy of the concept of responsibility will reveal a wide range of senses, making clear that the prevailing sense of responsibility as accountability of the subject, within a metaphysics of will and subjectivity, is but one narrow sense of the term, and perhaps not even the most primordial one. In fact, a simple, schematic and preliminary survey of various linguistic expressions points to the plural scope of responsibility, opening onto various problematics, questions and domains, left to be explored further.

The classic understanding of responsibility is captured in the expression 'being responsible for one's actions', which speaks of the autonomy of the subject, of self-legislation and self-ownership. It belongs to a semantics of power and appropriation, as it is about owning one's actions and owning oneself, about establishing an area of mastery and control. Responsibility has traditionally been associated with a project of appropriation, understood as the securing of a sphere of mastery for a wilful subject, a model one finds developed from Aristotle's discussion of the voluntary and responsible decision in Book III of *The Nicomachean Ethics* to Kant's discussion of transcendental freedom in the third antinomy and his understanding of enlightenment as self-determination and self-responsibility, and culminating, although not without some paradoxes and reversals, with Sartre's philosophy of hyperbolic responsibility. In that tradition, responsibility is understood in terms of the *subjectum* that lies at the basis of the act, as ground of imputation,[13] and opens onto the project of a self-legislation and self-appropriation of the subject. To be responsible in this context designates the capacity by a sovereign subject to appropriate itself entirely in an ideal of self-legislation and transparency. As Derrida put it, 'all the fundamental axiomatic of responsibility or decision (ethical, juridical, political), are grounded on the sovereignty of the subject, that is, the intentional auto-determination of the conscious self (which is free, autonomous, active, etc)' (WA, xix), an interpretation that is to be deconstructed.

One also speaks of 'being responsible for the consequences of one's actions', an important addition, for in the first instance (in being responsible for one's actions), the stress is essentially on the dimension of the past, as one is asked to answer for his or her past deeds, whereas to say that one is responsible for the consequences of one's actions implies that one is looking towards the future of the act, and that there can be a responsibility to the future and not only towards the past. In this sense, responsibility is being accountable for the future, for what has not yet happened! This is the emphasis placed by Hans Jonas in his famed *The Imperative of Responsibility: In Search of an Ethics for the Technological Age* (1985),[14] where the author argues that responsibility ought to be directed towards the future (what he calls a 'future-oriented ethics' [IR, 12–17] or also an 'ethics of the future' [IR, 25–31]) in the sense of preserving future generations in the face of human destructiveness. The Kantian formulations of ethics are said to need to include a future humanity (indeed, the very future of humanity!), as well as nature itself. Such future-oriented ethics would 'seek not only the human good but also the good of things extrahuman, that is, to extend the recognition of "ends in themselves" beyond the sphere of man and make the human good include the care of them' (IR, 8). In other words, the categorical imperative should be recast so as to include future humanity. As parents are responsible for their children (for Jonas, the parent-child relation is the archetype of responsibility),[15] human beings would be responsible for nature and for the future of humanity. Yet, there are different ways of conceiving of a responsibility towards the future, for it could be taken either as a way to calculate the effects of one's actions in the future and thus within the horizon of calculability and control, or it could be taken on the contrary as a responsible opening towards what remains incalculable in what is yet to come. Derrida speaks of a responsibility to the future, to the arriving of the *arrivant*, 'a future that cannot be anticipated; anticipated but unpredictable; apprehended, but, and this is why there is a future, apprehended precisely as unforeseeable, unpredictable; approached as unapproachable' (GD, 54). There would thus be a responsibility towards what has not yet happened, or to what is still coming. In Jonas' work, this implies a relation of caring towards the vulnerable. Such responsibility for the future is for Jonas based on a fear for the vulnerability of the earth. Jonas clarifies that he is not speaking of a 'duty arising from procreation' but of a 'duty to such procreation' (IR, 40). That duty for future mankind (which 'charges us, in the first place, with ensuring that there be a future mankind'! [IR, 40]), is based on the fragility of life. Human existence, Jonas writes, 'has the precarious, vulnerable, and revocable character, the peculiar mode of transience, of all life, which makes it alone a proper object of "caring"' (IR, 98). Another sense of responsibility is here introduced, based on care, and no longer authorship: when Jonas speaks of an attitude of protection towards nature, a responsible concern for its vulnerability or frailty, responsibility is taken in terms of respect, and care. We are responsible for what is in our care, not first as imputable subjects, but as caretakers. Care or concern, or respect, belong to semantic sets that are distinct, if not foreign, to accountability and its problematics of subjectivity and authorship. For Levinas, 'not doing violence to the other' constitutes the very meaning of ethics and responsibility. Vulnerability now appears as the new ground of responsibility, in the call not to do harm to the vulnerable.

This last sense leads us to give thought to a certain excess with respect to the subjective enclosure of the concept of responsibility. For, in contrast with responsibility for one's own actions and their consequences, and thus by extension for oneself, another expression speaks not of a responsibility for self, but instead of a 'responsibility for the other'. In such a context, it is clear that one can no longer maintain that the accountability of the subject constitutes the main sense of responsibility, for one is longer speaking about one's own actions and one's relationship to them. Responsibility is no longer about what I have done, but about another for whom I care and am concerned with, another towards whom I have obligations. As Emmanuel Levinas puts it, 'Usually, one is responsible for what one does oneself. I say, in *Otherwise than Being or Beyond Essence*, that responsibility is initially for the other' (Levinas 1985: 96).[16] This is ultimately what Levinas will call 'persecution': I have done nothing and yet I am responsible for the other. Levinas also severs the traditional relation between responsibility and the egological subject, overcoming the egological enclosure of responsibility, no longer assigned to the interests of the ego: I am now responsible for what is foreign to me, for 'what does not even matter to me' (EI, 95). What can be the ground of such an obligation? Certainly not my own self as subject and author: its measure is no longer the self-ownership of a subject, the return onto itself of the self, but the claim made on me by the other. The emphasis is displaced from the self towards the other, and the subject is overturned as subjected to the other. Thus, the ground of this obligation, if it is not the self, will have to be located in the other itself, and in a certain vulnerability of the other (his/her mortality, ultimately). This is of course the great divide that Levinas retraced and radicalized, between a responsibility for self and a responsibility for the other, leading to an ethics of otherness apart from all egology or egological thinking. As Derrida explains in *The Gift of Death*,

> Levinas wants to remind us that responsibility is not at first responsibility of myself for myself, that the sameness of myself is derived from the other, as if it were second to the other, coming to itself as responsible and mortal from the position of my responsibility before the other, for the other's death and in the face of it. (GD, 46)

This raises the question of the scope or the measure of responsibility, as it appears in the question: 'To whom or to what are we responsible?' For which other am I responsible, for whom or for what? Indeed, to answer, like Levinas, that the other is the one I am responsible for is only the beginning of the question: we know the Levinassian quandary discussed in its aporetic structure by Derrida in *The Gift of Death*: 'Tout autre est tout autre': every other is wholly other. I am therefore obligated to all others insofar as I am obligated to each and every other. How to discriminate between others if I am each time obligated to a singular other and thus bound in this singular responsibility to sacrifice all other others? For this expression, 'tout autre est tout autre', is a way of 'linking alterity to singularity' and 'signifies that every other is singular, that everyone is a singularity' (GD, 87). Are these others only human, as Levinas claimed, since the French word for the face, *visage*, is exclusively human? And how can one speak of determinable measure when a certain aporia, or sacrifice, seems to make the ethical experience impossible? As I respond to one singular other, I sacrifice all the other others, and I can only respond ethically by sacrificing or betraying ethics. 'I can respond only to the one (or to the One), that is, to the other, by sacrificing the other to that one... and I cannot justify this sacrifice' (GD, 70). This sacrificial space implies that as a consequence 'the concepts of responsibility, of decision, or of duty, are condemned a priori to paradox, scandal, and aporia' (GD, 68). The question of responsibility is thus opened from this aporia onto its own infinity, indefiniteness or undecidability.

This question is addressed frontally by Sartre, leading to a hyperbolic inflation of responsibility in his thought of existence: My responsibility, Sartre claims, is boundless, extends to 'all men' and everything concerns me. However, this hyperbolic inflation of responsibility proves to be nothing but the hyperbolic inflation of subjectivity since for Sartre everything that happens happens to me, and what happens to me happens through me. I am responsible for everything and for all as I project an image to be embraced by all. I am responsible for 'all men' in the sense that I carry the weight of the world on my shoulders, that is, that I embrace the whole world in my will. To that extent, Sartre does not perturb the traditional definition of responsibility as authorship but reinforces and extends it hyperbolically. He writes: 'We are taking the word "responsibility" in its ordinary sense as "consciousness" (of) being the incontestable author of an event or of an object' (Sartre 1992: 707). For Levinas as well, I am responsible for everyone, but in the opposite sense of Sartre, because for Levinas I am responsible as expropriated and hostage of the other's infinite demand.

One can take this question, 'To whom or to what are we responsible?,' in a different direction, questioning the very division between the human and the non-human that has structured the history of responsibility. For whom or for what is one responsible? Human beings, animals, things, nature, the world, the cosmos or universe, everything? In the words of Jean-Luc Nancy, 'For what are we responsible? ... responsible for being, for God, for the law, for death, for birth, for existence, ours and that of all beings?' (Nancy 1999: 1).[17] What is the scope or the range, the limits and measure of responsibility? Isn't it always taken in an excessive movement leading to an exceeding of the very anthropocentric enclosure, disturbing the demarcation between what would be a human and a non-human sphere? This excess would open onto what Nancy calls the singular plurality of being, in which the relation to an other is no longer governed by the human signified, or the human as transcendental signified. Nancy explains in *Being Singular Plural* that in being-with it is the matter of a communication between singularities, where no privilege to human Dasein can be granted. Responsibility exceeds the anthropocentric closure, and designates the between of singularities:

> If one can put it like this, there is no other meaning than the meaning of circulation. But this circulation goes in all directions at once, in all the directions of all the space-times opened by presence to presence: all things, all beings, all entities, every-thing past and future, alive, dead, inanimate, stones, plants, nails, gods – and 'human', that is, those who expose sharing and circulation as such by saying 'we'. (Nancy 2002a: 3).[18]

The human being does not constitute the centre of creation, Nancy insists. Instead, creation (that is, the way the world emerges and exists, *ex nihilo*) 'transgresses [*traverse*] humanity', so that 'in humanity, or rather right at [à même] humanity, existence is exposed and exposing' (BSP, 17). To that extent, there is no human sphere with its accompanying anthropocentric self-respon-sibility. As Nancy formulates it, the thought of the singular plurality of being would lead us to state the following with respect to the world: it is not a human world, but a world of the co-exposure of the human and the non-human. I would not be 'human', Nancy explains, if I did not 'have this exteriority "in me", in the form of the quasi-minerality of bone' (BSP, 18). And we 'would not be "humans" if there were not "dogs" and "stones"' (BSP, 18). Humanity is not the origin, centre, or finality of the world:

> It is not so much the world of humanity as it is the world of the non-human to which humanity is exposed and which humanity, in turn, exposes. One could try to formu-late it in the following way: humanity is the exposing of the world; it is neither the end nor the ground of the world; the world is the exposure of humanity; it is neither the environment nor the representation of humanity. (BSP, 18).

As one can see, the expression 'responsibility for the other' can explode the self-centred sense of responsibility in many directions, calling into question our most basic beliefs in the structure of being and its composition as well as in our conception of what it means to be human.

One also speaks of responsibility in the sense of 'carrying a weight', of 'shouldering' a burden. Ordinary language speaks of the connection between responsibility and weight, of responsibility as the carrying of a weight. However, what exactly weighs in the weight? Heidegger speaks of the human being as a being who is burdened or heavy with a weight, in a situation of care and concern, in contrast to the lightness or carelessness of irresponsible or inauthentic being. Heidegger evokes the fundamental 'burdensome character of Dasein, even while it alleviates the burden' (Heidegger 1953: 134). So-called 'moods of elation', which do alleviate the burden, are said to be possible only on the basis of this burdensome character of Dasein's being. The being of the there, Heidegger writes, 'become[s] manifest as a burden [*Last*]' (Heidegger 1953: 134). Heidegger defines Dasein as 'care', as concern: being is at issue for Dasein, it is a task of being, and is a weight I have to carry and be 'responsible for'. Responsibility as the carrying of the weight of existence is the originary phenomenon, and irresponsibility – making thing easy – is derivative.

Ultimately, the weight designates the facticity of existence, a facticity to which we are assigned and have to carry as our very finitude.

In Levinas' thought, the motif of weight marks the ethical situation of the finite subject as assigned (hostage!) to the infinite other, the assigning of a finite subject to the infinite demand of the other: what weighs in this case is the dissymmetry or incommensurability between the finite I and the infinite Other. The other's demand is greater than my capacities to respond, as finite I, and yet this is how I must respond. This appears in the motif of hospitality as welcome of the other: the welcome of the other is the finite welcome of an infinite. The subject welcomes or receives the other beyond its own finite capacities of welcoming. The call of the other is thus 'too much' to bear and weighs on the finite subject, an excess that cannot be an argument against ethical responsibility: it is not because I cannot materially do justice to the other that I am not obligated to him or her; there is no relationship between my capacities as a finite subject and the ethical responsibility that is mine. In fact, as Levinas says, dissymmetry is the law of responsibility, as it represents a responsibility for an other that necessarily exceeds my finite capabilities. This excess for the subject is the origin of responsibility and its weight. Furthermore, Levinas stresses that ethical responsibility is not chosen, is not the result of my decision or initiative, but is assigned to me, 'before freedom', by the other facing me, putting me in a situation of obligation. The weight is thus threefold: it is the weight of a dissymmetry between the infinite other and the finite subject; it is the weight of the passivity of an ethical obligation before freedom and choice; and finally, it is the weight of otherness itself: the otherness of the other weighs on me precisely insofar as the other remains other, never appropriable by me, exterior to me yet calling me to responsibility.

This weightiness, which seems to exceed all limits or measure (and it is in fact this very boundlessness that weighs), can nonetheless take two forms, at least: it can take the form, as in Levinas, of the finite self becoming hostage to the infinite other. In this last case, as we saw, the weight is the weight of otherness. But it can also take the Sartrean form, in which I carry the weight of the world on my shoulders in the sense that I embrace the whole world within my will. I am responsible for everything and for all men, says Sartre, like Levinas, who also writes that I am responsible, and more than all the others, but for opposite reasons. For Sartre, it signifies the absolutizing of the wilful subject taking over the whole world and being responsible 'for all men' insofar as I am the 'author' of the meaning of the world. For Levinas, it means the subjection of the finite subject to an infinite other. Because the subject is exposed to an alterity, the very possibility of appropriation is called into question. Weight would thus be the 'resistance' of what remains inappropriable for the subject, either absolutizing of the subject (Sartre) or radical expropriation and subjection of the subject (Levinas): in both cases, responsibility is infinite and overwhelming and the subject carries the whole weight of the world on its shoulders. The weight of responsibility can thus have the following senses: it can designate the absolute authorship of the free subject (Sartre), the dissymmetry of an infinite obligation of the other for a finite subject (Levinas), or the weight of finitude as exposure to the inappropriable (Heidegger).

Such resituating of responsibility opens the thematics of answerability and responsiveness, responsibility as 'responding to' or answering a call. Derrida considers that any sense of responsibility must be rooted in the experience of responding, and belong to the domain of responsiveness.[19] Responsibility is first and foremost a response, as its etymological origins, traceable to the Latin *respondere*, betray. Derrida distinguishes three types of responsiveness: there is 'to answer for' [*répondre de*]; 'to respond to' [*répondre à*]; and 'to answer before' [*répondre devant*]. Derrida gives priority to the 'responding to' as it mobilizes the inscription of an other to whom or to what I respond. One reads in *The Politics of Friendship*:

> One answers for, for self or for something (for someone, for an action, a thought, a discourse), before – before an other, a community of others, an institution, a court, a law). And always one answers for (for self or for its intention, its action or discourse), before, by first responding to: this last modality thus appearing more originary, more fundamental and hence unconditional. (Derrida 2005: 250)

The phenomenological senses of responsibility might be closer to a problematic of answerability than to one of accountability, which is too dependent on a metaphysics of subjectivity.[20] Responsibility first needs to be taken as a kind of response, as being assigned to a call. One thinks here, for instance, of Heidegger's call of conscience in *Being and Time*, and later the call or address of being to which one has to correspond, Heidegger going so far in *The Zollikon Seminars* as to claim: 'To be answerable to the claim of presencing is the greatest claim of humanity: ethics is this claim' (Heidegger 2001: 217). The motif of the call is also central to Levinas' definition of responsibility, the call of the other person, the other human, out of his or her vulnerability and mortality. One can also evoke here Jean-Luc Marion's problematic of the saturated phenomenon, and the call that this excess places on the called one (*l'interloqué*). For Jean-Luc Marion, in fact, the senses of responsibility as accountability of the subject, as well as the Levinassian sense of responding to the other's face, presuppose the original sense of responsibility as response to the call as such. In *Being Given*, he writes:

> Responsibility can now be redefined. (c) Nobody will deny that responsibility, understood as the property of a juridical 'subject' having to respond for his acts and an ethical 'subject' having to respond to what the face of the Other demands (to envisage him [*de l'envisager*] as such), can be deduced from the most general figure of the response to a call by a gifted [*un adonné*], and the call 'always arises from a paradox (saturated phenomenon)'. (Marion 2002: 293)[21]

Responsibility is then a response, not a spontaneous initiating, as Kant claimed. The subject is the recipient of the call, not a transcendental subject; we are respondents, not absolute beginners. For Kant, to be responsible means to be able to begin something absolutely. But as called, the subject can never begin anything, only respond. The I always comes after, always comes 'late', and its responsibility is that very delay in the form of the registering of and responding to the call. This is where one notes the crucial importance of the conception of the human being which is at the basis of a conception of responsibility: Kant thinks of the human being as a rational subject, and thus as origin ('transcendental freedom') and foundation. His concept of responsibility will bear these features. Heidegger thinks of the human, no longer as a subject, but as Dasein, that is, as a thrown existence (to be taken on responsibly). Similarly, with Levinas, the subject is understood as assigned to a call, as passivity: the subject is hostage of the other. Responsibility in this sense is not a matter of choice or inclination, but arises out of a demand placed on the subject, a demand that takes the form of a duty, of an ethical obligation, a call I cannot not answer. That demand needs to be answered: having to respond, to answer (duty, obligation), implies that one cannot not answer. In fact, not responding is already a kind of response. This is exactly how Heidegger would define inauthenticity: a not-responding (to the call of conscience) that nonetheless is a kind of response: 'responding in the form of not-responding' means being inauthentic.

This polysemic range reveals the unilateral nature of the understanding of responsibility as accountability of the subject, which is but one sense of the term, and perhaps not even the most primordial: having to respond to a call, exposure to the vulnerability of the other (the other as vulnerability), openness to the event of being as my own 'to be', having to take upon oneself the weight of responsibility, whether the weight of finitude, of otherness or of an essence-less existence – all these senses point to the experience of and exposure to the inappropriable. Responsibility becomes the experience of and response to this inappropriable character of existence and of the other. This, at least, is what a history of responsibility – that is, a genealogy of its senses – allows us to see.

François Raffoul is Professor of Philosophy at Louisiana State University. He is the author of *Heidegger and the Subject* (Prometheus Books, 1999), *A Chaque fois Mien* (Galilée, 2004), *The Origins of Responsibility* (Indiana University Press, 2010) and is completing a new monograph entitled *Thinking the Event*. He has co-edited several volumes: *Disseminating Lacan* (SUNY Press, 1996), *Heidegger and Practical Philosophy* (SUNY Press, 2002), *Rethinking Facticity* (SUNY Press, 2008), *French Interpretations of Heidegger* (SUNY Press, 2008) and more recently *The Bloomsbury Companion to Heidegger* (Bloomsbury, 2013, 2016). He has co-translated several French philosophers, in particular Jacques Derrida ('*Ulysses Gramophone: Hear Say Yes in Joyce*', in *Derrida and Joyce: Texts and Contexts*, SUNY Press, 2013), Jean-Luc Nancy (*The Title of the Letter: a Reading of Lacan* [1992], *The Gravity of Thought* [1998], *The Creation of the World or Globalization* [2007] and *Identity* [Fordham University Press, 2013]). He is the co-editor of a book series published by SUNY Press, entitled *Contemporary French Thought*.

Notes

1. Hereafter cited as GM, followed by page number. Nietzsche speaks of the 'long history of the origins of responsibility' [*Geschichte der Herkunft der Verantwortlichkeit*]. Earlier in the text, in the preface, Nietzsche had already mentioned his attempt at publishing hypotheses concerning 'the origin of morality' [*Ursprung der Moral*]; GM, 16.
2. Hereafter cited as WP, followed by page number.
3. Hereafter cited as P, followed by the page number.
4. Hereafter cited as HPP, followed by page number.
5. All translations are mine.
6. As Larry Hatab explains, 'The search for a decisive ground in ethics can be understood as an attempt to escape the existential demands of contention and commitment. Moral "decisions" and the sense of "responsibility" for decisions may in fact be constituted by the global *undecidability* of ethical questions'. Hatab 2008: 241.
7. Kant writes: 'The transcendental idea of freedom is far from constituting the whole content of the psychological concept of that name, which is for the most part empirical, but constitutes only that of the absolute spontaneity of an action, as the real ground of its imputability'. Kant 1998: A448/B476, p. 486.
8. Hereafter cited as GD, followed by page number. In fact, 'We must continually remind ourselves that some part of irresponsibility insinuates itself wherever one demands responsibility without sufficiently conceptualizing and thematizing what "responsibility" means; *that is to say everywhere*'. GD, 25.
9. Hereafter cited as BGE, followed by page number.
10. Hereafter cited as HH, followed by page number.
11. In *The Genealogy of Morals*, Nietzsche states: 'My desire, at any rate, was to point out to so sharp and disinterested an eye ... in the direction of an actual history of morality' [*wirklichen Historie der Moral*]. GM, 21.
12. Translation slightly modified (we substitute 'happening' for 'occurring'.)
13. In his *Doctrine of Right*, Kant thus explains that a person is 'a subject whose actions can be imputed to him', whereas a 'thing is that to which nothing can be imputed'. Kant 1999: 378.
14. Hereafter cited as IR, followed by page number.
15. Jonas claims that the very model or paradigm for conceiving of ethics is that of the solicitude of the parent towards his or her children. It is, he writes, 'the archetype of all responsible actions' (IR, 39). The parent-child relation becomes the archetype of all responsibility of humans towards other humans, towards the world, and towards the future of the earth.
16. Hereafter cited as EI, followed by page number.
17. Another translation, by Sara Guyer, is provided in *A Finite Thinking*, ed. Simon Sparks (Stanford, CA: Stanford University Press, 2003), pp. 287-99.
18. Hereafter cited as BSP, followed by page number.
19. See for instance P, 15, where Derrida uses the term 'responsiveness' in English in the original. Also see GD, 3.
20. In his book, *Ethics and Finitude*, Larry Hatab seeks to advance a notion of responsibility 'that can be characterized as "answerability" (cf. the German *verantwortlich*), rather than what I would call moralistic "accountability". With these formulations I mean to distinguish responsibility from autonomous agency and a related sense of accountability'. Hatab 2000: 185.
21. Translation modified.

References

Derrida, Jacques. 1995. 'Passions', in *On the Name*, ed. Thomas Dutoit. Stanford, CA: Stanford University Press, pp. 3–34.
———. 1996. *The Gift of Death*, trans. David Wills. Chicago, IL: University of Chicago Press.
———. 2004. 'Jacques Derrida, penseur de l'évènement' [Jacques Derrida, Thinker of the Event], interview by Jérôme-Alexandre Nielsberg', *l'Humanité*, 28 January 2004, http://www.humanite.fr/2004-01-28_Tribune-libre_-Jacques-Derrida-penseur-de-levenement.
———. 2005. *The Politics of Friendship*. London and New York: Verso.
Derrida, Jacques and Elisabeth Roudinesco. 2004. *For What Tomorrow...: A Dialogue*. Stanford, CA: Stanford University Press.
Hatab, Lawrence. 2000. *Ethics and Finitude*. Lanham, MD: Rowman & Littlefield.
———. 2008. *Nietzsche's On the Genealogy of Morals*. Cambridge: Cambridge University Press.
Heidegger, Martin. 1953. *Sein und Zeit*. Tübingen: Max Niemeyer Verlag.
———. 2001. *The Zollikon Seminars*, trans. Franz Mayr and Richard Askay. Evanston, IL: Northwestern University Press.
Jonas, Hans. 1985. *The Imperative of Responsibility: In Search of an Ethics for the Technological Age*. Chicago: University of Chicago Press.
Kant, Immanuel. 1998. *The Critique of Pure Reason*, trans. Paul Guyer and Allen W. Wood. Cambridge: Cambridge University Press.
———. 1999. *The Metaphysics of Morals*, in *Practical Philosophy*, ed. Mary J. Gregor. New York: Cambridge University Press.
Levinas, Emmanuel. 1985. *Ethics and Infinity*. Pittsburg, PA: Duquesne University Press.
Marion, Jean-Luc. 2000. 'The Saturated Phenomenon', in *Phenomenology and the 'Theological Turn'*. New York: Fordham University Press.
———. 2002. *Being Given: Toward a Phenomenology of Givenness*, trans. Jeffrey L. Kosky. Stanford, CA: Stanford University Press.
Merleau-Ponty, Maurice. 1964. *The Primacy of Perception*. Evanston, IL: Northwestern University Press.
Nancy, Jean-Luc. 1999. 'Responding for Existence', *Studies in Practical Philosophy* 1(1).
———. 2002a. *Being Singular Plural*. Stanford, CA: Stanford University Press.
———. 2002b. 'Heidegger's "Originary Ethics"', in François Raffoul and David Pettigrew (eds), *Heidegger and Practical Philosophy*. Albany, NY: SUNY Press, pp. 65–86.
———. 2008. *Dis-enclosure: The Deconstruction of Christianity*. New York: Fordham University Press.
Nietzsche, Friedrich. 1967. *On the Genealogy of Morals*, trans. Walter Kaufmann. New York: Vintage Books.
———. 1968. *The Will to Power*, trans. Walter Kaufmann and R.J. Hollingdale. New York: Vintage Books, Random House.
———. 1974. *The Gay Science*, trans. Walter Kaufmann. New York: Vintage Books.
———. 1977. *The Twilight of the Idols*, trans. Richard Polt. Indianapolis and Cambridge: Hackett.
———. 1986. *Human, all Too Human: A Book for Free Spirits*. New York: Cambridge University Press.

_____. 1989. *Beyond Good and Evil*, trans. Walter Kaufmann. New York: Vintage Books.

Raffoul, Francois. 2010. *The Origin of Responsibility*. Bloomington, IN: Indiana University Press.

Sartre, Jean-Paul. 1992. *Being and Nothingness: A Phenomenological Essay on Ontology*, trans. Hazel E. Barnes. New York: Washington Square Press.

Index

Z

Zande witchcraft, 145
Zigon, Jarrett, 23, 24, 69, 70, 73, 179, 180,
        183, 185, 186, 187, 219
The Zollikon Seminars (Heidegger), 245